W9-DCU-831

Redcoats

Recent scholarship has highlighted the significance of the Seven Years War for the destiny of Britain's Atlantic empire. This major study offers an important new perspective through a vivid and scholarly account of the regular troops at the sharp end of that conflict's bloody and decisive American campaigns. Fresh sources are employed to challenge enduring stereotypes regarding both the social composition and military prowess of the 'redcoats'. The book shows how the humble soldiers who fought from Nova Scotia to Cuba developed a powerful *esprit de corps* that equipped them to defy savage discipline in defence of their 'rights'. It traces the evolution of Britain's 'American Army' from a feeble, conservative and discredited organisation into a tough, flexible and innovative force whose victories ultimately won the respect of colonial Americans. By providing a voice for these neglected shock-troops of empire, *Redcoats* adds flesh and blood to Georgian Britain's 'sinews of power'.

A former newspaper journalist, Stephen Brumwell earned his Ph.D. in History from the University of Leeds in 1998. He is the author of several scholarly articles and co-author of *Cassell's Companion to 18th Century Britain* (Cassell: London, 2001). Dr Brumwell currently works as a free-lance writer in Amsterdam, The Netherlands.

For Mum and Dad

Redcoats

The British Soldier and War in the Americas, 1755–1763

Stephen Brumwell

CAMBRIDGE
UNIVERSITY PRESS

PUBLISHED BY THE PRESS SYNDICATE OF THE UNIVERSITY OF CAMBRIDGE
The Pitt Building, Trumpington Street, Cambridge, United Kingdom

CAMBRIDGE UNIVERSITY PRESS
The Edinburgh Building, Cambridge CB2 2RU, UK
40 West 20th Street, New York, NY 10011-4211, USA
10 Stamford Road, Oakleigh, VIC 3166, Australia
Ruiz de Alarcón 13, 28014 Madrid, Spain
Dock House, The Waterfront, Cape Town 8001, South Africa

http://www.cambridge.org

First published 2002

Printed in the United States of America

Typeface *Sabon* 10/12 pt. *System 3B2* [KW]

A catalogue record for this book is available from the British Library.

Library of Congress Cataloging in Publication Data

Brumwell, Stephen, 1960–
Redcoats : the British soldier and war in the Americas, 1755–1763 / Stephen Brumwell.
p. cm.
Includes bibliographical references (p.) and index.
1. United States–History–French and Indian War, 1755–1763–Campaigns. 2. Seven Years War, 1756–1763–Campaigns. 3. Great Britain. Army–History–French and Indian War, 1755–1763. 4. Great Britain. Army–Military life–History–18th century. 5. Soldiers–Great Britain–History–18th century. 6. Soldiers–North America–History–18th century. 7. Soldiers–West Indies–History–18th century. I. Title.

E199 .B89 2001
940.2′534–dc21 2001025491

ISBN 0 521 80783 2 hardback

Contents

List of illustrations

Figures

Sketch maps

Acknowledgements

This book stems from a deep-rooted interest in the redcoats and their experience of American warfare during the mid-eighteenth century. That fascination began some thirty years ago when the BBC televised an adaptation of *The Last of the Mohicans*. Although lacking a Hollywood-style budget, this wonderfully atmospheric and menacing production prompted much whooping and wielding of wooden tomahawks as schoolboy gangs re-enacted pivotal scenes across Britain's wastelands. By an uncanny coincidence, at much the same time the young persons' magazine *Look and Learn* devoted its back page to an equally evocative series on the exploits of 'Rogers' Rangers': written and illustrated by Ronald Embleton, each eagerly awaited installment heightened my curiosity about the 'French and Indian War' and those who waged it. A growing interest in the Georgian army was bolstered when, as a thirteen-year-old, I first read John Prebble's *Culloden* (London, 1961): this gripping and compassionate account of the bloody confrontation that ended the last Jacobite rebellion also demonstrated the possibility of viewing the past through the eyes of even the most humble protagonists. Although my exposure to higher education was long postponed, these early influences endured: many years later, when I was granted the opportunity to undertake postgraduate study, my research proposal was never in doubt.

In the course of researching and writing my doctoral dissertation, 'The British Soldier in the Americas, 1755–1763' (University of Leeds, 1998), and the book that evolved from it, I received assistance from many quarters. In the first instance, the project would not have been feasible without funding from the British Academy; I remain extremely grateful to that body for the chance to pursue my studies. In addition, a generous grant from the Henry E. Huntington Library at San Marino made it possible to conduct extensive research among that institution's manuscript collections. The courteous and prompt assistance I received from the Huntington's staff was typical of that encountered elsewhere; however, a particular mention should be made of the Public Record Office at Kew, and the Scottish Record Office (now the National Archives of Scotland) in Edinburgh, where much of my archival research was conducted.

Work upon published primary sources was largely undertaken within the Brotherton Library at Leeds, an experience that has left me in no doubt of the excellence of that institution's holdings: modern history specialist Neil Plummer and the staff of the Special Collections deserve thanks for their efforts on my behalf. At the School of History, University of Leeds, I owe a particular debt to John Childs, the supervisor of my postgraduate research, and to the former Chairman, John Morison. The two anonymous readers at Cambridge University Press gave guidance that proved crucial as I struggled to reshape my doctoral dissertation into a book; whilst I have not always heeded their advice, I remain very grateful for it. I am also obliged to those scholars who expressed an interest in my researches and who took the trouble to comment upon my findings. I would like to thank the following: Bill Speck, Stephen Conway, John Gooch, Pete Edwards, John Houlding, Patrick Bell, Jeremy Black, Edward Spiers, Hugh Cecil, Alan Murray and Andrew Mackillop. In addition, I much appreciated the encouragement given by Brian R. Sullivan, Julie Flavell and Jack Pole. I also wish to acknowledge the generosity with which Dr Houlding, Charles E. Brodine Jr and Gerry Orvis shared the results of their own researches.

Lord Ramsay very kindly granted me permission to publish material gleaned from the invaluable Dalhousie Muniments held in the National Archives of Scotland. I am likewise grateful to Arnold Publishers for allowing me to reproduce parts of an article that first appeared in *War in History*, V, 2 (April 1998) within Chapters 6 and 7 of my book. Two chapters originated as papers presented to the Military History Research Seminars organised in the School of History in Leeds under the auspices of Professors Childs and Gooch; parts of others first surfaced in papers given to the conferences on Early American History and Culture held at Brunel University in 1999 and at Sidney Sussex College, Cambridge, during the following year. The opportunity to present my ideas in this way before lively and informed audiences proved extremely useful, and I am grateful to the organisers, respectively Ken Morgan and Mike McDonnell, and Betty Wood and Tony Badger, for inviting me to speak. At Cambridge University Press, Social Sciences Publishing Director Frank Smith has proved an unfailing source of advice and encouragement since first agreeing to consider my work; it also gives me great pleasure to acknowledge the help of Social Sciences Editorial Assistant Alia Winters, who handled my frequent inquiries with courtesy and efficiency.

The Duke of Wellington once described the Battle of Waterloo as 'hard pounding': his words could equally well be applied to some of the more gruelling aspects of protracted research projects. For me, the pounding would have been all the harder without the convivial company of friends on both sides of the Atlantic: much that appears in these pages was first discussed informally over a pint or two with Craig Gibson, John Finlayson, Catherine Sladen, Robin Shackleton, Matt Spring and Tim

Harrison-Place. Many of the practical aspects of research were eased by others who provided accommodation at short notice. In London, Gary Houston, Katie Williams and Mark and Rosanna Duff all deserve my thanks for their continuing friendship and hospitality. My research trip to California was likewise made all the more enjoyable through the generosity of Sarah and Andy Ingersoll. While writing this book I have been very fortunate to enjoy the companionship of Laura Durnford; her unswerving support contributed greatly to its completion.

Finally I would like to make a special mention of my parents. As a history-obsessed youngster I was very lucky in possessing a father and mother willing to tolerate and even encourage this trait: indeed, barely a weekend of my childhood passed without a family excursion to some castle or other historic site prompted by my persistent pleading. The interest in the past that my parents kindled has never left me: I would therefore like to dedicate this book to them with affection and gratitude.

Note: Unless specified otherwise, all quotations retain their original spelling and punctuation; editorial insertions are placed within square brackets. Underlined passages in manuscripts are here indicated by italics. The army rank given to individuals reflects that relevant at the time of the incident concerned or quotation cited. The term 'rank and file' is used throughout in its mid-eighteenth century sense to denote private soldiers and corporals; sergeants and drummers were classed as non-commissioned officers.

Abbreviations used in footnotes

AB	Abercromby Papers, Huntington Library, San Marino
Add. MSS	Additional Manuscripts, British Library, London
ADM	Admiralty Papers, Public Record Office, Kew
BFTM	*Bulletin of the Fort Ticonderoga Museum*
BIHR	*Bulletin of the Institute of Historical Research*
CHR	*Canadian Historical Review*
CKS	Centre for Kentish Studies, Maidstone
CO	Colonial Office Papers, Public Record Office, Kew
DCB	*Dictionary of Canadian Biography*
DNB	*Dictionary of National Biography*
EHR	*English Historical Review*
GCM	General Court Martial
GD	Gifts and Deposits, National Archives of Scotland, Edinburgh
HMC	*Historical Manuscripts Commission, Reports*
JSAHR	*Journal of the Society for Army Historical Research*
LO	Loudoun Papers, Huntington Library, San Marino
MM	*Mariner's Mirror*
MVHR	*Mississippi Valley Historical Review*
MSS	Manuscripts
NAM	National Army Museum, Chelsea
NYCD	*Documents Relative to the Colonial History of the State of New York*
NYHSC	*New-York Historical Society, Collections*
PMHB	*Pennsylvania Magazine of History and Biography*
RH	Register House Series (microfilms), National Archives of Scotland, Edinburgh
WMQ	*William and Mary Quarterly* (Third Series)
WPHM	*Western Pennsylvania Historical Magazine*
WO	War Office Papers, Public Record Office, Kew

Introduction: Approaching the 'American Army'

On 9 April 1763, Major-General Jeffery Amherst, the Commander-in-Chief of Britain's land forces in North America, authorised a historic announcement from his headquarters in New York. Amherst had received a letter from the Secretary-at-War, Welbore Ellis, informing him of a resolution that had been unanimously agreed in the House of Commons four months previously: this expressed the thanks of the House to the officers of the Navy and Army for their 'meritorious and eminent services' to King and country during the war that had now ended after some seven years. Ellis expressed his personal satisfaction in transmitting this recognition of the 'good conduct, courage and zeal of the officers and soldiers of his Majesty's army', and requested that Amherst communicate this 'public mark of honour' to the men under his command. Amherst was not noted for displays of emotion, but the sentiments he conveyed through the General Orders issued that day were clearly heartfelt:

> The Commander in chief with the warmest gratitude must express to the officers and soldiers he has the honour to command the real pleasure and satisfaction he has in communicating to them this honourable testimony of their services, and he cannot omit on this occasion to signify to them that their constant steady good conduct and unwearied exertion of their abilities in carrying on the extensive and successfull war in this country, not only entitles them to his most sincere acknowledgements, but has imprinted on him such strong marks of affection and esteem for them, that their happiness and glory must always be inseperable from his.[1]

When Amherst first arrived in America five years earlier, British soldiers had not enjoyed such renown. Indeed, the wave of victories responsible for

[1] Orders dated New York, 9 April 1763, in *Journals of the Hon. William Hervey in North America and Europe, with Order Books at Montreal, 1760–1763* (Bury St Edmunds, 1906), pp. 182–83.

raising the reputation of the King's troops to dizzy new heights by 1763 only followed long years of frustrating setbacks which had seen the prestige of the redcoats plunge. During the course of that war British regulars had been employed in North America and the West Indies on a far larger scale than ever before. The gruelling and bloody campaigns in which ever growing numbers of redcoats participated ultimately forged a seasoned 'American Army' that had first conquered Canada and then stripped the Bourbons of their most prized Caribbean possessions.[2] One civilian observer considered the redcoats who sailed from New York for Martinique in 1761 to be 'extremely well disciplined' and 'full of life and courage';[3] the soldier and historian Thomas Mante agreed that the force sent subsequently against Havana was the 'finest army, for its numbers, in the whole world'.[4] Such famous victories were only secured through a lavish expenditure of manpower: the army agent John Calcraft mourned more than the demise of business when he commiserated with Amherst on the heavy casualties sustained in the year's West Indian operations, as 'that army was compos'd of the best soldiers which ever yet existed, & the Loss of such brave men cannot be too much Lamented'.[5]

These contemporary testimonies to the high quality of the 'American Army' are difficult to reconcile with the assessments of many modern historians. In particular, the seasoned and confident troops eulogised by men like Mante bear little resemblance to those redcoats who march through the pages of both 'popular' and scholarly accounts of the Seven Years War. Many such works offer an all-too-familiar picture of the British soldier and his world – a convenient snap-shot that invariably contains certain standard components. According to this well-worn stereotype, the British Army of the mid-eighteenth century was a starkly polarised society in which a rank and file recruited from the very bottom of the social pile soldiered under the command of men drawn from its aristocratic upper reaches. Down-trodden, cowed and resentful, the humble redcoats were kept to their duty by a savage disciplinary code:

2 For use of this title see, for example, letter from Lieutenant Nicholas Delacherois, 'Camp at the Havanna', 30 July 1762, in 'The Letters of Captain Nicholas Delacherois, 9th Regiment', ed. S. G. P. Ward, in *Journal of the Society for Army Historical Research*, LI (1973), 5–14; p. 9.

3 'A Letter from a Gentleman in New York to his friend in London' (no date), in *The Gentleman's Magazine and Historical Chronicle ... 1763* (February), p. 88.

4 Thomas Mante, *The History of the Late War in North America and the Islands of the West Indies, including the Campaigns of MDCCLXIII and MDCCLXIV against His Majesty's Indian Enemies* (London, 1772), p. 484. The author had himself served as Assistant Engineer at Havana.

5 Calcraft to Amherst, 13 November 1762, in WO (War Office Papers, Public Record Office, Kew)/34 (Amherst Papers)/99, fol. 127.

indeed, it was only fear of the lash that persuaded British soldiers to endure the cheerless conditions of army life and the bloody theatre of the battlefield. Drilled to a robotic level of efficiency and crammed inside gaudy and constricting uniforms, such men would march into the cannon's mouth if so ordered because the consequences of refusal were worse. Denied the most basic rights and any individual voice, British soldiers forfeited their very humanity; they were no more than automatons – faceless components in a rigid military machine. The popular image of the British Army's officers is equally unflattering: they were largely fops and fools; adept at manipulating a corrupt system, most of them had bought their way up the promotion ladder. Arrogant, unimaginative and unprofessional, their shortcomings were happily disguised by the ritualistic nature of eighteenth-century European warfare; under such prescribed conditions, shows of initiative were quite simply irrelevant. However, when removed from this familiar environment, and obliged to fight under different rules, such officers invariably led their hapless subordinates to disaster.

This hackneyed and hostile overview of the British Army has enjoyed a particular resonance in North America, for reasons which are not difficult to fathom: at a 'popular' level it fits snugly with the comforting knowledge that such 'professional' British redcoats were subsequently worsted by 'amateur' American patriots during the Revolutionary War; on another, it meshes with the work of modern American scholars who have chosen to view the Seven Years War through the eyes of the colonial populace that British regular troops were sent to defend. Seen from the perspective of a Massachusetts volunteer, or a Connecticut magistrate, the British soldier was indeed an unlovely creature. Not only did the rank and file's swearing, drinking and whoring horrify the God-fearing New Englanders, but their commanders sought to impose policies that threatened cherished liberties throughout the seaboard colonies. Of course, all of this unprecedented imperial interference might have been more bearable if the British Army had at least proved effective at its primary job of combating the French and their Native American 'Indian' allies. Yet in the colonists' opinion this had been far from the case: on the contrary, supercilious British officers had spurned the advice of their American counterparts and proved signally incapable of adapting their stilted and inflexible tactics to local conditions. The results were predictable: defeat after humiliating defeat at the hands of a numerically inferior foe.

The shattering reverses sustained by the redcoats during the dismal opening phases of the Seven Years War have long dominated popular perceptions of that conflict in America. Despite the efforts of a handful of respected scholars to prove otherwise, ultimate victory in that war continues to be attributed to anything but the prowess of the British Army.[6] After all, it is argued, colonial troops had done much to win their own freedom from the French and Indian menace, whilst the redcoats who triumphed at Quebec and elsewhere merely delivered a belated *coup de grâce* to defences that were already undermined by Bourbon indifference, the omnipotence of the Royal Navy and the alienation of Canada's traditional tribal allies. The consensus reached by recent scholars also suggests that Americans came away from the Seven Years War with a thoroughly jaundiced impression of both the British Army and the state it represented: the seeds sown by this animosity would all too soon bear bitter fruit and contribute to the rupture of Britain's Atlantic empire.[7]

These negative portrayals of the redcoats have proved so enduring because they contain an undeniable core of truth: the British Army of the eighteenth century *did* include hardened criminals; some of its malefactors *were* subjected to horrific floggings; a majority of officers *had* purchased their commissions; combat during the heyday of the smoothbore musket *was* typically characterised by formal close-range confrontations; embarrassing defeats *were* sustained in consequence of adherence to hidebound tactics. Again, damning modern assessments of the British Army in America remain rooted in certain undoubted facts, and those historians who view the redcoats as agents of discord in the Anglo-American world have assembled an impressive body of evidence to support their findings. While not seeking to dispute the existence of such tensions, this book none the less argues that the British Army contributed far more to winning the Seven Years War in the Americas than many historians have been prepared to concede: although thousands of locally raised 'provincial' troops served on the mainland, it was the regulars who

6 Although few in number, the British Army's champions in America have included some of the most distinguished historians to work on the pre-Republican era. See S. Pargellis, *Lord Loudoun in North America* (New Haven, 1933), and L. H. Gipson, *The British Empire Before the American Revolution* (15 vols, New York, 1936–70). Indeed, in 1946 Gipson dedicated Volume Six of this magisterial work 'to the thousands of soldiers from the British Isles who lie buried in unknown graves here in the New World as a result of the Great War for the Empire waged between the years 1754 and 1763' (*The Years of Defeat: 1754–1757*, v). John Shy subsequently observed: 'There is renewed emphasis on the fact that British regulars won the war, and it would not have been won otherwise'. See *Toward Lexington. The Role of the British Army in the Coming of the American Revolution* (Princeton, 1965), p. 86.

7 See A. Rogers, *Empire and Liberty: American Resistance to British Authority, 1755–1763* (Los Angeles, 1974); D. E. Leach, *Roots of Conflict: British Armed Forces and Colonial Americans, 1677–1763* (Chapel Hill, North Carolina, 1986), esp. pp. 76–166; F. Jennings, *Empire of Fortune: Crowns, Colonies, and Tribes in the Seven Years War in America* (New York, 1986), esp. pp. 204–22. Anglo-American friction forms a leitmotif of Fred Anderson's large-scale narrative, *Crucible of War. The Seven Years War and the Fate of Empire in British North America, 1754–1766* (New York, 2000).

campaigned throughout the Americas and increasingly bore the brunt of the actual fighting; the focus here is therefore upon the redcoats themselves.[8]

It is now widely recognised that the global conflict that encompassed both the gradual evolution and rapid destruction of the 'American Army' also defined the 'first British Empire'.[9] In acquiring vast new territories, Britain's armed forces had won victories that fuelled patriotic fervour and a growing sense of imperial destiny.[10] For the British Army itself the Seven Years War had likewise marked a watershed: the years after 1763 witnessed not only a dramatic expansion in the size of the peacetime establishment, but also saw increasing numbers of redcoats stationed overseas;[11] from a relatively modest organisation intended primarily for domestic security and limited European campaigning, the Army had been transformed into a sprawling instrument of empire. Despite the pivotal importance of the Seven Years War for Britain's progression to the rank of leading European imperial power, little scholarly attention has been devoted to those servicemen who actually waged it.[12] This book seeks to go some way towards redressing that imbalance by examining the personnel of the 'American Army'; the evidence presented challenges the enduring view of the British soldier in America, and suggests that such simplistic descriptions fail to reflect what was in reality a far more complex picture. Indeed, any deeper exploration of the British Army that operated in the Americas during the 1750s and 1760s reveals a social system characterised by distinctive rituals and relationships – one in which redcoats of all ranks emerge as individuals with voices of their own.

The campaigning experience of these soldiers was very different from that of those battalions despatched to the old battlefields of Flanders and

8 The provincial soldier has already received attention in several scholarly works. See F. Anderson, *A People's Army: Massachusetts Soldiers and Society in the Seven Years War* (Chapel Hill, North Carolina, 1984); J. Titus, *The Old Dominion at War. Society, Politics, and Warfare in Late Colonial Virginia* (Columbia, South Carolina, 1991); H. E. Selesky, *War and Society in Colonial Connecticut* (New Haven, 1990), esp. pp. 144–215.

9 See P. J. Marshall's introduction to *The Oxford History of the British Empire. Volume Two: The Eighteenth Century Empire*, ed. P. J. Marshall (Oxford, 1998), pp. 1–27; also L. Colley, *Britons: Forging the Nation 1707–1837* (New Haven, 1992), pp. 101–02.

10 K. Wilson, *A Sense of the People. Politics, Culture and Imperialism in England, 1715–1785* (Cambridge, 1998), pp. 196–8. E. H. Gould, *The Persistence of Empire. British Political Culture in the Age of the American Revolution* (Chapel Hill, North Carolina, 2000).

11 J. A. Houlding, *Fit for Service: The Training of the British Army 1715–1795* (Oxford, 1981), p. 7.

12 Just as the Royal Navy enjoyed the status of 'senior service' in Georgian Britain, so sailors rather than soldiers have attracted the greatest share of scholarly interest. Students of the army during the Seven Years War have little to set beside the detailed study of the Royal Navy contained in N. A. M. Rodger's *The Wooden World: An Anatomy of the Georgian Navy* (London, 1986).

Germany. In America, redcoats might be expected to endure both the bitter winters of Nova Scotia and the torrid heat of the Caribbean, with their attendant risks of frostbite or fever. These troops likewise faced the fatigue of negotiating exceptionally difficult terrain – ranging from the forests, lakes and mountains of the mainland wilderness to the dense tropical foliage and rugged volcanic landscapes of the West Indian islands. In addition, besides encountering the white-coated Bourbon regulars that generations of British soldiers had confronted in Europe, the redcoats who served in the Americas were also obliged to deal with more exotic foes – native 'Indians' and other irregulars who employed bewildering guerrilla tactics and paid scant regard to the conventions of 'civilised' warfare. Taken together, these conditions demanded high levels of endurance and adaptability, producing soldiers who compensated in courage and tenacity for what they lacked in parade-ground polish. In the opinion of the New York trader John Watts, it was the hard-bitten veterans of these punishing American campaigns who had clinched victory during the costly expedition against Havana. He wrote:

> Your Hyde Park Generals it's said treated them with great contempt, because they were not high dressd, they had been too long away from St: James' to be fashionable, hard labour, in the Woods & Batteaus had soild their Cloths & discomposed the smart Cock, yet without such Troops ... the Conquest had never been made, nor the place ours.[13]

As contemporaries on both sides of the Atlantic ultimately recognised, the challenge of American campaigning created a remarkably flexible force that proved capable of waging both the 'conventional' warfare of the Old World, and operating under the very different 'irregular' conditions of the New. The British Army only achieved victory through a painful and protracted metamorphosis: the arduous process by which the 'American Army' adapted itself under the impetus of local conditions forms the second major theme of this book. During its dynamic period of transformation, the 'American Army' acquired an ethos and tactical doctrine that set it apart from other British and European armies: the redcoat regiments that assaulted Martinique in 1762 were in many respects different from those sent into the wilderness seven years before. This same army was 'American' in more than just name: although the bulk of the regulars had been recruited in Britain, a significant minority were either natives of

[13] Watts to Moses Franks, New York, 27 October 1763, in *Collections of the New-York Historical Society, 1928: The Letter Book of John Watts, Merchant and Councillor of New York, January 1, 1762 – December 22, 1765* (New York, 1928), p. 92.

the North American colonies or recent immigrants from Europe. In consequence, many of the redcoat battalions in America exhibited a more diverse character than those employed elsewhere.[14] The American theatre of the Seven Years War also witnessed the British Army's first large-scale use of Scottish Highlanders, a phenomenon that has been identified as making an important contribution towards the formation of a 'British' national identity.[15] These factors rendered the 'American Army' a distinctive and influential organisation – one that merits detailed investigation.

Structure and sources

As regards structure, Chapter 1 narrates the operations of the 'American Army'; it traces the scale, scope and effectiveness of Britain's deployment of regular manpower in North America and the Caribbean between 1755 and 1763, so providing a broad context for the thematic chapters that follow: these present a detailed examination of the redcoats and their experience of warfare in the Americas. Themes explored include the recruitment and composition of the rank and file and officer corps; the implementation of discipline; the extent to which the army represented a distinct community with its own customs; and the degree to which soldiers were prepared to speak out in defence of their established rights. Subsequent chapters address the challenges that faced the British Army in America, and its efforts to overcome them. Coverage is given to the constraints that America's physical environment imposed upon military activity, and the cultural context of American warfare – in particular, the Army's contacts with the Indian tribes of the mainland and the impact of 'savagery' upon established European codes of behaviour in wartime. Two chapters address different aspects of the Army's operational response to 'American' warfare: the danger posed by 'irregulars' and the redcoats' attempts to neutralise them; and the extent to which conditions encountered in America bequeathed a lasting tactical legacy to the British Army. Although integrated within that organisation, the Scottish Highland battalions retained a distinct cultural identity; they are therefore accorded detailed analysis in their own right. The final chapter considers the demobilisation process and the subsequent fate of disbanded veterans; it

[14] It has been suggested that as many as 11,000 colonials saw service in British regular units during the Seven Years War. See Don Higginbotham, 'The Early American Way of War: Reconnaissance and Appraisal', in *William and Mary Quarterly* (Third Series), XLIV (1987), 230–73; p. 235.

[15] Colley, *Britons*, p. 103.

reassesses the place of the 'American Army' in history and legend, ventures some general verdicts regarding that force's wider significance as an agency of British empire and nationhood, and evaluates its unwitting role in the creation of the American republic.

The interpretations presented here rest upon a wide range of evidence. A particular effort has been made to reflect the views and experience of the 'common soldier', and thereby provide a voice for a figure all too often assumed to be mute. For example, in his study of Wellington's army, Sir Charles Oman noted the relative dearth of military memoirs surviving from the years before Britain's epic struggle with Napoleonic France. Oman conjectured that both the lost war with the rebellious American colonists, and the victorious global conflict it followed, had failed to spark the 'crusading' spirit that inspired the Iron Duke's soldier-scribes to record their experiences.[16] The lack of such 'voices from the ranks' has also been lamented by scholars dealing directly with the British Army of the eighteenth century. In his general survey of the subject, Colonel H. C. B. Rogers remarked upon the rarity of first-hand 'accounts of the life of the rank and file, particularly at the beginning of this period'.[17] Similarly, in a more specialised study of the Army's 'police' role, Tony Hayter regretted the paucity of memoirs, diaries and letters capable of adding flesh to the bare bones of the 'official' record; because neither 'the man in the ranks nor the man in the street wrote memoirs or correspondence', the picture had instead to be constructed 'from many scattered and oblique sources'.[18]

One object of this book is to suggest that, as far as the 'American Army' is concerned, such assessments are unduly pessimistic. Amongst the diverse sources consulted, the first-hand testimony of participants figures prominently: indeed, the voices of both officers and other ranks who fought through these costly campaigns still resonate from the pages of a surprising number of memoirs. These eyewitness sources vary greatly in

16 C. Oman, *Wellington's Army, 1809–1814* (London, 1912), pp. 3–6. Oman was 'quite certain that there was more writing going on in the army during the ten years 1805–1815 than in the whole of the eighteenth century' (ibid., p. 3).

17 H. C. B. Rogers, *The British Army of the Eighteenth Century* (London, 1977), p. 61.

18 T. Hayter, *The Army and the Crowd in Mid-Georgian England* (London, 1978), pp. 2–3. More recently, Alan Guy has emphasised the readiness of scholars to consult just such a diverse range of material in their efforts to shed light upon the Georgian soldiery. See *Colonel Samuel Bagshawe and the Army of George II, 1731–1762*, ed. A. Guy (London, 1990), p. 15. Dr Guy, whose own researches have done much to clarify the complexities of regimental administration, notes that the bulk of this work has addressed the period *after* 1760. Studies of army life in the reign of George III include S. Frey, *The British Soldier in America: A Social History of Military Life in the Revolutionary Period* (Austin, Texas, 1981); and G. Steppler, 'The Common Soldier in the Reign of George III, 1760–1793' (unpublished PhD thesis, University of Oxford, 1984).

nature and value, ranging from detailed contemporaneous journals to more impressionistic retrospective memoirs; some embrace picaresque adventures worthy of Thackeray's Barry Lyndon himself. Yet if read with a critical eye, such hitherto underexploited sources can shed a remarkable degree of light upon the personnel and campaigns of the 'American Army'.

Letters from private soldiers and NCOs occasionally surface amongst the papers accumulated by senior officers; however, the bulk of such collections comprise correspondence between fellow officers, along with material addressing aspects of army administration. Of the major collections consulted here, the papers of three successive commanders-in-chief, John Campbell, Lord Loudoun (1756–58), James Abercromby (1758) and Jeffery Amherst (1758–63), proved particularly valuable.[19] In addition, a mass of material concerning the period 1756–58 exists among the various official and personal papers relating to Brigadier-General John Forbes.[20] Another category of source material which deserves particular mention is the extant collections of orders issued within the 'American Army'. Examples of such 'orderly books' survive at various levels – army, brigade, garrison, regiment and even company – offering coverage for most theatres of operations between 1755 and 1763. Besides providing a contemporaneous record of efforts to regulate the activities of a given formation, orderly books shed light upon many facets of army life, frequently naming individuals of all ranks: as such, they go some way to bridge the gap between personal memoirs and correspondence, and those sources concerned purely with military administration.

In terms of official administrative records, the evidence relating to the 'American Army' initially appears both scanty and fragmentary; in certain instances, such as the tattered 'returns' of troops serving in America held at the Public Record Office, this description is quite literally true. Hanoverian Britain lacked the bureaucracy of its arch rival across the Channel; in consequence the official records cannot compete with the documents held in the Archives de la Guerre and quarried by André Corvisier for his study of the French soldier of the *ancien régime*.[21]

19 Loudoun Papers (LO) and Abercromby Papers (AB), Huntington Library, San Marino, California. Both the 'official' (WO/34) and the 'family' (Centre for Kentish Studies (CKS), Maidstone, U1350) Amherst papers have been consulted.

20 Much of Forbes's correspondence is gathered in the National Archives of Scotland, Edinburgh. See GD (Gifts and Deposits) 45 (Dalhousie Muniments)/2 and microfilms RH 4/86/1–2. Other important material has been published in *Writings of General John Forbes, Relating to His Service in North America*, ed. A. P. James (Menasha, Wisconsin, 1938).

21 See A. Corvisier, *L'Armée française de la fin du XVIIe siècle au ministère de Choiseul* (2 vols, Paris, 1964).

Despite such discouraging first impressions, upon closer acquaintance the War Office files yield valuable evidence. As Dr John Houlding has demonstrated, systematic analysis of such routine documents as marching orders and inspection returns can reveal much about the Army's role and efficiency. In addition, the registers of those veterans who applied for pensions from the Royal Hospital at Chelsea contain basic biographical information which goes far to compensate for the dearth of soldiers' discharge papers from the era of the Seven Years War.[22] The hefty ledgers of correspondence emanating from the office of the Secretary-at-War provide a helpful running record of administrative decisions. Less orderly, but more interesting for the purposes of the present book, are the letters and petitions sent to the War Office by individuals ranging from senior officers to soldiers' widows; these survive in collected form from 1756 onwards.[23]

Anyone studying the British Army in North America during the Seven Years War owes a debt to the pioneering work of Stanley Pargellis; his formidable scholarship underpinned an analysis of army administration that remains required reading. In the course of his researches, Pargellis noted the importance of another extensive range of War Office papers, the records of the Army's General Courts Martial; indeed, he observed that these minutes 'reconstitute the intimate details of army life more satisfactorily than any other kind of document'.[24] As with soldiers' memoirs and journals, provided that due caution is observed and selectivity exercised, the minutes of the General Courts Martial constitute an invaluable body of evidence; indeed, extensive work undertaken on these records for this study has only served to increase respect for Pargellis's assessment of their worth.

In combination, these varied personal and official documents provide a substantial reservoir of primary source material: this book employs such evidence to present a detailed reassessment of the redcoats and their experience of the Seven Years War in the Americas; in doing so it aims to illuminate a neglected and misunderstood society, and thereby place some flesh and blood upon the metaphorical 'sinews of power' of Hanoverian Britain's 'fiscal–military state'.

22 Both the chronological 'Admission Books' (WO/116) and the unit-based 'Regimental Registers' (WO/120) have been used. Discharge documents of men applying for pensions from 1787 onwards are in class WO/121.

23 See WO/4 (Out-letters, Secretary-at-War); WO/1 (War Office, In-letters).

24 Pargellis, *Lord Loudoun*, p. 370; WO/71 (Courts Martial, Proceedings).

1

Britain's war effort in the Americas

The events of the 'Great War for the Empire' in the Americas have long excited the attention of historians. Indeed, the signatures on the Treaty of Paris were barely dry before detailed accounts of the struggle appeared in print.[1] Since then, succeeding generations of historians on both sides of the Atlantic have continued to be drawn to the subject.[2] Such interest is understandable. The campaigns waged between 1755 and 1763 sprawled over thousands of miles, encompassed famous victories and humiliating defeats, and sported a *dramatis personae* ranging from the cowardly and incompetent to the heroic and inspired. In addition, for all its fluctuating fortunes, the conflict terminated in the effective elimination of France from the North American mainland. This decisive result was to have a major impact upon the balance of power on that continent – with momentous implications for the future of Britain's own American colonies.

The conflict that convulsed North America in the mid-eighteenth century was the final bout of an ongoing struggle between the English-speaking colonies and French Canada that had begun some sixty years previously. Since 1689, when William III confronted Louis XIV and triggered a 'Second Hundred Years War', the formal European campaigns had each spawned their savage offshoots involving the

1 See John Entick, *The General History of the Late War, Containing its Rise, Progress and Events, in Europe, Asia, Africa and America* (5 vols, London, 1763–64); Anon, *An Impartial History of the Late Glorious War* (Manchester, 1764). Mante's *History of the Late War* provides the best overview of the American campaigns.

2 An ambitious recent narrative is Anderson, *Crucible of War*. The most detailed modern treatment remains Gipson's *British Empire Before the American Revolution*. Volumes VI–IX (1946–56) cover what Gipson dubbed 'the Great War for the Empire'. For all its prejudices and occasional liberties with the sources, Francis Parkman's *Montcalm and Wolfe* (2 vols, Boston, 1880) offers a vivid account. The strong Anglo-centric perspective of Parkman, and indeed Gipson, can be balanced by consulting Guy Frégault, *Canada: The War of the Conquest*, trans. M. M. Cameron (Toronto, 1969). For a briefer treatment see D. E. Leach, *Arms for Empire: A Military History of the British Colonies in North America, 1607–1763* (New York, 1973), pp. 351–510. The role of Indians is emphasised in Jennings, *Empire of Fortune*, and I. K. Steele, *Warpaths: Invasions of North America* (New York, 1994), pp. 179–247.

American colonies of the rival powers. Hence the Wars of the League of Augsburg and the Spanish and Austrian Successions were mirrored across the Atlantic in spasms of fighting that the English colonists remembered by the names of their monarchs – King William, Queen Anne and King George. Such confrontations proved bloody enough, but were to be dwarfed by the scale of the closing phase of the struggle.

The friction that sparked the Seven Years War grew from Britain's increasing disquiet over France's territorial ambitions on the northern and western fringes of its mainland American colonies. Continuing tension led to bloodshed amidst the backwoods of the Upper Ohio during the summer of 1754. As the storm clouds gathered, some British politicians were quick to appreciate that the looming war was likely to prove more serious than its predecessors. On 16 December, Secretary-at-War Henry Fox warned the House of Commons that the American colonies would become embroiled in a conflict 'very different from any they were ever engaged in before'. Instead of 'a parcel of wild Indians, or a few French militia', the colonists could now expect to face French regulars – the same veterans who had sometimes worsted British troops in Flanders during the War of the Austrian Succession. Against such opponents, Fox added, 'a much more exact discipline will be necessary on our side, than ever was necessary in any war heretofore carried on by any of our colonies in America'.[3] It was in an effort to bolster colonial defences with just such an injection of discipline that the ministry headed by Thomas Pelham-Holles, Duke of Newcastle, had already approved a reinforcement of two regiments of regular troops under Major-General Edward Braddock, who was to serve as commander-in-chief in North America.[4] Further orders were issued for the re-raising within America itself of a brace of regiments which had served during the previous war, and been disbanded at its close.[5]

This initial response did not represent any significant change in traditional attitudes to colonial defence: the government had no plans for

[3] *Proceedings and Debates of the British Parliaments Respecting North America, 1754–1783*, eds R. C. Simmons and P. D. G. Thomas (6 vols, New York, 1982–87), I, p. 36.

[4] Braddock's battalions were Sir Peter Halkett's 44th Foot and Thomas Dunbar's 48th Foot. When ordered upon American service in October 1754, both were on the weak 'Irish' establishment of 310 rank and file. Before embarking from Cork they were to be raised to 520 each by drafts of 420 men drawn from regiments in Great Britain and Ireland. In America, both battalions were to be further augmented to 730 by local recruiting. In February 1755, orders were issued for yet another augmentation to 1,040 rank and file. See Henry Fox to various correspondents, War Office, 3 October 1754 to 3 February 1755, in WO/4/50, pp. 50; 66; 158 (unless specified otherwise, all correspondence from the Secretary-at-War or his clerks originates from the War Office).

[5] William Shirley's 50th Foot and Sir William Pepperrell's 51st Foot (Fox to Robert Ince, ibid., p. 50).

any large or long-term commitment of regular manpower in North America. Previous military emergencies in the Americas had likewise been countered by the despatch of regulars intended to stiffen the resolve of the colonial militia, or to cooperate with the armies of volunteer 'provincials' that were habitually raised for specific operations by the individual colonies.[6] The British Army's performance on these occasions had rarely proved impressive.[7] Once such crises passed, the majority of these regular troops were typically withdrawn, leaving small garrisons in their wake. For example, Nathaniel Bacon's Virginian rebellion of 1676 had shaken the home government sufficiently to send a task force of more than 1,100 soldiers to restore order.[8] Although these redcoats arrived too late to participate in quelling the unrest, some of them remained behind to discourage future disorder. At the same period, similar penny-packets of regulars were permanently based in New York, Jamaica and the Leeward Islands. During the first half of the eighteenth century, the British Army's presence in North America and the Caribbean had gradually increased as an ever-growing number of settlers sought protection against such external foes as the French, Spanish or native Indians, and the internal threat posed by their own expanding slave populations. In 1715, following the Treaty of Utrecht, Britain's military establishment in the Americas numbered almost 2,000 men. By 1754, that total had doubled.[9] Such figures sounded impressive enough, but the units involved were too scattered to act effectively. After 1750, three battalions were concentrated in Nova Scotia to watch over a resentful Acadian populace: however, the remainder of the North American mainland had to depend upon seven 'independent companies' based in the particularly vulnerable frontier colonies of New York and South Carolina. In the Caribbean and North Atlantic, Britain's regular presence consisted of two regiments and a pair of independent companies. Many of these redcoats had been manning their remote outposts for decades: neglected by the home government, their military efficiency was often dire. Commenting upon the condition of the 40th and 45th Foot in Nova Scotia, James Wolfe observed that they had been 'so long in this Country, & hence imbibed so many bad Habits,

6 Unlike the militia – those able-bodied men obliged to defend their communities in crisis situations – the provincials served for pay and were raised for designated campaigns only. However, as it embraced most of the adult male population, the militia theoretically provided the pool of manpower from which the provincials were recruited.

7 See, for example, J. Childs, 'Secondary Operations of the British Army During the Nine Years War, 1688–1697', in *JSAHR*, LXXIII (1995), 73–98.

8 W. E. Washburn, *The Governor and the Rebel: A History of Bacon's Rebellion in Virginia* (Chapel Hill, North Carolina, 1957), p. 95.

9 Shy, *Towards Lexington*, pp. 24; 29; 34–45.

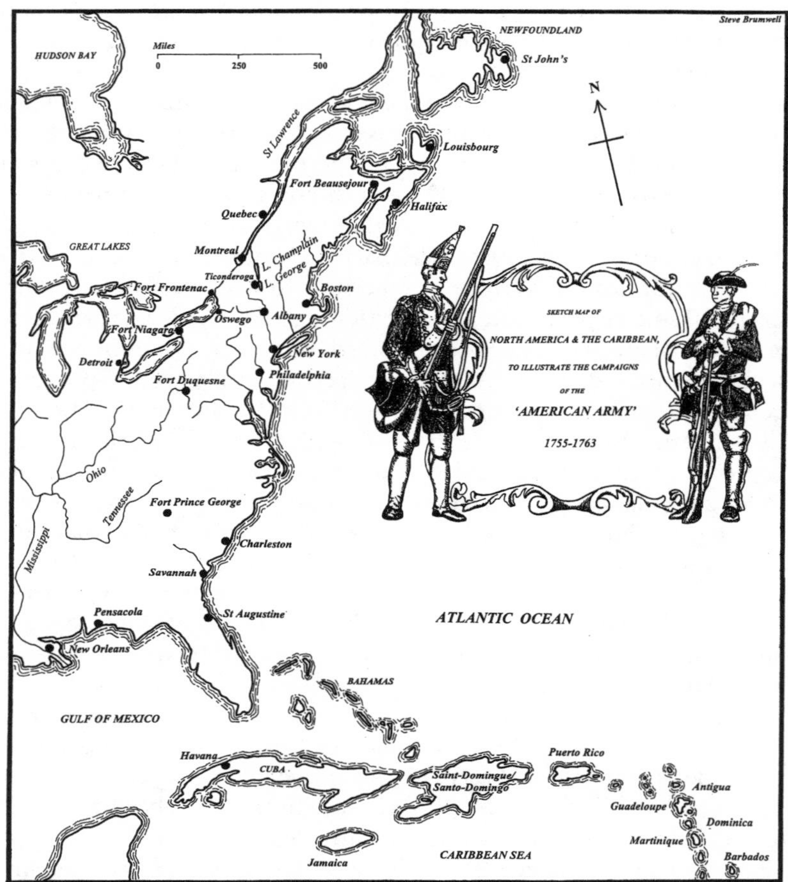

Map 1 North America and the Caribbean, to illustrate the campaigns of the 'American Army', 1755–63.

that No good can be made of them'.[10] The reputation of the West Indian battalions was equally poor: high mortality from local diseases rendered the Caribbean a dreaded posting for officers and men alike. On the eve of the 'Great War for Empire', Britain's military presence in the Americas was plainly inadequate in terms both of quantity and quality.

10 See 'General Wolfe's Scheme for Improving the Colony [Nova Scotia] . . . 1758 or 1759' in *The Northcliffe Collection* (Ottawa, 1926), p. 111. The 40th had served in the province, without relief, since its formation in 1719 (ibid., p. 109). For the notoriously inefficient New York regulars see S. Pargellis, 'The Four Independent Companies of New York', in *Essays in Colonial American History, Presented to Charles McClean Andrews by his students* (New Haven, 1931), pp. 96–123.

Defeat and demoralisation

The reinforcement represented by Braddock's two British battalions arrived at Virginia's Potomac River in March 1755; they were to form the back-bone of the army designed to execute one thrust of Britain's North American strategy for that year. Bolstered with American recruits, and supported by locally raised provincials, this command was to push through the wilderness of Pennsylvania to strike the French post of Fort Duquesne at the Forks of the Ohio. The two regular regiments raising in America were to mount a second expedition supervised by William Shirley, the lieutenant-governor of Massachusetts, and Braddock's second-in-command. According to the plan, once Braddock had captured Fort Duquesne, he was to unite with this northern army and march against the French fortress of Niagara. In addition, Colonel William Johnson, the newly appointed superintendent to the northern Indian tribes, was to lead an army of provincials from New York against Crown Point. Finally, French incursions in Nova Scotia were to be countered by an expedition to Fort Beauséjour in the Bay of Fundy.

By May, Braddock's force had begun assembling at Fort Cumberland, Maryland.[11] The expedition finally marched on 10 June, having been delayed by the sluggish response of the colonial authorities to requests for transport and supplies. This failure of local governments to give whole-hearted support to the efforts of the British Army was to become a familiar complaint in the coming war years. Braddock rapidly encountered other obstacles that were to dog subsequent British commanders obliged to operate in the wilderness beyond the settlements of the eastern seaboard colonies: chief among them was the immense logistical problem of negotiating the mountainous and wooded terrain that divided him from his goal, while carrying sufficient supplies to feed his men and draught animals, and enough artillery to pound the objective into submission. It was in an effort to hasten his progress that Braddock decided to leave his heavy baggage and part of the troops at the Little Meadows under the command of Colonel Thomas Dunbar of the 48th Foot, and press on with a picked force including the original core of regulars brought from Ireland. Despite his enduring reputation as a blundering martinet, Braddock spared no effort to secure his column from surprise, and hostile Indians who attempted to menace its flanks were baffled. After a laborious approach march, Braddock's force neared its objective on 9 July. By the early afternoon

[11] On the Braddock expedition see P. E. Kopperman, *Braddock at the Monongahela* (Pittsburgh, 1977).

the troops had successfully negotiated a hazardous double crossing of the Monongahela River. Soon after, Braddock's advance-guard collided with a force of some 850 French and Indians sent from the Fort. After an initial exchange of fire the Indians flanked the British column, seizing an area of dominating high ground that the advance-guard under Lieutenant-Colonel Thomas Gage had neglected to secure. In the ensuing bush-fight Braddock's regulars became disordered by the unfamiliar wooded conditions and 'irregular' tactics of their opponents. Unlike their concealed assailants, the close-packed redcoats provided a perfect target. One survivor recalled:

> They need not have taken sight at us for they Always had a large Mark, but if we saw of them five or six at one time [it] was a great sight and they Either on their Bellies or Behind trees or Runing from one tree to another almost by the ground.[12]

After some three hours of such confused fighting, Braddock's men succumbed to panic. They broke and fled, taking their mortally wounded general with them. Out of the 1,469 men with Braddock that day, nearly two-thirds were killed or wounded.[13] The disaster was compounded by a shameful panic at Dunbar's camp, resulting in the wholesale destruction of much-needed munitions; that officer subsequently withdrew the remnants of his regulars to premature 'winter quarters' in Philadelphia, so exposing the frontier settlements to the attentions of French and Indian raiders.

The dispiriting outcome of Braddock's expedition was already known when Shirley's northern offensive got under way in late July. Shirley, who had now assumed the mantle of commander-in-chief, headed west from Schenectady on 24 July with about 2,000 regulars and provincials.[14] He reached the key trading station of Oswego on Lake Ontario without opposition, but supply problems and heavy desertion prevented the expedition from getting anywhere near its objective of Niagara. Meanwhile, Johnson's army of 3,000 New England provincials advanced northwards from Albany, constructing Fort Edward before cautiously proceeding to the southern end of Lake George. On 8 September, Johnson encountered a Franco-Canadian army commanded by Major-

12 'Journal of Cholmley's Batman', in *Braddock's Defeat*, ed. C. Hamilton (Norman, Oklahoma, 1959), p. 29.

13 *Military Affairs in North America, 1748–65: Selected Documents from the Cumberland Papers in Windsor Castle*, ed. S. Pargellis (New York, 1936), p. 114.

14 Shirley had his own and Pepperrell's regiments, together numbering about 1,600, and some 500 New Jersey provincials. See J. A. Schutz, *William Shirley; King's Governor of Massachusetts* (Chapel Hill, North Carolina, 1961), pp. 201; 206.

General Jean-Armand Baron de Dieskau.[15] Unlike Braddock, Dieskau could boast extensive combat experience: this did not prevent him ending the day as a wounded captive after his force was worsted at the confused and rambling battle of Lake George. Despite their unexpected victory, Johnson's provincials grew increasingly dejected and homesick. News that the French had taken the opportunity to fortify Ticonderoga, at the northern head of Lake George, persuaded Johnson to abandon the campaign against Crown Point and instead consolidate his position at the opposite end of the lake by constructing Fort William Henry. Of all the British expeditions mounted that summer, only the small-scale Nova Scotia operation achieved its stated objective. Lieutenant-Colonel Robert Monckton led 2,000 provincials and 280 regulars against Fort Beauséjour. After some desultory skirmishing with the French and their allied Indians, that post was bombarded into surrender on 16 June and renamed Fort Cumberland in honour of the captain-general of the British Army, William Augustus, Duke of Cumberland.

The opening year of campaigning had proved inauspicious for British arms. Observers were quick to blame Braddock's defeat on the cowardice of his redcoats, noting that they were the same men who had fled so disgracefully before Jacobite clansmen at Prestonpans a decade earlier.[16] The regulars' conduct at the Monongahela was contrasted unfavourably with that of the Virginian provincials, who 'behav'd like Men and died like Soldiers'.[17] Indeed, such limited successes as had been secured that summer stemmed largely from the efforts of the 'amateur' provincials rather than the red-coated 'professionals': after all, the force sent to the Bay of Fundy was overwhelmingly composed of Massachusetts volunteers, whilst Johnson's provincials had vanquished Dieskau without the aid of the British Army. This situation prompted some pundits to question the very concept of deploying British regulars in North America. Such 'old English officers and soldiers', one commentator argued, 'must always engage upon unequal terms, for want of knowing the method of fighting which is peculiar to this country'.[18]

15 Dieskau's force numbered about 1,500, of whom 220 were regulars from 'Old France' and the remainder Canadian militia and Indians. See 'Battle of Lake George, 8th September, 1755', in *Documents Relative to the Colonial History of the State of New York*, ed. E. B. O'Callaghan and B. Fernow (15 vols, Albany, 1853–87), X, 335.

16 *Gentleman's Magazine, 1755* (August), p. 380. In fact, only one of Braddock's battalions, Halkett's 44th, had fought at Prestonpans. At that time it was numbered the 55th. See K. Tomasson and F. Buist, *Battles of the '45* (London, 1962), p. 59.

17 George Washington to Robert Dinwiddie, Fort Cumberland, 18 July 1755, in *The Writings of George Washington*, ed. J. C. Fitzpatrick (39 vols, Washington, 1931–44), I, 149. Washington, himself a Virginian, had served as an aide-de-camp to Braddock.

18 *Gentleman's Magazine, 1755* (October), p. 474.

The campaigning season of 1756 none the less saw the arrival of fresh British battalions in North America: Charles Otway's 35th Foot and Lord John Murray's 42nd Regiment of Highlanders – the 'Black Watch' – landed at New York in June along with Major-Generals James Abercromby and Daniel Webb.[19] These officers were to act under John Campbell, Earl of Loudoun, who replaced Shirley as commander-in-chief in North America. By the time of Loudoun's arrival in July 1756, the reputation of the regulars had sunk so low that a provincial army destined for Crown Point under Major-General John Winslow initially refused to serve alongside the redcoats. According to Benjamin Franklin, they feared that 'Regulars join'd with them, would claim all the Honour of any Success, and charge them with the Blame of every Miscarriage'.[20] Friction between regulars and provincials was fuelled by mutual suspicion: in particular, the official ruling that reduced general and field officers of the provincials to the status of senior captains when serving with the regulars generated deep resentment amongst the colonials.

Neither the reinforcements from Britain, nor the regular troops raising in America, played any part in the great disaster of 1756. Dieskau's successor, Major-General Louis-Joseph Marquis de Montcalm, wasted little time before striking at the English colonies.[21] On 14 August the important entrepôt of Oswego, which was garrisoned by about 1,700 regulars and provincials, capitulated after a feeble resistance. Oswego's fortifications had proved so inadequate in the face of the French cannonade that the sickly defenders were obliged to build batteries from old pork barrels. As one officer recalled, the garrison 'lay so much exposed, that the Enemy could see the Buckles in our Shoes'.[22] A handful of the garrison were killed during the siege, and more were murdered following the surrender after the French proved unable to control their Indian allies: the remainder were sent to Canada as prisoners-of-war. In what was to become a familiar strategy of aggressive defence, Montcalm decided against a further advance, instead contenting himself with destroying the Oswego complex before withdrawing to Montreal.

19 Orders were issued for each of these battalions to be augmented with some 500 men before they sailed for America, raising them to a theoretical establishment of 1,040 rank and file. See Secretary-at-War, William Wildman, Viscount Barrington to Robert Ince, 27 January 1756, in WO/4/51, p. 158; Barrington to Fox, 18 February, in ibid., p. 203. Lord Barrington succeeded Fox at the War Office in November 1755, continuing there until March 1761, when he was replaced by Charles Townshend.

20 To Sir Everard Fawkener, New York, 27 July 1756, in *Military Affairs in North America*, p. 185.

21 Montcalm fielded 3,100 regulars, Canadians and Indians ('Campaign of 1756 in Canada', in *NYCD*, X, 468).

22 'Journal of the Siege of Oswego' in *The Military History of Great Britain, for 1756, 1757 . . .* (London, 1757), p. 38.

The expansion of regular manpower

The Oswego débâcle, following on the heels of Braddock's defeat, was responsible for a decisive change in Britain's attitude towards the defence of her American possessions: from the autumn of 1756 ministers reacted to events across the Atlantic by ordering a dramatic expansion of the King's troops in North America. Back in January the Cabinet had already approved a scheme to recruit a further four battalions of regulars within the colonies themselves. It was intended that this 'Royal American Regiment' should be raised amongst the Protestant German settlers of Pennsylvania. The final composition of this sprawling formation proved far more motley, but the original plan reflected a general policy that sought to fill the ranks of the regular regiments in America with colonial recruits.[23] The attractiveness of such initiatives was only enhanced by an acute dearth of volunteers in Britain. Indeed, the manpower crisis at home had proved so worrying that a Recruiting Act was passed to 'press' the 'idle able-bodied' into the Army and marines. The previous summer had already witnessed a controversial plan to recall those 'out-pensioners' of Chelsea Hospital who remained capable of shouldering a musket and employ them on garrison and other duties, so releasing more robust troops for service elsewhere.[24]

Endorsed by the Duke of Cumberland, the drive to gain recruits in the American colonies had initially enjoyed considerable success: Stanley Pargellis has estimated that during the opening two years of the war some 7,500 men were enlisted in America by British regiments, compared with 4,500 regulars sent from Britain itself.[25] From the summer of 1756, after the official declaration of war against France, that situation began to change. In contrast to the opening phase of the conflict, the overwhelming majority of the regulars in North America now hailed from the mother country. In September, orders were issued for Richard O'Farrell's 22nd Foot, along with drafts of men drawn from twelve battalions in Ireland, to be sent as reinforcements to America.[26] The priority placed upon increasing the regular presence across the Atlantic was further highlighted in the New Year with a novel move to raise two battalions of Scottish

[23] Initially numbered the 62nd Foot, the Royal American Regiment became the 60th when the 50th and 51st were 'broken' in 1757. On the raising of this unit see Pargellis, *Lord Loudoun*, pp. 61–67.

[24] *The London Gazette*, no. 9,500, 5–9 August 1755.

[25] Pargellis, *Lord Loudoun*, pp. 108–109.

[26] Barrington to Lt-Col. Lawrence, Governor of Nova Scotia, 20 September 1756 (WO/4/52, p. 249).

Highlanders specifically for American service.[27] Early in the summer of 1757, the American command received a substantial addition of seven more battalions of regular troops.[28] In August a further reinforcement was authorised, theoretically consisting of 2,380.[29] By the autumn of 1757 there were 21 battalions and seven independent companies of regulars on the North American continent – a total of 20,268 officers and men.[30]

In all, during 1757 some 11,000 regulars were sent from Britain to America: the same period witnessed the former flood of colonial recruits dwindle to a trickle, with just 1,200 men being raised.[31] This dramatic reversal resulted from several factors. First, the recruiting parties of 1755–56 had enjoyed such rich pickings in the colonies because they faced few of the legal restrictions that curbed their activities in Britain. From the summer of 1756 that situation altered with the introduction of legislation intended to appease colonial opinion by regulating such thorny issues as the widespread recruitment of indentured servants.[32] In Pennsylvania, the Army's enlistment of 'a great Number of Bought Servants' had provoked a strongly worded protest from the province's elected representatives: they considered that this interference with their legal property and rights constituted 'a manifest and grievous Injustice & Oppression'.[33] The new law sought to mollify masters, allowing them to retrieve errant servants by refunding the enlistment money; it also offered financial compensation – at a level to be fixed by two local justices of the peace – to cover a recruit's remaining period of indenture. Far from defusing the crisis, the act backfired by providing a legal basis for resisting recruitment. As 1756 drew to a close Loudoun was already pessimistic about the prospects for recruitment in America: in Pennsylvania the army had 'hitherto reapt very little benefit

[27] Both battalions were to consist of 1,040 rank and file under Lieutenant-Colonel Commandants Archibald Montgomery and Simon Fraser. See *London Magazine or Gentleman's Monthly Intelligencer, 1757* (January), pp. 41–2.

[28] These comprised the second battalion of the 1st Foot ('The Royal Regiment' or 'Royal Scots'), and the following regiments: 17th, 27th ('The Inniskilling Regiment'), 28th, 43rd, 46th and 55th. The 2/1st was on the establishment of 1,040 rank and file, all the others at 730.

[29] There were nine companies of Highlanders plus drafts of 40 men from each of 37 battalions in England and Ireland. See Barrington to Colonel Whitmore, 11 August 1757, in WO/4/54, p. 311.

[30] See 'Monthly Return of His Majesty's Forces in North America', 24 October 1757, in GD 45/2/13/3. Of the 18,385 'effective' rank and file, only 14,254 were actually fit for duty.

[31] Pargellis, *Lord Loudoun*, p. 109.

[32] *An Act for the Better Recruiting of His Majesty's Forces on the Continent of North America; and for the better Regulation of the Army, and preventing of Desertion therein* (Boston, 1756).

[33] 'The Humble Address of the Representatives of the Freemen of Pennsylvania', to Lt-Gov. Robert Hunter Morris, 11 February 1756 (LO 819).

from the act relating to Servants, from the general resistance of the People, and the Justices insisting, they are the judges of the Sum the man is worth to his Master'; things were no better in New England, where 'the People of the Country give every discouragement, Publickly and Privately, to prevent the People from Enlisting'. Loudoun added that the situation was exacerbated because militiamen balloted for service in the provincials were prepared to pay 'very high Premiums' for substitutes to enlist in their place.[34]

Loudoun's fears were well justified: in coming months regular recruiting officers faced an increasingly uphill struggle in attracting colonial volunteers for their battalions. For example, in January 1758 Captain John Cosnan of the 45th Foot doubted that his recruiting parties in Boston would enjoy any success, owing to 'so great a backwardness to the King's service'.[35] That same month, Lieutenant-Colonel John Donaldson of the 55th Foot told how his recruiting officer had complained of 'ill usage' from 'ye people in Connecticut, and of their taking all measures in their power to obstruct him in raising men'.[36] The handful of recruits enlisted by such efforts proved incapable of redressing the steady wastage sustained by the regulars through combat, sickness and desertion.

The nadir of British prestige

Most of those redcoats that Loudoun commanded in the summer of 1757 were gathered for an expedition against the great French fortress of Louisbourg on Cape Breton, which was viewed as the key to the St Lawrence Valley. In contrast to previous campaigns, which had sought to safeguard British territory, this ambitious operation marked the onset of an aggressive strategy aimed at the very heart of French power in Canada. Loudoun's plans coincided with political changes across the Atlantic which saw the replacement of the Newcastle administration with a new ministry fronted by William Pitt and William Cavendish, Duke of Devonshire – a government superseded soon after by the famous Pitt–Newcastle coalition. The Louisbourg expedition mustered at Halifax,

34 Loudoun to Henry Fox, begun Albany, 22 November, finished New York, 26 December 1756, in CO (Colonial Office Papers, Public Record Office, Kew)/5 (America and West Indies)/48, fol. 8.

35 Cosnan to Adjutant-General John Forbes, Boston, 18 January 1758 (GD 45/2/24/5).

36 Donaldson to Forbes, Albany, 28 January 1758, in GD 45/2/26/4.

Nova Scotia in early July.[37] However, this impressive force was never employed against its target. Loudoun's operation was aborted owing to Britain's inability to secure local superiority at sea – a crucial mistake that would not be repeated.

That same summer, while Loudoun lingered at Halifax, Montcalm exploited the temporary reduction of British manpower in New York to attack the colony's northern frontier. He accordingly assembled a powerful army of regulars, militia and Indians and descended upon Fort William Henry.[38] The garrison of regular and provincial troops, under the command of Lieutenant-Colonel George Monro, mounted a valiant resistance in the teeth of a heavy bombardment, but when Major-General Webb refused to stage the requested relief expedition from nearby Fort Edward, they were forced to capitulate.[39] In recognition of their stubborn defence, and in contrast to the less resolute garrison of Oswego, Monro's men were granted the honours of war by the victors. Such niceties of European warfare meant nothing to Montcalm's Indian allies. Frustrated by a lack of loot and scalps, these warriors fell upon the prisoners in an incident immortalised by James Fenimore Cooper as the 'massacre' of Fort William Henry.[40] Once again, Montcalm decided against a further advance. He destroyed the extensive fortifications and retired.

The continuing impotency of British arms was underscored in November when 300 Indian and Canadian raiders advanced down the Mohawk Valley and burned the settlement of German Flats: the regular garrison of Fort Herkimer, on the opposite bank of the river, proved incapable of intervention. Despite the vast influx of regular troops during 1757, the campaigns of that year had done nothing to enhance their reputation. Indeed, in the eyes of some colonials, the growing numbers of redcoats had only worsened the situation. As one commentator

[37] There were thirteen battalions of regulars plus a composite unit drawn from the three Nova Scotia regiments. The total of all ranks, including 297 men of the Royal Artillery, was 11,996 (Returns, Halifax, 3 August 1757 in GD 45/2/12/1). There were also 500 American 'rangers'. See *An Historical Journal of the Campaigns in North America for the Years 1757, 1758, 1759, and 1760, by Captain John Knox*, ed. A. G. Doughty (3 vols, Toronto, 1914), I, 41.

[38] Montcalm's army totalled 8,019, including some 2,000 Indians. See *Adventure in the Wilderness: The American Journals of Louis Antoine De Bougainville, 1756–60*, ed. C. Hamilton (Norman, Oklahoma, 1959), pp. 152–3.

[39] The garrison numbered 2,372. Of these, 842 were redcoats of the 35th, the 3/60th and the New York Independents. There were also 24 men of the Royal Artillery and 95 rangers. The 1,400 provincial troops were from Massachusetts, New Jersey, New Hampshire and New York ('State of the Garrison of Fort George [Fort William Henry] and of the Troops encamped at the Intrenchment 9th August, 1757', in *NYCD*, X, 621–5).

[40] See I. K. Steele, *Betrayals: Fort William Henry and the 'Massacre'* (New York, 1990).

observed, 'the more we are strengthened from Great Britain, the more ground we lose against the French'; he added that this 'great number of regular troops have been of no service for want of proper management'.[41] That December regular recruiting parties in Pennsylvania ran almost as much risk at the hands of the inhabitants as they had from the French and Indians: several redcoats of the New York Independents were badly beaten by a gang at Kennet in Chester County. Violence had erupted after the local tavern keeper John Baldwin damned Loudoun and his army for a 'parcell of Scoundrells' who had proved nothing more than a burden to the country.[42]

Discredited by the dismal outcome of events, Loudoun was replaced as commander-in-chief in North America in early 1758 by James Abercromby. Despite the disasters of 1756–57, Loudoun had none the less done much to create the administrative and logistical basis for future success. Denied the aid of significant numbers of Indian allies, Loudoun had been obliged to explore alternative methods of furnishing the British Army with troops capable of tackling wilderness conditions: to this end he had employed locally raised 'rangers' and also encouraged redcoat volunteers to serve with them – a trend that soon led to the emergence of regular light infantry units in North America. Indeed, Loudoun's legacy provided the sound foundations from which the ministry dominated by Pitt was to mount a more vigorous war effort in America.[43] Yet for all his efforts, Loudoun had never been able to win the ungrudging cooperation of the various colonial governments in assembling supplies and approving the services of provincial troops. This situation was changed early in 1758, when Pitt's ministry made significant concessions aimed at securing concerted colonial support for the war against France. Continuing gripes over the relative rank of regular and provincial officers were largely silenced by greatly improving the status of the latter. Financial incentives achieved a virtual revolution in the colonial attitude towards raising provincials to serve alongside the redcoats: in future Britain would arm and feed troops voted by the colonies for coming campaigns. Although the provinces were

41 'Letter from a Correspondent at New York, dated August 26, 1757', in *Gentleman's Magazine*, 1757 (October), pp. 442–3.

42 Sworn statement of Sergeant James Jobb in LO 5011, enclosed in Captain Charles Cruikshank to Loudoun, Wilmington, 14 December 1757 (LO 5012).

43 Pitt's enduring reputation as the chief architect of victory in the 'Great War for Empire' has been challenged by scholars who instead regard him as the public face of a talented ministerial team that included the commander-in-chief Sir John Ligonier, First Lord of the Admiralty Lord George Anson, and even the much maligned Duke of Newcastle. The key role of the former is emphasised in R. Whitworth, *Field Marshal Lord Ligonier: A Story of the British Army, 1702–1770* (Oxford, 1958). For a detailed reassessment of the ministry as a whole see R. Middleton, *The Bells of Victory: The Pitt–Newcastle Ministry and the Conduct of the Seven Years War, 1757–1762* (Cambridge, 1985).

required to raise, clothe and pay their soldiers, even these costs would theoretically be refunded by Parliament in due course.

Although the schemes formulated by the 'Great Commoner' and his colleagues met with mixed fortunes, Britain's North American campaigns of 1758 were none the less destined to prove a crucial turning-point in the conflict. In a triple-pronged strategy, Abercromby was to strike north from Albany to Lake Champlain, whilst Major-General Jeffery Amherst headed an amphibious attack against Louisbourg and Quebec, and Brigadier-General John Forbes mounted a fresh effort to capture Fort Duquesne. Together, these ambitious operations envisaged the deployment of some 24,000 regulars and another 22,500 provincials.[44]

Before outlining the campaigns of 1758, it is necessary to assess the magnitude of the task faced by those British commanders destined to attack Canada. At first glance, the sheer numbers of redcoats and provincials earmarked for the assault upon the northern bastion of New France suggest that the English enjoyed an overwhelming superiority. In terms of regular troops, the discrepancy between Britain and France was especially marked. By the crucial summer of 1758, Britain had assembled 23 battalions of regulars on the North American continent.[45] Since 1755, just twelve battalions of professional soldiers had been sent to Canada from France. At full paper strength, which they never reached, these units were supposed to amount to some 6,600 officers and men. The paucity of France's commitment of troops to North America is all the more striking when it is appreciated that the years between 1757 and 1762 saw her regular forces reach a maximum strength of almost 330,000.[46] By contrast, Britain's far higher allocation of regulars to the American theatre stemmed from a much smaller establishment.[47] In addition to the *troupes de terre* sent from France, by 1757 Canada also fielded 64 independent companies of regulars, the *compagnies franches de la marine* – so called because they were administered by the Navy Department responsible for

44 See CO/5/50, fols 55–6: 'Distribution of His Majestys Forces in N. America for the Campaigns 1758 according to the Returns of 24th February 1758', signed by James Abercromby, 28 April 1758.

45 There were also the seven independent companies, and a newly raised unit of five companies known as Gage's Light Infantry (the 80th Regiment of Light Armed Foot).

46 L. Kennett, *The French Armies in the Seven Years War: A study in military organisation and administration* (Durham, North Carolina, 1967), p. 77.

47 Estimates presented to Parliament in December 1759 envisaged a regular army of 109,000 men for the coming year. See R. Middleton, 'The Recruitment of the British Army, 1755–1762', in *JSAHR*, LXVII (1989), 226–38; 236.

the colonies. These units, which were often employed on garrison duty, represented a theoretical total of about 4,000 trained troops.[48]

Compared with their opponents, French commanders could therefore deploy relatively few regulars. However, the white-coated professionals were not the only forces available for the defence of Canada: in periods of crisis they could be supplemented by some 15,000 militia. These civilians-in-arms represented a more valuable resource than the term 'militia' suggests. Canada was a frontier society geared to warfare. In marked contrast to the English colonies, where the militia had all too often decayed, Canadian men were expected to play an active role in defending their homeland.[49] Although lacking the discipline necessary to face British redcoats on the open battlefield, these unpaid militiamen could none the less be relied upon to man defensive positions. More importantly, many Canadians had acquired extensive experience of wilderness conditions through war or trade with the neighbouring Indian tribes: as such, they provided French armies with a pool of skilled irregulars who were equally adept at aiming a musket or paddling a canoe; in consequence, the military usefulness of these hardy *habitants* exceeded that of the bulk of provincial troops raised by the English colonies. In addition, New France could call upon the services of fluctuating numbers of Indian allies, drawn from a heterogeneous range of tribes. Although often unpredictable, these warriors were born guerrilla fighters whose fearsome reputation exerted an intimidating effect out of all proportion to their numbers.

Other factors worked to offset the disparity in manpower between the Anglo-Americans and the French, and to ensure that the contest was by no means as unequal as it might at first appear. Indeed, as some British officers were quick to appreciate, when it came to mounting offensive operations in North America, mere numbers could sometimes prove more of a hindrance than a help. Unwieldy armies were an embarrassment when it came to navigating the unsettled interior: the logistical nightmare of assembling and transporting the supplies required to feed large expeditions frequently delayed the onset of operations until the summer campaigning season had been truncated to a brief few months. A further consideration serving to counter the numerical inferiority of New France stemmed from the fundamental character of the conflict. The war against

48 There were a further 36 companies in Louisiana, some of which participated in operations in the Ohio theatre. On the French regulars see R. Chartrand, *The French Soldier in Colonial America* (Ottawa, 1984); W. J. Eccles, 'The French Forces in North America during the Seven Years War', in *Dictionary of Canadian Biography*, ed. F. G. Halpenny (13 vols, Toronto, 1966–94), III, xv–xxiii; xvii.

49 For the 'military ethos' within Canadian society, see 'The Social, Economic, and Political Significance of the Military Establishment in New France', in W. J. Eccles, *Essays on New France* (Toronto, 1987), pp. 110–24.

Canada has been viewed as a siege writ large, in which the beleaguered French 'garrison' consequently enjoyed the substantial strategic advantage of operating upon interior lines of communication.[50] Particularly important was the continuous watercourse running from Louisbourg on the Atlantic coast, via the St Lawrence River to the posts on the Great Lakes; this and other waterways permitted the rapid assembly of troops where they were most needed, either for defence or to launch opportunist strikes against vulnerable British targets. In combination, these factors go far to explain why the conquest of Canada required repeated applications of seemingly overwhelming force.

The turn of the tide

Two of the expeditions mounted by the Anglo-Americans in 1758 enjoyed signal success. Like Loudoun before him, Amherst assembled a powerful army at Halifax. As had been the case in 1757, the Louisbourg expedition was composed almost entirely of regular troops.[51] The redcoats were given careful instruction in the techniques of amphibious landings: this diligence paid off on 8 June when they staged a remarkably successful assault upon defences at Gabarus Bay.[52] Although the French were 'intrenched up to their Chin along the Shore', the signal was given to land. At this:

> the whole set off with the greatest eagerness, and a Terrible fire began on both Sides, that, nothing was Seen or heard for one hour but the thundering of Cannon and flashes of lightening, where the never daunted Spirits of British Soldiers landed and forced their way through the Batteries and breastworks.[53]

Conspicuous for his gallantry and energy during this hazardous assault and the subsequent siege operations was James Wolfe, described by one officer as 'ye most in defatigable active man I have ever heard of'.[54] Unfavourable weather delayed the landing of the siege artillery,

50 Shy, *Toward Lexington*, pp. 87–8.

51 The fourteen battalions of regulars (2/1st, 15th, 17th, 22nd, 28th, 35th, 40th, 45th, 47th, 48th, 58th, 2/60th, 3/60th and 78th), with a detachment of Royal Artillery, totalled 12,659. There were also five companies of rangers at 538 of all ranks. See 'Troops destined for the Siege of Louisbourg, May 24th, 1758', in CO/5/53, fol. 93.

52 See J. M. Hitsman and C. C. J. Bond, 'The Assault Landing at Louisbourg, 1758', *Canadian Historical Review*, XXXV (1954), 314–30.

53 'Journal of Richard Humphrys' (Add. MSS 45,662), pp. 10; 13.

54 'Diary of Captain Philip Townsend, 22nd Foot, 1756–58', NAM MSS 8001–30 (unpaginated), entry for 22 July 1758.

but by 19 June British guns were pounding the fortifications. The French garrison under Augustin de Boschenry de Drucour offered a spirited defence, and on the night of 9 July made a sortie in force. Despite initial success, this sally was beaten back with severe losses. Such efforts were merely attempts to postpone the inevitable, and the battered fortress surrendered on 26 July. Four battalions of the *troupes de terre*, and another 24 companies of colony regulars, became prisoners-of-war. Louisbourg's defenders had none the less delayed Amherst for long enough to scupper any possibility of pressing forward to Quebec that summer.

The original plan of operations was further disrupted when the army under Abercromby experienced costly and dispiriting failure before the French lines at Ticonderoga. Abercromby had eventually assembled a numerous and confident force of 15,000 regulars and provincials.[55] Encamped at the southern end of Lake George beside the scorched ruins of Fort William Henry, Abercromby's troops were drilled under the supervision of the expedition's charismatic and popular second-in-command, Brigadier-General George Augustus, Lord Howe. The army was eager for battle with the French: one officer reported that 'from the Spirit & looks, both of Regulars and Provinciall Troops I am certain we shall drub the rascalls'.[56] By 4 July, sufficient bateaux had been assembled to transport Abercromby's formidable army along Lake George. At the northern end of the lake, Montcalm had concentrated eight battalions of regulars around Fort Ticonderoga, or Carillon as it was known to the French. These men worked frenziedly to complete a defensive line across the peninsula on which the fort itself was situated. On 6 July, while Montcalm's troops were building their defences, Abercromby's army made an unopposed landing at the head of the Lake. The Anglo-Americans formed columns and began to march through the woods towards the fort. French patrols were brushed aside, but in the course of the skirmishing Lord Howe was killed; this bewildering forest fighting threw the British columns into confusion, and the troops were obliged to regroup at their original landing-place. The army started out again on the following day, and by 8 July Abercromby considered himself ready to attack. Having received intelligence that the French were expecting a major reinforcement, and convinced that the position could be taken by direct infantry assault, Abercromby decided against bringing up his artillery and blasting Montcalm's breastwork to pieces. Although the

55 There were 6,367 regulars and 9,024 provincials (Abercromby to Pitt, Camp at Lake George, 12 July 1758, in *London Magazine*, 1758 (August), p. 426).

56 Lt-Col. Francis Grant, 42nd Regiment, to his brother, Sir Ludovick Grant MP, Fort Edward, 16 June 1758, in GD 248 (Seafield Muniments)/49/1/81.

French defences were incomplete, and left an unguarded flank, Abercromby ignored this weakness and instead ordered his men to storm the breastwork with the bayonet.[57] The result was carnage. Montcalm's defences were screened by a dense abatis of tangled and sharpened branches; those soldiers who struggled through this barrier in repeated efforts to reach the enemy were shot down by men they could scarcely see. One officer wounded during the attack recalled: 'The fire was prodigiously hot, the slaughter of officers very great, almost all wounded, the men still furiously rushing forwards without any leaders.'[58] After more than four hours of futile bloodshed, Abercromby finally called off the assault. For all his heavy losses, Abercromby retained the potential to regroup and attack again: instead, he withdrew his army to its old camp; there, the morale of officers and men plummeted alongside the reputation of their general.

Despite the disaster at Ticonderoga, troops drawn from Abercromby's army did score one significant success: Colonel John Bradstreet led 3,000 men, mostly provincials, up Lake Ontario, pausing briefly at the ruins of Oswego before moving on to besiege the French bastion of Frontenac. Bradstreet's force proved sufficient to overawe the undermanned and undergunned fort. Crucial supplies and ships were destroyed in a blow that damaged French credibility in the eyes of their Indian allies, and ruptured the vulnerable supply route to the isolated posts of Niagara and Fort Duquesne. By the end of 1758 the latter fort had also fallen to British arms. Throughout the spring and early summer, Brigadier-General Forbes had assembled an army of about 6,000 regulars and provincials, along with a substantial contingent of 800 allied Cherokee warriors.[59] Forbes's expedition was subject to frustrating delays, a factor that prompted most of the Indians to decamp in disgust. Forbes moved cautiously towards his objective, using a different route from that followed by Braddock three years before, and anchoring his advance upon fortified supply depots. A misguided attempt to surprise the fort, headed by Forbes's friend, Major James Grant, was bloodily repulsed by

[57] The French breastwork was defended by 3,526 men. Apart from 250 Canadians and fifteen Indians, all were regulars. See *Adventure in the Wilderness*, p. 231.

[58] 'Narrative', enclosed in Captain Charles Lee, 44th Foot, to Miss Sidney Lee, Albany, 16 September 1758, in *Collections of the New-York Historical Society, 1871: The Lee Papers, Volume I, 1754–76* (New York, 1872), p. 13.

[59] Under the original 'Distribution of His Majesty's Forces in N. America for the Campaigns of 1758', Forbes was to command some 1,854 regular infantry and artillery, plus 5,000 provincials (CO/5/50, fols 55–6). According to a 'General Sketch' of the troops under Forbes' command, dated at Shippensburgh on 1 September 1758, a total of 6,334 regulars and provincials were participating in the campaign. Of these, more than 800 provincials had been detached to guard the frontiers. See RH 4/86/1 (microfilm – no piece references).

the French and their Indian allies on 14 September. Despite this discouraging setback, by early October Forbes's advanced troops had established a camp at Loyal Hannon, where they soon rebuffed a raid aimed at capitalising upon Grant's defeat. Deprived of tribal backing by a negotiated settlement, the French garrison was obliged to abandon the post, and an ailing Forbes arrived on 25 November to claim Fort Duquesne for Britain. The dying general renamed the outpost Fort Pitt in honour of the statesman whose name was already being linked with the revival of British fortunes in North America.

The campaigns of 1758 not only marked a turning-point in the war; they also witnessed an upsurge in the prestige of British regulars. The great morale-boosting victory of that summer, the capture of Louisbourg, had been the work of regulars alone, whilst the grimly determined Forbes had demonstrated that an officer schooled in the conventional warfare of Flanders could also prove willing to absorb the new lessons of the wilderness. Ironically, it was the crushing defeat at Ticonderoga that had done most to enhance the reputation of the regulars: although the bungling Abercromby could be castigated for 'murthering a parsell of Fine Souldiars that was willing to jeopard their Lives for their Counteries Service', the valour demonstrated by his redcoats on that bloody day earned widespread praise.[60] For example, the New Yorker John Watts had heard that Abercromby's defeat stemmed from his soldiers' desire to 'wipe off the Stain of their former Inactivity'. It was the regular troops who 'bore the heat of the action', and suffered accordingly. Despite the disappointment of the setback, Watts consequently found it hard to be critical of soldiers who had 'behaved so gallantly, and Sacrificed their Lives for us'.[61] The provincials serving in Abercromby's army had also proved unstinting in their admiration for the redcoats' conduct during the attack.[62] Although the traditional rivalry between regulars and provincials could still be rekindled upon occasion, as demonstrated by wrangling over the responsibility for Major Grant's defeat before Fort Duquesne, even here there were signs that attitudes were beginning to mellow. Indeed, while vigorously refuting claims that Grant's downfall stemmed from the disobedience of a provincial officer, and drawing attention to the sometimes dismal performance of the regulars in recent campaigns, one

60 John Lloyd to Henry Lloyd, Stamford, 27 July 1758, in *Collections of the New-York Historical Society, 1927: Papers of the Lloyd Family of the Manor of Queens Village, Lloyd's Neck, Long Island, New York 1654–1826, Volume Two, 1752–1826* (New York, 1927), p. 554.

61 Watts to Richard Peters, New York, 17 July 1758, in RH 4/86/1. The regulars sustained 1,610 killed, wounded and missing, compared with a total of just 334 for the provincials (See WO/1/1, fol. 199).

62 See Anderson, *A People's Army*, pp. 147–9.

colonial correspondent none the less conceded that his countrymen were 'not insensible of the worth and bravery of the British troops in general', recognising the 'amazing valour' they had shown at the landing on Cape Breton and their 'good conduct on other occasions'.[63]

Provincial troops played an active combat role in the army under Forbes and had captured Frontenac with little assistance from the regulars. Yet the usefulness of most of the colonial volunteers that Pitt's open-handed initiatives had summoned into the field that summer was less apparent. In fact, Abercromby's Ticonderoga campaign had been retarded for weeks by his strict instructions to await the arrival of the provincial regiments. The delay allowed the French to push forward reinforcements and construct the defensive lines before which the General's army was cut to pieces. When they finally materialised, the provincials placed an unprecedented strain upon the army's already overburdened transport and supply system.[64] Yet the provincials' efficiency as soldiers scarcely justified the priority placed upon them: for example, orders issued just days before the assault upon Ticonderoga required the provincial regiments to draw up with intervals between each company 'to avoid geting in heaps as much as possible'.[65] As such evidence reveals, the New Englanders of 1758 were virtually untrained, and their brief stint of active service ensured that they remained so.[66] From that summer onwards there was a marked tendency for the colonial volunteers to be relegated to such support roles as the construction of roads and forts, the transportation of provisions by land and river, and the manning of strong-points: as Lieutenant-Colonel James Robertson put it in a comment often taken to epitomise the scornful attitude of the British officer towards Americans, the provincials could labour upon 'the works that in inhabited Countrys are perform'd by Peasants'.[67] Such tasks were crucial to the British war effort, but the widespread employment of the provincials in these fatigue duties also ensured that the grimmer business of fighting was increasingly viewed as the speciality of the redcoated regulars.[68]

63 Letter from 'A New Englandman', 9 May 1759, in *Gentleman's Magazine, 1759* (May), pp. 223–4. For the contribution that prompted this riposte, see 'Letter from an Officer who attended Brigadier Gen. Forbes . . .', in ibid. (April), pp. 171–4.

64 See Pargellis, *Lord Loudoun*, pp. 354–5; also M. J. Cardwell, 'Mismanagement: The 1758 British Expedition Against Carillon', in *Bulletin of the Fort Ticonderoga Museum*, XV, 4 (1992), 237–91.

65 General Orders, 3 July 1758 (AB 407).

66 Anderson, *A People's Army*, pp. 75–7.

67 Robertson to John Calcraft, Schenectady, 22 June 1760 (LO 6251).

68 Anderson, *A People's Army*, pp. 142–3; C. P. Stacey, 'The British Forces in North America during the Seven Years War', in *DCB*, III, xxiv–xxx; xxviii. By contrast, the Canadian militia played an *increasing* combat role during 1759–60. See M. L. Nicolai, ' "A Different Kind of Courage": The French Military and the Canadian Irregular Soldier during the Seven Years War', in *CHR*, LXX (1989), 53–75.

Annus mirabilis

The successes gained during the summer of 1758, in particular the capture of Louisbourg, persuaded Pitt that the time was now ripe to widen operations to embrace France's West Indian colonies. The islands of Martinique, Guadeloupe and St Domingue were not only centres for the lucrative sugar trade, but also provided havens for the French privateers that preyed upon Anglo-American shipping. It was therefore decided that the aged but experienced Peregrine Hopson should be appointed major-general to command a force of about 7,000 regulars in an expedition against the islands.[69] Hopson's force sailed from Plymouth on 12 November 1758, and by mid-January of 1759 the fleet lay off Martinique's chief harbour of Fort Royal. After Commodore John Moore's warships had cannonaded neighbouring shore batteries into silence, an advance party of regulars was successfully landed on the evening of 16 January. Martinique's regular garrison was paltry, and the militia undisciplined: the real strength of the island lay in its formidable natural defences.[70] As Hopson's redcoats probed forwards they found their progress barred by sheer ravines; heavy brush and sugar cane plantations provided cover from which the island's defenders waged effective guerrilla warfare. If Hopson's siege guns were to be brought into action against the citadel of Fort Royal it would be necessary to maintain a precarious communication from the landing place to the French fortifications: in the face of the harassment already encountered this plan was considered untenable. Just a day after landing the troops were re-embarked, having suffered about one hundred killed and wounded.

A fresh proposal to attack Martinique's principal settlement of St Pierre was abandoned as likely to result in heavy casualties, and on the advice of Moore it was decided to switch the expedition's attentions to Guadeloupe. Naval firepower silenced the defences of the leading town of Basseterre, permitting the infantry to land unopposed on 24 January. The port's major bastion – also named Fort Royal – and the adjoining lines had been evacuated by the defenders, who retired to carefully prepared defensive positions amidst the island's rugged interior. As Fort Royal was

69 There were two 'old' regiments, the 3rd ('The Buffs') and the 4th ('The King's Own'), plus five newly raised corps (61st, 63rd, 64th, 65th and the seven companies of Highlanders destined to form the 2/42nd). These would be joined by elements of the 38th Foot from Antigua. On this expedition see M. T. Smelser, *The Campaign for the Sugar Islands, 1759: A Study of Amphibious Warfare* (New York, 1955).

70 According to one of the island's defenders, the regular garrison of Fort Royal consisted of just 250 infantry and artillerymen. See 'Journal of a French Officer at Martinico . . . ', in *London Magazine, 1759* (July), p. 361.

repaired to receive a British garrison, Hopson's unseasoned troops began to sicken and die at an alarming rate. Victims of the Caribbean environment included Hopson himself, who succumbed to fever on 27 February and was replaced by Major-General John Barrington. The new commander had long cherished the idea of transferring operations to the opposite, or 'Grand Terre', side of the island, where a party of marines and Highlanders had already secured a harbour bridgehead by storming Fort Louis on 14 February. Leaving a regiment to garrison Fort Royal, Barrington evacuated the remainder of his sickly command to Fort Louis on 6 March. From this base Barrington employed naval transports to ferry detached commands under Brigadiers John Clavering and Byam Crump against objectives scattered around the island. These roving forces proved remarkably successful, and by 21 April the island's defenders were ready to sue for terms. No sooner had the capitulation been signed on 2 May than a messenger informed the inhabitants of the tardy appearance of reinforcements from Martinique consisting of 600 regulars and 2,000 'Buccaneers', complete with cannon and spare arms. Upon learning that Guadeloupe had already surrendered, these troops re-embarked. As a relieved Barrington reported to Pitt, Guadeloupe had been conquered 'by great perseverance, and changing intirely the Nature of the war, by carrying it on by Detachments'. Barrington praised the efforts of his officers and the bravery of the troops, who 'got the better of every Obstacle' and 'Forced the Enemy in all their Entrenchments, and Strong Passes'.[71]

For the coming campaigns on the mainland, it was decided to repeat the three-pronged strategy that had enjoyed partial success in 1758. With the incompetent Abercromby now recalled, the high command was inherited by Amherst. Like his predecessor, Amherst was charged with attacking Canada via the traditional invasion route of Lakes George and Champlain. At the same time an amphibious task-force under Major-General James Wolfe was to besiege Quebec, whilst Brigadier-General John Prideaux headed an advance upon Niagara. Such extensive operations required a major commitment of manpower. Like Loudoun before him, Amherst had rapidly discovered that recruitment within America was insufficient to match attrition, and he therefore relied largely upon reinforcements from Britain to keep his battalions up to strength. Amherst was consequently delighted to learn of a ministerial decision to send him

71 Letter from Headquarters in the Capesterre, Guadeloupe, 9 May 1759, in *The Correspondence of William Pitt, when Secretary of State, with Colonial Governors and Military and Naval Commissioners in America*, ed. G. S. Kimball (2 vols, London, 1906; repr. New York, 1969), II, 100.

700 Highlanders for the 42nd Foot, plus 2,150 drafts to recruit the other regular battalions, observing that there was 'more than room' for these men.[72] In particular, the army destined for the St Lawrence under Wolfe was desperately short of manpower. Indeed, since the capture of Louisbourg the battalions allocated to Wolfe's expedition had lost three times as many men as they had raised.[73] Within just weeks of this decision, all of those reinforcements originally earmarked for Amherst's army were instead diverted to Hopson's Caribbean expedition. It was not until the summer of 1759 that Amherst eventually received reinforcements from the troops that had conquered Guadeloupe. However, instead of the contingent of almost 3,000 men that Amherst had originally anticipated, just 693 drafts were sent, whilst the Highlanders had now been depleted by casualties to 507. Some of the men had died on the passage from Guadeloupe; many others were sick. In fact, Amherst reported, just 350 of the drafts were actually fit for service.[74] The inadequacy of this contribution can be appreciated when it is realised that the troops in North America were then some 4,500 rank and file short of their theoretical establishment.[75]

Of the campaigns mounted during 1759, Wolfe's unexpected conquest of Quebec, which climaxed in the young General's death in the very hour of victory, boasts a dramatic appeal that has long overshadowed the other British successes of that 'Year of Miracles'.[76] It had originally been intended that Wolfe should have 12,000 men for his campaign, but the army assembled at Louisbourg amounted to just over two-thirds of that total. However, the quality was high: as was becoming typical for operations involving difficult amphibious manoeuvres, the army was once again composed almost entirely of regulars.[77] Wolfe was seconded by a trio of brigadiers – George Townshend, Robert Monckton and James Murray. By 27 June 1759, Wolfe's troops had been transported up the St Lawrence

72 Amherst to Lord Barrington, New York, 19 January 1759, in WO/1/5, fol. 35.

73 There were 1,558 lost and 525 recruited. See 'Embarkation Return of His Majesty's Forces, destined for an Expedition in the River St Lawrence, under the command of Major General Wolfe, Neptune at Sea, June 5, 1759', in CO/5/51, fol. 67.

74 Amherst to Barrington, Camp of Crown Point, 10 August 1759, in WO/1/5, fol. 62.

75 The army in America was supposed to number 27,330 of all ranks, compared with an actual total of 21,874. See 'Abstract' of returns in North America, 1759 (WO/17(Returns)/1489/5).

76 For the Quebec campaign see C. P. Stacey, *Quebec 1759: The Siege and the Battle* (Toronto, 1959).

77 Wolfe was given ten battalions plus a composite unit, the 'Louisbourg Grenadiers', formed from the élite companies of the three battalions left in garrison there. There were also six companies of rangers and a detachment of the Royal Artillery. The total of all ranks (except staff and drummers) 'fit for duty' was 8,535. See CO/5/51, fol. 67. The only provincials involved were 300 'pioneers' who joined the army before Quebec.

River by a fleet of 49 warships commanded by Vice-Admiral Charles Saunders, and landed unopposed on the Isle of Orleans, some three miles below Quebec. The city was shielded by strong natural defences and entrenchments manned by a substantial army of about 15,000 men under Montcalm.[78] In the course of July the bulk of Wolfe's troops were shifted from their initial position: British artillery batteries were established at Point Lévis, on the south bank of the St Lawrence opposite the city itself, with another camp sited on the north bank in a position divided from the main French troop concentration at Beauport by the river and falls of Montmorency. Faced with a seemingly impregnable objective, Wolfe struggled with the task of engaging the defenders under conditions favourable to his regulars. An attempt to ford the Montmorency River on 26 July encountered sufficient resistance to convince Wolfe that he must look elsewhere. On 31 July, Wolfe accordingly orchestrated an amphibious assault on the Beauport lines, supported by land with troops from the Montmorency camp, in the hope of luring the defenders into a major confrontation. Although the men were eventually landed as planned, they attacked too soon and were thrown back with heavy losses. The survivors withdrew in good order, hoping that the jubilant French would be encouraged to quit their defences, but, as one participant recalled, 'the Poltroons, who were twice our numbers, dared not to come down to us, though often invited by the hats waved at them from our general officers and troops'.[79] As the siege dragged on, a sickly and frustrated Wolfe was reduced to bombarding the city into ruins and torching the down-river hamlets. Since their arrival before Quebec, Wolfe's soldiers had frequently become embroiled in vicious bush-fights with the enemy's Indians and militia. Such clashes saw British troops matching the brutalities of their opponents. As Brigadier Townshend wrote to his wife, the campaign had degenerated into a 'Sceene of Skirmishing Cruelty & Devastation'.[80]

Wolfe remained convinced that the only answer to the conundrum was another attempt to breach the Beauport lines. By contrast, the General's increasingly truculent brigadiers were equally certain that the solution lay *above* the city itself. British troops had already made sporadic amphibious

[78] Of these, about 2,650 were from the *troupes de terre*. The remainder included militia and between 1,000 and 1,200 Indians. Brigadier-General François-Charles de Bourlamaque, defending the Lake Champlain front against Amherst, had another 3,000 men, more than half of them regulars. See Stacey, *Quebec, 1759*, pp. 43–4. Montcalm now held the rank of Lieutenant-General and commanded all the troops in Canada. Before his promotion, Montcalm had remained subordinate to the Governor-General of New France, Pierre de Rigaud, Marquis de Vaudreuil.

[79] *An Accurate and Authentic Journal of the Siege of Quebec*, p. 23.

[80] Townshend to Charlotte Lady Ferrers, 6 September 1759, in *Historical Manuscripts Commission: Marquess of Townshend Manuscripts* (London, 1887), p. 309.

raids in this region with mixed success, but if a larger force could be established there, the brigadiers argued, Quebec's supply lifeline would be severed, so obliging Montcalm to emerge and fight. Although this was at odds with his own plans, Wolfe quickly accepted the brigadiers' scheme. Accordingly, on 3 September the camp at Montmorency was evacuated and the troops transferred to Point Lévis. Wolfe's initial intention was to land his army on the north bank of the St Lawrence some eight miles above Quebec. However, upon examining the ground in person, Wolfe noticed the potential for landing at a cove just two miles from the city. In the early hours of 13 September, Wolfe put this modified version of the brigadiers' plan into operation. Owing to a combination of skilful planning and incredibly good luck, Wolfe's boats reached their objective unmolested. An advance-guard of light infantry scrambled up a scrubby cliff; the rest of the force negotiated a less precipitous path. By dawn, Wolfe had 4,500 redcoats arrayed on the Plains of Abraham facing the city walls. A stunned Montcalm gathered a roughly equal number of regulars and militia from the Beauport camp and rushed them to counter the threat. Given the weak condition of Quebec's fortifications and the lack of provisions to sustain a close siege, the French general had opted to engage Wolfe in the open. Montcalm's decision in favour of a battlefield confrontation has prompted accusations of rashness. Where the French commander can be more safely criticised is in failing to await the arrival of a force of more than 2,000 crack troops under his subordinate, Colonel Louis-Antoine de Bougainville, who were operating to the north, in the British rear. After a bout of skirmishing, during which Canadians and Indians subjected Wolfe's line to a harassing fire, Montcalm's motley force trotted forwards to the attack. Enduring the French musketry, Wolfe's redcoats held their own fire until, in the words of one of them, the enemy were 'within Forty Yards of the point of our Bayonets ... at which time we poured in such a discharge; and which we continued with such a regular briskness, as was visible to all, by the good effect it produced'.[81] This devastating fusillade was seconded by a vigorous pursuit, although elements of the defeated army made stubborn efforts to cover its retreat. In the course of the brief battle Wolfe sustained three wounds, the last of which proved fatal. Montcalm also received a mortal injury. Although the bulk of Montcalm's army escaped to fight another day, Quebec itself surrendered on 18 September.

Compared to the high drama of the events on the St Lawrence, Amherst's methodical advance from Albany appeared a plodding affair.

81 'Memoirs of John Johnson', in *The Siege of Quebec and the Battle of the Plains of Abraham*, eds A. G. Doughty and G. W. Parmelee (6 vols, Quebec, 1901), V, 104.

The complex logistical preparations for the campaign and the sluggishness of the provinces in mustering their men had delayed the onset of operations until 21 July. However, the impressive force of 11,000 regulars and provincials that moved once again across the familiar waters of Lake George apparently held great confidence in its new commander. Writing before the start of the campaign, one officer had no doubts that the 'Conqueror of Louisburgh, will give a good account of Ticonderoga'. He added: 'Our General is beloved by his Soldiers, Honourd and Esteemed by his officers, Carful of mens Lives and healths, in short, He is the man I would chuse to serve under, of any I know in the service'.[82] Amherst's army landed at the French end of the Lake with little opposition. The breastwork upon which Abercromby's men had flung themselves in vain a year before was now abandoned without a struggle as Bourlamaque's troops retired to the fort itself. While Amherst established siege lines and bombarded the stronghold, the garrison gradually withdrew to Crown Point via Lake Champlain. On the evening of 26 July, the remainder of the defenders left and fired the fort. Days later, Amherst's scouts informed him that Crown Point had also been evacuated. Bourlamaque and his men fell back to a strong position at Île aux Noix on the Richelieu River. Although he had hoped to push onwards to Montreal, so supporting Wolfe's efforts on the St Lawrence, Amherst lacked the naval force necessary to secure the navigation of Lake Champlain. Unable to advance from Crown Point, he set his carpenters to the laborious task of building the vessels required to blast the puny French navy from the Lake while his soldiers began work on an extensive new fort.

Although Amherst failed to proceed against Canada that year, the smallest expedition of the summer had enjoyed spectacular success. At the beginning of July an army of some 3,000 men had sailed from Oswego towards Fort Niagara, reaching its objective undetected on 6 July.[83] Despite the 'most Shocking Delays' caused by the incompetence of the engineers in directing the siege works, within a week British ordnance was none the less inflicting considerable damage upon the

82 Major Alexander Campbell, 77th Regiment, to his father, John Campbell, Fort Edward Camp, 19 June 1759, in GD 87 (Mackay of Bighouse Muniments)/1/85. A return of the troops embarked at Lake George on 25 July 1759 gives a total for all ranks of 11,133, of which 5,854 were regular infantry and artillerymen and 5,279 provincials. See 'Amherst's Personal Journal' (CKS, U1350/014) p. 51.

83 There were three battalions of regulars (44th, 46th and 4/60th), plus two regiments of New York provincials and a body of allied Indians ('Distribution of the Troops for the Campaign of 1759', in ibid., p. 41). Most of the 4/60th and half of the provincials were left at Oswego. For this operation see B. L. Dunnigan, *Siege, 1759: The Campaign Against Niagara* (Youngstown, New York, 1986).

French defences.[84] When the commander of the expedition, Brigadier Prideaux, was killed accidentally on 20 July, the direction of operations fell to Sir William Johnson, the vanquisher of Dieskau in 1755. A relief force scrambled together from the French posts in the far west was confronted and defeated on 24 July in a short, sharp fire-fight outside the fort at La Belle Famille. Niagara's commander, Captain Pierre Pouchot, surrendered next day. The outer defences of fortress Canada had now been breached, so clearing the way for an assault upon its citadel in the New Year.

The conquest of Canada

Before Amherst could instigate his final campaign against Montreal, fighting erupted on other fronts. Increasing friction between settlers and the Cherokees of the Carolinas prompted the despatch of a punitive expedition into that tribe's mountainous homelands under the command of Colonel Archibald Montgomery.[85] Although this force baffled a Cherokee ambush, and succeeded in burning several Indian towns, supply and transport problems obliged Montgomery to withdraw before the job of pacification was completed. That task was only accomplished by a second expedition in 1761. This larger column, of some 2,600 regulars and provincials, was commanded by Lieutenant-Colonel James Grant – the same officer who had been defeated and captured by Indians at Fort Duquesne three years previously.[86] Grant's force rebuffed a Cherokee attack on 10 June and proceeded to destroy fifteen towns and 1,500 acres of Indian corn: this devastation proved sufficient to bring the hostiles to the peace table.

At Quebec, the spring of 1760 saw Wolfe's victory of the previous September come close to being unravelled when the French gathered the bulk of their available manpower, including all eight of the regular line battalions, in a bold effort to recapture the city. Rather than endure a siege, Brigadier-General Murray sallied forth with his outnumbered and sickly garrison. In an extremely hard-fought encounter at Sainte-Foy on

84 Captain Allan Maclean to Lt-Col. Frederick Haldimand, camp before Niagara, 14 July 1759, in Add. MSS., 21,728, fol. 29.

85 Montgomery's regulars numbered about 1,300 men (Amherst to Pitt, New York, 8 March 1760, in *Correspondence of Pitt*, II, 263). By the time it left Fort Prince George on 28 May, the column had been reinforced to some 1,700 by rangers, provincials and Catawba Indians. See D. H. Corkran, *The Cherokee Frontier: Conflict and Survival, 1740–62* (Norman, Oklahoma, 1962), p. 208.

86 Grant commanded about 1,400 regulars, 700 South Carolina provincials, 400 rangers, and 100 Indians (ibid., p. 246).

28 April, Murray was defeated by Major-General François-Gaston, Duc de Lévis, and driven back into Quebec with heavy losses.[87] This unexpected blow demonstrated the continuing capacity of Canada's outnumbered defenders to concentrate their resources and strike swiftly against the colony's divided assailants. In seeking battle at Sainte-Foy, Murray had gambled with recklessly high stakes: as one British officer observed, had Quebec's defenders surrendered, the French 'wou'd again have had a Superiority in america'.[88] Happily for the Anglo-American war effort, Murray's garrison held out until the arrival of a Royal Navy squadron in the St Lawrence obliged the French to abandon the siege in mid-May.

The long-suffering defenders of Quebec participated in the final, inexorable advance on Canada. Three British armies, comprising more than 17,000 regulars, provincials and allied Indians, were destined to converge on Montreal: Murray from Quebec, Brigadier-General William Haviland from Lake Champlain, and Amherst via Lake Ontario.[89] The bulk of the remaining French regulars were positioned to defend the route allocated to Haviland. Of the trio of commands, the main army under Amherst faced the most determined opposition, being obliged to capture the island stronghold of Fort Lévis. Heavier casualties were sustained subsequently at the hands of Canada's formidable natural defences: on 4 September Amherst lost more than 80 men, drowned in negotiating the notorious Cedar rapids. One officer recalled that the experience of witnessing 'fellow creatures floating on the wrecks and you passing them not being able to assist would pierce the most obdurate heart'.[90] Murray's column was the first to reach the objective: within three days, the trio of British commands all menaced Montreal. In the face of overwhelming odds, Vaudreuil capitulated on 8 September 1760. Denied the honours of war because of the atrocities perpetrated by their Indian allies during earlier campaigns, the depleted French regulars burned their regimental colours rather than surrender them to the victors.[91] This final act of defiance signalled the end of hostilities on the North American mainland.

87 For the battle of Sainte-Foy, see below, pp. 255–61.

88 Lt-Col. Robertson to Calcraft, Schenectady, 22 June 1760 (LO 6251).

89 Amherst's command of 10,142 regulars and provincials and 706 allied Indians was the largest by far. Haviland's force of regulars and provincials totalled about 3,400 while Murray's command, which was composed of regulars alone, numbered 4,011. See 'Amherst's Personal Journal', pp. 82–3; 87; 96.

90 Thomas Stirling to his brother William Stirling of Ardoch, Camp at Montreal, 9 September 1760, in GD 24 (Abercairny Muniments)/1/458/1.

91 Hard service and desertion had reduced the French regulars to about 3,500. The eight battalions of *troupes de terre* now numbered just 2,302 officers and men, while two battalions of brigaded colony regulars amounted to another 1,168 of all ranks. See 'State of the ten French Battalions at Montreal which Capitulated 8th Sept 1760 . . .', in 'Amherst's Personal Journal', pp. 91–2.

Historians have typically viewed New France's defeat at the hands of the Anglo-Americans as a *fait accompli*: after the 'watershed' year of 1758, they argue, diverse factors interlocked to render the struggle so one-sided that the military collapse of Canada was merely a matter of time. According to these scholars, Pitt's allocation of unprecedented resources towards a single-minded pursuit of victory in America, the ascendancy of the Royal Navy and the disaffection of New France's Indian allies all combined to assure Canada's fall.[92] By contrast, the redcoats' role in this triumph has been marginalised to the extent that their efforts scarcely register on the credit side of the balance. Indeed, in the words of Francis Jennings, the 'British military system and its commanders were simply rotten': this dire organisation only disguised its deficiencies by fielding huge armies that ultimately overwhelmed the opposition by 'sheer weight'. Although victorious at Quebec and Montreal, the redcoats had done no more than exploit the breakthrough that this massive application of manpower had inevitably yielded.[93]

As a primary objective of the present book is to suggest that these same campaigns saw the formation of a formidable and effective 'American Army', it is necessary to assess the contribution of the redcoats in relation to those reasons commonly cited for the downfall of New France. In terms of resources, at a fundamental level it is clear that the Pitt–Newcastle ministry placed increasing emphasis upon the American war at the very time that Versailles was neglecting Canada for the European theatre: as this chapter has demonstrated, one obvious consequence of such priorities was an unprecedented concentration of redcoats in North America. In addition, Pitt's determination to maximise the manpower of the hitherto uncooperative American colonies had made it possible – indeed obligatory – for his generals to field large armies. Although the redcoat battalions remained woefully undermanned, and the provinces rarely raised the quotas required of them, in purely numerical terms the dice remained loaded against Canada. Yet, as even the most superficial survey of military history reveals, numbers alone offer no guarantee of victory. For British commanders in America, the mass levies of provincials called forth by Pitt's financial incentives proved a mixed blessing. The lamentable quality of the New Englanders assembled for Abercromby's Lake George campaign of 1758 has already been noted: if anything, British officers complained, the provincials enlisted subsequently were even worse. As with Abercromby's ill-fated offensive, the continuing inability of the provinces to raise their men in good time, and the logistical problems that such unwieldy contingents

92 See for example, Anderson, *Crucible of War*, pp. 236–9; 412; 453–5.
93 Jennings, *Empire of Fortune*, p. 211.

served to exacerbate, delayed two successive campaigns against New France.[94]

The shortcomings of the provincials as soldiers did not go unnoticed by British officers: their blistering criticisms have provided ready ammunition for modern scholars keen to highlight tensions between Britons and Americans.[95] But these comments were not merely expressions of blind prejudice against 'inferior' colonials; they also represented the verdicts of professional soldiers seeking victory in a long, bloody and frustrating war. Such regulars remained ready to praise those provincials whose behaviour merited recognition. For example, the Virginia Regiment emerged from Forbes's punishing campaign against Fort Duquesne with a high reputation, and thereafter continued to earn plaudits from senior British officers.[96] Again, when Colonel John Johnston of the New York provincials was killed at Niagara in 1759, he was 'agreed on all Hands to have been the greatest Loss'. One regular officer mourned Johnston as 'the best head & heart we had in this small army'; in consequence, his death far outweighed that of the expedition's British commander, Brigadier-General Prideaux.[97] If applause of this kind remained rare, it was for the simple reason that most provincials increasingly resembled armed labourers rather than true combat troops.

An over-emphasis on provincials was one legacy of ministerial intervention in the American war; another detrimental consequence for British commanders in America was Whitehall's unusually close involvement in the formulation of strategy. Such interference merely hindered British officers in their conduct of operations. As the capable Forbes observed in February 1758, the 'immense distance' between Britain and North America, allied to the precariousness of the Atlantic crossing, made 'all orders and directions for the conduct of affairs on this great Continent, almost unnecessary unless of a very general nature'. When Forbes wrote, Lord Loudoun had already drawn up his own plan of operations for the coming campaigning season. In Forbes's opinion, Loudoun's blue-print promised 'to give the French the greatest stroke they have mett with in North America'.[98] The strategy thrashed out by Loudoun during that winter ultimately yielded victory over Canada, although success would

94 See for example, Captain James Abercrombie to Loudoun, New York, 16 April 1759 (LO 6090); and Robertson to Calcraft, Schenectady, 22 June 1760 (LO 6251).

95 For a selection of comments by regular officers see Leach, *Roots of Conflict*, 130–32.

96 Titus, *Old Dominion at War*, pp. 126–7; 133.

97 See Richard Huck to Loudoun, 4 August 1759 (LO 6134); Captain Allan Maclean to Colonel Robertson, Camp before Niagara, 22 July 1759 (LO 6127).

98 Copy of a letter to the 'Duke of B–d [Bedford]', New York, in Forbes's hand, undated but *c.* mid-February 1758 (RH4/86/1). See also Loudoun to Commodore Lord Colville, New York, 8 February 1758 (LO 5554).

require not one campaign but three. This hiatus stemmed partially from New France's natural strengths, but it also reflected inertia resulting from the direction of strategy from afar. Each winter and spring, as they awaited the arrival of packet-ships bringing their orders from London, British commanders were left twiddling their thumbs, or, if Amherst's officers are to be believed, kicking up their heels at a round of balls and routs.[99] When they finally arrived, the orders formulated by Pitt and his colleagues were couched in terms that left little scope for initiative and effectively hobbled the men on the spot: the fatal consequences of Abercromby's close adherence to his detailed instructions have already been noted. Amherst received equally comprehensive orders for the operations of 1759;[100] although given some leeway regarding the execution of his own campaign from Albany, it was only in the following year that the full implications of such restrictive control sank home in Whitehall: in 1760 Amherst was allowed discretion 'to concert the properest measures for pushing the operations of the next campaign' from his 'knowledge of the Countries thro' which the War is to be carried, and from emergent circumstances not to be known here'.[101] This evidence suggests that the benefits of Pitt's dynamic leadership were less obvious to the soldiers fighting his American campaigns than they have appeared to modern historians: far from smoothing the path to victory, by burdening his commanders with too many provincials and circumscribing strategy the 'Great Commoner' had in fact added to the task facing the 'American Army'.

Turning to the second factor habitually cited for Canada's fall, the might and reach of the Royal Navy was undeniably significant. Seapower underpinned Britain's ability to maintain a far-flung conflict in the Americas; naval blockades denied New France reinforcements and supplies, including the trade goods required to retain the allegiance of her Indian allies; it was likewise the Royal Navy's warships that escorted task-forces to their objectives and naval officers who orchestrated amphibious landings. However, Georgian Britain's maritime supremacy was never as obvious as patriotic historians of the Dreadnought era subsequently believed. A failure to secure local naval superiority off Cape Breton had foiled Loudoun's grand expedition of 1757, whilst the sudden appearance of a French squadron in the Caribbean in March 1759 obliged Commodore Moore to shift his fleet from Guadeloupe, so depriving General Barrington of naval support. It was only in November 1759, two months after Wolfe's conquest of Quebec, that Admiral Hawke's

[99] See letters from James Robertson and James Abercrombie to Loudoun, New York, 3 and 4 February 1759 (LO 6039; 6041).

[100] Pitt to Amherst, Whitehall, 29 December 1758, in *Correspondence of Pitt*, I, 432–42.

[101] Same to same, Whitehall, 7 January 1760, in ibid., 237–42; 238.

destruction of the Brest fleet amidst the storms and shoals of Quiberon Bay finally scotched lingering fears for the security of Britain itself.[102]

Where the armed forces of mid-Georgian Britain were concerned, 'combined operations' meant exactly that.[103] Close liaison between the services was therefore essential for victory. Although the Royal Navy represented a major mobile resource of both man- and firepower, what made it so decisive in America was the unprecedented degree of cooperation between sailors and redcoats. As Lieutenant Thomas Webb of the 48th Foot noted, a 'Unanimity and Harmony', which had been 'but too much neglected' in the past, was conspicuous at Louisbourg in 1758.[104] During subsequent combined operations throughout the Americas, British soldiers continued to match the exacting standards of the 'Senior Service'. Whilst acknowledging the key role of sea power for British victory in the American campaigns of the Seven Years War, it therefore remains important to recognise the redcoats' growing expertise in amphibious warfare; this included a unique proficiency in the notoriously hazardous business of assaulting a hostile shore.[105]

Historians of the Seven Years War in the Americas have also emphasised the decisiveness of shifting tribal allegiances for the success of the Anglo-American war effort. Indian support for Canada clearly slackened after 1757, when warriors from the 'Far West' returned to their villages bearing lethal trophies from Fort William Henry: scalps taken from smallpox victims were credited with wreaking havoc throughout the *pays d'en haut*;[106] in addition, it is argued that Montcalm's high-handed treatment of his assorted Alonquian and Iroquoian allies did nothing to endear them to New France.[107] This situation was compounded in 1758 by Bradstreet's elimination of Frontenac – a post deemed crucial for maintaining the allegiance of the western nations – and the defection of the Ohio tribes at the Treaty of Easton. The steady decline of Indian support for New France was matched by a corresponding growth in Britain's ability to muster tribal allies. However, Canada had begun the conflict with a virtual monopoly of Indian support, and even after 1758, warriors

102 The limitations of Georgian seapower are addressed in *The British Navy and the Use of Naval Power in the Eighteenth Century*, eds J. Black and P. Woodfine (Leicester, 1988), and *Parameters of British Naval Power 1650–1850*, ed. M. Duffy (Exeter, 1992).

103 R. Harding, *Amphibious Warfare in the Eighteenth Century: The British Expedition to the West Indies, 1740–42* (Woodbridge, Suffolk, 1991), p. 169.

104 [Thomas Webb] *A Military Treatise on the Appointments of the Army ... Proposing Some New Regulations ... which will be particularly useful in carrying on the War in North America* (Philadelphia, 1759), ii; ix.

105 See below, pp. 236–45.

106 [Captain Alexander Monypenny, 55th Foot] to John Forbes, Camp at Lake George, 26 June 1758 (GD 45/2/93/4).

107 Steele, *Warpaths*, pp. 204–5; 212.

from many nations continued the fight against the Anglo-Americans: Benjamin West's imagination notwithstanding, there were no Indians with Wolfe at Quebec; by contrast, Montcalm continued to enjoy the services of more than 1,000 warriors. With Indians, as with other combatants, it was never simply a question of numbers. Just as compact commands of specialised rangers or armed boatmen were vastly more valuable in the wilderness than sprawling contingents of raw and sickly provincials, so small, manageable bands of Indians were preferable to the heterogeneous hordes that had joined Montcalm in 1757; that general's aide-de-camp, the future explorer Louis Antoine de Bougainville, observed in 1756 that it was 'better to have on hand only a specified number of these mosquitoes, who would be relieved by others'.[108] The same lesson was learned by British soldiers. When the large contingent of Cherokees and Catawbas with Forbes's army in 1758 had dwindled to 200, Colonel Henry Bouquet observed that even this number was 'preferable to 500 rogues who do nothing but filch our presents without rendering any Service'.[109] In another important sense the 'Indian factor' should not be overplayed: with few Indian allies during its early campaigns, the British Army had no option but to look elsewhere for 'irregulars'. By 1758 British commanders could already field useful light troops of their own; although by no means the equals of Indians in the woods, they none the less demonstrated the extent to which the 'American Army' had developed a capacity to wage war in the wilderness independent of tribal allies.[110]

Such evidence suggests that the British Army's role in the conquest of Canada was far from negligible. For all that historians have depicted the event as a foregone conclusion, the rotten trunk of New France did not simply topple of its own accord; it had to be felled, and whilst influential scholars remain reluctant to acknowledge the fact, those wielding the axe to greatest effect wore the red coat of the regulars.

The twilight of the 'American Army'

Victory in Canada freed British troops to pursue operations on other fronts. However, years of tough campaigning had taken a heavy toll of Amherst's regular battalions. In the autumn of 1760, Amherst learned

108 *Adventure in the Wilderness*, p. 60.

109 Bouquet to Forbes, Fort Loudoun, 16 June 1758, in *The Papers of Henry Bouquet*, eds S. K. Stephens, D. H. Kent, A. L. Leonard and L. M. Waddell (6 vols, Harrisburg, 1951–94), II, 97.

110 See below, Chapters 6 and 7.

that his army was to receive a reinforcement from England of some 2,000 new-raised men.[111] Such raw troops were better than nothing, although they did little to meet the manpower demands of an army in which the regulars were now almost 7,000 men below establishment. As Amherst emphasised, there was a 'great number of men wanted to compleat the Army, which cannot be recruited by enlisting men in this Country, owing to the vast bounty money the Provincials give to raise their men'.[112] Indeed, by pledging to reimburse the provinces for whatever it cost to raise their own troops, Parliament had effectively scuppered the recruitment of regulars in North America.

Despite these continuing problems, in December Amherst was warned to be ready to act against either the Gulf of Mexico or Martinique. By early 1761 the Cabinet had opted for another West Indian campaign. The expedition against Martinique was delayed until September 1761, to avoid the devastating hurricane season. Meanwhile, Amherst was instructed to send 2,000 of his regulars to Guadeloupe, ready for an attack upon the 'neutral' island of Dominica. Although the designated force was dispersed by storms, enough troops rendezvoused under the expedition's leader, Brigadier-General Andrew Lord Rollo, to effect a landing near the chief town of Roseau and rout the local militia.

The major operation against Martinique was led by another veteran officer, Major-General Monckton. He commanded 13,000 men, largely drawn from the North American mainland, but also including troops from the West Indies, Belle Isle in the Bay of Biscay, and Britain itself.[113] Once again, British naval superiority permitted the landing on 16 January 1762 to proceed unmolested under the cover of heavy broadsides. Within two days the entire army had been safely disembarked at Cas des Navières, some four miles west of Fort Royal. The French, consisting of regulars and militia, were entrenched on the formidable height of Morne Tartenson.[114] On 24 January, élite forces of British grenadiers and light infantry stormed this position, pushing the defenders back to an even stronger one at Morne Garnier. Three days later the French defenders

111 Amherst to Barrington, Crown Point, 18 October 1760, in WO/1/5, fol. 132.

112 Ibid., fol. 133.

113 From Guadeloupe and Antigua, detachments of the 4th, 38th and 65th; from Dominica, 22nd, 77th, 94th; from North America, 15th, 17th, 27th, 28th, 35th, 40th, 1/42nd, 2/42nd, 43rd, 48th, 3/60th; from Europe, 69th, 1/76th, 2/76th, 90th, 98th, 100th. There were also two companies of American rangers and ten of 'Barbadoes Volunteers'. The total including artillerymen was 13,288 (Returns, Carlisle Bay, 24 December 1761, in WO/17/1489/12).

114 Intelligence sent to Pitt in May 1761 reported Martinique's defenders as 8,770 'hommes' including regulars, militia and both free and enslaved blacks. See 'Etat Géneral des Compagnies De Milice qui se Trovent dans l'isle de la Martinique', in CO/110 (Guadeloupe)/1, fols 239–40.

launched an unexpected sally against the British batteries. The stratagem misfired as the sortie was not only repulsed but pursued so closely that the redcoats entered the lines of Morne Garnier along with the fleeing French. One British soldier reported:

> They were pursued by the troops with the utmost eagerness up Morne Grenier, by every path, road, practicable to run walk or creep up by, which put the Heroes in such a fright, that they abandoned their works, Cannon, heights & passes as fast as they saw a red coat in sight.[115]

Deserted by the island's militia, the regulars besieged in the citadel of Fort Royal surrendered on 4 February.

While the Martinique operations were under way, Spain had belatedly entered the fray in support of her beleaguered Bourbon relatives. Within days of Britain's declaration of war against her old enemy on 4 January, George Earl of Albemarle was given the rank of lieutenant-general and appointed to command the troops on an expedition against Havana.[116] The naval forces were placed under Vice-Admiral Sir George Pocock. Albemarle was to deploy some 14,000 troops drawn from Martinique and England: once established on Cuba, he expected to receive a further reinforcement of 4,000 from Amherst's mainland army. These troops, including some provincials, were to be returned to Amherst at the conclusion of the Cuban mission. They were then to form part of a force of 8,000 men that Amherst was to lead against New France's remaining southern territory of Louisiana – a paper plan that reckoned without the ravages of the West Indian 'sickly season'. Brigadier-General Haviland was one veteran who dreaded the consequences of a 'Spanish War'; writing from Martinique on 20 March, Haviland warned Amherst that officers and men alike had already begun to drop: he feared they would soon be joined by many more of the General's 'good old americans'.[117]

By 6 June the British flotilla had appeared off the port of Havana, to the consternation of the unsuspecting inhabitants. Next day, after naval gunfire had subdued the shore batteries, the troops were landed at Coximar, several miles east of the city. On 8 June a substantial Spanish force which included cavalry – an arm that had scarcely been seen on the North American mainland or in previous Caribbean campaigns – took up a strong position to contest the route to Havana. The Spanish troopers charged, but, in the words of a British officer, 'showed bad discipline and

115 Captain Harry Gordon, 1st Battalion Royal American Regiment, to Colonel Henry Bouquet, 'Fort Royal in Martinico', 18 February 1762, in Add. MSS 21,648, fol. 39.

116 On this expedition see *The Siege and Capture of Havana 1762*, ed. D. Syrett (London, 1970).

117 See WO/34/55, fol. 117.

great cowardice and were immediately drove off'.[118] The key to Havana was the powerful stronghold of El Morro – sited high above the eastern mouth of the harbour and popularly regarded as impregnable. However, El Morro, and much of the port it guarded, was itself commanded by the heights of La Cabana. This crucial position boasted only sketchy defences and was stormed by British light infantry and grenadiers on 11 June. Four days later a detachment of 2,800 infantry and marines under Lieutenant-Colonel William Howe landed near the mouth of the Chorera River and established posts facing the western side of the city. Albemarle's siege lines progressed only slowly, hampered by dense scrub, thin soil and disease. Despite these handicaps, by the end of June the siege batteries were nearing completion. The garrison responded by launching two attacks early on the morning of 29 June. Both parties retired after meeting a fierce reception. By early July, British batteries were in action against El Morro. Within days the exhausted besiegers suffered a disheartening setback after their main battery was consumed by fire. Sickness, coupled with the exertions of labouring under fierce heat, was now inflicting a far heavier toll than Spanish lead or steel. One private soldier, James Miller of the 15th Foot, recalled:

> The fatigues on shore were excessive, the bad water brought on disorders, which were mortal, you would see the mens tongues, hanging out parch'd like a mad dogs, a dollar was frequently given for a quart of water; in Short by dead, wounded, and sick, the army were reduced to two reliefs, and it was supposed that we should be obliged to reimbark without taking the place.[119]

With sailors from Pocock's warships employed to man the batteries, the siege lines continued to inch forward, prompting a trio of Spanish sorties in the early hours of 22 July. All were checked. In late July the first of the much-needed reinforcements from Amherst arrived: in return, Albemarle despatched the remains of four battalions who were now unfit for duty. On 30 July 1762, El Morro was successfully mined: in the resulting

118 Letter by Lieutenant Nicholas Delacherois, 9th Foot, 'Camp at the Havanna', 30 July, 1762, in 'Letters of Nicholas Delacherois', *JSAHR* (1973), p. 9. Estimates of Havana's defenders range from 5,000 to 10,000. However, the garrison included three regular regiments of foot and another of dragoons, plus marines and artillerymen. Seamen were available from ships in the harbour, while there were large numbers of militia and other irregulars both in Havana itself and in the surrounding region (*Siege and Capture of Havana*, xxi).

119 'Memoirs of an Invalid' (CKS, U1350/Z9A), p. 65. Some 5,366 soldiers were lost at Havana between 7 June and 18 October, 1762, representing about 40 per cent of the troops present; of these, just 560 were killed in action or died of wounds, compared with no less than 4,708 who succumbed to disease. See *Siege and Capture of Havana*, p. 305.

confusion a British storming party mounted the breach and gained the castle after a bout of hand-to-hand fighting. The next objective, the smaller La Punta fort on the opposite side of the harbour mouth, was battered into submission on 11 August. Faced with the prospect of an assault and subsequent sack, Havana capitulated. The surrender came none too soon for the British Army: Havana had been conquered at a high price – the virtual destruction of the 'American Army' that had humbled French power in North America and the West Indies.[120] John Watts, who witnessed the return of the survivors, hoped that this 'wofull reduction of the Havanna' would secure a favourable peace, as it had 'entirely broke the heart of the stoutest little Army in the world'.[121]

While the costly Havana operations were under way, the French launched a surprise attack on Newfoundland, the base for a lucrative fishery. In early May a squadron of five warships carrying some 800 regular troops slipped through the Royal Navy's Brest blockade to arrive off Newfoundland on 24 June.[122] Fort William at St John's was garrisoned by a small detachment of the 40th Foot and Royal Artillery: this neglected and dejected command soon surrendered without a siege, even though the French possessed no artillery. News of the raid reached Amherst at New York on 15 July. Two months earlier, Amherst had been strongly opposed to plans to take further troops from the mainland for operations elsewhere, considering 'it very imprudent to send one single man more out of the Country'.[123] Now, with the bulk of his redcoats fighting in the West Indies or scattered in remote garrisons, the General was obliged to scour far and wide for sufficient soldiers to counter the unexpected threat to the north. Amherst's manpower crisis obliged him to employ some of the invalids who had recently arrived at New York from Martinique. These 'recovered men' were subsequently joined by detachments from the garrisons of Halifax and Louisbourg to form a task-force of 1,559 soldiers commanded by the General's younger brother, Lieutenant-Colonel William Amherst.[124] On 11 September, Lt-Col. Amherst rendezvoused at sea with a flotilla under the commander-in-chief of the North

120 By autumn Albemarle's army numbered just 5,774 'effective' rank and file, of whom only 1,039 were actually fit for duty (Returns, Havana, 24 October 1762, in WO/17/1489/21).

121 Watts to Moses Franks, New York, 27 October 1762, in *NYHSC: Letter Book of John Watts*, p. 92.

122 See E. W. H. Fyers, 'The Loss and Recapture of St John's Newfoundland, in 1762', in *JSAHR*, XI (1932), 179–215.

123 Amherst to Secretary-at-War Charles Townshend, New York, 12 May 1762, in WO/1/5, fol. 231.

124 Besides the 'recovered men' organised as two companies of light infantry, there were ten companies of regulars, and five of Massachusetts provincials. See Fyers, 'Loss and Recapture of St John's Newfoundland', *JSAHR*, XI (1932), 192.

American squadron, Commodore Alexander Lord Colville. Two days later, Amherst's troops landed near St John's, pushed through dense woods and secured the strong post of 'Kitty Vitty'. This position, and Fort William itself, was dominated by Signal Hill. On 15 September two of Amherst's light companies scaled a precipice to dislodge a superior force of French grenadiers from the summit. When Amherst subsequently brought up his mortars and began shelling the fort, the French commander, Joseph Louis Comte d'Haussonville, surrendered his garrison of 770 regulars as prisoners-of-war. By 19 October, William Amherst was back in New York, having mounted an operation notable for efficient cooperation between the land and sea services, and which clearly demonstrated the quality of the veteran 'American Army'.

Peace was signed in February 1763, but that summer brought a fresh challenge for Jeffery Amherst as a dangerous war erupted among the Indian tribes of the western frontier. With the Havana troops reduced to a feverish handful, and other units disbanding or contracting to the reduced peacetime establishment, Amherst was hard pressed to counter the threat.[125] A succession of small posts was captured, while Detroit and Fort Pitt were besieged by substantial Indian forces.[126] Amherst scraped together sufficient troops to send relief expeditions to both of these posts. The first, under the command of the General's aide-de-camp, Captain James Dalyell, reached Detroit at the end of July. However, in a move that overrode the advice of the garrison commander, Major Henry Gladwin, Dalyell decided on a night sortie against the besieging Indians on 31 July.[127] Dalyell's force was ambushed by warriors led by the Ottawa war chief Pontiac, and driven back into Detroit with considerable losses. Reinforcements for Fort Pitt won through after the relief column under Colonel Henry Bouquet clashed with the Ohio Indians at Edge Hill near the stream of Bushy Run.[128] After a

125 Shy, *Toward Lexington*, pp. 113–25.

126 For the Indian war of 1763–64 see H. Peckham, *Pontiac and the Indian Uprising* (Princeton, 1947); also R. White, *The Middle Ground: Indians, Empires and Republics in the Great Lakes Region, 1650–1815* (Cambridge, 1991), pp. 269–314.

127 Dalyell's command numbered 276 regulars of all ranks. On its composition and fate, see two letters from Detroit, both dated 8 August 1763, in *The Pennsylvania Gazette*, no. 1811 (8 September 1763). Pontiac's warriors were estimated at about 400 ('Journal of Pontiac's Conspiracy', in *The Siege of Detroit in 1763, comprising the Journal of Pontiac's Conspiracy and John Rutherfurd's Narrative of a Captivity*, ed. M. Quaiffe (Chicago, 1958), pp. 3–215; 204.

128 Bouquet's force numbered about 500, consisting of the remnants of the 42nd and 77th regiments of Highlanders, plus a handful of the 1/60th and some rangers. The British considered that they had been attacked by a roughly equal number of Indians. See D. Daudelin, 'Numbers and Tactics at Bushy Run', in *Western Pennsylvania Historical Magazine*, LXVIII (1985), 153–79. For a contemporary narrative of Bushy Run, and of Bouquet's subsequent Muskingum campaign, see [William Smith] *An Historical Account of the Expedition Against the Ohio Indians in the year MDCCLXIV ...* (London, 1766).

fierce combat on 5–6 August, the hard-pressed Bouquet finally scattered his opponents. Bouquet won a much-heralded victory, but his losses prevented the pursuance of offensive operations against the Indians. Groups of these warriors retained the capacity to inflict considerable damage: on 14 September a band of Seneca ambushed a supply convoy near Niagara, then massacred the two companies of regulars who marched to its assistance.[129] Amherst returned to England in late 1763 with his reputation in tatters: his successor Lieutenant-General Thomas Gage – the man who had led Braddock's advance-guard some eight years before – inherited a messy and inglorious Indian war. That bloody chapter only closed in 1764, when Indian resistance crumbled in the face of tribal disunity and well-armed expeditions led by Colonels Bradstreet and Bouquet.

The contemporary reputation of the redcoats

Before 'Pontiac's War' had run its course, events far from the troubled frontiers were beginning to attract the attention of British politicians. Throughout the seaboard provinces, Whitehall's decision to retain a substantial peacetime army of redcoats in North America – and to secure colonial revenue to help pay for it – had triggered determined opposition. Resistance against future imperial efforts to tax the colonies would lead ultimately to war and American independence from Britain.

As has been noted, historians probing the roots of this dramatic rift have shifted their attention from the notorious flash-points of the 1760s and 1770s and delved back to the era of the 'Great War for Empire'. There is no doubt that the early years of warfare against New France were all too often characterised by squabbling amongst the Anglo-Americans. However, it is equally clear that when the tide of the conflict started to turn from the summer of 1758 onwards, and determined efforts were made to tackle those issues that had originally outraged colonial opinion, so attitudes towards the British Army also began to change. Parliament's largesse transformed the disposition of the provincial assemblies, whilst antagonisms over such issues as the quartering of troops in private houses subsided as compromise solutions were reached. There was even evidence that British and American soldiers were learning to get along with each other: according to one New Englander, Amherst's campaign of 1759 had proved 'happy beyond all former ones', not least because

129 More than 80 men were killed in this ambush, largely from the 80th Foot. See *London Magazine*, 1763 (November), p. 604.

> those disquieting Distinctions which were heretofore made between Regulars and Provincials, and at which our People took such Umbrage, are not this Year allowed of, but the whole has been treated as one Corps, amongst whom the greatest Harmony and Unanimity has subsisted.[130]

Above all, it was the British Army's improved performance on campaign that underpinned a sea-change in opinion: waves of colonial acclaim – expressed in letters, newspaper correspondence and sermons – greeted the exploits of the redcoats on the North American continent and in the Caribbean. Louisbourg's fall had hinted at what was to come. Amongst the literary efforts inspired by 'British Valour' upon that occasion was a poem by the Harvard graduate John Maylem, whose couplets drew favourable comparisons between Amherst's triumph and the siege of Troy.[131] But it was the conquest of Quebec that opened the floodgates. Wolfe's near-miraculous victory inspired a vintage crop of sermons from colonial pulpits. That preached by Andrew Eliot at Boston on 25 October 1759 – a day of public thanksgiving in Massachusetts – highlighted popular themes. Eliot observed that the siege was attended with difficulties 'insurmountable to any, but a General of such heroic fortitude and consummate skill, such fine officers, and such intrepid soldiers'.[132] To embattled New Englanders, the long struggle against Catholic New France had sometimes generated a crusading zeal; in the fiery sermons of their preachers, it was but a small step from Canada to Canaan. For all its regrettable habits, the triumphant British Army clearly enjoyed divine approval: after all, was it not God who had endowed General Amherst with the admirable qualities that allowed him to preserve a 'good Agreement' between his redcoats and provincials?[133] Whilst the credit for all victories ultimately rested with the Lord of Hosts himself, British regulars had undoubtedly been prominent among His earthly instruments. Some sermons explicitly acknowledged the primacy of the redcoats at the sharp end of the Anglo-American war effort: speaking before Governor Thomas Pownall and the Massachusetts Council on 16 October 1759, Samuel Cooper noted that the province's own troops had 'chearfully supplied in the

130 See 'Extract of a letter from a Gentleman in the colony of Connecticut to his friend in London, dated Nov 16 [1759]', in *Derby Mercury*, 1–8 February 1760.

131 *The Conquest of Louisbourg: A Poem by John Maylem, Philo-Bellum* (Boston, 1758), p. 12.

132 Andrew Eliot, *Sermon Preached . . . For the success of the British Arms this Year* (Boston, 1759), pp. 35–6.

133 Nathaniel Appleton, *A Sermon Preached [upon] the Surrender of Montreal, and All Canada* (Boston, 1760), pp. 23–4.

Garrisons of Louisbourg, and Nova Scotia, the Place of some of those veteran British Regiments, by whose Valor the Conquest of that American Carthage was obtain'd'.[134] Wolfe's glorious death provided an opportunity to remember other British officers who had given their lives for King and Country. A natural candidate for such deification was Lord Howe – already a firm favourite of the Massachusetts men when slain at Lake George in 1758. More surprising was the elevation of the much-maligned Braddock to the pantheon of Britain's fallen warriors. Through the words of Jonathan Mayhew, the curmudgeonly Coldstreamer now became 'a brave English general ... whose untimely fall can hardly be too much lamented'.[135]

This chorus of contemporary approval for the British Army and its leaders offers a striking contrast to the assessments of modern historians. Whatever colonial Americans may have thought of British soldiers and the government they represented in 1757, by 1763 the successes gained at Louisbourg, Quebec, Martinique and Havana had done much to redeem the reputation of the King's troops and to enhance the prestige of the mother country. Few colonials could doubt Britain's determination to safeguard and augment her American possessions: in 1760, the preacher Thomas Foxcroft called upon his congregation to bless George II for 'his Paternal Goodness in sending such effectual Aids to his American Subjects'.[136] That commitment had been expressed most conspicuously through a lavish distribution of regular troops to the American theatre. In January 1759, no less than 32 battalions of redcoats were serving in North America and the West Indies: at the same period, Britain's contribution to the allied army in Germany amounted to just six battalions of infantry and fourteen squadrons of horse.[137]

Victory over France and Spain had demonstrated both the fighting efficiency of these redcoats and the awesome power of the British state. There is evidence that the achievements of the 'American Army' evoked not only widespread recognition but also considerable shared pride amongst the colonial population. For example, in the autumn of 1759 one New York civilian wrote to 'congratulate' his father on the 'Glorious S[uc]cess of *our* Troops in the Reduction of Quebeck', in which '*our*

134 Samuel Cooper, *Sermon Occasioned by the Reduction of Quebec* (Boston, 1759), ix.

135 Jonathan Mayhew, *Two Discourses Delivered October 25th, 1759 ... For the Success of His Majesty's Arms* (Boston, 1759), pp. 18; 21.

136 Thomas Foxcroft, *A Sermon Preached ... On Occasion of the Surrender of Montreal, and the Complete Conquest of Canada ... by the Blessing of Heaven on his Britannic Majesty's brave Troops, under the auspicious Conduct of that truly great and amiable Commander, General Amherst* (Boston, 1760), p. 23.

137 Sir Reginald Savory, *His Britannic Majesty's Army in Germany During the Seven Years War* (Oxford, 1966), pp. 465–6.

Heroick Generall Mr Wolfe' had lost his life.[138] As Jonathan Mayhew had put it, Wolfe had died far from his native land, 'yet near one which would glory might it be said, that "this man was born here!" '.[139] A spirit of joint endeavour likewise lay behind the decision of Massachusetts – soon to prove the very crucible of anti-British sentiment – to pay for a substantial monument in Westminster Abbey to the memory of Lord Howe.[140] Another colony that was destined to prove a breeding-ground for revolutionary notions had likewise paid tribute to deserving British soldiers. On 14 March 1759, when Brigadier-General John Forbes was buried in the chancel of Philadelphia's Christ Church, Pennsylvania's governing élite turned out in force, following the coffin 'two by two' in an impressive show of respect.[141] The services of another regular soldier were recognised in 1765, the year of the Stamp Act riots, when the General Assembly of Pennsylvania voted its 'sincere and hearty Thanks' to Henry Bouquet. This address praised Bouquet's conduct during the recent wars with the French and Indians, in particular at 'the remarkable Victory over the savage Enemy, united to oppose you, near Bushy Run ... owing, under God, to your Intrepidity and superior Skill in Command, together with the Bravery of your Officers and little Army'. The grateful representatives proceeded to laud Bouquet for his 'constant Attention to the Civil Rights of his Majesty's Subjects in this Province'.[142] Such language is all the more remarkable when it is remembered that bickering over the recruitment of indentured servants had once caused Pennsylvanians to view the British Army as a sinister menace to liberty and property, and to express their outrage in very different words.

Whilst it would be naive to argue that redcoats and colonists had learned to coexist in a state of harmony, the evidence none the less suggests that the very real tensions between British soldiers and Americans apparent during the opening years of the 'Great War for the Empire' had largely relaxed at its triumphant conclusion. If, as is now widely accepted, the end of that conflict saw Americans identifying more

138 Henry Lloyd II to Henry Lloyd, Boston, 13 October 1759, in *NYHSC: Papers of the Lloyd Family*, II, 573. The italics are mine. See also Shy, *Toward Lexington*, pp. 143–8.

139 Mayhew, *Two Discourses*, p. 63.

140 According to the inscription, the memorial was erected as a 'testament' of esteem from the officers and soldiers of Massachusetts Bay. Howe's younger brothers, Richard and William, commanded Britain's sea and land forces during the opening years of the Revolutionary War.

141 Details of Forbes's funeral, and a laudatory obituary, appeared in the *Pennsylvania Gazette*. Given in *Writings of Forbes*, pp. 301–2.

142 Address of the Representatives of the Freemen of the Province of Pennsylvania, 15 January, 1765, cited in Francis Parkman, *The Conspiracy of Pontiac* (2 vols, Boston, 1880), II, 407–8.

closely with Britain than ever before,[143] then no small share of responsibility for this remarkable *rapprochement* lies with the redcoats of the 'American Army': during long years of warfare the British Army had rehabilitated not only itself but also the state that it represented. It was the subsequent decision to tax the colonists, coupled with the employment of soldiers to uphold royal authority, that swiftly squandered the credit accumulated at such heavy cost: within a decade such policies had transformed the bold heroes of Quebec into the bloody butchers of Boston.

143 See J. P. Greene, 'The Seven Years War and the American Revolution: The Causal Relationship Reconsidered', in *The British Atlantic Empire Before the American Revolution*, eds P. Marshall and G. Williams (London, 1980), pp. 84–105; 98–9. Also M. K. Geiter and W. A. Speck, 'Anticipating America: American Mentality before the Revolution', in *Britain and America: Studies in Comparative History, 1760–1970*, ed. D. Englander (London, 1997), pp. 26–47; 41; and J. Shy, 'The American Colonies, 1748–1783', in *Oxford History of the British Empire*, II, pp. 300–324; 306; 308.

2

Gone for a soldier

In Britain, as in the Thirteen Colonies, the Army's unexpected victories during the Seven Years War had prompted widespread jubilation. At Bath, for example, Wolfe's conquest of Quebec was marked in lavish style: the spa's uncrowned monarch, Richard 'Beau' Nash, ordered his personal cannon to be fired and gave a ball at 'Mr Simpson's'. Amongst the less genteel populace of nearby Bradford-on-Avon the celebrations were more spontaneous: there, the 'glorious News' triggered 'the greatest Rejoicings ever known in the Memory of Man'. The church bells had already rung for two days before official confirmation of the news caused the townsfolk to gather at 'The Swan'. After drinking many 'loyal Healths', the crowd progressed to the marketplace, where a vast bonfire had been constructed. Warmed to patriotic fervour by this victory blaze, the multitude gave three cheers, raising their tankards once again to 'their brave Countrymen in America, and the immortal Memory of their late brave Commander General Wolfe'. For all their obvious enthusiasm, Bradford's celebrations had proved remarkably orderly: indeed, despite the dense crowds, and 'the large Quantities of Strong Beer' consumed, *Boddely's Bath Journal* was able to assure its readers that 'not the least Accident happen'd'.[1]

Enthusiasm for British victories should not be confused with enthusiasm for Britain's Army. In the immediate wake of such successes as Quebec, Louisbourg and Martinique, the redcoats enjoyed the esteem of their countrymen:[2] the outbursts of patriotic celebration that marked these events have been taken to indicate that Englishmen were beginning to view their professional army in the positive light hitherto reserved for the Royal Navy.[3] But the victory bonfires had barely subsided before these sentiments gave way to indifference: at the Oxfordshire village of

[1] *Boddely's Bath Journal, 1759*, p. 172 (Monday 22 October).

[2] Hearing of Quebec's fall, the Sussex grocer Thomas Turner observed: 'I think in this affair our generals, officers and common men have behaved with uncommon courage and resolution, having many and great difficulties to encounter before they could bring the city to surrender.' See *The Diary of Thomas Turner, 1754–1765*, ed. D. Vaisey (Oxford, 1984), p. 191.

[3] Wilson, *Sense of the People*, p. 196.

Nuneham Courtenay, where the Reverend James Newton 'Treated the Ringers & my Servants & Labourers with two Black Jacks of Ale for the good News of taking Quebec', the Army's deeds in Canada were all too soon eclipsed by the prowess of his cat 'Tyger', who had killed 'an abundance of mice' at the taking in of the wheat rick.[4]

Whilst the first two Georges expressed an abiding interest and pride in their army, such views were not shared by their subjects; indeed, distrust of the soldier went to the very core of the national character.[5] For all his triumphs across the globe, the redcoat remained a sinister and despicable figure in the eyes of his countrymen. To a nation that revelled in an imaginary superiority over its continental neighbours – authoritarian, Catholic regimes bolstered by sprawling permanent armies – the professional soldier was both unnecessary and un-English. In the eyes of those educated men who followed political debate in pampthlets and newspapers, a standing army posed a genuine threat to cherished English liberties; in the hands of an unscrupulous despot, such redcoats could easily become the shock-troops of tyranny. Lingering suspicion of the military surfaced during the ritualised debates surrounding the annual passage of the Mutiny Act by which Parliament permitted the Army's continued existence. Pundits who warned against the spectre of military rule had their examples ready to hand from the previous century: the military dictatorship enforced by the hardened veterans of Cromwell's New Model Army, and the absolutist tendencies suggested by the Army's expansion under the pro-Catholic James II. The Seven Years War has itself been identified as a turning point in English attitudes towards the Standing Army: an issue that was very much alive in the reign of George II subsided under his successor, not least because of the pride generated by the redcoats' impressive performance on battlefields from Germany to America.[6] Despite a growing acceptance of the Army by the governing élite, such sentiments clearly failed to percolate through the mass of British society. Men lower down the social scale had their own reasons for disliking the soldiery. Before the barrack building programmes of the French Revolutionary and Napoleonic Wars, soldiers were commonly billeted upon ale-houses and stables in the midst of a

4 *The Deserted Village: The Diary of an Oxfordshire Rector James Newton of Nuneham Courtenay 1736–86*, ed. G. Hannah (Stroud, 1992), pp. 61; 67.

5 J. Hayes, 'The Royal House of Hanover and the British Army, 1714–60', in *Bulletin of the John Rylands Library*, XL (1957–58), 328–57; C. Barnett, *Britain and Her Army, 1509–1970: A Military, Political and Social History* (London, 1970), pp. 165–8. See also A. J. Guy, 'The Army of the Georges 1714–1783', in *The Oxford Illustrated History of the British Army*, eds D. Chandler and I. Beckett (Oxford, 1994), pp. 92–110.

6 P. Langford, *A Polite and Commercial People, England 1727–1783* (Oxford, 1989), p. 689.

resentful populace. In Ireland, where a separate military establishment was maintained in an effort to disguise the true size of the Army from its critics, soldiers on the march were sometimes foisted upon families too poor to provide for them. As one soldier observed, the parish constable responsible for allocating billets was usually reluctant to antagonise the 'Squire, Parson, Gentleman, or able Farmer, by sending so disagreeable a Thing to their Houses as a Red Coat, not considering their Valour at Culloden Mure, & c'.[7]

Above all, it was the very factor responsible for exhausting the Army's hard-won prestige in America after 1763 that had traditionally denied it an enduring place in the affections of Britons themselves: just as ingrained colonial suspicions of the military were rekindled by the use of redcoats to curb civil disobedience, so the Army's popularity at home was fatally compromised by its peacetime role of heavily armed police force. Whether waging guerrilla warfare against well-organised gangs of smugglers, or dispersing starving mobs with butt, bayonet and bullet, the redcoated infantryman or dragoon was the ultimate defender of the state.[8] Thus it was that in the spring of 1757, as Lord Loudoun pondered his instructions to assault Canada, other British soldiers were campaigning far closer to home. In Cornwall, where a long, hard winter had prompted widespread unrest, Lieutenant Charles Campbell of 'The Buffs' led a detachment in pursuit of a band of rampaging tin-miners. Campbell's lively account of the episode suggests an exciting jaunt. In their efforts to overtake the tinners, Campbell's command had been obliged to requisition horses and transform themselves into makeshift cavalry. As Campbell reported to his colonel, George Howard, this curious scene 'would have given Mr Hogarth an opportunity to exercise his genious, had he seen us'. After a brief skirmish the tinners had been dispersed with the loss of seventeen prisoners and a piece of red flannel 'stiled their bloody flag'. In the Lieutenant's opinion, there was 'no more to be done with these Tinners, than to pursue them briskly, as they don't seem inclinable to stand soldiers'.[9]

Other redcoats evinced less enthusiasm for such duties: Private James Miller of the 15th Foot clearly loathed them. Miller could take pride in his service at Louisbourg, Quebec, Martinique and Havana, but his

7 Anon, *The Case of the Infantry in Ireland ...* (Dublin, 1753), pp. 13–14. In the mid-eighteenth century there were some 12,000 soldiers in Ireland. See A. J. Guy, 'The Irish Military Establishment, 1660–1776', in *A Military History of Ireland*, eds T. Bartlett and K. Jeffery (Cambridge, 1996), pp. 211–30; 216.

8 See Hayter, *Army and the Crowd in Mid-Georgian England*; Houlding, *Fit for Service*, pp. 57–90; P. Muskett, 'Military Operations Against Smugglers in Kent and Sussex, 1698–1750', in *JSAHR*, LII (1974), 89–110.

9 Campbell to Howard, Truro, 2 May 1757, in WO/1/974, pp. 153–4.

regiment's role in the winter of 1772 brought him nothing but shame. Posted to the Scottish Lowlands, the men of the 15th 'were order'd out, on several disagreeable duties Vizt quelling of mobs, and trifling riots'. The confrontations 'always ended in blood', and Miller felt they should have been handled by the civil authorities without military assistance.[10] Miller's commander at Quebec had expressed a similar dislike for police work. During the autumn of 1756, Lieutenant-Colonel James Wolfe headed a detachment sufficient 'to beat the mob of all England collected'. Wolfe's troops were on hand to overawe the broad-cloth weavers of Gloucestershire, who had been driven to desperation by wage cuts that left them starving. To Wolfe, the weavers' grievances seemed just; the prospect of using force against them caused him 'a great deal of concern'.[11]

Like Wolfe, the dashing Lieutenant Campbell did not return from the American war. But whereas Wolfe achieved immortality at Quebec, Campbell succumbed ingloriously to disease on Guadeloupe.[12] Yet even the patriotic sentiments aroused by Wolfe's heroic death proved incapable of reversing his countrymen's prejudice against the redcoat. Indeed, such negative perceptions continued to dominate civilian attitudes into the heyday of the Victorian Empire: like generations of redcoats before him, Kipling's 'Tommy' knew the old truth that hostility towards the Army only abated when the drums of war began to roll.[13] This chapter examines the recruitment and backgrounds of the men who staffed the redcoat battalions of Britain's 'American Army' of the Seven Years War; it seeks to challenge perceptions that not only dominated the outlook of eighteenth-century Englishmen, but continue to influence the assessments of modern scholars.

Recruiting the regulars

In Georgian Britain soldiering in the ranks was deemed a low-caste occupation: besides being unpopular, soldiers were also poor. The private's pay of 8*d*. a day before stoppages compared unfavourably with all but the most humble members of society. Those who sought to

10 'Memoirs of an Invalid', p. 12.

11 Wolfe to his mother, from Sodbury, 24 October 1756, and Stroud, November 1756, in B. Willson, *The Life and Letters of James Wolfe* (New York, 1909), pp. 304; 306.

12 *London Magazine, 1759* (June), p. 338.

13 Kipling's poem 'Tommy' first appeared in the *Scots Observer* on 1 March 1890. See *The Complete Barrack-Room Ballads of Rudyard Kipling*, ed. C. Carrington (London, 1973), pp. 31–3.

organise England's population into a stratified hierarchy accordingly placed the 'common soldier' near the very bottom of the pile, below unskilled labourers and above only the 'cottagers, paupers and vagrants'.[14] As one redcoat complained, the private soldiers of the army were 'treated in a very disrespectful manner, exposed to many hardships, and by the meanness of their pay are put to the greatest inconvenience to subsist'.[15] Despite society's disdain for the professional soldier, the British Army none the less sought to fill its ranks with 'volunteers'; this optimistic outlook was maintained until the introduction of conscription in 1916. Although the 'press' was applied periodically in the eighteenth century as an emergency wartime measure, the vast majority of redcoats were enlisted – in theory if not always in reality – with their own consent. Regiments were filled by the time-honoured method of 'beating up' for recruits through the despatch of detachments into the towns and countryside. Recruiting parties typically consisted of a subaltern accompanied by a trusty and convivial sergeant, a musician to drum up a crowd, and several other smartly equipped veterans. The scenes that ensued when these squads touted for custom at hiring fairs and taverns offered ample inspiration for playwrights, cartoonists and balladeers. Such works exploited the striking difference between the smooth-tongued recruiter and his gullible prey: they also contrasted the extravagant promises of fabulous wealth and martial glory that emanated from the recruiting officer with the harsh realities of gruelling service, meagre pay and crippling wounds.

Recruiting parties were supposed to observe basic standards of character and physique, although these fluctuated according to supply and demand. The 'ideal' is represented by instructions to regular officers recruiting in Pennsylvania in 1755 who were warned against enlisting 'Irish, or any other Country', unless it was certain they were Protestants. In addition, recruits were to be 'straight and well made, broad shouldered ... none but shall measure 5 Feet 5 Inches without shoes, from 16 to 20, and 5 Feet 6 from 20 to 35'.[16] Instructions issued by Lord Loudoun two years later for all the regiments in America were less particular; whilst they prohibited the enlistment of Frenchmen, deserters, or any men aged under eighteen or over 40, it was now sufficient that recruits should be 'free from ruptures, Convulsions & Infirmitys', and in

14 Gregory King in 1688 and Joseph Massie in 1759 both gave the annual income of the private soldier's family as £14. The same surveys recorded the income of labourers or husbandmen as £15 in the earlier year, rising to £16 in 1759. See D. Hay and N. Rogers, *Eighteenth-Century English Society* (Oxford, 1997), pp. 19–20.

15 Anon, *A Soldier's Journal* (London, 1770), p. 172. The author identifies himself only as 'Jonas'.

16 F. T. Nichols, 'The Organization of Braddock's Army', in *WMQ*, IV (1947), 124–47; 139.

every way 'fit for Service'. None were to be enlisted under the height of five feet five inches, except for 'growing lads', who could be taken at five feet four. If possible, recruits were to be enlisted for 'life': otherwise men should be enlisted for 'a term of years (not less than three) or During the present War, with a promise that they will not be Obliged to serve out of America'.[17]

In terms of physique, many recruits fell short of even these undemanding standards. This was quite literally the case with a consignment of drafts received by the 46th Foot in 1763. Of 150 soldiers whose height was recorded, no less than 63 (42 per cent) were under five feet five inches in height; they included the diminutive Christopher Richey, who at five feet none the less towered above Daniel Frank, who measured just four feet six inches tall. Aged 30 and 36 respectively, neither of these veterans of the Royal Americans could be classified as 'growing lads'. The same list also reveals the presence of soldiers recruited at an advanced age: 60-year-old Robert Plunket had enlisted in the 44th Foot just five-and-a-half years earlier, whilst Archibald McKaye was 52 when he joined the same regiment in 1754.[18] The officer receiving these drafts considered them to be 'most Excessive bad in every Respect', although it is unlikely that they were uniquely so: in time of war, when men were scarce, 'show' took second place to serviceability. This was particularly true in America, where the formal confrontations of Flanders were all too rare. As Colonel John Forbes observed at New York in 1757,

> the middle of a warr is not a time to beautify Regts and if any size is taken in England that can carry a muskett, there can be no reason for refusing them here, where from behind a tree a pigmy may kill a Polyphemus ... for I am told and have always heard the strength of Armies reckoned from the numbers of Fire arms, and Not the height and strength of mankind.[19]

Some slippage in physical standards was a natural consequence of the exigencies of a rapidly expanding conflict; another result was the presence of recruits drawn from categories specifically excluded under the recruiting instructions. Despite the eighteenth-century Englishman's morbid fear

17 Recruiting Instructions, Albany, 16 November 1757 (GD 45/2/18/1A). Individual regiments also issued their own more rigorous specifications to recruiters: the 45th Foot's party in Boston was told that recruits were 'to be straight, with broad shoulders, good limbs, & healthy complexion, free from all blemishes or bodily infirmities whatsoever, none under 16 years of age, or above 35, and none under 5 feet 5 inches high, except growing lads under twenty' (Instructions from Major A. Murray, Halifax, 20 October 1757, in GD 45/2/24/1B).

18 Return of drafts, Niagara, 5 October 1763, in WO/34/22, fols 203–4.

19 Forbes to Loudoun, 10 December 1757, in *Writings of Forbes*, p. 23.

of 'Popery', an organisation that relied heavily upon Irish manpower inevitably included a significant contingent of Catholics. For example, Lord Loudoun was convinced that Irish recruits who had deserted from the 50th and 51st Foot at Oswego were 'mostly Roman Catholicks'. Despite the best efforts of their commanding officers, Loudoun also suspected the presence of Catholics amongst the Irishmen of the 44th and 48th Regiments.[20] Two redcoats who distinguished themselves at the siege of Havana, Barney Carrol and William King, must have concealed their true faith while in the Army; this emerged when they were later convicted for slashing a victim during an attempted robbery in London. Carrol and King 'suffered' at Tyburn on 31 July 1765; as the editors of *The Malefactor's Register* explained to their readers, the last words of the brutal pair remained obscure, as they were 'attended by a priest of their own persuasion'.[21] According to the clergyman who attended his execution in September 1756, the deserter Patrick Dunn of the 35th Foot was himself a 'romish Priest'; in consequence, the Galway-born Dunn 'dy'd a strict Papist'.[22]

Foreign deserters and turn-coats also found their way into the redcoat battalions of the 'American Army'. Upon the fall of Louisbourg, out of 402 men of the French Voluntaire Etranger regiment who remained fit for duty, no less than 131 were enlisted by British units.[23] Amherst subsequently proved reluctant to absorb such defectors. When Governor Francis Bernard of New Jersey told Amherst of his hopes of recruiting the colony's provincial regiment with German and Swiss Protestants from among French prisoners-of-war, the General's response was lukewarm, as 'no dependance' could be placed upon such men. Amherst explained: 'so soon as We come near to the Enemy, or to their Territories Numbers of them would immediately Desert to them'.[24]

Whatever their appearance or origin, likely recruits were entitled to an enlistment bounty; in Britain this was typically a 'guinea and a crown', and in the American continental colonies a roughly equivalent sum represented by a 'Pistole and a Dollar'. The crown was for drinking the King's health, while the guinea was usually withheld to provide the recruit with

20 Loudoun to Cumberland, Albany, 29 August 1756, in *Military Affairs in North America*, p. 232.
21 Anon, *The Malefactor's Register; or, the Newgate and Tyburn Calendar . . . from the year 1700 to Lady-Day 1779* (5 vols, London, 1779), IV, 275–9.
22 'The Diary of Rev. John Ogilvie 1750–1759', ed. M. W. Hamilton, in *BFTM*, X, 5 (Feb. 1961), 331–85; 375.
23 See 'State of the Garrison of Louisbourg', and note of 'Germans & Prodestants from the Volontaires Etrangers', in Amherst to Pitt, Camp near Louisbourg, 10 August 1758 (CO/5/53, fols 148; 154).
24 Bernard to Amherst, Amboy, 14 March 1760, in CO/5/58, fol. 76; Amherst to Bernard, New York, 16 March 1760, in ibid., fol. 78.

provisions during the march to the regiment, and to supply basic items of clothing, or 'necessaries', upon joining the corps. After a man had made his initial pact with the recruiter, this officer had four days to take him before a justice of the peace for formal attestation. At this point a recruit could still change his mind – provided that he repaid his bounty plus an extra pound of 'smart money' for the trouble caused.[25]

Such was the theory, and in England, where the Army was closely monitored, recruiters who failed to observe certain standards were likely to earn a swift rap across the knuckles. In America, recruiters for the regulars initially employed a range of tactics that their Old Country counterparts could only dream of. Some indication of these recruiting practices comes from the minutes of the General Courts Martial held within the 'American Army'. An example is provided by the case of James McDonell, tried in 1757 for deserting from Captain Peter Wraxall's New York Independent Company. Shortly before his recruitment McDonell's wife had died, leaving him to care for two young children. It was while travelling to collect money due to him from property in Pennsylvania and North Carolina, with which he hoped to support his family, that McDonell met an acquaintance who made him drunk. McDonell testified to what happened next:

> Whilst he was in liquor, Corporal Holmes with a Recruiting Party of the aforesaid Company, happening to be in the House, fell in with him, as he was told next morning, being that night so Drunk that he doth not remember seeing a red coat in the house, and was greatly Surprised in the Morning, when the said Corporal told him he was enlisted, and giving him at the same time, either a pint or half a pint of Stewed Rum.

On recovering his senses, McDonell offered the corporal no less than £16 to let him go, but to no avail. When brought before the justice for attestation, McDonell originally refused to take the oath, but on being told that he must swear to be faithful to King George, deemed it his patriotic duty to comply. McDonell subsequently quit the company at Fort Hendrick in a bid to alleviate the distressed condition of his offspring. Although Corporal Holmes confirmed McDonell's testimony, and despite the fact that McDonell enjoyed a high character in his neighbourhood, he was found guilty and sentenced to 200 lashes.[26]

In the scramble for colonial manpower, recruiting sergeants had few qualms about enlisting men who were already serving in other units. For

25 A. J. Guy, *Oeconomy and Discipline: Officership and administration in the British Army, 1714–63* (Manchester, 1985), p. 124.

26 General Court Martial (hereafter GCM), Fort Edward, 13 July 1757, in WO/71/65.

example, John Butler of the 50th Regiment was charged with deserting in New York in May 1756, then enlisting in Hopson's 40th Foot under a different name. In defence, Butler claimed that 'he was made very drunk by a man Employ'd to recruit for another Regiment who put a Dollar in his hand, and afterward lock'd him up in a room'. On sobering up, Butler explained that he was already enlisted, and returned the money given to him when drunk, along with all save six shillings of his bounty money.[27] Disney Lynch, who was charged with deserting from the 2/60th and enlisting in Captain William Ogilvie's New York Independent Company under a false name, claimed that when he was left behind by his regiment, Corporal Adam Berger of the Independents had made him drunk, forced money upon him and insisted that he enlist with *him*. Lynch added that when he proceeded to sign the attestation papers in his own name, the officer of the Independents in attendance, Lieutenant Archibald McCawley, had objected.[28] It is interesting that a similar allegation against Berger was made in 1761 by another man he enlisted for Ogilvie's company during 1757. John Fisher, who was charged with deserting from the company in May 1760, said that he had originally enlisted in the 46th Foot, but 'being left behind in the Jersey's, was trappaned into the Independents'.[29]

Even more revealing was the case of Jeremiah Collins, who was enlisted on four separate occasions within six months. Collins had originally been recruited by Corporal Edward Proud of the 48th Foot at Philadelphia in October 1755, only to abscond that same night. At the end of February 1756, Collins enlisted with the 50th at Dutch Creek, but deserted within a few days. On 20 March, Collins joined the 44th at New Town, Chester County. Once again, he swiftly disappeared. At the beginning of April, Corporal Proud claimed Collins from another party of the 48th which had again enlisted him at Philadelphia. Collins was at best criminally irresponsible, and at worst a professional 'bounty-jumper'; however, there is a ring of truth in his explanation that 'he told them all that he was Inlisted with Corporal Proud of the Forty Eighth Regiment and that he was in Liquor all the different times that he Inlisted and they forc'd the money upon him'.[30]

Although recruitment in America became more closely regulated from the summer of 1756 onwards, dubious recruiting techniques persisted

27 He was none the less found guilty and sentenced to 500 lashes. See GCM, Oswego, 4 August 1756, in WO/71/44.

28 Lynch received a death sentence. See GCM, Fort George, New York, 28 September 1757, in WO/71/66.

29 'Trepanning' – an allusion to the surgical technique of boring a hole into the skull of a patient to release cranial pressure – was a slang term for entrapment.

30 Not surprisingly, this defence failed to sway the court, who sentenced Collins to death (GCM, Albany, 19 May 1756, in WO/71/43).

long after. In 1762, James Davison of the 27th Foot was sent sick to the continent from Martinique and was amongst the 'recovered men' assembled to wrest St John's from the French. In the wake of the successful Newfoundland expedition, Davison was ordered back to Havana with several other soldiers, only for his transport to be captured by a Spanish frigate and carried to Cuba. Eight days later Davison escaped to St Eustatius, where he joined the crew of an English privateer. Davison slipped away from that vessel at the Connecticut port of New London. In a development that was understandable given his recent odyssey, Davison soon entered a public house, and 'got much in Liquor' in company with William Lee of the 15th Foot. The landlord gave each of the drunken pair a dollar, adding that they were now enlisted in the 2nd Battalion of the Royal Americans. Davison maintained that this process had gone ahead, even though he told the landlord, both before and after receiving the dollar, that he was already a soldier in the 27th. He had said the same when brought before the JP and refused to be attested. Eventually, the stubborn Davison was taken to General Amherst himself. Amherst sent Davison back to Havana to serve in his own regiment, the 15th Foot.[31]

Although the British Army of the Seven Years War was technically a 'volunteer' force, the redcoat battalions none the less contained a significant number of recruits who had been thrust into the ranks without their consent. Such men were the fruits of the 'Recruitment Acts' of 1756 and 1757: these measures, 'for the Speedy and Effectual Recruiting of His Majesty's Land Forces and Marines', permitted the conscription, or 'pressing', of the unemployed. Similar emergency legislation had been enacted during the Wars of the Spanish and Austrian Successions and would be used again when fighting erupted between Britain and its North American colonies.[32] According to the 1756 Act, those liable for 'pressing' were defined as 'such able-bodied men as do not follow or exercise any lawful calling or employment, or have not some other lawful and sufficient support and maintenance'. Recruits should not be under seventeen or over 40, under five feet four inches tall without shoes, or a known 'papist'. Officers receiving recruits were to pay twenty shillings to the parish or town officials for every man produced. Such men were to be enlisted for five years. Under the terms of the 1757 Act, anyone providing information leading to the enlistment of a suitable recruit would now receive half the sum to be paid to the parish officers. This Act introduced

31 Davison was acquitted of desertion. See GCM, Havana, 28 February 1763, in WO/71/73.

32 See A. N. Gilbert, 'Army Impressment During the War of the Spanish Succession', *Historian*, XXXVIII (1976), 689–708; also S. Conway, 'The Politics of British Military and Naval Mobilization, 1775–83', *English Historical Review*, CXII (1997), 1179–201; 1181–4.

a £3 bounty for volunteers, who would serve for three years, or the duration of the war if that lasted longer.[33] Some historians have stated that the Army employed forcible recruitment to the same extent as the Royal Navy, but the land press was in fact implemented for limited periods to meet specific manpower requirements:[34] once those targets had been met, the press would be lifted by public announcement. For example, the press of spring 1756 initially aimed to fill the ranks of the ten new regiments being raised since January. In March, the High Sheriffs of those counties where these units had their headquarters were required to summon the commissioners responsible for implementing the Act. Each of the regiments was allocated two or more counties from which they were to receive men selected by the commissioners. Officers were to inform themselves of the times and places of the commissioners' meetings, and 'then & there to receive, such Impress'd Men as the Commissioners, and your Officer or Officers shall judge to be such, as are Intended to be Entertained as soldiers in His Majestys service'.[35] Within a month, eight of the new regiments had either neared nor completed their establishments, and any men picked up were to be sent to the marines instead. The press was to be lifted from 1 May.[36]

Although of limited duration, impressment proved capable of generating considerable numbers of men. Besides filling new units, pressed men also served to swell formations expanding from the low peacetime establishment before embarking upon active service. In March 1756, as Otway's 35th Foot prepared to sail for America, it received no less than 500 of those pressed that spring – an influx that doubled the regiment's strength.[37] The scale and thoroughness of the 1756 press emerges from a remarkable account written by one of those snared in its dragnet. In a letter to his parents, this anonymous private soldier of the 35th described how he was 'press'd in London', along with 'a great many more creditable Persons ... to serve his Majesty as a Soldier in North America'. The writer's fatalistic tone suggests the inevitability of this outcome: 'For above a Year before I left London, I durst not look out at Night, nor Walk the Streets in the Day, for Fear of being press'd, seeing so many go before me: But it happen'd to be my Turn at last'.[38]

33 *The Scots Magazine, 1756* (March), p. 114; ibid., 1757 (February), pp. 61–2.

34 Sir John Fortescue assumed that the Press Act was renewed annually for the remainder of the war. See *A History of the British Army* (13 vols, London, 1899–1930), II, 573–4. In fact, no such press was enforced after 1757 owing to increasing parliamentary opposition and the revival of the Militia.

35 Barrington to the commanding officers of nine regiments, 11 March 1756, in WO/4/51, pp. 257–60. The tenth, Perry's 57th (later 55th) Foot, was based in Scotland.

36 *London Gazette*, no. 9576 (20–24 April 1756).

37 Loudoun to Daniel Webb, London, 27 March 1756 (LO 974).

38 Letter from Quebec, 7 October 1759, in *Derby Mercury* (30 November to 7 December 1759).

Across the Atlantic Lord Loudoun subsequently struggled to hammer this reluctant material into shape: that autumn he informed the Duke of Cumberland that the 35th were 'entirely Raw Officers and Soldiers, and everything new to them: the prest Men, I dare not yet trust so near the Enemey'.[39] Indeed, six of them promptly deserted together to the French. Their taste of freedom proved all too brief. Two deserters surrendered after losing their way in the wilderness; the other four were found wandering by Captain Robert Rogers and his rangers. All six were sentenced to death.[40]

Many of the 'idle' swept up by the press were just such material as hardship habitually drove into the Army: it has been argued that the press therefore served largely to stimulate ordinary recruiting by prompting men to volunteer and thereby qualify for bounties.[41] Whilst some recruits no doubt opted to 'jump' before they were 'pushed', the impact of compulsion should not be underrated. For example, a list of men raised for the 34th Foot in 1757 shows 90 pressed men, as against just 38 volunteers.[42] Regimental officers appointed to liaise with the commissioners of the press were frequently castigated for rejecting recruits who did not conform to their own standards. As a result, officers grudgingly accepted many pressed men who were plainly unfit for service: nineteen men discharged by the 35th Foot in 1757 included nine who had been pressed.[43] Pressed men did not necessarily make bad soldiers: according to their commanding officer, none could have behaved 'with more coolness, and Resolution' than the six companies of the 35th who helped to defend Fort William Henry in 1757.[44] John Moor, a pressed man who was charged with desertion in 1764, was given a good 'character' by his officers, having behaved well despite being placed in a company containing 'a great number of disorderly men'. Moor, who had been drafted into the 28th Foot from the disbanding 4th Battalion of the Royal Americans in August 1763, told how

> he was Pressed into His Majesty's service in the Town of Froome, in England in the year 1756, and Served in His Majesty's 3 regt,

39 Letter dated Albany, 3 October 1756, in *Military Affairs in North America*, p. 239.

40 GCM, Albany, 20–22 September 1756 and GCM, Fort Edward, 9 October 1756, in WO/71/44.

41 Houlding, *Fit for Service*, p. 118.

42 'Return of the Imprest Men and Volunteers, Rais'd for the 34th Regiment of Foot in the County of Essex', in Capt George Barry, 50th Foot, to Barrington, Brentwood, 3 April 1757 (WO/1/973, p. 23).

43 'Return of the Men listed in Europe & Press'd Men Discharged & not Recommended' (GD 45/2/35/4).

44 'Memorandum' by Lt-Col. George Monro, Albany, 1 November 1757 (LO 5309).

> and has Served in several regiments, having been Drafted from one to another, and having frequently complained & remonstrated against it, has, ever since he could find no redress, been very uneasy.[45]

The case of the unfortunate Moor serves as a reminder of the third method by which the British Army staffed units on active service. Drafting – the transfer of soldiers from one unit to reinforce another – was particularly important in meeting the manpower targets of the regiments serving in America, where, as has been seen, local recruiting proved grossly inadequate from 1757 onwards. The system was deplored by officers at the time, and has since been identified by historians as detrimental to donor and recipient alike: units receiving drafts were required to assimilate large numbers of strangers, whilst those drafted lost scarce manpower. The results played havoc with training and unit cohesion.[46]

When a regiment was reduced or disbanded, it was common for those men who were not entitled to their discharge to be transferred to another unit. Drafting could also occur when a battalion was rendered so ineffective by the fortunes of war that a decision was taken to 'break' it. Such proved the fate of the short-lived 50th and 51st Regiments, which had been raised in North America as Shirley's and Pepperrell's in 1754–55. The bulk of these battalions were captured at Oswego in the summer of 1756 and taken to Canada as prisoners-of-war; from there, batches were despatched across the Atlantic in cartel ships for eventual exchange with French servicemen held in British prison camps. The King had decided to reduce both regiments as from Christmas Eve 1756, and the majority of those 400–500 men who had arrived back in England by the onset of the New Year were ordered to be drafted into the 2nd Battalion of the 1st Foot, or 'Royal' Regiment before it embarked for America.[47] However, the planned reduction was delayed because some of the Oswego garrison remained captive in France, whilst those companies which had been detached at the time of the Oswego fiasco were still on duty in North America.[48] Of the latter, 247 were rounded up and confined in Boston's Castle William before being turned over to the Royal American Regiment on 7 March 1757.[49] The Oswego diaspora proved yet more protracted:

45 GCM, Montreal, 26 June 1764, in WO/71/74. Moor, who must have served in The Buffs at Guadeloupe, was sentenced to 1,000 lashes, although Thomas Gage subsequently reduced this to 500.

46 Houlding, *Fit for Service*, pp. 120–25; Guy, *Oeconomy and Discipline*, pp. 126–7.

47 Barrington to the Earl of Home, 3 February 1757, in WO/4/53, p. 166.

48 Barrington to the Earl of Dartington and Lord Viscount Dupplin, 30 April 1757, in WO/4/54, p. 14.

49 WO/1/1, fols 82–3.

throughout the winter members of the ill-fated garrison continued to trickle into English ports from Canada and France.[50]

Drafts were supposed to consist of 'unobjectionable men' who would prove acceptable to their new units. Despite the fact that donor regiments were expected to pay for rejected drafts, and to replace them, in many cases those officers ordered to make drafts embraced the opportunity to shed their least useful men – new recruits, the superannuated, misfits and 'bad characters'. For example, before Hopson's expedition against the West Indies, James Wolfe's 67th Foot was obliged to give 168 drafts to The Buffs and another 32 to the 61st Foot. These were to be 'unexceptionable men', and Wolfe's own battalion would receive £5 compensation for each of them.[51] However, Lieutenant-Colonel Trapaud of The Buffs subsequently reported that of the drafts received from Wolfe's, no less than 51 had been rejected as 'unfit for present service': 41 of these men had assorted ailments, while the other ten were too weak even to shoulder their muskets. Those men who *had* been accepted included ten deserters from the French Army enlisted on the coast of Normandy during Lieutenant-General William Bligh's recent expedition. Eight of these were actually British soldiers taken prisoner earlier in the war; the other two were Germans.[52] Wolfe's attempt to purge its undesirables misfired: the day after receiving Trapaud's complaint, Barrington warned the commanding officer of the 67th to complete the draft with the required number of serviceable men.[53]

The commanding officers of units destined to receive such transfusions of manpower were understandably wary that their regiments would become contaminated by poor material. For example, Brigadier-General Byam Crump, the governor of Guadeloupe and Lieutenant-Colonel of the 4th Foot, was in dire need of reinforcements but none the less dreaded the effect of an influx of substandard drafts upon the island's garrison. Crump warned Barrington that unless care was taken to prevent 'frauds', the three Guadeloupe regiments would be ruined. He therefore pleaded that Barrington would take the garrison under his protection, 'particularly the King's Own Regiment and not suffer that Corps, which at Culloden saved the Kingdom and upon all occasions has behaved with distinction, to be filled with the refuse of other Regiments'.[54]

50 See also C. T. Atkinson, 'A Colonial Draft for the Royals in 1757', in *JSAHR*, XVI (1937), 215–17.

51 Barrington to Wolfe et al., 27 September 1758, in WO/4/56, p. 269.

52 Trapaud to Barrington, Hilsea Barracks, Portsmouth, 13 October 1758, in WO/1/975, p. 301.

53 WO/4/56, p. 368.

54 Crump to Barrington, Guadeloupe, 24 October 1759, in WO/1/19, fol. 36. The King's Own had indeed experienced fierce fighting at Culloden. See Tomasson and Buist, *Battles of the '45*, pp. 156–60.

On occasion, the common practice of using a draft to off-load the unwanted had the unofficial sanction of the authorities. In the summer of 1757, when reinforcements for America were assembled by drafts from 37 battalions in Great Britain and Ireland, King George II had directed Lord Ligonier to ensure 'that the worst men should be draughted'.[55] Cumberland added the qualification that these should be 'recruits tho' servicable men', as trained soldiers were too scarce to be spared at that time.[56] The drafts began arriving at New York in early December 1757.[57] Of the 1,000 disembarked with Colonel Whitmore, 910 were split between six battalions: the other 90 'either Deserted, died or were returned unfit for service by the Surgeons of the Hospital'.[58] Many of these drafts had been sent out with poor clothing. Indeed, Loudoun had been obliged to 'new cloath' no less than 578 men who 'otherwise would have been naked'.[59] Of the drafts, 146 had been incorporated into the 44th Foot. The testimony of one of these men, Hugh Morrison, is revealing of both the nature of the drafts, and the failure of their parent regiments to equip them properly. Morrison swore that he had joined the 8th Foot as a recruit in May 1757, only to be drafted for America within three months. He had received no clothing from his original unit except 'an Old Coat & an Old Waistcoat'.[60]

Like pressed men, drafts were liable to resent such cavalier treatment. For example, Charles Hussey, who was charged with desertion from the 48th Foot in March 1756, entered that regiment as a draft from the 20th Foot before it sailed to America.[61] Another man of the 48th, Robert Banks, left his regiment at Boston in May 1759, as it was under orders to embark for the St Lawrence with Wolfe. Like Hussey, Banks had joined as a draft.[62] As with the pressed men, there was nothing to prevent a draft from becoming a good soldier. John Campbell, who was acquitted on a charge of desertion in 1758, had been drafted from Handasyde's 16th Foot to the 3rd Battalion of the Royal Americans. While in the 60th he had behaved extremely well – so well, in fact, that his officer, James

55 Barrington to Col Whitmore, 11 August 1757, in WO/4/54, p. 311; Barrington to Cumberland, Cavendish Square, 8 July 1757, in *Military Affairs in North America*, p. 381.
56 Ibid., p. 386.
57 R. Middleton, 'A Reinforcement for North America, Summer 1757', in *Bulletin of the Institute of Historical Research*, XLI (1968), 58–72; 67.
58 Return of the drafts received from England with Colonel Whitmore, Albany, 27 May 1758, in WO/1/1, fol. 192.
59 Maj.-Gen. Abercromby to Barrington, Albany, 27 May 1758, in ibid., fol. 188.
60 Affidavit enclosed in Lt-Col. Thomas Gage to Abercromby, Albany, 21 May 1758, in ibid., fol. 196.
61 GCM, Albany, 11 June 1756, in WO/71/43.
62 GCM, Havana, 20 September 1762, in WO/71/72.

Dalyell, took Campbell with him when he secured a captain's commission in Gage's Light Infantry.[63]

Personnel (i): The men in the ranks

Having examined the Army's recruiting techniques, it is necessary to assess the material such efforts yielded. Britain's 'voluntary' enlistment suited an era that prided itself upon protecting the liberty of the individual; not everyone agreed that this was beneficial for the British Army. The system's critics included the man who was arguably the most successful British soldier spawned during the course of the 'Second Hundred Years War'. Despite his victories over Napoleon and his marshals, the Duke of Wellington considered that French conscription was superior to Britain's voluntary enlistment. Whilst the former gathered 'a fair sample of all classes', the latter produced an army composed of 'the mere scum of the earth'.[64] Wellington's notorious verdict has long coloured the popular image of the private soldier in the Georgian era, prompting accusations of shameful ingratitude towards the men he led to victory from Assaye to Waterloo.[65] Other British soldiers had employed equally unflattering vocabulary to describe the private soldiers of the 1750s and 1760s: in the opinion of Guadeloupe's Governor Campbell Dalrymple, they included 'the scum of every county, the refuse of mankind'.[66] Like Wellington, James Wolfe ultimately owed his reputation to the fighting qualities of the humble redcoat: he also shared the Duke's capacity to subject that figure – or, indeed, anyone else – to withering criticism. Commenting on Braddock's defeat, Wolfe had no hesitation in blaming the disaster upon 'the cowardice and ill-behaviour of the men'. Wolfe pondered: 'did ever the Geneva and p[ox] of this country operate more shamefully and violently upon the dirty inhabitants of it under the denomination of soldiers?'[67] Elsewhere, Wolfe castigated Braddock's

63 GCM, Albany,16 May 1758, in WO/71/66.

64 Comment made at Sudbourn, 4 November 1831, in Philip Henry, 5th Earl Stanhope, *Notes of Conversations With the Duke of Wellington. 1831–1851* (4th edn., London, 1889), p. 14.

65 See, for example, Oman, *Wellington's Army*, p. 42. However, while observing that the British Army attracted its fair share of petty criminals and drunkards, to the extent that it was scarcely possible to 'conceive such a set brought together', Wellington none the less considered it 'wonderful that we should have made them the fine fellows they are' (Conversation at Deal Castle, 11 November 1831, in Stanhope, *Notes of Conversations With Wellington*, p. 18).

66 Campbell Dalrymple, *A Military Essay*...(London, 1761), p. 8.

67 Wolfe to his father, Southampton, 4 September 1755, in Willson, *Life and Letters of Wolfe*, p. 274.

unfortunate redcoats as 'Rascals' and 'canaille'.[68] Recruits raised for Wolfe's own regiment were 'terrible Dogs to look at', who would have to be trained to fight at night, 'that the Enemy may think 'em better than they realy are'.[69] In the following year Wolfe was even more scathing about the garrison of Portsmouth, whom he described as 'vagabonds that stroll around in dirty red clothes from one gin-shop to another ... dirty, drunken, insolent rascals'.[70]

In the eyes of another officer, Bennett Cuthbertson, the men who provided the Army with its recruits were bumbling rustics of child-like simplicity. Cuthbertson, who wrote an influential book on regimental administration, believed the private soldier to be incapable of completing even the most basic task without supervision, remarking that 'Soldiers are not to be depended on in anything, let it be ever so much for their advantage.' Such men also needed to be cured of the 'Stubborn disposition which characterizes the peasants of most countries' and broken of their 'awkward clownish ways'.[71] Cuthbertson's attitude to the rank and file emerges clearly in his discussion of recruitment, a tricky business requiring 'a certain degree of humour and address' – talents 'not to be expected in the generality of Soldiers'. When it came to enlisting recruits, officers should always make their own judgement of a man's age, as 'the common people are in general so ignorant in this point, that it is absurd to take a peasant's word, for being only twenty five'.[72] This image of the private soldier as stolid yokel is likewise apparent in a letter from James Murray, the Lieutenant-Colonel of the 15th Foot. Reporting his plans to embellish the regiment's headgear by adding a 'Hatband and Tassel a la Hanoverian', Murray had no fear of thereby transforming his men into dandies. Indeed, Murray wrote,

> I am of oppinion there is no danger of making an English soldier too much so, on the contrary I have ever found it almost impossible to conquer the Cloonesh [clownish] Disposition so remarkable in the lower sort of People in this Island.[73]

Such comments should not be taken out of context: they reflect the hierarchical nature of English society in the eighteenth century and reveal only

68 Wolfe to the Duke of Richmond, Winchester, 25 October 1755, in 'Some Unpublished Wolfe Letters, 1755–58', ed. R. Whitworth, *JSAHR*, LIII (1975), 65–86; 68.

69 Same to same, Cirencester, 19 January 1757, in ibid., p. 80.

70 Wolfe to Lord George Sackville, Portsmouth, 7 February 1758, in Willson, *Life and Letters of Wolfe*, p. 357.

71 Bennett Cuthbertson, *A System for the Compleat Interior Management and Oeconomy of a Battalion of Infantry* ... (Dublin, 1768; corrected edition, Bristol, 1776), pp. 111; 107; 163.

72 Ibid., pp. 55; 59.

73 Murray to Jeffery Amherst, Maidstone, 7 June 1757 (CKS, U1350/013/4).

one side of the officer's attitude to the rank and file. If officers sometimes viewed their men as 'children' it was because convention dictated that they should themselves adopt the role of 'parent'. Just as the country squire ideally demonstrated a fatherly concern towards his forelock-tugging labourers, so many army officers tempered their haughty scorn for the 'lower orders' with a paternalistic interest in the well-being of their men. Even the unbending Cuthbertson stressed the obligation of officers to act as 'a sort of guardians to the Men in their respective Companies'.[74] The officers of the 15th Foot adopted this role in 1757 when the battalion was based in Kent. With provisions expensive locally, great care had been taken to ensure that the soldiers' money was spent in the best possible way. In the very same letter in which he had derided his men as 'clowns', Lieutenant-Colonel Murray reported that the battalion's officers had 'display'd great humanity, going themselves to market with their men & every one striving who can do and think best for the relief of the poor Soldier'.[75] For all his intemperate outbursts against the redcoat, Wolfe remained capable of displaying a genuine concern for the man in the ranks. On arriving at Portsmouth following the siege of Louisbourg, Wolfe found that 72 invalids from the regiments involved in the campaign had been disembarked without any preparations for their reception. In consequence, Wolfe reported, 'these Poor Creatures are likely to Suffer every kind of distress, being put on Shoar, with out Billets or Quarters'. Wolfe had urged measures to ensure these veterans were given shelter.[76] Such attention apparently gained Wolfe the devotion of his men. Sergeant James Thompson of Fraser's Highlanders claimed that Wolfe acted as a 'father' to him, and remembered that it was the General's custom to address his men by the title of 'Brother Soldier'. Indeed, Wolfe was 'so kind and attentive to the Men, that they would have gone through fire and water to have served him'.[77] Thompson was recalling events of 70 years before, and it is tempting to dismiss such anecdotes as the sentimental reminiscences of an old man. Yet confirmation of Wolfe's paternalism, and the affection it inspired, is provided by a letter written within weeks of his death. According to Lieutenant Henry Browne of the 22nd Foot, the General's fall prompted universal grief amongst the troops: 'even the Soldiers dropt tears, who were but the minuet before driving their Bayonets through the French'. Browne compared the army to 'a family

74 Cuthbertson, *Interior Management*, p. 156.

75 CKS, U1350/013/4.

76 Wolfe to Barrington, Portsmouth, 4 November 1758, in WO/1/975, p. 275.

77 'Anecdote of Wolfe's Army – Wolfe, the Soldier's Friend – as related by a volunteer of Fraser's Highlanders', in GD 45/3/422, fols 481–3.

in tears & sorrow which had just lost their father, their friend & their whole Dependance'.[78]

Despite their frequent criticisms of the redcoat's faults, most officers agreed that with proper leadership the British soldier represented fine military material. For example, Humphrey Bland, the author of what was probably the most popular military manual of the mid-eighteenth century, praised the fighting spirit of the redcoats. Bland considered that the 'Common Soldiers' of the British Army were less susceptible to panic than those of any other European nation: 'For the English are naturally Active, Strong, Bold and Enterprising; always ready to go on to Action; but impatient when delay'd or kept back from it'.[79] Bland's verdict carries more than a whiff of the xenophobic disdain that eighteenth-century Englishmen habitually displayed towards their foreign neighbours; its basic truth was none the less acknowledged by many of those men who officered the 'American Army'. Just days before his death on the Plains of Abraham, when painful illness and frustrating setbacks might have been expected to sharpen his tongue, Wolfe proved unstinting in praise of his redcoats. He wrote: 'Our poor soldiery have worked without ceasing, and without murmuring; and as often as the enemy have attempted upon us, they have been repulsed by the valour of the men'.[80] Commanders often took pains to convey such sentiments to their troops. For example, in the wake of the misguided assault upon the French lines at Ticonderoga, James Abercromby issued general orders thanking the officers and men for their 'gallant behaviour'. The commanding officers of each corps were to take care that their men were informed of this.[81] Following the storming of Morne Tartenson on Martinique in 1762, Robert Monckton announced that he was 'highly sensible of the valour of the Troops he has the honour to command; the gallant behaviour which they have shewn this day will do honour to their Country, and ever distinguish them as Britons'.[82]

Irresponsible, drunken, oafish and occasionally heroic, when viewed solely through the eyes of his officers the redcoat in the ranks remains a two-dimensional figure. Yet it is possible to flesh out this image through the use of other sources. First, much information can be gleaned from

78 Browne to his father John Browne esquire, Louisbourg, 17 November 1759 (NAM MSS., 7808-93-2).
79 Humphrey Bland, *A Treatise of Military Discipline* . . . (5th edn., Dublin, 1743), p. 143.
80 Wolfe to the Earl of Holderness, on board the *Sutherland* at anchor off Cape Rouge, 9 September 1759, in Willson, *Life and Letters of Wolfe*, p. 474.
81 Orders, Lake George, 10 July 1758, in 'The Monypenny Orderly Book', *BFTM*, XII, 6 (October, 1970), 434–61; 442.
82 Orders, Martinique, 24 January 1762, in 'Hamilton Notebook' (NAM MSS, 6707–11), p. 261.

official documents. Inspection reports yield much basic data: besides supplying comments on the regiment's appearance, parade performance and general efficiency on a given day, they also provide details of officers' commissions and breakdowns of the nationality, age, size and service of the men. For example, when Amherst's 15th Foot was reviewed at Shroton Camp by Sir John Mordaunt on 13 October 1756, it was formed largely of Englishmen in their twenties, of between five feet six inches and five feet eight inches in height, who had been recruited over the previous two years. Mordaunt noted that the men were 'Young and Well Sized'; it was 'A Good Regiment', 'Well disciplined', 'Properly appointed' and therefore 'fit for Service'.[83]

Such documents reflect the state of units on home service. However, an overview of the Army in North America itself can be gained from an extensive series of regimental returns ordered by Loudoun during the summer of 1757.[84] Like the British inspection reports, these provide the 'vital statistics' of the formation concerned.[85] The broad outlines revealed are unmistakable: some 60 per cent of Loudoun's regulars were men in their twenties and teens, of five feet seven inches or under in height, who had been in the Army for two years or less. Yet this clear majority of recruits was at least partially balanced by a hard core of veterans who were mature in both age and experience: indeed, nearly one in five of Loudoun's redcoats had accumulated service dating back a decade or more to embrace the War of the Austrian Succession.

Amongst the most revealing data furnished by the 1757 returns is a detailed breakdown of the ethnic composition of each battalion. Once again, the overall patterns are clear: 'English' recruits – a term embracing Welshmen – contributed just 30 per cent of the manpower. Together, Scots and Irish represented more than half of the total: this statistic becomes more striking when it is appreciated that the combined populations of Scotland and Ireland in the 1750s fell far short of England's.[86] It comes as no surprise to observe that both the Black Watch and Archibald Montgomery's 1st Highland Battalion were composed exclusively of Scots, or that the 2nd Battalion of the 1st Foot, or 'Royal Scots', included a significant contingent of their countrymen. More puzzling at

83 No less than 82 per cent of the 15th Foot's personnel were 'English'. See WO/27(Inspection Returns)/4.

84 See Appendix: Tables 1–6.

85 Unlike returns surviving for units in Britain, they do not include the comments of inspecting officers regarding the unit's appearance and drill.

86 See Appendix, Table 5. Estimates for *c.* 1755 reckon the population of England and Wales as at least 6 millions; Scotland possessed about 1.25 millions, whilst Ireland held some 3 millions. See W. J. Hausman, 'The British Economy in Transition, 1742–1789', in *British Politics and Society from Walpole to Pitt, 1742–1789*, ed. J. Black (London, 1990) pp. 53–79; 59.

first glance is the clear majority of the same nationality in Perry's 55th Foot, a unit with no obvious Scottish affiliation. Yet this phenomenon can be explained by the fact that the regiment was in Scotland during the enforcement of the 1756 Press Act, and was allocated the pressed men of seven Lowland and Highland shires.[87] In addition, the town of Perth had offered 'a Guinea & a half' to every man enlisting in the 42nd or Perry's at that time – a gambit indicative of the sometimes blurred relationship between pressing and volunteering.[88] Such stratagems clearly worked: in America, the daughter of one of its officers observed that the 55th 'might be considered as a Scotch regiment'.[89] Again, whilst the high proportion of Irishmen in the 27th, or 'Inniskilling', Regiment reflects regional ties, the even larger percentage of that nation in Bragg's 28th Foot and other nominally 'English' battalions is at first surprising – until it is remembered that these units had sailed for America after long years on the 'Irish Establishment'.

The 1757 returns are especially valuable for the light they shed upon the levels of American-born recruits, and of foreigners enlisted on both sides of the Atlantic. Although these categories combined represent only 15 per cent of the whole, in certain units their contribution was undoubtedly significant. Whilst the Royal American Regiment never attracted the preponderance of German Protestants that its advocates had envisaged, in 1757 foreigners and Americans none the less formed between one-third and one-half of all four battalions. The Regiment's chief promoter, Colonel Jacques Prevost, had certainly received instructions to 'repair to Germany to raise as many men as he is able', although the exact number of recruits harvested in Europe remains unclear.[90] In 1758 Loudoun called for an official inquiry to examine the Regiment's ramshackle recruiting accounts; Prevost – by common consent the most unpopular officer in America – had claimed sums of money for men who had never even left Germany; 'others by Mistake have been by Different Names Charged twice, tho' the same Persons'.[91] For all Prevost's skulduggery, sufficient recruits were enlisted upon the European continent and in America to lend the corps an individual identity: its diverse composition is reflected in those veterans of the 60th who sought Chelsea pensions. 'Typical' redcoats like the Leeds clothier Jeremiah Cocker and Limerick labourer Lot Connor had served alongside more exotic comrades: Michael Frieshop, a

87 Barrington to Perry, 29 March 1756 (WO/4/51, p. 325).
88 Humphrey Bland to Loudoun, Edinburgh, 1 April 1756 (LO 999).
89 *Memoirs of an American Lady . . . By Mrs Anne Grant* (London, 1808; repr. New York, 1901), part I, 64. Grant's father was Duncan MacVicar, an officer in Montgomery's Highlanders and then the 55th.
90 See Prevost's recruiting schemes of February 1756, in LO 2576 and 2577.
91 Loudoun to Abercromby, London, 9 June 1758 (AB 340).

Norwegian wigmaker; Sergeant John Weilsenger, a cook from Anhalt Dessau; and John Horn, a Philadelphia cobbler.[92]

As has been seen, the tempo of recruitment for the regulars in North America fluctuated wildly, with the frenzied enlistments of 1755 and 1756 countered by a subsequent dearth of volunteers. Colonial recruits were therefore concentrated within those units that had arrived in America before 1757, or were actually raised within the colonies themselves: for example, William Shirley, the colonel of the 50th, maintained that more than 1,000 of the men enlisted for his own regiment and Pepperrell's 51st were recruited within the 'four Governments of New England'.[93] The 1757 returns reflect these trends. Outside the ranks of the 60th, 'Natives of America' cluster in the 40th and 47th – both part of the pre-war garrison of Nova Scotia – the indigenous New York Independent Companies, and the 48th Foot that had arrived with Braddock. The 48th seemingly acquired a distinctly 'American' character: in December 1762, as Albemarle prepared to sail to England from Havana, he recommended that units returning to the continent in the spring should include that regiment, 'as it is Compos'd of a great number of Americans enlisted for a Term of Years which Time is elaps'd and the Soldiers are become extremely anxious and impatient to return home'.[94] Battalions arriving in America after 1756 recruited relatively few locals: of 569 men of the 58th Foot at Quebec in December 1759, just 23 (4 per cent) had been recruited in America.[95] A belated and short-lived injection of colonial manpower came in June 1762, when Amherst's regular battalions were reinforced by provincial volunteers.[96] The 58th's share was some forty Massachusetts men enlisted to serve 'for one year in America only': these New Englanders had only been tempted into the regulars by hefty bounties comparable with those available to provincial recruits.[97]

92 See WO/116/5, fols 6; 27; 31; 43.

93 Petition of Shirley to King George II, 3 January 1757 (WO/1/4, fol. 192).

94 'Instructions for the Hon. William Keppel Major General . . .', in CO/117 (Havana)/1, fols 257–8. Of 374 discharged soldiers sent to North America from ten Havana battalions, no less than 137 (37 per cent) were from the 48th Foot (WO/34/55, fol. 316).

95 See 'Succession Book, 58th Foot, 1756–1803' (WO/25(General Registers)/435). This invaluable document provides background details for many hundreds of recruits. Muster rolls confirm the presence of 569 of these at Quebec on 24 December 1759. The present study draws upon this 'sample' for information about the Army's personnel. For a detailed examination of this source, see S. Brumwell, 'Rank and File: A Profile of One of Wolfe's Regiments', in *JSAHR*, LXXIX (spring 2001), 3–24.

96 Of the 4,000 'recruits for completing the Regular Corps' required by Amherst, only 788 were actually raised. See *The Journal of Jeffery Amherst. Recording the Military Career of General Amherst in America from 1758 to 1763*, ed. J. C. Webster (Toronto, 1931), pp. 277–80; 331.

97 That month the 'American Army' was offering bounties of £6 sterling, plus £5 New York currency, for short-term recruits. See Thomas Irwin to Amherst, Portsmouth (New Hampshire), 22 June 1762 (WO/34/90, fol. 233).

As the furore over the recruitment of indentured servants demonstrates, many men enlisted by the British Army in America were themselves recent immigrants rather than genuine natives. When Captain John Cosnan of the 45th Foot scoured Boston's hinterland for likely material in 1758, he reported that the men 'picked up here are generally Irish, such as have been the fishing season at Newfoundland'.[98] Irishmen formed the largest single group of those men enlisted by recruiting parties in New England during the winter of 1757–58.[99] Of the 58th Foot's handful of 'Americans', only five were actually born in the colonies. Such evidence suggests that the proportion of American recruits in the British Army should not be exaggerated: indeed, the most telling argument against inflating their number is the vociferous civilian opposition towards regular recruiting parties. Yet enough of King George's colonial subjects took his shilling to lend a distinctive character to several units and give added significance to the title '*American* Army'; and whilst Noah Flood of Gage's Light Infantry probably represents an extreme case, these Ezekials, Solomons and Ichabods also imparted an unmistakable New England flavour to muster-rolls dominated by the homelier Christian names of the Old Country.[100]

The racially mixed population of Britain's North American colonies offered other potential sources of manpower that the Army proved less ready to tap. Recruiting instructions issued by William Shirley during his brief stint as commander-in-chief warned not only against enlisting Frenchmen, Catholics and runaway servants, but also any 'Negro, Mulato, or Indian'.[101] Whilst the British Army already had a tradition of recruiting black men and boys as drummers and regimental musicians, it made no effort to enlist them as private soldiers. By contrast, there is ample evidence that both free and enslaved blacks shouldered arms in provincial regiments and ranging companies.[102] Like blacks, 'domesticated' Indians from the settled coastal colonies served in the provincials: amidst the mayhem following the fall of Fort William Henry, Montcalm's tribal allies had 'Hauled out the Indians & Negroes belonging to the Provincial Regiments'.[103] As will be seen, the British Army repeatedly

98 Cosnan to Colonel John Forbes, Boston, 18 January 1758 (GD 45/2/24/5).

99 Of 80 enlisted, there were 39 Irish (49 per cent), 28 Americans, six English and seven foreigners (Dutch, German, Spanish and Portuguese). See recruiting returns of the 'Royal', 28th, 40th, 45th and 47th, from 10 November 1757 to 5 March 1758, in LO 4657; 5581; 5690; 6853; 6883; 6894; 6919; 6923; 6924; 6933; 6935; and GD 45/2/24/3; 45/2/35/8–9.

100 Flood was sentenced to 1,500 lashes for desertion. See General Orders, New York, 26 May 1762, in CKS, U1350/016/2 (no page or folio refs).

101 'Recruiting Instructions', 1755 (LO 727).

102 S. A. Padeni, 'Forgotten Soldiers: The Role of Blacks in New York's Northern Campaigns of the Seven Years War', *BFTM*, XVI, 2 (1999), 152–69.

103 'Transactions at Fort William Henry', in LO 6660, p. 11.

sought to employ both 'domesticated' and 'wild' Indians as irregulars, yet its policy towards their integration within the regular battalions was less consistent. Despite Shirley's directions to the contrary, some Native Americans undoubtedly did wear the redcoat of King George. Reporting an outbreak of smallpox in the garrison at Portsmouth, England in 1757, General Hopson blamed the contagion on drafts from Shirley's and Pepperrell's given to the Royal Regiment; those infected included an 'Indian Squaw, [who] was Wife to an Indian, a Soldier, turned over among others into the Royals, & who, Since He came here, died of ye Small pox'.[104] During the following winter, as desperate recruiting officers trawled Massachusetts for manpower, Captain Cosnan of the 45th quizzed John Forbes whether 'it wou'd be agreeable to my Lord [Loudoun], that We shou'd enlist Indians, as Lt Phillips has been offerr'd some in this province'. Having gained the clarification he sought, the Captain replied: 'I Have now acquainted all the Officers they may now take Indians, that come within their instructions'.[105] Yet by 1762 attitudes had changed. That year an apprehensive Lieutenant John Elliott of the Royal Regiment was obliged to confess his 'very great error' in enlisting three Indians for the regulars: Elliott assured Jeffery Amherst that he would never again deviate from his orders.[106] It is tempting to speculate that the General's prejudices ended a practice which had contributed another distinctive strand to the already motley fabric of Britain's 'American Army'.

More about the redcoats who campaigned across the Americas can be learned through anaylsis of another valuable cache of official documents, the registers of those soldiers examined at Chelsea Royal Hospital to establish whether or not they qualified for a pension in consequence of wounds or long service. The Chelsea registers record much the same information included upon a soldier's discharge certificate: name, age, length of service, the nature of the 'complaint' upon which the application was grounded, place of birth, and in most cases, occupation before joining the Army. In the vast majority of cases, applications reflect the mundane rigours of military life: men are frequently described as 'old and infirm', 'worn out with hard service', and most commonly of all, simply 'worn out'. However, the pension rolls also reveal the consequences of combat: the great engagements of the British Army, such as Fontenoy in 1745 and Minden in 1759, are marked by waves of applications from maimed veterans of the regiments involved. The out-pension records naturally

104 Hopson to Barrington, Portsmouth, 27 March 1757, in WO/1/973, p. 536.

105 Cosnan to Forbes, Boston 26 January and 16 February 1758 (GD 45/2/24/6 and LO 5611).

106 Elliott to Amherst, Boston, 3 May 1762 (WO/34/90, fol. 160).

contain a high proportion of superannuated men who cannot be taken as representative of their comrades as a whole; however, by examining the applications of men 'selected' by the random process of having been wounded at approximately the same time it is possible to gain a more accurate cross-section of the men in the ranks at a given moment, from which some general conclusions can be drawn.

Three 'samples' will be examined here, concentrating upon men wounded at Braddock's defeat in 1755, Louisbourg in 1758, and at Guadeloupe in the following year.[107] Taking the Monongahela casualties as representative of those redcoats who marched into the wilderness, it emerges that they were typically well-seasoned and mature soldiers. Although Braddock brought both his regular regiments up to strength by recruiting in North America itself, no colonials were among those applying for a Chelsea pension in 1756. This fact lends weight to the contention that the men surveyed here were all Monongahela casualties, as it is known that when Braddock made his final march to Fort Duquesne he left his raw local recruits behind and pushed on with his 'old' troops.[108] In general, the men wounded at Louisbourg were younger than those employed under Braddock, reflecting the broad profile of the extensive 1757 returns; by contrast, the Guadeloupe group mirrored the Monongahela wounded in both age and service. If all three samples are combined, the following profile appears for the 'typical' man in the ranks: age 31.8 years; service, nine years; age upon enlistment, 22.8 years. What emerges consistently from these figures is the fact that private soldiers typically enlisted in their early twenties: this is confirmed by a larger sample of 130 men of the 58th Foot who were subsequently examined for Chelsea pensions. The service records of these men reveal an average enlistment age of 22.7 years.

Of the 83 sampled casualties from the Monongahela, Louisbourg and Guadeloupe, 'occupations' are recorded for all save six. Of these the largest single group consisted of unskilled manual workers who described themselves as either 'labourer' or 'husbandman'. The next largest category musters men involved in textile production. The synonymous trades of shoemaker and cordwainer, along with tailors, also represent significant clusters. Striking corroboration for this general pattern is provided by the 'Succession Book' of the 58th Foot, which lists occupations for all

107 See Appendix, Table 7.

108 Kopperman, *Braddock at the Monongahela*, pp. 177–8. Americans recruited for the 44th and 48th who were wounded in subsequent actions did apply for Chelsea pensions. For example, Thomas Janvier of the 48th, examined on 23 December 1760 after being wounded at Quebec, was a 36-year-old shoemaker from Pennsylvania. He had served for five years and four months (WO/120/4, p. 576).

save eleven of 569 men identified as serving in America on Christmas Eve 1759.[109]

The fact that so many soldiers possessed an 'occupation', or even 'trade', at the time of their enlistment invites speculation regarding the factors that prompted such men to forsake civilian life for the hard and despised calling of the soldier. In her pioneering study of the British soldier during the American Revolution, Sylvia Frey sought to match such data to displacement resulting from changes in agriculture and growing industrialisation.[110] In times of extreme hardship, such as the notoriously grim winter of 1756–57, broad economic causes probably underlay many enlistments; however, great care should be taken in attempting to relate the former occupations of soldiers to more specific trends. The evidence examined above strongly suggests that the composition of the mid-Georgian infantry mirrored that of the workforce in general. Hence the high proportion of labourers and husbandmen – Cuthbertson's 'peasants' – reveals the prevalence of casual workers in what remained a predominantly rural economy. Such men were guaranteed work during the summer's harvest, but often lacked employment at other times. Likewise, the high proportion of weavers in the ranks was a natural consequence of the traditional importance of textiles to the local economies of many British regions.[111] It is unlikely that such men owed their enlistments to the introduction of labour-saving machinery: recent research into the Georgian economy suggests that technological advances in textile production only began to have a significant impact in the opening years of the nineteenth century.[112] Instead, the presence of soldiers from such varied backgrounds in the battalions under Wolfe and Amherst probably indicates a more general precariousness of employment among labourers and artisans alike.[113]

As the number of jobless usually exceeded the vacancies in the ranks, it plainly required something more for a man to take the King's shilling. In the vast majority of cases it is only possible to guess at the reasoning behind enlistments: however, in an era when it was not unusual for craftsmen to toil for fourteen hours a day, the sheer drudgery of civilian life should not be dismissed as a motivating factor.[114] The hard lot of

109 Appendix, Table 8.

110 See Frey, *British Soldier in America*, pp. 6–16.

111 The 'Succession Book' of the 58th Foot includes former weavers from throughout Britain.

112 J. Rule, *The Vital Century. England's Developing Economy, 1714–1815* (London, 1992), pp. 103–4.

113 On the economic background to recruitment see Steppler, 'The Common Soldier in the Reign of George III', pp. 31–8.

114 See J. Rule, *The Labouring Classes in Early Industrial England, 1750–1850* (London, 1986), p. 132.

indentured servants in Pennsylvania and Maryland certainly left them susceptible to the blandishments of regular recruiting sergeants. Some of these labourers had more personal reasons for quitting their bondage: the 'many Recruits' drummed up by Braddock's battalions also included several 'that had been Kidnapped In England and Brought Over hear and Sold to the Planters'.[115] According to a Scottish soldier who had himself been abducted as a child and sold in the colonies, such servants frequently encountered 'barbarous Treatment' that left them ready to run at the first opportunity.[116]

The surviving accounts of those private soldiers who wrote memoirs of their service reveal that for some men at least, a craving for adventure and variety was undoubtedly significant. For example, 'Jonas' attributed his enlistment in John Huske's 23rd Foot to a 'rambling disposition'. A native of Oxford, 'Jonas' had attended school until the age of twelve, before being apprenticed to an 'agreeable business'; despite this secure and comfortable existence, he none the less enlisted at the age of fifteen, without consulting his parents.[117] In the case of another teenaged recruit, James Miller, boyish notions of adventure led him to the Army. Miller recalled: 'From the earliest recollection, the hearing of a drum beat, set the heart on fire! A soldier, in my Idea, must be the first of mortals, being the guardian of his country.' The young Miller subsequently went out of his way to attract the attention of soldiers, finally succeeding in 1756, when 'at a very tender age' he was enlisted for Amherst's 15th Foot by a civilian recruiting agent, or 'crimp'.[118] For Henry Grace, military service provided an escape from an unpleasant situation of his own making. At the age of ten Grace had gone to Winchester College in preparation for a career in the clergy. However, during the course of the next six years Grace travelled the well-trodden path into 'idleness' and 'bad company'. The consequence, Grace noted, was 'the Displeasure of my Tutor, and the Hatred of my Schoolfellows'. He therefore 'took a Resolution to enlist for a Soldier' in the first regiment that came to Winchester, which happened to be Peregrine Lascelles's 47th Foot.[119] The mere fact that these soldiers recorded their experiences for posterity suggests that they were untypical of the men in the ranks, and the same may hold true for their motivation. The youth of all three writers should also be considered: it is probable that

115 'Journal of Cholmley's Batman', in *Braddock's Defeat*, pp. 10; 12.

116 *French and Indian Cruelty; Exemplified in the Life and Various Vicissitudes of Fortune, of Peter Williamson, a Disbanded Soldier ... Written by Himself* (York, 1757), p. iii.

117 *A Soldier's Journal*, p. 2.

118 'Memoirs of an Invalid', pp. 8–9.

119 *The History of the Life and Sufferings of Henry Grace, of Basingstoke in the County of Southampton. Being a Narrative of the Hardships He Underwent During Several Years Captivity Among the Savages in North America ... Written by Himself* (Reading, 1764), pp. 3–4.

soldiers who enlisted from impulse, boredom or a sense of adventure were more likely to be footloose teenagers than more mature men with domestic commitments.

As regimental returns indicate, many units embarking on active service consisted overwhelmingly of inexperienced recruits. For example, when Anstruther's Regiment was reviewed in September 1756 the inspecting officer noted that the men's clothing had become badly worn owing to constant drilling, and because the 'new raised' troops had little experience of caring for their uniforms.[120] However, most units also mustered a number of old hands who had soldiered before. The 'Succession Book' of the 58th Foot shows that besides the drafts received from other units, a significant number of men recruited by the regiment already possessed a record of service in formations ranging from the Guards to the Scots Brigades in Dutch service.[121] Such evidence of *re*-enlistment is revealing: it suggests that for some men at least, the Army provided a secure and familiar alternative to the uncertainties of civilian life. The extent to which soldiers could become 'institutionalised' is indicated by the case of Isaac Jameson, who was charged with desertion from the 28th Foot in 1764. Jameson claimed that he had not been in his right senses since injuring his head after falling down a draw well at Trois Rivières three years previously: if he had been in full possession of his faculties, he would never have contemplated deserting from an army in which he had already served for thirteen years. Indeed, he had 'no other way of getting his bread, but by Serving as a Soldier'.[122] Duncan Cameron, who had fought at Dettingen and Fontenoy before being shot through the leg 'and cut and hack'd in a miserable Manner' at Culloden, might have been forgiven for turning his back upon the Army after being discharged in 1748. But as Cameron explained, necessity drove him to re-enlist: 'not having accustomed myself to hard Labour, I soon was obliged to enter into my old Employ of a Soldier for a Livelihood'.[123] In other cases disillusionment with life outside the Army prompted re-enlistment. Such was the experience of 'Jonas' upon returning to Oxford after his discharge from the 4th Foot in July 1763: he remained until the following January, 'when things not turning out to my expectations, I went to London, and again enlisted in my old regiment, being desirous of going back to the West Indies'.[124]

[120] Of 688 men present, 608 (88 per cent) had service of one year or less. See Review of the 60th (58th) Foot, Plymouth Dock, 30 September 1756 (WO/27/4).

[121] Of the 569-man sample of those at Quebec in December 1759, some 36 (6 per cent) had served in other units before entering the 58th.

[122] GCM, Montreal, 5 April 1764, in WO/71/74.

[123] *The Life, Adventures, And Surprising Deliverances of Duncan Cameron, Private Soldier in the Regiment of Foot, late Sir Peter Halket's* (3rd edn., Philadelphia, 1756), p. 9.

[124] *A Soldier's Journal*, pp. 167–8.

For all its dangers and hardships, army life clearly exerted a powerful hold over a substantial number of men.

Although drawn overwhelmingly from the 'labouring classes', the redcoat battalions mustered men of widely varied intellect and outlook. As instructions issued to recruiting officers concerned themselves with physical appearance rather than mental ability, the Army enlisted some men who conformed to Cuthbertson's patronising descriptions of doltish yokels; their presence is clear from the records of the Army's General Courts Martial. When Asey Johnson of Shirley's Regiment was tried for desertion at Oswego in August 1755, the court members heard that he was prone to irrational behaviour. They found Johnson guilty of desertion, but 'on Consideration of his being a poor, simple, ignorant fellow, as appears by his Tryal', acquitted him.[125] Similarly, James Dunworth of the 44th Foot, who earned 600 lashes for desertion, had his sentence remitted by General Abercromby 'in consideration of his Simplicity'. Major Eyre of the 44th told the court that Dunworth had been mocked by other men in the company who viewed him as 'a Poor simple Man and a fit Object of Ridicule'.[126] Again, when William Webber of the 17th Foot was charged with marauding on Cuba the court soon decided that it was unnecessary for him to proceed with his defence 'as he appeared to them to be an Idiot'. This opinion was readily confirmed by Webber's company commander and the court declined passing sentence.[127]

Journals and letters written by 'common soldiers' reveal that the infantry battalions also included men of considerable intelligence and perception: the relative rarity of these documents should not be taken as evidence for unusually low levels of literacy, but rather reflects the poor survival rate of such material. For example, in May 1758, Lieutenant John Knox heard that more than 40 letters for the officers *and* soldiers of the 43rd Foot had been received by the post office at Halifax, Nova Scotia.[128] Indeed, promotion to the rank of corporal or sergeant was conditional upon a candidate being able to 'read and write in a tolerable manner';[129] as a result, a minimum of between six and eight men within every company were required to be literate. Of the 569-man sample from the 58th Foot in 1759, no less than 97 – roughly one soldier in six – subsequently achieved the rank of sergeant or corporal in that regiment. Of course, aptitude with a quill was not the only quality required for such promotion: as indications of literacy levels in the ranks these figures should therefore be treated as conservative. A more accurate impression of literacy can be

125 GCM, Oswego, 22 August 1755, in WO/71/42.
126 GCM, Albany, 16–18 May 1758, in WO/71/66.
127 GCM, near 'Cajamar [Coximar]', Cuba, 28 June 1762, in WO/71/71.
128 *Knox's Journal*, I, 171.
129 Cuthbertson, *Interior Management*, p. 5.

gauged from surviving administrative documents, for example, the account book of Major James Clephane's company of Fraser's Highlanders, kept at Halifax in May 1758. Each of the 111 men serving in the Major's company was required to sign, or make his 'mark', in acknowledgment of the accuracy of the account. Of the 88 men for whom such evidence survives in the book, 35 (40 per cent) could write their own names.[130] Another sample drawn from later in the century reflects a comparable ratio: out of 47 infantry privates whose discharge documents were presented at Chelsea Hospital on 12 May 1787, eighteen (38 per cent) carried the recipient's signature, whilst the other 29 bore a 'mark'.[131] Such evidence suggests that more than one-third of the men in the ranks had at least some knowledge of reading and writing, a figure matching literacy levels among the 'labouring poor' in general.[132]

A more limited number of soldiers boasted considerable education. For example, the polished penmanship of Corporal Thomas Innes of the 17th Foot led to his appearance before a General Court Martial on a charge of attempting to provoke mutiny through a seditious letter. Innes, who denied writing the threatening note, told the court that 'like other lads he had Tryed when at School to write two or three different hands'.[133] William Vernon of the 3rd Foot, who published a volume of poetry in 1758, was clearly exceptional. Vernon's sonnets were pitched at a sophisticated audience, with subscribers including his colonel and many of the battalion's officers.[134] It is probable that Vernon's comrades would have preferred the more robust stanzas of Ned Botwood, a sergeant of grenadiers in Lascelles's 47th Foot, whose rollicking ballad 'Hot Stuff' was written for the Quebec expedition of 1759.[135] Other men had relied on literacy for their livelihood before joining the Army: John Johnson, the 58th Foot's chronicler of the Quebec campaign, described himself as a 'writing master', while Moses Pullen of the 48th, who was wounded at the Monongahela, had previously been a 'Scribbler'.[136] As the case of Henry Grace indicates, some 'common soldiers' came from more privileged backgrounds than were customary for the rank and file. It was not unknown for certain impulsive 'gentlemen' to shoulder a musket in the ranks. Frustrated in his hopes of securing a commission in the Guards, James

130 GD 125/34/6.
131 In WO/121/1 (no page or folio numbers).
132 These have been estimated at between 30 and 40 per cent. See J. Rule, *Albion's People: English Society, 1714–1815* (Harlow, 1992), p. 140.
133 GCM, Camp at Lake George, 20 June 1759, in WO/71/67.
134 *Poems on several Occasions, by William Vernon, A Private Soldier in the Buffs* (London, 1758), p. ix.
135 Botwood was killed during the botched attack at Montmorency on 31 July 1759. See L. S. Winstock, 'Hot Stuff', in *JSAHR*, XXXIII (1955), 2–4.
136 For Johnson see WO/23/435, fols 125–6; for Pullin, WO/116/5, fol. 4.

Boswell had toyed with 'multitudes of wild schemes' that included enlisting as a 'private man'. For Boswell, 'good sense prevailed', and all thoughts of soldiering were soon submerged in his usual round of casual wenching and stimulating conversation.[137] Others took the plunge. Grace's comrades in the 47th included Corporal John Price Gwinett, brother 'to a Gentleman of considerable estate & character in Glamorganshire' who 'went from His Friends & Listed' when aged about seventeen.[138] In 1757 Loudoun's Adjutant-General, Colonel John Forbes, was petitioned to retrieve Edward Burlton, a young man expected to inherit 'a very pretty fortune', who had been 'imprudent enough to inlist as Common Soldier' in Murray's 46th Foot. The lad's uncle had enlisted the support of none other than Sir John Ligonier in the hope that Edward could be 'excused the duty of the Common men' until he gained a commission.[139] The presence of such men serves as a further warning against the dangers of attempting to reduce the redcoat battalions to a uniform mass of humanity.

Personnel (ii): The officer 'corps'

For soldiers possessed of sufficient education, experience and inclination, there remained the chance of acquiring the King's commission with its associated status of officer and gentleman. Before examining the fortunes of those redcoats who were promoted from the ranks, it is necessary to say something about the character and outlook of the 'corps' such men aspired to enter. Owing to the ascendancy of the purchase system, the bulk of commissions were bought for agreed fees.[140] Although purchase occasionally permitted the rapid advancement of men with more money than merit, the prevalence of such cases should not be exaggerated. Indeed, about one-third of all commissions were awarded without purchase to deserving candidates: these provided promotion for officers of proven value, and offered a route into the officer corps for suitably qualified NCOs. Such former rankers added a minute knowledge of regimental administration to a body that was already characterised by a high degree of professionalism: after a careful study of the service records of officers from a selection of regiments, Dr John Houlding has concluded

137 Entry for 26 December 1762, in *Boswell's London Journal 1762–1763*, ed. F. A. Pottle (London, 1950), p. 107.

138 See letter recommending Gwinett to Loudoun, [February?] 1756 (LO 2582).

139 Dr P. Burlton to Forbes, London, 14 March 1757 (GD 45/2/32/2).

140 See A. Bruce, *The Purchase System in the British Army, 1660–1871* (London, 1980), pp. 22–40.

that the Army was 'led by an officer corps of the most considerable experience, made up of men who, by and large, entered the service for life and got on by steady, competent service'.[141]

This verdict is supported by an examination of the officer corps in the 'American Army'. When Arthur Morris arrived in America in 1757 as lieutenant-colonel of John Forbes's 17th Foot, he had served in the regiment for 'near thirty eight years' with 'close attendance' to his duty. For Morris, soldiering in the 17th was a family tradition: his father and brother had both died while captains in the regiment.[142] Such men frequently possessed considerable experience of active service. For example, Thomas Jocelyn, who obtained a captaincy in the Royal American Regiment in 1757, had purchased his ensigncy in The Buffs fifteen years earlier Jocelyn fought at Dettingen in 1743 and bought a lieutenancy in the regiment soon after. He served in the ensuing campaigns of the War of the Austrian Succession, and 'receiv'd a shot thro' the Body at Laufeld', after which the Duke of Cumberland had obtained him a company in the regiment. At the peace, Jocelyn was reduced with the additional wartime companies, remaining idle until 1755 when he was sent to America as a captain in Shirley's. Although on detachment when Oswego fell, Jocelyn was 'broken' along with his regiment. He subsequently gained a company in the Royal Americans, but despite being one of the 'eldest' captains in America, entered the 60th as the youngest in terms of seniority within the regiment. Given his poor prospects, Jocelyn hoped to be recommended to General Amherst for 'Redress and Promotion'.[143] The petition proved fruitless: Jocelyn held the same rank in July 1759 when he was killed defending a convoy from Indian attack.[144]

Another seasoned veteran was Paulus Aemelius Irving, who distinguished himself at the head of Amherst's 15th Foot during the Quebec campaign. Irving had obtained his ensigncy back in April 1741:[145] by the time he arrived in America in 1758 he had already seen action in Flanders and on the disastrous expedition to Carthagena. Such experience proved invaluable at Quebec, as Sergeant James Thompson of Fraser's Highlanders recalled. Skirmishing near Point Lévis had unsettled the troops: faced with a scene of confusion, the senior officer with the column, who lacked Irving's service experience, requested the Major to assume command. Cramming his trade-mark wig into his pocket and drawing his sword, Irving calmly restored order among the battalions.[146] The

141 Houlding, *Fit for Service*, p. 115.
142 Morris to Col. John Forbes, Albany, 13 December 1757, in GD 45/2/21/10.
143 Memorial of Jocelyn to Brig.-Gen. John Forbes (undated, but *c.* autumn 1758), in GD 45/2/33/4.
144 John Stanwix to Amherst, Camp at Fort Bedford, 14 August 1759, in CO/5/56, fol. 233.
145 For the dates of Irving's commissions as ensign, lieutenant and captain, see WO/27/4.
146 J. R. Harper, *The Fraser Highlanders* (Montreal, 1979), pp. 77–8.

Major's coolness under fire was in evidence once again on 28 April 1760, when the 15th Foot helped to cover the retreat of Murray's army after it was worsted at Sainte-Foy. Years later, James Miller of the battalion remembered how the Major ordered the men to turn about and fire volleys at the pursuing French. In the bustle, Irving risked losing his trusty wig; 'he however put it under his arm, with great Sang froid, and said "damn the old wig", a name by which he is known, to this day, by the old souldiers'. Indeed, the 'brave Veteran' Major Irving had endeared himself to officers and men alike.[147]

The wide-ranging American campaigns of the Seven Years War provided many other officers with the opportunity to accumulate experience of service under a variety of conditions. By the Caribbean operations of 1762, the 'American Army' fielded seasoned officers like Eyre Massy, who came to America in 1757 as Major to the 27th Foot. Massy first 'purchas'd a pair of Colours' in that regiment in the 'year Forty'.[148] In 1759, Massy had been wounded at the head of the 46th Foot while directing the musketry that ended French hopes of relieving Niagara. After the fall of Martinique, when Massy finally sought leave to settle his affairs in Ireland, he claimed to be the only field officer in America who had never been absent from his corps. Not for Massy the comforts of headquarters: indeed, he had spent his entire American service 'in the Woods' and 'would rather be in ye worst Frost in america with my Corps, than at New York without it'.[149] Again, Captain-Lieutenant Vernon Hawley of the 35th Foot boasted an impressive combat record when he appeared before a General Court Martial at Havana in July 1762. Hawley was charged with disobeying orders, insulting the adjutant, and showing disrespectful behaviour to his commanding officer, Major John Maunsell. Captain-Lieutenant Hawley disliked being 'humbugged' by adjutants and majors of brigade; he told the court how he had been

> for some time past on very hard duty, & was but just come off Fatigue at the time, that he was called upon again for Duty; and from Wearyness, and want of sleep, and Refreshment, was perhaps not Sufficiently Master of himself to act with all the propriety he might.

A court member, Captain Roger Spendlove of the 43rd, swore to Hawley's courage at Quebec on 13 September 1759, and 'at the passing the Ravines in Martinico the 24th January last in the Face of the Enemys Redoubts,

147 'Memoirs of an Invalid', pp. 38–9.
148 Memorial of Massy to Loudoun, November 1757 (LO 4480).
149 Lt-Col. Massy, 27th Foot, to Amherst, Fort Royal, Martinique, 16 February 1762, in WO/34/55, fol. 72.

and Batteries, on both which occasions the Prisoner acted with the Grenadier Company'. As Spendlove put it, 'he never desired a better Officer on smart Service'. Hawley's effectiveness in a fight had been demonstrated more recently when he helped to repulse the Havana garrison's 'grand sortie' of 29 June. Lieutenant-Colonel Thomas Trougheir of the 72nd Foot and Major Francis Ogilvie of the 9th both praised Hawley's spirited resistance – opinions confirmed by the large number of Spanish bodies found scattered about his position. The fiery Hawley, who had also campaigned in Nova Scotia, remained keen for action and apologised to the court for consuming time that could be 'so much more gloriously employed'.[150]

Like the men they led, British officers of the mid-eighteenth century reflected a wide ethnic mix: if anything, representatives of Britain's peripheries were even more conspicuous at officer level than amongst the rank and file. Indeed, Englishmen represented less than a quarter of those officers serving under Loudoun in 1757 – a smaller proportion than either the Scots or those drawn from Ireland's Protestant ascendancy. The clustering of American and foreign officers in those units that mustered relatively high concentrations of their humbler countrymen is logical enough, as is the total monopoly of Scots in the Highland battalions.[151] However, the unusually high numbers of Scots and Irish in America in 1757 remains sufficiently striking to warrant further comment.[152] Officers from Scots and Irish backgrounds were prominent in the British Army throughout the eighteenth century.[153] Both nations possessed strong traditions of military service abroad, ranging from the Scots Dutch brigades to the 'Wild Geese' employed by the Bourbons; for the Scots at least, this mercenary heritage, combined with economic pressures at home, may go far to explain the phenomenon.[154] More generally, it has been suggested that the poverty of the 'Celtic fringe' in relation to England provided its gentry with greater incentives to seek their fortunes overseas.[155]

Whilst the presence of numerous Anglo-Irish officers in the 'American Army' excited little contemporary comment, the influx of Scots prompted

150 GCM, 'camp near Fort Mauro [El Morro]', Cuba, 10–14 July 1762, in WO/71/71.

151 See Appendix, Table 6.

152 John Houlding's survey of 3,234 British officers on service across the globe in 1757 reveals a very different pattern from the 'American Army': English, 45.3 per cent; Irish, 27.3 per cent; Scots, 24.3 per cent; foreigners, 1.7 per cent; and Americans, 1.4 per cent. I am grateful to Dr Houlding for generously supplying me with these data.

153 See M. Odintz, 'The British Officer Corps, 1754–1783' (unpublished PhD dissertation, University of Michigan, 1988), p. 211.

154 J. Hayes, 'Scottish Officers in the British Army 1714–63', in *Scottish Historical Review*, XXXVII (1958), 23–33; 23; for the Irish dimension see T. Bartlett and K. Jeffery, 'An Irish military tradition?', in *A Military History of Ireland*, 1–25; esp. 10–13.

155 Colley, *Britons*, pp. 128–9.

a degree of grumbling: in 1758, Major-General Webb sought to sow discontent by suggesting that the Army in America was a 'Scotes Expedition' which left English and Irish officers disadvantaged in the promotion stakes.[156] Yet it would be misleading to place undue emphasis upon ethnic tensions. For example, Lieutenant John Knox noted how the saints' days of the English, Irish, Scots and Welsh were all respected by officers and men alike: garrison colours were hoisted in honour of the occasion; according to custom, the soldiers of the relevant country were advanced pay to celebrate, their comrades assuming their duties while they did so. Commenting upon the 'greatest mirth and good humour' that marked St Patrick's Day at Fort Cumberland, Nova Scotia in 1759, Knox felt moved to add 'that the army are such strangers to national reflections, that they are not even heard of among the private soldiers'. Knox, who was himself an Irishman, could only wish that such aspersions 'were as sensibly and politely avoided by all other ranks of people'.[157] As will be seen, Britain's officer corps included prickly individuals who were not above picking a fight by uttering the very 'reflections' that Knox abhorred; however, the relative rarity of such incidents suggests that the Army constituted a professional fraternity in which the prejudices of the outside world could not be tolerated; as a subsequent chapter will suggest, it thereby nurtured notions of 'Britishness' that would take far longer to root amongst civilians.

The mid-Georgian officer corps was also characterised by a degree of social diversity: younger sons of the nobility and landed gentry possessing both wealth and influence rubbed shoulders with men lacking either, but who none the less came from 'good' families – the professions, trade or clergy. Regardless of the wide differences in their means, these officers theoretically shared a common status that set them apart from the men they commanded: they all enjoyed the background, outlook and education of 'gentlemen'. Men who failed to match this standard were unlikely to prosper. For example, Lieutenant-Colonel Murray of the 15th Foot was determined to rid the regiment of 'that Hibernian clod' Ensign Frederick Bolton. As an exchange with another ensign had failed to transpire, Murray feared that Bolton would 'Continue to embarrass poor No 15'.[158] In the following year, Lieutenant-Colonel Morris of the 17th Foot was equally anxious to jettison another bad apple, Lieutenant John Gregory. Along with Ensign Henry Robinson, Gregory had become embroiled in 'a little Fray' with the Under-Sheriff of Albany who had

156 Loudoun to the Duke of Argyll, 14 February 1758 (LO 5599).
157 *Knox's Journal*, I, 141–2; 294–5. On similar celebrations during the Revolutionary War, and their significance for the Army's role as ethnic 'melting pot' see S. Conway, *The British Isles and the War of American Independence* (Oxford, 2000), p. 192.
158 Letter dated Salisbury, 20 March 1757 (CKS, U1350/013/2).

arrested the pair for debt. In order to save them from jail, and the regiment from disgrace, Morris had been obliged to endorse Robinson's bills. An exasperated Morris reported the affair to his colonel, John Forbes, observing that whilst Robinson remained young enough to 'reclaim', Gregory was beyond redemption: the Lieutenant's behaviour was so bad that he represented a 'discredit to the Corps'.[159] To the evident relief of Morris, Forbes approved of Gregory selling his lieutenancy to Ensign George Swetenham. Morris had settled the price at 250 guineas, 'which is a very low price for a Lieutenancy, but as much as he deserves, having no merit in any shape, which I freely told him'. Indeed, during his two years with the regiment Gregory had 'behaved in such a manner, as to be despis'd by the Corps'.[160]

Unlike Gregory, most officers were acutely aware of their character and reputation. In consequence of this heightened sensitivity, duelling was endemic. A careless word uttered over the claret could lead inexorably to a dawn 'meeting' with swords or pistols. The code of behaviour that governed an officer's actions left little choice in the matter: although an officer who fought a duel breached the *Articles of War*, the man who refused a challenge risked committing the far more heinous crime of cowardice.[161] This situation is illustrated by the case of Ensign Charles Shirreff of the 45th Regiment, who was tried for sending a challenge to Ensign William Wetherhead of the 47th Foot. The case arose from a trivial dispute over a garden which both officers shared at Fort Cumberland, Nova Scotia. Wetherhead had refused to 'meet' Shirreff unless the challenge was put in writing and specified the weapons to be employed. Shirreff duly obliged:

> Sir, As I am Certain in many things You have endeavoured to hurt my Character, and have done it this day, by setting forth among the Officers of this Garrison, that I behaved like a dirty Rascal, for which I must insist upon your making me a proper acknowledgement before the Officers of the Garrison, or if not, that you will meet me tomorrow morning, with your Sword, behind the Hutts, I am sir, your humble Servt, Charles Shirreff.

On receiving Shirreff's note, Wetherhead promptly delivered it to the fort's commanding officer, Lieutenant-Colonel Montague Wilmot of the 45th Foot. In his defence, Shirreff admitted writing the letter, but in

159 Letter from Albany, 13 March 1758 (GD 45/2/21/19).

160 Morris to Forbes, Albany, 3 April 1758 (GD 45/2/21/22).

161 For a discussion of this 'honour code', see A. N. Gilbert, 'Law and Honour Among Eighteenth-Century British Army Officers', in *The Historical Journal*, XIX (1976), 75–87; also Odintz, 'British Officer Corps', pp. 508–36.

view of Wetherhead's comments, considered he had no option. He told the court: 'I conceived I should be unworthy to bear His Majesty's Commission, if I did not endeavour to clear up my Reputation.' Although Shirreff was found guilty, and sentenced to be cashiered, it was clear that the court members endorsed his behaviour. They considered that Shirreff endured 'very gross & bad Treatment' from Wetherhead and had attempted everything in his power to obtain 'proper Concessions' before resorting to a challenge. Indeed, had he not acted as he did, the court believed that Shirreff 'might have fallen into a breach of the 23rd Article of the 15th Section of the *Articles of War*' – conduct unbecoming an officer and gentleman. The court had also heard Wilmot's testimony that Shirreff had invariably behaved 'as an Officer and Gentleman' who was always keen to volunteer for patrols. They unanimously recommended Shirreff for clemency: the appeal did not go unheeded, and Loudoun reinstated him. Wetherhead, who was charged the following day with having 'aspersed the character of Ensign Shirreff in a manner unbecoming an Officer and Gentleman', encountered a very different response and was discharged from the King's service.[162]

Even where a duel resulted in death, the officer who 'killed his man' in defence of his honour was unlikely to face conviction. An example is provided by the case of Lieutenant James Grandidier and Captain-Lieutenant Peter Van Ingen. Both officers served in the Royal American Regiment, but this 'long acquaintance' failed to prevent a duel in which the latter was fatally wounded. The confrontation arose from an incident over supper at Van Ingen's New York lodgings, which was witnessed by another officer of the regiment, Ensign Edward Barron. Van Ingen, who was drunk, 'damned all the Germans, saying they were a Parcell of Rascalls, and imposing Scoundrells'. Like many other officers in the 60th, Grandidier was himself a German and wondered whether Van Ingen had any gripe against *him*. Van Ingen intensified the tirade, calling Grandidier a 'Coward, and worthless Fellow', and eventually striking him in the face. Grandidier ignored this provocation, but told Barron:

> I Suppose you have a droll Notion of my Behaviour, but Captain Van Ingen is in Liquor, and I am sober, I'll endeavour tomorrow to convince you that I am a Gentleman, and will clear my character as such to my Brother Officers.

Next morning, when Grandidier confronted Van Ingen, and demanded satisfaction, Van Ingen replied that he had treated him as he deserved, and was ready to 'fight him with what weapons he chose'. Soon after break-

162 GCM, Fort Cumberland, 2–3 September 1757, in WO/71/66.

fast, Barron heard that Van Ingen had been dangerously wounded. In defence, Grandidier claimed that Van Ingen had behaved like a 'mad Man'. He hoped it would appear to the court that 'no one could have acted otherwise than I did, that I have comported myself like a Gentleman, a Man of honor, and like one not unworthy the Commission with which His Majesty has been pleased to distinguish me'. Grandidier was found not guilty.[163] Reporting this 'unfortunate affair' to the Secretary-at-War, Amherst emphasised that Grandidier was 'forced to what he did', and appeared so 'unblameable' that he had been honourably acquitted by the court.[164]

Officers who fraternised with the lower ranks were viewed as breaching a social code. For example, when Thomas Murray's 46th Foot was in Ireland under orders for embarkation to America, Captain Mathew West was placed under arrest by the regiment's commanding officer, Lieutenant-Colonel Samuel Bever, for participating in 'shamefull Bestialities with some infamous Women in company with, and in presence of many of the private Soldiers'. According to the Lord Lieutenant of Ireland, John Russell, Duke of Bedford, such behaviour was 'totally unbecoming an Officer and a Gentleman' and made it impossible for any officer to serve alongside West. In consequence a court of inquiry was held to investigate the matter: the findings were sent to the Duke of Cumberland, who decreed that West should be superseded.[165]

Despite such segregation between those 'gentlemen' who held the King's commission and the 'common soldiers' they commanded, some men who began their army careers in the ranks none the less succeeded in bridging a social chasm to don the sash and gorget of the officer. In particular, the onset of a new war with France led to the expansion of the Army and created a demand for officers with sufficient experience to train large numbers of raw recruits – a role for which callow youths, however well bred, were clearly unsuited. In January 1756, when ten new regiments were created, the ensigns appointed to Perry's 57th (55th) Foot at Stirling included Sergeants George Coventry and Hugh Rose.[166] Of the 32 ensigns appointed to the sprawling Royal American Regiment that March, three were former non-commissioned officers.[167] That summer, another 49 men who were serving either as senior NCOs in infantry battalions or as 'Private Gentlemen' in the Horse Guards were appointed as lieutenants,

163 GCM, Camp on Staten Island, 26 October 1761, in WO/71/71. Nowhere in these minutes is the actual duel described.

164 Amherst to Charles Townshend, New York, 27 November 1761, in WO/1/5, fol. 213.

165 Bedford to Barrington, Woburn Abbey, 13 December 1758, in WO/1/975, pp. 163–4.

166 Unlike these former NCOs, the other five ensigns appointed to the regiment were all described as 'Gent[lemen]'. See *London Gazette*, no. 9548 (20–24 January 1756).

167 Ibid., no. 9657 (20–23 March 1756).

mostly to the second battalions that had been ordered for fifteen regiments.[168] It was significant that these men had been 'appointed' rather than 'promoted': they had not purchased their commissions in the usual manner, or made the customary progression from the rank of ensign. This difference was spelled out in 1758, when the second battalions became separate, numbered regiments. Those lieutenants 'made from Serjeants at the forming of the 2nd Battalions' were to go into the new regiments which were likely to be disbanded at the peace. These men had already been 'acquainted that they were not to rise higher, but to be put on half Pay, upon Reduction'.[169] They had been elevated because of their knowledge of drill and regimental paperwork: the importance of such experience to units undergoing rapid expansion was emphasised when Sergeant Anthony Hixon of Duroure's 4th Foot – a man who had behaved remarkably well at the siege of Minorca in 1756 – was made a lieutenant in Walsh's 49th Foot at Jamaica. Barrington informed Colonel Walsh that the appointment had been made because of Hixon's usefulness in 'training the new Levies'.[170]

The distinction between those men who had purchased their commissions in the recognised fashion and those 'appointed' because of their value as drill-masters or administrators is clear from the case of Lieutenant Thomas Grant of the 23rd Foot. Grant had bought an ensigncy in the unlucky 51st Foot in October 1755, only to be taken prisoner with the regiment at Oswego in the following summer. After a stint on half-pay, Grant was appointed to a lieutenancy in the 23rd – the 'Royal Regiment of Welch Fuziliers' – in September 1757. Upon the division of the two battalions into distinct regiments, Grant elected to stay with the 23rd rather than transfer into the 68th – a choice that gained the approval of his lieutenant-colonel and the officers of both battalions. Despite this consensus, the colonel of the 23rd, General John Huske, ruled that Grant could not serve in his battalion, having been 'Made from a Serjeant' in one of the South Carolina Independent Companies. Grant stuck to his guns: not only was he out of the Army when he purchased, but he had also obtained his commission *before* the raising of the second battalion. In consequence, Grant argued, he could not be classed as one of the 'Lieutenants made from Serjeants' and hoped that Barrington would therefore obtain him his proper rank – that is, as a bona fide officer.[171]

168 Thomas Sherwin and Barrington to various commanding officers, 17 September to 1 October 1756 in WO/4/52, pp. 232–76.
169 Barrington to the commanding officers of fifteen regiments of foot, 5 May 1758, in WO/4/55, p. 491.
170 Letter of 18 June 1757, in WO/4/54, p. 142.
171 Undated memorial [1758] of Grant to Barrington, in WO/1/974, p. 217. In a note on the reverse, Barrington mentioned that Grant was willing to serve in the 68th, and he was to be posted accordingly.

Promotion from the ranks might be barred if a candidate possessed an 'inappropriate' background. For example, when a vacant ensigncy arose in the 1/60th, Major Walters recommended Sergeant-Major George Butrick, who had his 'money ready', and was in other respects a 'Deserving Man'. Amherst had no objection to filling the vacancy in Butrick's name – provided the battalion's commanding officer, Henry Bouquet, approved. However, Bouquet pointed out that Butrick had come to the Royal Americans from Lord Loudoun's Regiment, where he had served as a private or corporal, having been recommended because of his skill as a tailor, 'in which capacity he was received and employed in the Battalion'. Had Major Walters been aware of Butrick's history, Bouquet felt sure he would never have thought him suitable for an officer. Amherst agreed with these 'well-grounded' objections, and accepted Bouquet's suggestion that the vacant commission should instead go to Edward Hubbard, a volunteer with the battalion who had previously served as a lieutenant in the Virginia provincials.[172]

'Volunteers' were young 'gentlemen' who served as cadets in the hope that this practical experience of military life would help to secure than an ensign's commission when a vacancy arose. Some volunteers purchased their 'colours', but those who distinguished themselves in action could win commissions without paying a penny. Despite their youth, volunteers frequently took heavy risks in search of such recognition. The nephew of Captain John Wrightson of the Inniskilling Regiment was just sixteen when he accompanied his uncle to America in 1757: within months the lad was killed and scalped by Indians near Ticonderoga while out on scout with Major Robert Rogers and his rangers.[173] James Henderson, a volunteer in the 22nd Foot, earned an ensigncy through his presence at the dramatic high point of Wolfe's Quebec expedition. Henderson, who served the campaign with the 'Louisbourg Grenadiers', was alongside the young general when he sustained his third and final wound. In a letter to his uncle, Henderson claimed to have carried the stricken Wolfe to the rear, where he died in his arms. Henderson initially feared that his prospects of advancement had expired with the general,

> But it Pleased God to Rease me up Friends in All the Survifing Genl Officers, And in Particular in Gen. Monckton Who, upon his First Taking the Command, Inquired for the Volinter that Distinguished him Self so Much on the 13th Septr With Gen.

[172] Amherst to Bouquet, New York, 27 November 1760 and 2 March 1761; Bouquet to Amherst, Fort Pitt, 20 December 1760 (Add. MSS 21,634, fols 37; 42; 39).

[173] Undated memorial (*c.* 1762–63) of Wrightson to Governor William Rufane of the 76th Foot at Martinique (WO/1/19, fol. 224).

Figure 1 Edward Penny's *The Death of General Wolfe* (1763) shows the stricken general being tended by surgeon Thomas Wilkins of the 35th Foot. Wolfe is supported by Volunteer James Henderson, while Lieutenant Henry Browne indicates the rout of the French; both men belonged to the 22nd Foot and served the Quebec campaign with the 'Louisbourg Grenadiers'. Courtesy of the Ashmolean Museum, Oxford.

> Wolfe As he thought it A Duty Incombant on him in Honour to Gen. Wolfe's Memory to Provide for that Gentleman.

Within days Henderson received a commission in the 28th Foot.[174] John Peebles, who was appointed surgeon's mate to the Second Virginia Regiment of provincials in 1758, had to wait longer for his opportunity.[175] In the summer of 1763, while surgeon's mate in Montgomery's Highlanders, Peebles obtained permission to serve with the regiment as a volunteer.[176] The only volunteer with Bouquet's relief

174 'A Letter Describing the Death of General Wolfe', in *EHR*, XII (1897), 762–3. The letter is dated Quebec, 7 October 1759. Henderson is pictured in Edward Penny's 1763 painting of the General's death, having advised the artist on the accuracy of the scene. See Fig. 1.

175 Peebles's first commission as surgeon's mate describes him as 'Gentn'. See GD 21 (Cunningham of Thorntoun Muniments)/674.

176 Capt. James Dalyell to Maj. Lobel, New York, 14 June 1763 (GD 21/488).

expedition to Fort Pitt, Peebles was dangerously wounded during the fierce encounter at Bushy Run.[177] Peebles already enjoyed a high reputation for his services at Newfoundland during the previous year; despite the reduction of officers with the general peace, Amherst was confident that the King would approve of his decision to grant him an ensigncy in the 42nd Regiment with 'no fees to pay'.[178]

Volunteers were drawn from the same strata of society that provided the bulk of the officer corps and, in theory at least, already possessed the qualities of a gentleman. However, while happy enough to give ensigns' commissions to those sergeants considered to be 'Proper Persons', Amherst was wary about the general concept of promotion from the ranks, having too often seen the 'ill Consequences' of it. In the case of one sergeant recommended for a commission, Amherst was plainly unenthusiastic. He wrote: 'I made strict enquiry about him and I should be glad to make him a Quarter master, but I cannot approve of making him an Ensign.'[179] Although the role of quarter-master, like that of adjutant, was often undertaken by a serving subaltern, both positions were considered to be especially suitable for former NCOs.[180] Competent quarter-masters were essential to regimental efficiency, but the suspicion lingered that they were not quite 'real' officers. This emerges clearly from an exchange between Lieutenant-Colonel John Beckwith, the commanding officer of the 44th Foot in 1764, and the battalion's quarter-master, Thomas Tricket. Beckwith had called Tricket an 'impertinent fellow' during a row regarding a garden fence. Standing on his dignity, Tricket told Beckwith, 'I am a Gentleman, & have a Commission', to which Beckwith uttered the crushing retort, 'a Quarter Master is no Gentleman'.[181]

Even if a sergeant possessed a suitable 'character' for promotion, he still required the necessary funds to live in the style appropriate for an officer. For example, Sergeant-Major Charles Bevill of the 3/60th had been recommended to Amherst by no less a person than Lord Barrington. Although Barrington did not generally approve of commissions being given to sergeants, he had received such strong assurances that Bevill was a 'remarkable good man' that he hoped Amherst could provide for

177 Bouquet to Amherst, Fort Pitt, 11 August 1763, in Add. MSS 21,634, fols 358–9.

178 Amherst to Bouquet, New York, 25 August 1763, in WO/34/41, fol. 122.

179 Amherst to Brig.-Gen. Gage, New York, 20 March 1761, in WO/34/7, fol. 26.

180 Indeed, the spurned Sergeant-Major Butrick was commissioned as quarter-master to William Howe's 46th Foot on 15 March 1764 (*The Army List*, 1765).

181 See GCM, Montreal, 14 May 1764, in WO/71/74. Beckwith, a quarrelsome 'Yorkshire man', appears to have been a singularly unpleasant and unpopular officer: Captain Charles Lee of the 44th described him as a 'petty Caligula' and 'an abandon'd miscreant' (Lee to Miss Sidney Lee, Philadelphia, 1 March 1760, in *NYHSC: Lee Papers*, I, 28–9.

him.[182] Bevill was well known as a reliable and diligent soldier, who had demonstrated his courage in the face of the enemy at Fort William Henry and Louisbourg.[183] Even this combination of powerful connections and outstanding service proved insufficient to compensate for Bevill's lack of funds: as Amherst explained, it was impossible to give the valiant Sergeant-Major a regular commission as he was 'Circumstanced'.[184]

Although formidable, such social and financial barriers to promotion were not insurmountable, as is demonstrated by the career of Richard Humphrys of Bragg's 28th Foot. The first surviving muster rolls for the 28th Foot, dated at Quebec, 1 October 1760, show that Humphrys was a private soldier in Captain Arthur Browne's company. In the following muster, Humphrys appears as a corporal. The heavy casualties sustained through illness in the West Indies in 1762 gave Humphrys his next step on the promotion ladder: the muster of Major Ralph Corry's company for six months from October 1762 to April 1763 shows that he was now a sergeant, although listed as 'sick'.[185] Humphrys remained in this capacity for thirteen years, until the outbreak of warfare with the American colonies brought his promotion to ensign. The demands of a rapidly escalating conflict apparently provided Humphrys with his chance: within three years he had risen to lieutenant.[186] This rank represented the limit of Humphrys's progress in the 28th Foot. Subsequent promotion was more sluggish: when Humphrys finally obtained a captaincy in 1786, it was in the remote and unglamorous Bengal Engineers.[187]

A man like Humphrys probably owed his promotion to the pressing demand for officers versed in regimental routine. Others gained commissions in recognition of extraordinary feats of courage or leadership. According to orders issued at Quebec in March 1760, Sergeant John Fraser of the 48th Foot had been appointed as ensign in the regiment, 'having distinguished himself in the field'. Significantly, Fraser had been recommended by his colonel as 'qualified in every respect, to act up to the dignity of an Officer'.[188] Fraser was clearly a useful officer and rose swiftly within his own corps, gaining a lieutenancy in August 1762, and achieving the rank of captain in December 1770.[189] Another sergeant to win a

182 Barrington to Amherst, Cavendish Square, 15 December 1758 (CKS, U1350/036/52).

183 Maj. Prevost to Amherst, Halifax, Nova Scotia, 6 May 1759 (CKS, U1350/036/52A – in French).

184 Bevill declined a commission in the rangers. After Amherst gave him 'as much Money as he wanted', he instead opted to seek his fortune on Guadeloupe. See Amherst to Barrington, Camp at Fort Edward, 19 June 1759 (CKS, U1350/038/8).

185 WO/12/4416 (Muster Rolls 28th Foot, 1759–76), fols 7; 15; 63.

186 Commissions dated 29 October 1776 and 13 January 1779. See *Army List*, 1778; 1779.

187 *The East India Kalendar or Asiatic Register . . . 1794* (London, 1794), p. 48.

188 *Knox's Journal*, II, 357. Fraser was commissioned as ensign in the 48th Foot on 10 March 1760 (*Army List*, 1762).

189 See ibid., 1764 and 1771.

commission in recognition of his bravery was Alexander Fraser of the 'Royal' Regiment. Following the fall of Havana, Sergeant Fraser was appointed quartermaster to a newly raised troop of light dragoons as a reward for being the first of the storming party to penetrate the El Morro fortress.[190] Outnumbered by the defenders, some members of the forlorn hope had initially fallen back, but Sergeant Fraser and a handful of men 'withstood the attack of a multitude of Spaniards, and by their gallant behaviour kept possession of the breach till the rest returned to the charge'. Yet the same fighting spirit that carried Fraser through the maelstrom of a hotly contested breach soon proved his downfall. Fraser's wife was conducting an affair with Corporal James Dunn of the 48th Foot; the quartermaster had therefore requested that either he, or his rival, should be transferred, 'as he could not bear to see or do duty with a man who used him so basely'. The plea was ignored, with consequences fatal to both men when they chanced to meet soon after: overcome by 'rage and jealousy', Fraser drew his sword and stabbed Dunn. The corporal died of his injuries and the gallant Fraser was hanged for the murder.[191]

As the tragic case of Sergeant Fraser indicates, far from resembling faceless automatons the soldiers of the 'American Army' were individuals possessed of all-too-human emotions. Evidence presented in this chapter likewise suggests that the enduring 'popular' perception of the redcoats requires modification in other important respects. Rather than relying upon the 'dregs' of society to fill its ranks, the Army mustered recruits drawn from a wide cross-section of the 'lower orders', ranging from labourers to skilled craftsmen. The reasoning behind enlistments likewise varied, although economic hardship undoubtedly motivated many. Britain's infantry battalions were far from homogeneous in other ways: genuine volunteers soldiered alongside those 'conscripted' under the Press Acts, while a medley of regional accents reflected the enlistment of recruits from all corners of the British Isles. Across the Atlantic, this ethnic mix was spiced by a smattering of Germans, Dutch and Swiss, along with a significant minority of men born in the colonies themselves. Although non-British recruits were largely concentrated in certain units, their presence none the less contributed to the distinctive corporate identity of the 'American Army'.

190 This unit, 'Captain Nutterville's Light Troop', was the only force of regular cavalry raised by the British Army during the American campaigns of the Seven Years War, although two troops of mounted 'rangers' in crown pay operated on the Georgia frontier.

191 See *Scots Magazine, 1763* (Appendix), pp. 723–4. Also GCM, Havana, 25 April 1763 (WO/71/73).

Once again, the 'popular' modern view of the British officer is at odds with the contemporary evidence addressed here. Like the rank and file, the officer corps was more socially diverse than the deep-rooted stereotypes suggest: although 'gentry' backgrounds predominated, the corps provided scope for the advancement of able candidates of humbler origins. Although it is always possible to find exceptions to the rule, most of these men were far removed from the blundering incompetents of cliché. Indeed, many officers were already highly experienced when they arrived in America, and subsequently added to their professional knowledge by long years of practical soldiering under demanding local conditions. For all their ingrained prejudices, such officers recognised the potential of the men under their care and sought to provide them with the leadership they deserved: had any other attitudes prevailed, the British Army could never have learned to fight and win the war in the Americas.

3

Following the drum

Of all those ingredients that constitute the enduring image of the British Army in North America, none is more potent than the savage discipline under which the redcoats soldiered. Historians concerned with highlighting the cultural dichotomy between Old World regulars and New World provincials have devoted particular attention to a code that placed a heavy reliance upon corporal and capital punishment. The undoubted severity of the Army's discipline has generated much pungent prose: the redcoats were 'literally whipped into shape' under a regime that advocated the 'torture' of the 'lower class' rank and file by 'upper class' officers content to command through fear rather than respect.[1] Provincial troops who witnessed the inhuman treatment meted out to their fellow 'Englishmen' grew conscious that 'a coercive disciplinary system was the engine that drove the British army, and that the blood of common soldiers was its lubricant'. Repeated exposure to such brutal spectacles led colonial soldiers to a disturbing but understandable conclusion – that the mother country's interpretation of individual liberty differed markedly from their own.[2] It is assumed that the redcoats were cowed by the Army's discipline: unlike the provincials, who viewed their voluntary military service in terms of a 'contract' liable to become null and void if breached by the imposition of unacceptable duties, 'the repressive disciplinary system of the regular army' left its humble rankers powerless to protest at their own grim lot.[3]

Modern assessments of the British Army's discipline during the Seven Years War are founded upon indisputable facts, and there will be no attempt to dispute them here. However, it would be misleading to suggest that coercion alone proved capable of governing the redcoats' conduct. Such men belonged to a distinct community with its own self-imposed codes of behaviour; for all its notorious harshness, official discipline was but one of the factors responsible for regulating the regulars. Indeed, as evidence presented in this chapter will demonstrate, far from being intimidated into slavish obedience by the fearsome sanctions ranged

1 Jennings, *Empire of Fortune*, pp. 208–10; 422.
2 Anderson, *Crucible of War*, p. 286–8.
3 Leach, *Roots of Conflict*, p. 123.

against them, British soldiers remained remarkably ready to defy the Army's discipline in defence of their hallowed 'rights'. No less than the New England provincials with their 'contracts' and 'covenants', the redcoats retained a keen awareness of the terms and conditions under which they had enlisted to serve King George. Both individuals and groups proved willing to voice their grievances through written petitions and 'direct action': the officer who failed to consider the legitimate complaints of his men did so at the risk of propagating disaffection and mutiny.

Discipline

By the era of the Seven Years War the redcoated British soldier had acquired the nickname of 'Lobster'.[4] This epithet was scarcely flattering, although it remained preferable to another that had also gained currency: 'bloody back' was a soubriquet that passed scornful judgement upon the Army's ready recourse to the cat-o'-nine-tails. That both nicknames were deemed derogatory is indicated by their employment in Boston during the confrontation that triggered the 'massacre' of 5 March 1770; on that occasion townsfolk goaded redcoats with the jeering challenge 'Come on you rascals, you bloody backs, you lobster scoundrels, fire if you dare ...'[5]

Such jibes reflected the reality of army life. As has been conceded, the redcoats of the 'American Army' soldiered under a strict discipline; scholars who have studied military justice in the Georgian era fail to agree on whether it became less so over the course of the eighteenth century, thereby reflecting an awareness of the humanitarian values emanating from the Enlightenment.[6] It is certainly true that traditional military punishments such as 'running the gauntlet' – where an offender was beaten by his comrades – fell into abeyance as the century progressed, but the same period witnessed the consolidation of equally brutal methods. Scholarly analysis of declining 'annual lash averages' should not detract from the underlying fact that the discipline of the British Army was harsh,

4 The title was apparently coined in April 1740 following an article in *The Craftsman* recording a hypothetical conversation between 'Thomas Lobster, soldier, and John Tar, mariner'. See Fortescue, *History of the British Army*, II, 582–3.

5 'A Narrative of the Late Transactions at Boston', in Lt-Col. William Dalrymple to the Earl of Hillsborough, Boston, 13 March 1770, in *Documents of the American Revolution 1770–83, Colonial Office Series*, ed. K. G. Davies (21 vols, Shannon, Ireland, 1972–81), II, 65.

6 S. Frey, 'Courts and Cats: British Military Justice in the Eighteenth Century', in *Military Affairs*, XLIII, 7 (February 1979), 5–11. For a contrary view to Frey's 'softening-of-justice' thesis see A. N. Gilbert, 'The Changing Face of British Military Justice, 1757–1783', in *Military Affairs*, XLIX, 2 (April 1985), 80–84.

and remained so until the abolition of flogging in 1881. The concept of leniency is likewise difficult to reconcile with the verdicts of the Army's General Courts Martial: the gallows, firing-squad, and above all the lash were all employed with depressing regularity in a spectacularly unsuccessful effort to discourage infringements of the *Articles of War*.

In an age accustomed to casual brutality the Army's discipline remained capable of shocking those civilians who witnessed its implementation. George Durant, the paymaster on Hopson's West Indian expedition, was outraged by the sight of two marines being flogged 'with that dreadful Instrument of cruelty a Cat o' Nine Tales'.[7] As already noted, the severity of punishment in the regular regiments in America likewise horrified provincial troops accustomed to a milder regime.[8] For the redcoats themselves, floggings were a fact of army life and accepted as such. Whilst hardened to the spectacle of corporal punishment, the man in the ranks might none the less register concern when such blood-letting appeared excessive. Duncan Cameron of the 44th Foot recalled that when Braddock's battalions recuperated at Wills Creek after their defeat at the Monongahela, 'there was Court-Marshall, upon Court-Marshall, and the most cruel Whippings succeeded them as ever I beheld ... some were whipp'd for good Reason, some for little, but, in general, they were too severe'.[9] Lashings were administered by the drummers; although they were classed as non-commissioned officers and paid four pence more a day than the private soldiers, such unpleasant duties ensured that drummers remained at the base of the regimental hierarchy.[10] Most officers considered this savage system to be justified. Bennett Cuthbertson reflected a widely held view when he observed that 'Subordination, and strict Discipline, cannot (from the general depravity of the Soldiery) be properly supported, without having recourse to the severest punishments.'[11] Even a humane man like the surgeon Robert Hamilton, who was plainly sickened by the frequent punishments he was obliged to attend, could agree that such strictness was 'absolutely necessary, for the proper behaviour, and subordination of the privates'.[12]

7 See 'George Durant's Journal of the Expedition to Martinique and Guadeloupe, October 1758 – May 1759', ed. A. J. Guy, in *Army Records Society: Military Miscellany I* (Stroud, 1997), pp. 1–68; 26 (entry for 23 December 1758).

8 See Anderson, *A People's Army*, pp. 138–40. When operating alongside the redcoats, the provincials were themselves subject to regular discipline.

9 *Life of Cameron*, p. 14.

10 Hence it was regarded as a privilege for drummers to be permitted to shoulder a musket in the ranks. For example, the 'Succession Book' of the 58th Foot records that on 12 July 1760, Thomas Chilton, '4 yrs a Drumr in this Regt', was 'now allow'd by Coll Howe to carry arms' (WO/25/435, fols 110–12).

11 Cuthbertson, *Interior Management*, p. 119.

12 Robert Hamilton, *The Duties of a Regimental Surgeon Considered* ... (2 vols, London, 1787), II, 25.

Although floggings were common enough, the lash was not the only method used to enforce discipline. Most miscreants were disciplined less harshly and more informally by verbal reprimands, 'manual correction' or 'minor punishments'; it was only serious crimes and persistent offenders that warranted the closer scrutiny of Regimental or General Courts Martial.[13] However, even this lower tier of discipline could involve considerable violence. According to 'Jonas', summary beatings were a common punishment for trifling mistakes on the parade-ground: 'When in the field, if you do not comprehend the officers instructions, presently tis bougre, rascal, villain, scoundrel, with a volley of oaths .... Neither are the officers back-ward of making use of canes and sticks, with very little provocation'.[14] Some relatively minor offences were punished less brutally. For example, when John Byrns of the 44th Foot plunged into the Hudson River at Albany to retrieve a cask of cordial spirits, he was put in the 'Bread & Water house for dirtying his coat'.[15] More serious transgressions earned solitary confinement in the 'Black Hole', 'generally a small, damp, dark, confined place', where inmates had nothing but straw to lie on.[16] Considerable use was made of non-corporal punishment designed to shame offenders: for example, John Knox records the case of a grenadier of the 43rd Foot who went missing when his party was ambushed near Annapolis Royal in Nova Scotia in December 1757. Upon his return, the man was court-martialled and found guilty of cowardice. In a punishment which Knox considered to demonstrate 'great discernment in the members of that court', the prisoner was dubbed a notorious coward and sentenced to ride the wooden horse for half an hour every day for six days, 'with a petticoat on him, a broom in his hand'. In addition, a paper was pinned on his back bearing the words 'Such is the reward of my merit'. This humiliating display provoked the 'inexpressible mirth of the whole garrison, and of the women in particular'.[17] A regimental order issued during the siege of Quebec on 22 August 1759 reveals use of a similar technique upon two

13 G. A. Steppler, 'British Military Law, Discipline, and the Conduct of Regimental Courts Martial in the Later Eighteenth Century', in *EHR*, CII (1987), 859–86; 863.

14 *A Soldier's Journal*, pp. 177–8. The prevalence of 'manual correction' is underlined by the following advice to subalterns from an old officer: '*Never beat your Soldiers*, it is unmanly. To see, as I have too often done, a brave, honest old soldier, battered and banged at the caprice and whim of an arrogant officer, is really shocking to humanity' (*Gentleman's Magazine*, 1760 (July), p. 304).

15 GCM, Albany, 2 November 1757, in WO/71/66.

16 Hamilton, *Regimental Surgeon*, II, 70.

17 *Knox's Journal*, I, 128–9. The 'wooden horse' was a traditional secondary punishment, consisting of an acute-angled structure which a soldier was obliged to straddle. The experience could prove painful – particularly if muskets or other weights were tied to the offender's ankles. In this instance, the punishment achieved its purpose: the same man subsequently 'approved himself a remarkable gallant soldier' (ibid.).

soldiers who had panicked while on outpost duty the previous night. Their colonel decreed 'that they shall stand an hour at ye necessary house [latrine], each with a woman's cap upon his head this evening, as a small punishment for the dishonour they have brought upon the corps and their brother soldiers'. In future, the pair were to march in the front of all parties with unloaded muskets.[18]

Before a man was brought to a Garrison or Regimental Court Martial it was customary for a 'court of inquiry' to examine whether there was any charge to answer. Most sentences meted out at this level were milder than those encountered at General Courts Martial. For example, a Garrison Court Martial at Montreal on 10 February 1761 gave 100 lashes to John Blake for 'selling spirituous licquor to soldiers contrary to order, particularly to a young boy a drummer'.[19] Daniel Bateman, of Captain Ogilvie's Independent Company, who had been confined in the main guard for brawling in the streets and selling his 'necessaries', was sentenced to 200 lashes by a Garrison Court Martial at Albany.[20] However, Regimental Courts Martial were sometimes accused of exceeding their powers by trying cases that should technically have gone before a General Court: upon occasion they could also award severe punishments.[21] At Quebec on 5 October 1759, Thomas Ledbetter of the 35th Foot appealed against the finding of a regimental court that had sentenced him to 600 lashes.[22]

General Courts Martial, which had the power to impose severe floggings or capital sentences, represented the last resort of military discipline. Despite this, such tribunals were held regularly throughout the American campaigns of the Seven Years War, dealing with many hundreds of cases. A wide range of offences was tried: cowardice in the face of the enemy, mutiny, theft, striking a superior, ungentleman-like conduct, murder and rape. But one crime above all others dominated proceedings: desertion was the scourge of all eighteenth-century armies, but it posed a particularly serious threat to the British forces in America, where recruits were so hard to find. Because desertion often peaked in the weeks before a fresh campaign, expeditions assembled in areas where the opportunities to abscond could be limited: just as regiments bound for the coast of

18 *General Orders in Wolfe's Army during the Expedition up the River St Lawrence, 1759: Literary & Historical Society of Quebec, Historical Documents* (Fourth Series, Quebec, 1875), p. 43.

19 'Brigade Order Books', in *Hervey's Journals*, p. 141.

20 Orders, Albany, 31 July 1761 (CKS, U1350/016/2). Just two weeks previously a General Court Martial at Albany had awarded Bateman 1,500 lashes for desertion (WO/71/68).

21 A. N. Gilbert has argued that soldiers brought before regimental courts enjoyed less legal protection than would have been the case with a General Court Martial. See 'The Regimental Courts Martial in the Eighteenth Century British Army', in *Albion*, VIII (1976), 50–66.

22 See 'Orderly books at Quebec', in *Northcliffe Collection*, p. 177.

France customarily encamped on the Isle of Wight, so the 'American Army' employed Staten Island in New York harbour as the jumping-off point for its operations in the Caribbean. The high command experimented with a variety of approaches in an effort to stem the steady drain on manpower. Mass executions and floggings were alternated with amnesties or 'Acts of Grace' which provided deserters with an opportunity to return unpunished. In January 1759, Amherst issued a general pardon to all deserters who had subsequently re-enlisted in other units serving in America: these men could remain where they were, whilst any other deserters who rejoined their colours by the beginning of March would likewise avoid retribution. In early May, as he readied his expedition against Ticonderoga, Amherst took a different tack: the General now warned that he was 'determin'd not to show mercy to any one Man, that can be such a Scoundrell to desert His King & country, during the Campaigne'.[23] Neither severity nor lenity solved the desertion dilemma. In fact, there was no easy answer to a phenomenon that could be triggered by a bewildering variety of factors. For some soldiers, desertion was a spontaneous reaction to ill-treatment: Peter Cloyne of the 51st Foot decamped in disgust the day after an incident during a march in hot weather. When Cloyne stepped aside to take a drink of water, an officer beat him over the head with a gun, 'so that the Blood run down in several places'. In other cases, grievances of longer standing were to blame: Frederick Muller and Roger Camps of the 4th Battalion of the Royal Americans deserted because part of their rations was given to them in turnips. In addition, neither Muller nor Camps ever received any pay for the fifteen weeks spent at sea while on passage from Europe to America, although both had been obliged to pay twice in one year for their camp equipment. Less predictable influences were also at work: when Thomas Knee of the 48th Foot deserted in June 1761 he explained that 'his Passion for a Girl in Canada induced him to take the step he did'.[24]

Most frequently, however, it was the momentary irresponsibility engendered by alcohol that underlay desertions.[25] Joseph Chase, Ezekiel Howard and Parker Smith of Shirley's 50th Foot went absent from camp after a drinking session in Schenectady. In a joint petition to the court the three explained that 'happening to drink more than common, and not being accustomed to hard drinking [they] were unluckily tempted by the

23 'Monypenny Orderly Book', *BFTM* (June 1971), pp. 163; 183.

24 See GCMs, Philadelphia, 21 January 1757 (WO/71/44); Fort Edward, 26 February 1759 (WO/71/67); Staten Island, 24 October 1761 (WO/71/71).

25 The importance of drink as a trigger factor for desertions is emphasised in A. N. Gilbert, 'Why Men Deserted from the Eighteenth-Century British Army', in *Armed Forces and Society*, VI, 4 (summer, 1980), 553–67; 560–61.

Devil, & strength of Licquor, to absent ourselves from Camp'.[26] If this trio really were such strangers to topeing they were untypical of their comrades. Indeed, it has been suggested that alcohol abuse reached 'epidemic' proportions in the British Army of the eighteenth century, raising the possibility that 'most soldiers were habitual drunkards'.[27] Heavy drinking certainly lay at the root of most army crime; indeed, it is unusual to find a court case in which alcohol does not play some part. In more ways than one, strong drink proved to be a great leveller: the private soldier who strayed while 'out of his senses' with New England rum was scarcely different from the subaltern whose sudden inclination for duelling was fuelled by brandy and Madeira. Such equality was in evidence following the fall of Havana, when hard drinking under a tropical sun contributed to the Army's rocketing mortality rates. As James Miller of the 15th Foot recalled,

> It was very usual, to meet Officers, and soldiers, drunk every hour of the day! The inhabitants were astonished at our excesses, and consider'd Englishmen, as beings weary of life ... certain it is, that many fell martyrs by sacrificing to Bacchus! [28]

The inevitability of widespread drunkenness was acknowledged in regimental orders issued by the 44th Foot in April 1755. These observed that drunken soldiers who were reprimanded by officers or sergeants frequently used 'Insolent Expressions' which were 'fare from their sober thoughts And Wholy Occationed by the Effects of Liquor': as such language could incur heavy punishment, drunks were therefore to be confined immediately and only dealt with when sober.[29] If followed to the letter, these humane and realistic orders must have saved many a man of the 44th from the lash or worse. Such enlightened attitudes were clearly exceptional: in consequence, many soldiers came before a General Court Martial for offences committed while drunk. For example, Thomas Franklin of the 43rd Foot received 1,000 lashes after a fracas at Havana with Ensign James Robertson of his regiment. Robertson had been enjoying a musical performance in the company of some Spanish ladies when the charming scene was interrupted by the appearance of the inebriated Franklin gawping in at the window. When Robertson told Franklin to clear off, the veteran muttered an insolent response. Venturing outside, Robertson struck Franklin several times with the flat of his scabbarded

26 All three were found guilty of desertion and sentenced to 1,000 lashes each (GCM, Oswego, 22 August 1755, in WO/71/42).

27 P. E. Kopperman, '"The Cheapest Pay": Alcohol Abuse in the Eighteenth-Century British Army', *Journal of Military History*, LX, 3 (July 1996), 445–70; 445; 449.

28 'Memoirs of an Invalid', pp. 72–3.

29 'Halkett's Orderly Book', in *Braddock's Defeat*, p. 75.

'hanger'; during the ensuing scuffle the ensign was thrown to the ground. Franklin was eventually arrested when Lieutenant Horatio Barbet of the 15th Foot arrived on the scene. In a defence that could have issued from the mouth of many a soldier, Franklin told the court that he was 'so much in Liquor, that he does not recollect any thing that passed that Evening'.[30]

As Cuthbertson noted, punishments were 'as much intended for examples, to deter others from transgressing, as to reclaim the persons on whom they are inflicted'.[31] In consequence, punishment was meted out in public before as many witnesses as possible. For example, when a court martial at Fort Edward sentenced Thomas Smith of Captain Cruikshanks's Independent Company to receive 1,000 lashes, it was specified that he was to receive 110 lashes at the head of each of nine different units of regulars and provincials.[32] It was customary for a surgeon or his mate to attend the punishment to offer expert advice on how many lashes a man could endure without endangering his life. Men who were unable to 'take' all of their allotted punishment at one time were none the less obliged to suffer the remainder upon their 'recovery'. This was apparently the case with the unfortunate Smith: soon after Colonel Roger Townshend was informed that the man of Cruikshanks's company 'who recd but a part of his Punishment some time ago, is now able to receive the remainder of it whenever the General thinks proper to order it'.[33]

Floggings proved frequent enough to merge with the routine of camp life. Executions were rarer, but far from uncommon. Indeed, on occasions when desertion posed a particular problem considerable numbers of death sentences were enforced. At a General Court Martial at Albany on 19 May 1756, no fewer than fifteen soldiers were sentenced to death for desertion. Of these men, at least ten are known to have been hanged.[34] Similarly, a court held at Oswego on 8–9 August 1760, on the eve of Amherst's advance upon Montreal, returned ten death sentences. Following these verdicts, a gallows was erected and four of the malefactors were executed that same evening; the army embarked upon the lake next morning.[35] More usually, the ultimate penalty was reserved for men deemed to be beyond redemption – serial deserters and 'notorious offenders'. Such 'bad characters' had often been pardoned on previous occasions. For example, John Rhode's chequered past caught up with him when he was convicted

30 GCM, Havana, 19 May 1763, in WO/71/73.
31 Cuthbertson, *Interior Management*, p. 122.
32 GCM, Fort Edward Camp, 11 June 1759, in WO/71/67; Orders, Fort Edward, 14 June 1759, in CKS, U1350/016/1, fol. 12.
33 Benjamin Mace to Townshend, 20 June 1759, in RH 4/98/2 (formerly GD 224/297/6).
34 WO/71/43; 'Proceedings of the Campaign in North America, 1756', in *Hervey's Journals*, pp. 20–21.
35 See WO/71/46; *Journal of Amherst*, p. 226; 'Brigade Order Books', in *Hervey's Journals*, p. 106.

of theft. The court had originally decreed that Rhode, of the Royal Americans, should receive 2,000 lashes before being drummed out of the regiment in disgrace. However, upon learning that he was an 'old Offender and lately pardoned for desertion', the members considered even this punishment to be insufficient and instead sentenced him to death.[36] When a soldier was found wandering at Saratoga and brought into Lake George Camp on 12 July 1759, Amherst ordered a court martial for the following morning. The General recorded the outcome in his journal: 'as it was his second desertion, I thought myself obliged to approve the sentence and order the execution at twelve at the head of the Picquets'.[37] James McMahon of the 44th Foot, who was sentenced to death for robbing soldiers of their shoe-buckles while they slept, was clearly a hardened criminal.[38] This fact emerged at McMahon's execution, when he confessed to the errors of his ways in a model dying speech that could have been ghost-written by the 'Ordinary' of Newgate himself. According to a provincial chaplain, before he was 'hove off' the ladder by the hangman, McMahon warned his comrades against the comprehensive catalogue of sins – 'gaming, robbery, theft, whoring, bad company-keeping, etc' – that had brought him to such a 'shameful untimely death'.[39] Like McMahon, Thomas Bayley of the 17th Foot had demonstrated the skills of the professional pick-pocket. He was charged with robbing his comrade John Stevenson of four dollars that had been contained in a pocket book. Sergeant-Major Thomas Chace and Sergeant Norman Deane reported that Bayley had previously been condemned to death for robbery at Louisbourg, only to receive a pardon. It was also believed that Bayley had attempted robbery on the road to Philadelphia, 'having fired his peice at some Country People', an action that earned him 1,000 lashes. The NCOs added the damning verdict that Bayley possessed 'a most Infamous Character in the Regiment'.[40] Unlike McMahon, Bayley felt disinclined to dedicate his last minutes of life to the moral improvement of his fellow soldiers. On the contrary, he proved 'very loath to die' and refused to kneel before the firing squad. Despite being pinioned hand and foot, Bayley continued to struggle: he was finally shot to death after being tethered to a log.[41]

36 GCM, Fort Edward, 14 September 1757, in WO/71/66.

37 *Journal of Amherst*, p. 135.

38 GCM, Lake George Camp, 21 July 1758, in WO/71/66.

39 'Journal of Reverend John Cleaveland, June 14, 1758 – October 25, 1758', in *BFTM*, X, 3 (1959), 192–233; 203.

40 GCM, Lake George Camp, 13 July 1759, in WO/71/67. On 20 July 1759, Amherst noted: 'I was forced to have a notorious Thief of Forbes [17th Foot] who was pardoned under the Gallows at Louisbourg shot' (*Journal of Amherst*, p. 141).

41 Account of Lemuel Wood, 20 July 1759, in Anderson, *A People's Army*, p. 139.

In the best traditions of Georgian justice, executions were carefully stage-managed in an effort to maximise the impact of the occasion.[42] Such public punishments were intended to impress spectators with a suitable sense of the law's awful majesty. But just as the holidaying crowds of Londoners at Tyburn habitually transformed 'hanging days' into irreverent 'fairs', so even military executions could fall short of their instigator's ideals. For example, a hanging at Nutting Island, New York in May 1757 prompted unruly scenes: not only was the Provost-Marshal Robert Webster insulted by off-duty soldiers assembled to watch the execution, but his hangman was pelted with stones and dirt. After the executioner had done his work, and was being escorted down to the waterside, 'a Crowd came about them', obliging the corporal's guard to fix bayonets and form a protective cordon. The corporal and six other soldiers were subsequently tried for neglecting to shield the Provost from abuse and failing to identify any of those responsible for the 'outrage': all were cleared of the charges against them. Webster's grim calling seemingly alienated the officers composing the court: William Bleakney of the 22nd Foot, a spectator charged with hurling a 'chip' of wood at him, was likewise acquitted.[43]

Where more than one death sentence was imposed, it was customary for use to be made of reprieves. When eleven deserters were sentenced to hang at Oswego in July 1760, one of them, John Jones of the 1st New York Regiment of provincials, was pardoned upon condition of serving the Provost as hangman during the coming campaign. At this, the remaining prisoners were to be told that the time had come for them to die, and they were to make their peace with God. When all had prayed, James Guinens of Colonel Fitch's Regiment was to be hanged. Only after this event were the surviving nine to be pardoned, 'in hopes this example will be sufficient warning to them never to desert again, and likewise put a stop to any more desertions during this Campaign'.[44] Commanders, particularly those troubled by continuing manpower problems, sometimes considered a well-timed display of mercy to be more beneficial than an execution. For example, at Albany on 10 November 1757, Loudoun pardoned Robert Ploughman of the 46th and John Henly of the 55th – both capitally convicted for desertion – 'in hopes that Lenity will have a better effect upon the Troops than the severity of Punishment'.[45] Other men owed their lives to a fluke of fate: five soldiers destined to die for desertion

42 For the nature and objectives of such public punishment see P. Linebaugh, 'The Tyburn Riot Against the Surgeons', in D. Hay et al., *Albion's Fatal Tree: Crime and Society in Eighteenth-Century England* (London, 1975), pp. 65–117.

43 See GCM, New York, 16 May 1757, in WO/71/44.

44 Amherst to Col. Haldimand, Camp at Oswego, 29 July 1760, in Add. MSS 21,661, fol. 78.

45 General Order Books of Loudoun's Commands, in RH 4/86/1.

at Oswego on 18 September 1755 were pardoned because news of William Johnson's victory at Lake George had arrived the previous night.[46] On other occasions pardons were issued under more traumatic circumstances. A deserter of Otway's regiment who was strung up at Fort Edward on 12 October 1756 was reprieved after the rope from which he was suspended snapped on two successive occasions.[47] A similar incident probably explains the respite awarded to Thomas Hunter, a grenadier in the 44th Foot who was sentenced to hang for desertion at Montreal on 12 November 1762. Five days later Major-General Thomas Gage pardoned Hunter, owing to 'an accident, which happened at the Intended Execution ... which I hope may have that Influence over his mind, as to engage him to become a good subject to his King hereafter'.[48] Hunter's brush with death failed to achieve the desired reformation of character. In the New Year he was once again sentenced to death for desertion: this time there was no 'accident'. Luck played an even more prominent role through the practice of requiring two or more condemned men to throw dice, with the 'loser' forfeiting his life. For example, when William Davis of the 58th Foot and Daniel Coleman of the 43rd were sentenced to death for robbing the King's stores at Quebec, Governor James Murray decreed that the pair should 'Cast Lots' for their lives. Murray would reprieve the man whom fortune had favoured 'till his Majesty's Pleasure be further Known'.[49] Several days later, Lieutenant John Knox witnessed the scene when Davis and Coleman threw 'dice for life'. Knox reported:

> eleven was the lucky number, which fell to the lot of a soldier of the forty-third regiment, who, it was remarked, did not discover the least satisfaction upon the occasion, either by his complexion or otherwise: the other poor fellow was instantly executed, and behaved quite undaunted, though with great decency.[50]

Persistent offenders like Thomas Hunter could expect little mercy. Men who deserted to the enemy were also unlikely to survive the attentions of a General Court Martial. In such cases, further ignominy might be added to the sentence. For example, in early August 1759, when deserter George Edwards of the 17th Foot was captured near Ticonderoga clad in enemy uniform, his own regiment was required to erect a gallows: Edwards was to be executed immediately, 'in his French Coat, with a Label on his Breast

46 'A Journal of the March of Shirley's Regiment from Boston to Niagara, 1755', in *Hervey's Journals*, pp. 1–17; 15.

47 'Proceedings of the Campaign in North America, 1756', in ibid., p. 43.

48 WO/71/72.

49 GCMs, Montreal, 22 January 1763 (WO/71/72); Quebec, 13 December 1759 (WO/71/46).

50 *Knox's Journal*, II, 310.

"Hang'd for Deserting to the French"'.[51] John Boyd of the 28th Foot, who had deserted from Wolfe's army at Quebec in the summer of 1759, served subsequently in the French regiment of Béarn and was believed to have fought against the British at the battle of Sainte-Foy. Although Boyd strenuously denied firing 'a shot at the English the 28th [of April 1760]', the court found him guilty and ruled that as he was 'a most heinous offender, having deserted his post', he should be 'hang'd in chains for the same, on the very spot where he appeared in arms against those Colours which he had sworn to Defend'.[52]

Just as an unsavoury reputation might sign a man's death warrant, so a previous good 'character' could save the skin of a soldier's back, or even his life. Thomas Leonard and William McArran of the 47th Foot, who deserted upon the regiment's arrival at Boston following the siege of Louisbourg, were both pardoned a flogging after it was heard that they had helped to defend the transport ship that was taking them to New York when it was attacked by a French privateer.[53] When John Collings of Gage's Light Infantry was tried for desertion, he applied to his officer, Lieutenant John Hall, for a character reference: Hall testified that he knew Collings to be an 'orderly and Brave Soldier by many Instances'. He had also heard Collings's 'Gallant behaviour near Fort Anne particularly mentioned by the Officers present in that affair'.[54] Collings was sentenced to death, but, as another man of Gage's had already been capitally convicted by the same court, Amherst pardoned him in recognition of his former bravery, and in the hope that one example would prove sufficient to end desertion in the regiment.[55] Peter Francis of the 47th Foot, who was charged with deserting from Sainte-Foy on the last day of 1759, escaped a severe flogging even though he had been seen at Quebec wearing the white coat of the French regulars. Francis told the court that he had been captured by Indians while going to see his Canadian mistress, and was obliged to serve with the French or 'rott in Gaol'. Called as a character witness, Sergeant John Curry testified that in his time with Lascelles's Francis had always behaved well, and had often served upon outposts at the exposed camp of Montmorency. Captain Samuel Gardner of Lascelles's recalled that he had once attempted to have Francis transferred into his company, but his existing officer 'liked him so well, as he did not

51 'Monypenny Orderly Book', *BFTM* (July 1932), p. 249; GCM, Ticonderoga, 3 August 1759, in WO/71/67.

52 GCM, Quebec, 26 October 1760, in WO/71/68.

53 GCM, Fort George, New York, 15 January 1759, in WO/71/67.

54 This fight, in which a mixed force of regulars and rangers clashed with Canadians and Indians, took place on 8 August 1758. See *The Journals of Major Robert Rogers, containing an account of the several excursions he made under the Generals who commanded upon the continent of North America during the late war* (London, 1765), pp. 117–19.

55 GCM, Fort George, New York, 16 January 1759, in WO/71/67.

chuse to part with him'. Although found guilty as charged, and sentenced to receive 1,000 lashes, James Murray subsequently ordered that Francis should be forgiven 'at the Intercession of the President in the Name of the Court'.[56] However, a good 'character' did not always guarantee a pardon: for example, Andrew Yeats, a deserter from Montgomery's Highlanders who was subsequently found serving in the ranks of the 'Jersey Blues' received 1,000 lashes despite glowing references from officers of his original battalion. Lieutenant Robertson said Yeats had always behaved well, 'Particularly with Major Grant at Fort de Quesne where he turned out Volunteer to Cover a party that went to Burn a Loghouse Close to the Fort'.[57] Edward Spark, who deserted from the 3/60th at Martinique after a three-day drinking bout with two sailors, testified in his own defence that he had been in the army for 23 years, having 'been at almost all the Sieges in America during the War' and served in the 36th Foot during the War of the Austrian Succession. His sergeant told the court how Spark had 'turned out a Volunteer' during the attack on the French redoubts in January 1762, and had 'behaved Gallantly, and like a good soldier'. Spark's service record probably saved his life: although the court awarded him 1,000 lashes, he was spared the death penalty routinely allotted to deserters from the Havana garrison.[58]

As these cases demonstrate, the 'character' that a man acquired during his army service was quite literally a matter of life and death. But it was not only in the eyes of his officers that such reputation counted: also important was a soldier's standing amongst his comrades. This can be seen clearly in the case of Samuel Norbury, a grenadier of the 40th Foot who was found guilty of desertion in 1761. Along with three other men convicted for the same offence, Norbury was ordered to prepare for death. General orders issued three days later announced that Norbury had been reprieved owing to the intervention of his fellow soldiers. Amherst explained: 'He receives his pardon on account of his former good behaviour as a Soldier, set forth in a Petition from the Granadiers of three Regiments & on their promises, that he will hereafter approve himself deserving of this Mercy.' The 40th was to be under arms that afternoon, when the pardon would be read to Norbury at the head of the regiment.[59]

56 GCM, Quebec, 27 July 1761, in WO/71/70. Captain Gardner was himself a member of this court.

57 GCM, Fort Edward Camp, 11 June 1759, in WO/71/67. It was unfortunate for Yeats that his former colonel, Archibald Montgomery, was court president.

58 GCM, Havana, 16 March 1763, in WO/71/73.

59 Orders, Staten Island, 13 and 18 September 1761, in U1350/016/2. Although the minutes of the General Court Martial at which Norbury was sentenced are missing from the series at the Public Record Office, it is likely that he was one of the 'Louisbourg Grenadiers' – formed from the élite companies of the 22nd, 40th and 45th regiments – who distinguished themselves under Wolfe at Quebec. It may also be significant that Norbury was sentenced on 13 September – the anniversary of Wolfe's victory on the Plains of Abraham.

Just as a steady man like Norbury attracted the support of his comrades, so those men who strayed beyond the bounds of acceptable behaviour were ostracised. For example, such conduct counted heavily against Thomas McNeal of the 43rd Foot when he was court-martialled for desertion; he claimed to have served at 'seven sieges' and always behaved well, but another soldier of the 43rd, Lathan Rice, testified that the men of the regiment often abused McNeal and called him 'informer' because he had reported a woman who sold liquor.[60] Thomas Hunter – the grenadier of the 44th Foot pardoned after an 'accident' at his intended execution – blamed his subsequent desertion upon the derision he endured from his comrades. In defence, Hunter claimed that he had been victimised by the aptly named Sergeant Gall, who had punched and kicked him, while 'reviling him with his former Misfortunes' and predicting that he would be hanged. In addition, Hunter had suffered 'other aggravations & upbradings from the private Men of the Company he came from'.[61] Cowardice in the face of the enemy incurred particular opprobrium: Corporal William Cox of the 22nd Regiment was jeered by fellow soldiers who witnessed him quitting his post at Havana, thereby allowing two Spaniards to poison the well he was supposed to be guarding.[62]

Motivation and morale

Such evidence suggests that the fear of official army discipline was by no means the only control upon behaviour in the ranks; for all the efforts of the Provost-Marshal with his lash and noose, in the last resort a redcoat's desire to retain the respect of his comrades may have exerted a more powerful influence over his conduct both in camp and upon the battlefield. Historians of the British Army of the eighteenth century have offered differing verdicts on the importance of comradeship and shared pride in regimental traditions as motivating factors for the rank and file. In her study of the British soldier of the 1770s and 1780s, Sylvia Frey suggests that both combined to promote group solidarity, thereby producing an army composed of a 'brotherhood of men'.[63] Mark Odintz likewise considers that 'regimental loyalty and identification' was 'perhaps the most significant feature of British military life' at that time, with 'unit pride' exerting a profound influence over officers and men alike.[64] This

60 McNeal was sentenced to death. See GCM, Havana, 9 February 1763, in WO/71/73.
61 GCM, Montreal, 22 January 1763 (WO/71/72).
62 Cox was sentenced to 500 lashes and reduced to the ranks. See GCM, camp near 'Fort Mauro [El Morro]', Cuba, 15 July 1762, in WO/71/71.
63 Frey, *British Soldier in America*, p. 112.
64 Odintz, 'British Officer Corps', pp. 17; 434–45.

emphasis upon comradeship and *esprit de corps* has failed to convince Alan Guy, whose researches among the extensive papers of Colonel Samuel Bagshawe have produced very different conclusions: in Bagshawe's correspondence the rank and file are mere 'commodities, to be recruited, drilled, managed, disposed of when worn out or reluctantly drafted into other units'.[65] Such rapid turnover of manpower, Guy argues, was hardly conducive to fraternity.[66]

Evidence examined in the course of researching this book supports the contention that unit loyalty played an important role in motivating the redcoat. Whilst it is impossible to deny the prevalence of drafting in the British Army of the eighteenth century, it is also necessary to remember that for every soldier who found himself transferred from one unit to another in bewildering succession, there were others who spent all or most of their military career in a single regiment. This was particularly true of those battalions which possessed sufficient seniority in the line to avoid disbandment at the close of hostilities. In contrast to such 'young' corps as Bagshawe's own 93rd Foot, which was little more than a feeder unit for other regiments, these were unlikely to be drafted wholesale with the coming of peace. Even where drafting did occur, the men selected were often those who had been received as drafts from other units, so leaving a rump of veterans who spent their entire service – from enlistment to death or discharge – in the same regiment. Of the December 1759 sample of 569 men from the 58th Foot, it can be established that the majority (316 men; 55.5 per cent) served out their entire period of enlistment in that regiment. This compares with 213 men (37 per cent) who had either entered as drafts or were subsequently drafted to other units.[67] Indeed, when the 58th Foot helped to defend Gibraltar during the great siege of 1779–83 it included a leavening of veterans who had fought with Wolfe on the Plains of Abraham.[68]

When finally recommended to Chelsea, such survivors could look back on two world wars and nearly three decades of soldiering in what had recently become 'The Rutlandshire Regiment'. The service accumulated by other men was even more extensive: John Smith, a grenadier in the 4th Foot, had served in the King's Own for 34 years when he came before the Chelsea Board in 1788. Smith's 'long service' had not left him unscathed. Besides sustaining a wounded leg in the fighting on Martinique during the Seven Years War, Smith was also shot through the thigh at Concord on 19

65 *Colonel Bagshawe and the Army of George II*, p. 15.

66 A. J. Guy, 'The Army of the Georges', in *Oxford Illustrated History of the British Army*, p. 94.

67 In the remaining 40 cases the information is insufficient to determine ultimate fate.

68 No less than 48 (8 per cent) of the 569 men in the December 1759 sample remained with the 58th when Gibraltar was blockaded.

April 1775 on the opening day of the American War of Independence.[69] Equally interesting is the case of Sergeant Abraham Cooper, who was recommended to Kilmainham Hospital when discharged at Dublin on 4 June 1784. Cooper had served in the 5th Foot for 30 years and eight months. Although he had seen no American service during the 'Great War for Empire', Cooper had ample experience of that conflict's European campaigns, having suffered a wound to the groin at St-Cast on the French coast in 1758, and another in the right leg at Warburg in Germany two years later. Besides his injuries, Sergeant Cooper was understandably 'Worn out by Long Service' in a regiment which had also fought at Bunker Hill and in the Caribbean during the Revolutionary War.[70]

In some units such continuity fostered a genuine *esprit de corps*. In his ballad 'Hot Stuff', Ned Botwood clearly emphasised his pride in his own regiment, Lascelles's 47th Foot, stressing that though they now wore the same uniforms as Shirley's disgraced 50th, it would be dangerous to confuse them with the dejected defenders of Oswego:

> When the Forty-seventh Regiment is dashing ashore,
> When bullets are whistling and cannon do roar,
> Says Montcalm, 'Those are Shirley's, I know their lapels'.
> 'You lie,' says Ned Botwood, 'We are of Lascelles!
> Though our clothing is changed, yet we scorn a powder-puff;
> So at you, ye bitches, here's give you Hot Stuff.'[71]

The premature attack at Montmorency in which Botwood was killed apparently resulted from keen rivalry within a battalion of the Royal American Regiment. Captain David Ochterlony, who commanded 200 men of the 2/60th at the landing, had been positioned to the left of the battalion's grenadier company, which was massed with the other grenadiers of the army. Ochterlony called over to Captain Gustavus Wetterstrom that although his men were not grenadiers, they would be the first to storm the redoubt that was the objective of the assault. With the grenadiers 'taking fire' at Ochterlony's boast, the entire command dashed forward without orders in a race for the redoubt.[72] In such a competitive

69 Smith's discharge certificate does not specify whether he was wounded on Martinique in 1759 or 1762: the grenadier company of the King's Own was engaged on both occasions. WO/121/5 (Board of 23 December 1788).

70 Aged 44 when discharged, Cooper must have joined the 5th Foot when a lad of just thirteen or fourteen years old. See WO/119/1, fol. 23.

71 Winstock, 'Hot Stuff', *JSAHR* (1955), p. 4.

72 This anecdote is related in an early manuscript history of the Royal Americans, the 'Memoir of Major Patrick Murray'. It is likely that Murray, who served in the regiment from 1770 to 1793, had the account from veterans of the Seven Years' War. See Lewis Butler, *Annals of the King's Royal Rifle Corps: Volume One, The Royal Americans* (London, 1913), p. 292.

atmosphere, it followed that 'notorious offenders' brought dishonour not only upon themselves, but also reflected badly on those men who shared their uniform. For example, Neal Cosgrove of the 43rd Foot, who had been confined for three months on suspicion of theft, later deserted, owing to 'many hardships' and the fact that his sergeant had threatened to strip the distinctive regimental facings from his coat, 'as he thought him a Scandal to the Corps'.[73]

Soldiers who transgressed the *Articles of War* could expect swift retribution; yet some officers were beginning to appreciate that discipline might also be served by rewarding the worth of the 'steady' soldier, who would thereby act as a model for his comrades. Conspicuous acts of gallantry might earn the private soldier a gratuity from his officers: when Captain Peter Pigou of the 43rd Foot was shot dead in an ambush in Nova Scotia, Sergeant Cockburne returned under fire to retrieve his possessions; in recognition of his courage, this 'brave fellow' was rewarded with five guineas and Pigou's laced hat.[74] There was no officially recognised system of awards for gallantry in the eighteenth century, or even a general issue of campaign medals before Waterloo;[75] however, the mid-Georgian Army was none the less developing methods of motivating the rank and file by giving official recognition for good behaviour. In the immediate aftermath of the Seven Years War, Bennett Cuthbertson had recommended the establishment of a graded 'order of merit' for the men in the ranks. Under this system a soldier who had spent at least seven years 'employed in the closest attention to military duty', without having 'incurred the censure of a Court-Martial', would qualify to receive a special medal from his commanding officer at the head of the regiment.[76] Although there is no evidence for such schemes in the 'American Army', they were certainly in existence later in the century. By 1789, the 7th Foot, or 'Royal Fusiliers', had developed a carefully graded system of awards. For example, when George Friskin was discharged at Edinburgh Castle on 9 May, he was dignified with the title of 'Veteran'. Friskin, who was 42 years old, had served for 22 years without appearing before a court martial in two decades. A slater from Perth, Friskin was 'worn out in the Service', having been 'Wounded in the Head & in the Body at the Battle of the Cow Pens in North Carolina & suffered much by long Confinement when Prisoner'. This record secured Friskin's admission as a member of

73 GCM, Crown Point, 25 July 1761, in WO/71/68.

74 *Knox's Journal*, I, 123.

75 Although officers and men of the New Model Army received medals after Cromwell's victory over the Scots at Dunbar in 1650, Waterloo was the first action for which the government provided a verified award to *all* soldiers present. See E. C. Joslin, A. R. Litherland and B. T. Simpkin, *British Battles and Medals* (London, 1988), p. 86.

76 Cuthbertson, *Interior Management*, p. 128.

the sixth class of the 'Badge of Distinction', and likewise gained him the 'Order of Merit' for fidelity and distinction.[77] According to Cuthbertson, another method of 'promoting a spirit of good behaviour' among the men was to ensure that the funerals of such 'Soldiers of Merit and Real worth' were marked by a suitable degree of ceremony.[78] Although casualties of battle or epidemic could expect to be tumbled into a common grave, when circumstances permitted all due respect should be shown. There is evidence for such rites in the 'American Army'. For example, when a man of Fraser's Highlanders died at Fort Stanwix in January 1759, he was interred with military honours: ten men from each of the four companies in garrison were to follow the corpse; twelve soldiers would fire over the grave.[79]

Other factors commonly used to explain military motivation remain less convincing when applied to the redcoats of the Seven Years War. Historians have noted how that conflict spawned 'patriotic societies' by means of which wealthy civilians were able to flaunt both their philanthropy and nationalism. For example, Jonas Hanway's 'Society for the Encouragement of the British Troops in Germany and North America' tapped a rich vein, rapidly raising more than £7,000 to provide comforts for serving soldiers and support for their widows and orphans.[80] Britain's officer corps was dominated by men from the same 'middling' and 'upper' class backgrounds as those who backed such ventures; the frequent expressions of patriotism, nationalism and downright xenophobia amongst officers are therefore unsurprising. For example, an exuberant teenaged subaltern wrote from Martinique on 27 February 1762:

> We are now in full Possession of the whole Island: see what we Britons can do! We hope to drive the World before us ere this War be over, and myself to be an old Captain. I brought in eight Prisoners; but had the Misfortune to have a Grenadier killed, a brave Fellow, worth 100 Frenchmen.[81]

Such men sometimes credited their humbler subordinates with similar sentiments: in the wake of the Revolutionary War, one former field officer contrasted the rootless and mercenary rankers of the Prussian Army with the higher-spirited British soldiery, who acted 'from the love of fame, and

77 See Chelsea Board of 13 June 1789, in WO/121/6.

78 Cuthbertson, *Interior Management*, p. 158.

79 Orderly Book, Fort Stanwix, 11 November 1758 to 30 January 1759, in GD 125/34/7, fol. 41.

80 See Langford, *A Polite and Commercial People*, p. 489; Colley, *Britons*, 91–2; J. Hanway, *An Account of the Society for the Encouragement of British Troops in Germany and North America* (London, 1760).

81 *Felix Farley's Bristol Journal*, 17 April 1762.

their country'.[82] However, whilst individual redcoats might voice a conventional loyalty to their monarch, and mutinous units take pains to emphasise a continuing personal allegiance to the state they had sworn to serve, there is little evidence to suggest that the rank and file of the 'American Army' were driven by any deeper sense of patriotism. Even those rare 'patriotic' statements that survive must be interpreted with caution. For example, when John Holland of the 46th Foot was tried for desertion at Havana in 1763, the court members expressed curiosity about a scar visible on his wrist; Holland explained that 'he received that Wound at Ticonderoga & was discharged, and recommended to Chelsea for the same, but finding himself able to serve his King & Country, he Enlisted again as a private Soldier'.[83] Holland was haggling for his life, and it would be unwise to read too much into his words. Once again, although the unknown soldier who wrote to his mother from Quebec in October 1759 considered himself 'not the worse Man' for being able to serve 'King and Country in so troublesome a time', it is worth remembering that he was only in America because he had been 'pressed' into the 35th Foot against his inclinations.[84] Although the introduction of short-term periods of service during the Seven Years War may have attracted recruits whose enlistments were not primarily motivated by economic hardship, the notable absence of patriotic sentiments among the rank and file in America warns against exaggerating the influence of 'King and Country' upon the ordinary redcoat's morale and behaviour.

Neither were the redcoats bouyed up by religious zeal. Unlike their Cromwellian forbears in the New Model Army, the British regulars of the Seven Years War were no psalm-singing host of the Godly. As has been noted, to their contemporaries amongst the New England provincials the redcoats all too often appeared deliberately God*less*. Regulars of all ranks were noted for irreverence: this flagrant Sabbath-breaking and voluble cursing shocked colonists who took their own religion seriously.[85] In contrast to the provincials, who were bombarded with a veritable barrage of sermons, the regulars rarely heard or even saw their own regimental chaplains. Following the conquest of Guadeloupe, Governor Byam Crump informed Lord Barrington: 'Our new friends the French take us for atheists, as we have ne'er a Chaplain amongst us

82 *Military Sketches. By Edward Drewe, late Major of the 35th Regt of Foot* (Exeter, 1784), p. 45.

83 GCM, Havana, 1 March 1763, in WO/71/73.

84 *Derby Mercury*, 30 November to 7 December 1759.

85 Anderson, *People's Army*, pp. 117–18. For religion as a motivating factor amongst the provincials see ibid., pp. 155–7.

nor any signs of public Worship.' Although Crump believed that a 'good Clergyman' would be of 'great comfort' to the sick, he would rather go without than endure the calibre of cleric customarily sent out.[86] Typical of such uninspiring material was John Dick, the deputy chaplain to the Royal Regiment in 1757. Weakened by a fever that had left him with 'an observable impediment in his speech and a great weakness in his nerves', Dick felt unable to face another Nova Scotian winter. Peregrine Hopson was reluctant to comply with this plea for leave, as there was only one other chaplain to minister to the ailing Halifax garrison. When Dick renewed his application, Hopson relented, comforted in the knowledge that the deputy appeared to be 'one of the oddest or mortals'.[87] Of a different stamp was the Reverend Michael Schlatter, who had offered his services to the Royal Americans in an unofficial capacity: besides preparing deserters for death, Schlatter had preached to that regiment's polyglot battalions in both English and German, with the happy result that the men had begun to 'Slacken with their rash and unneccessary expressions'.[88] The 60th also benefited from the ministrations of John Ogilvie, the dedicated missionary to the Mohawks. Amherst could only wish that the example set by Ogilvie's 'constant attendance, and unwearied diligence in the discharge of his duty' was followed by other army chaplains.[89] Despite the unswerving efforts of men like Ogilvie, the British Army in America was clearly unripe for religious awakening. Periodic attempts to raise the moral tone proved unsuccessful. For example, as part of a comprehensive disciplinary crack-down at Havana in 1763, off-duty soldiers were directed to attend weekly church parades cleanly dressed and with their hair neatly powdered. Subsequent orders reveal that old habits died hard: men were forbidden to 'play at Ball against any of the Churches', while patrols were established to quell the drunken riots that proved particularly prevalent on Sundays.[90] If, as Jonathan Clark has contended, the Church of England exerted a crucial control over Georgian society, its deferential creed went unheeded by that unruly congregation, the 'American Army'.[91]

86 Letter of 4 October 1759, in WO/1/19, fol. 34.

87 Dick to Hopson, Halifax, 19 October 1757 (LO 4671); Hopson to Loudoun, Halifax, 23 October and 25 December 1757 (LO 4693 and 5087).

88 Schlatter to Loudoun, Philadelphia, 4 February 1758 (LO 5538).

89 Amherst to Barrington, New York, 9 December 1760 (WO/1/5, fol. 138).

90 See NAM MSS 9212/73 (Order Book of Henry Moore, 48th Foot): Orders 12 February, 14 May, 28 May 1763.

91 J. C. D. Clark, *English Society 1688–1832: Ideology, Social Structure and Political Practice During the Ancien Regime* (Cambridge, 1985).

The Army as community

Evidence examined in Chapter 2 has already suggested that, for some men at least, the Army represented a familiar environment that offered an alternative to the vagaries of civilian life. In a general sense, the Army provided the soldier with a 'home'; this notion of 'community' was strengthened by other influences operating at regimental level. Although regional affiliations were not introduced until 1782, and even then meant little in an era when regiments lacked depots and remained largely itinerant, eighteenth-century battalions did include groups of men who hailed from the same immediate locality. If the 58th Foot was typical, in many cases these men must have been neighbours or work-mates before joining the army. Men enlisted by that regiment in the spring of 1756 included twelve recruits from the city of Worcester, among them a trio of glove-makers. Similarly, the eight Bromsgove recruits included three 'nailers'. The regiment's substantial contingent of Scots numbered seven men from the tiny township of Tain on the north-east coast. Of the recruits raised by the Earl of Sandwich at the same period, no less than six came from the remote fenland fastness of Ely, where four of them had worked as potters and another as a brickmaker. Four of the Ely men (of whom two, John and Thomas Field, were probably brothers) soldiered in the same company.[92] The existence of clusters of men who had known each other before their enlistment would surely have heightened the regiment's role as 'community'.

There is also evidence that the men who served in the 'American Army' formed a society characterised by broader ties and relationships; some indication of their nature can be gained from an incident aboard a transport ship at Halifax, Nova Scotia before Loudoun's unsuccessful Louisbourg expedition of 1757. One night, James Car of the 22nd Foot began making a great disturbance amongst his 'Comrades'. When urged to go to bed, the drunken Car responded with threats. Car ultimately inflicted a deep gash on the wrist of James Jones, leaving him 'terribly cut, and his Bed in a Gore of Blood'. After dressing Jones's wound, the surgeon's mate Nicholas Power asked Car how he could use a 'Brother Soldier' with such barbarity. At his trial, Car denied any personal malice to Jones, claiming to be 'out of his Senses with Liquor' at the time of the incident. Indeed, Car told the court, 'no Man can be less inclined to do a Brother Soldier an Injury than he is'. The case reveals not only the strong sense of community amongst 'Brother Soldiers' but also the existence of other more ritualised contacts that served to cement the ties of comradeship: when questioned by the wary Jones, Car had responded with the

92 All six were recruited between 21 and 26 March 1756.

assurance that he was a 'Mason'. Jones then asked Car to prove this fact by revealing the number of steps in 'Jacob's ladder'.[93] A similar fraternity existed amongst the sergeants. This is clear from the trial of three non-commissioned officers of the 'Royal' Regiment, who were charged with robbery at Louisbourg. Sergeant-Major John Stedman explained that on a trip into the shattered fortress with his two 'Brother serjeants' he had picked up a few English books in a ruined house. Sergeant William Finney said that he had taken two volumes – 'The Universal Pocket Book' and a spelling book 'at which all his Brother Serjeants laughed when he produced them in the Ring'.[94] Like the private soldiers, the sergeants saw themselves as members of a distinctive 'brotherhood', in this instance apparently accompanied by an informal 'sergeants' mess'.

The Army's sense of community was reinforced by the close proximity in which soldiers lived, both on campaign and in more settled barracks and billets. Within a regiment, each company was divided into messes – usually of six men – who ate together and shared a tent when in the field. This system was encountered by the newly enlisted 'Jonas', who arrived on the Isle of Wight in May 1758 to find several regiments already encamped in a 'canvas town'. Besides straw to lie on there were two blankets: to prevent one man obtaining a greater share of these than another, the blankets were sewn together at each end, so forming a wide tube into which the men crept. As 'Jonas' explained, the men usually lay 'head and feet, three one way and three the other; which, according to the cleanliness and health of your comrades, or the contrary, is more or less disagreeable'.[95]

Soldiers could therefore talk of 'sleeping' with their comrades without a hint of embarrassment. The extent to which contacts between the men went beyond 'comradeship' is difficult to establish. Consenting homosexual relationships are impossible to quantify from the available evidence, whilst the surviving records of General Courts Martial in the 'American Army' yield just two allegations of sexual assault by one soldier upon another. In an age in which proven 'unnatural acts' carried the death

93 Car received 500 lashes for 'barbarously and cruelly' cutting Jones (GCM, Halifax, 5 August 1757, in WO/71/66). According to John Knox, the detachment of the 43rd Foot at Annapolis Royal, Nova Scotia in 1757–58 included a busy Freemasons' lodge, while the garrison of Quebec in December 1759 included 'several lodges' (see *Knox's Journal*, I, 183; II, 313).

94 The trio were found guilty of 'great irregularity' and reduced to the ranks. However, on the recommendation of the court members, all three were pardoned and reinstated. See GCM, camp near Louisbourg, 6 August 1758, in WO/71/66.

95 According to 'Jonas', it was an established rule that the oldest soldier slept at the far end of the tent and the most junior nearest the door where anyone coming in or out was likely to trample upon him. Worse still, explained Jonas, recalling his own days as a recruit, 'as some of the men at night will not go beyond the tent door, you often suffer from their evacuations, as was the case with me' (*A Soldier's Journal*, pp. 4–5).

penalty, and when civilians sentenced to the pillory for lesser offences risked being stoned to death by outraged mobs, it is highly unlikely that such incidents would have escaped notice.[96] In the first of the two extant cases, heard at Havana on 23 September 1762, Sergeant John Lye of the Royal Americans strenuously denied making sexual advances towards Sergeant Henry Mitchell of the 35th. Lye claimed that Mitchell had fabricated the complaint after they argued over a blanket when making up a bed. Sergeant Lye was acquitted after the court heard character references: Lieutenant James Miller of the 60th testified that Lye was married with a wife in the barracks, and was 'never suspected of anything so infamous as criminal Conversation with Men'; Sergeant-Major John Armstrong said he had never known Lye to be suspected of sodomy, and had indeed slept alongside him while out on command.[97] Charles McHoennan of the 44th Foot was charged with the attempted sodomy of a mess-mate, James Smith. Like Lye, McHoennan claimed that the allegation was groundless and malicious. Indeed, McHoennan assembled ten soldiers willing to depose that 'they have all been at different times the Prisoner's Comrades in Quarters or Tent Mates, having lain in Bed or Tents with him more or less during near Six Years. These men had not known McHoennan to be guilty of any similar accusation 'except the Prisoners' having once [been] accused before in the like manner by one Charles Couse a soldier near two years ago'. On that occasion McHoennan had been acquitted, but the taint of previous misconduct, although unproven, seems to have convinced the court of his guilt: he was sentenced to 1,000 lashes and ordered to be drummed out of the regiment.[98] By contrast, the evidence against Lieutenant-Colonel Thomas Bowyer of the 63rd Foot at Guadeloupe, who was accused by his own regiment of having made 'some sodomitical attempts' upon three officers of the corps, was overwhelming.[99] However, as an officer and a gentleman, Bowyer was able to avoid being brought before a General Court Martial: faced with the unequivocal findings of a court of inquiry, Bowyer requested permission to resign his lieutenant-colonelcy 'in such manner as shall be most suitable to my present unhappy circumstances'.[100] Reporting this 'very extraordinary affair', the island's governor, Campbell Dalrymple, explained that he had accepted Bowyer's resignation after considering his 'services, his

96 On the brutal treatment of those convicted of homosexual acts see F. McLynn, *Crime and Punishment in Eighteenth-Century England* (Oxford, 1989), pp. 283–5.

97 WO/71/72.

98 Gage subsequently reduced the punishment to 500 lashes. See GCM, Montreal, 18 July 1763, in WO/71/73.

99 Court of Enquiry, Marigole, Guadeloupe, 18 May 1762, in WO/1/19, fols 106–7; 116–17.

100 Bowyer to Dalrymple, Capesterre, Guadeloupe, 18 May 1762, in ibid., fol. 108.

familly, & connections', thus saving him the 'ignomy of a public tryal' and protecting the 'character' of the young gentlemen who had been the object of the colonel's attentions.[101] As Dalrymple observed, the case was indeed extraordinary. From the available evidence, it is hard to disagree with N. A. M. Rodger's verdict regarding homosexual activity in the mid-eighteenth-century Navy; he found it 'difficult to believe that there can have been any serious problem with a crime so much detested, but so seldom mentioned'.[102]

Soldiers in search of more orthodox liaisons enjoyed considerable scope. The 'American Army' was far from being a masculine preserve: on the North American continent and in the West Indies alike soldiers had ample opportunity for contact with members of the opposite sex. During the 1759 Caribbean campaign, while recuperating after a fever, George Durant 'Made Love to a French Negress', discovering that 'a Black at Gardaloup & a white in Drury Lane differ'd only in Complexion as their Sentiments & *winning ways* seem'd pretty much the same'.[103] In addition to the inhabitants encountered in such settled areas, numbers of women accompanied the battalions virtually everywhere they served; they were often described simply as 'women' in official orders, a blanket term that fails to distinguish between soldiers' wives and unofficial 'camp followers'. Some of these women were undoubtedly prostitutes: orders issued during Braddock's march to the Monongahela warned that every soldier or woman found out of bounds without a pass would receive 50 lashes and be marched through the camp to 'expose' their behaviour. Women with Braddock's column were also obliged to submit to medical examination in an effort to prevent the spread of venereal diseases.[104] Such treatment should not be taken as evidence that prostitution was the norm. Many army women were legally married or involved in stable, common-law relationships.[105] It was also possible for women who followed the Army in an informal capacity to find a husband in the ranks: on 18 October 1758, one provincial private recorded rather unsympathetically how 'this afternoon their was a Lobster Corperel married to a Road Island whore'.[106]

101 Dalrymple to the Secretary-at-War, Guadeloupe, 30 May 1762, in ibid, fol. 110.

102 Rodger, *The Wooden World*, p. 81.

103 'George Durant's Journal', *Army Records Society, Military Miscellany, I*, p. 43 (entry for 17 February 1759).

104 'Halkett's Orderly Book', in *Braddock's Defeat*, pp. 98; 109.

105 P. E. Kopperman, 'The British Command and Soldiers' Wives in America, 1755–83', in *JSAHR*, LX (1982), 14–34; 14.

106 'Lemuel Lyon, Military Journal for 1758', in *The Military Journals of Two Private Soldiers, 1758–1775*, ed. A. Tomlinson (Poughkeepsie, New York, 1855; repr. New York, 1971), pp. 39–40.

In his study of the army women, Paul Kopperman suggests that they served as an irritant to the high command and were only grudgingly tolerated.[107] However, there is evidence that the presence of a limited number of women was viewed as beneficial and actually encouraged. For example, during the summer of 1757, when drafts were ordered to America from regiments in Britain and Ireland, Edward Whitmore suggested that it was 'proper, and for the good of His Majesty's Service, that five or six women for every hundred Men be permitted to Embark'.[108] Similarly, when Peregrine Hopson's West Indian expedition gathered in the following autumn, it was deemed 'necessary' that ten women per company should embark with the six regiments due to sail from England. As each of these battalions consisted of nine companies, no less than 540 women were to accompany the expedition.[109] In both these instances the women concerned were to be given provisions. Among those battalions serving in the Americas during the Seven Years War it was customary to allow rations to be drawn for a specified number of women per company. In May 1755, Braddock's regulars were permitted rations for six women in each company; a return of Captain Charles Baillie's grenadier company of Fraser's Highlanders, made at Stratford, Connecticut on 14 December 1757, lists seven 'Women Victualled with the Company'.[110]

On certain occasions women were specifically forbidden from accompanying the troops. Before the campaigns on Lake George under Abercromby in 1758 and Amherst in 1759, instructions were issued that no women should take the field: instead, just three or four women per company – depending upon whether the battalion theoretically consisted of 700 or 1,000 men – were to receive provisions at Albany.[111] During the gruelling expedition against the Cherokees in 1761, Lieutenant-Colonel James Grant assured Amherst: 'I have not allowed a single Woman to follow the Camp and if any of them are found near it, they are drummed out directly.'[112] Similarly, when troops were sent from the continent to reinforce the besiegers of

107 Kopperman, 'Soldiers' Wives', *JSAHR* (1982), p. 16.

108 Whitmore to Barrington, 25 August 1757, in WO/1/973, p. 1,185.

109 Barrington to Secretary to the Admiralty, John Clevland, 18 October 1758, in WO/4/56, p. 387.

110 'Halkett's Orderly Book', in *Braddock's Defeat*, pp. 89–90; GD 125/22/17/20.

111 In both instances, victualling was conditional upon these women serving as nurses in the General Hospital when required: those refusing this duty would be struck off the ration list. See 'Monypenny Orderly Book', *BFTM* (December, 1969), p. 339; ibid., (June 1971), p. 184.

112 Letter from Camp at Monk's Corner, 30 March 1761, in WO/34/47, fol. 57.

Havana, no women were to go because only a 'short Expedition' was envisaged.[113]

Women were commonly found on active service, and not infrequently in the thick of the fighting; they certainly numbered among the casualties sustained at Braddock's defeat in 1755. A soldier who survived the frantic retreat across the Monongahela recalled how 'an Indien Shot one of our Wimen and began to Scalp her' before her husband killed the warrior.[114] Women were similarly in the line of fire during the Caribbean campaign of 1762. Before the French sortie from Martinique on 27 January, the 2nd Battalion of the Royal Highland Regiment had pitched its tents on the banks of a rivulet. Lieutenant John Grant recalled: 'our Women had arrived and were comming to wash when three shells appeared quickly an[d] burst'. That summer Grant also witnessed women in the front line at Havana. Shortly after clearing a house in the suburbs of its Spanish defenders, Grant's command returned to find the building ransacked of spoils that included brocaded dresses and velvet suits. The 'Soldiers wives and camp followers' were already cavorting in this plundered finery, being 'equipped most amuzingly in their borrowed plumes'.[115] Many of the Army's women had plainly seen considerable active service as they followed the drum. One such woman, Martha May, described something of her experiences in an appeal to Lieutenant-Colonel Henry Bouquet. Mrs May had been incarcerated at Carlisle, Pennsylvania for abusing Bouquet 'to a High degree' after her husband – 'an Old Soldier' – had been taken out of the ranks and confined. She explained that the verbal broadside stemmed from love for her 'Poor Husband' rather than any ill-will towards 'so good a Colonel'. Her letter added: 'I have been a Wife 22 years and have Traveld with my Husband every Place or County the Company Marcht too and have workt very hard ever since I was in the Army.' Mrs May hoped to be pardoned 'that I may go with my Poor Husband, one time more to carry him and my good Officers water in ye Hottest Battle as I have done before'.[116]

Although obliged to act as nurses when required, the function that gained the army women their official recognition was their role in laundering the clothes of officers and men. The importance of this service to the Army was not lost on some women. At Fort Stanwix in the spring of 1759,

113 Orders, New York, 24 May 1762, in CKS, U1350/016/2. In the case of the 58th Foot this directive was ignored: when the battalion sailed for Cuba it was accompanied by 71 women and children. See 'State of His Majesty's 58th Regiment of Foot when taken Prisoners by the French, July 21st 1762', in WO/1/5, fols 309–10. Other women arrived at Havana with the regiments from Martinique.

114 'Journal of Cholmley's Batman', in *Braddock's Defeat*, p. 31.

115 'Journal of Lieutenant John Grant, 42nd Foot, 1758–62' (RH 4/77), pp. 76; 92.

116 Letter dated Carlisle, 4 June 1758, in *Papers of Bouquet*, II, 30.

Major James Clephane of Fraser's Highlanders took a stern line after he received complaints that the garrison's women were overcharging the men for doing their washing by demanding twice the customary rate. In consequence, on 13 March, the Major ordered that 'no Woman Presume to take more than one Penny for a Shirt, and one Penny for Each Waistcoat'. Women daring to charge higher rates would be cut off the 'List of His Majesty's Provisions'.[117]

Just as the men of the redcoat battalions ranged from the steady and reliable to the drunken and criminal, so a similar variety existed amongst their women. Evidence from the records of the General Courts Martial demonstrates the diversity of women encountered in the ranks. At one extreme was Mary Savage, wife of a soldier in the 2/60th and described by one of the battalion's officers as 'an irregular disorderly Woman'. This unflattering description led a court to disbelieve her claim, no doubt accurate, that she had been raped by three men of the battalion during a drinking spree. Very different was the lot of another army wife, Sarah Emerson, whose husband William was a private soldier in the 35th Foot. Mrs Emerson possessed considerable personal wealth: cash stolen from her strong-box included two 'doubleoons', for which she had paid £11 sterling, plus eleven dollars local currency and some silver change. More surprisingly, Mrs Emerson had her own servant, 'Mrs Owens', who had called out that 'her Mistress' had been robbed by a 'Blackamore'. Evidence from the courts martial reveals that many business-minded women accumulated considerable wealth by establishing themselves as sutlers or money-changers – a role that made them a tempting target for thieves. For example, William Garway of the 17th Foot was charged with robbing the money-changer Jenny Drinnon of 'upwards of fourteen Pounds Sterling'. Another witness in the case, Peggy Armstrong, was both a sutler and a money-changer.[118] Such activities did not always enjoy official approval, particularly where the retail of rum eroded the discipline of the troops: at the siege of Louisbourg, Admiral Edward Boscawen blamed the army women for selling rum and causing widespread drunkenness. He wrote to Amherst: 'I wish that pernicious liquor banished from your camp, I know the women of the Highlanders, & the Royals to be notorious sutlers.'[119] At Fort Stanwix, the long-suffering Major Clephane warned the 'Married Women' of the garrison that should any of them be discovered selling rum, he would not only 'turn them out of their Hutts; But will

117 Orderly Book, Fort Stanwix, 1 February to 9 April 1759 (GD 125/34/4, fol. 14). Women who accompanied Braddock's expedition also banded together in an effort to obtain 'Exorbitant Wages' ('Halkett's Orderly Book', in *Braddock's Defeat*, pp. 76–7.

118 See GCMs, Quebec, 25 September 1761 (WO/71/71); Fort Edward, 15 July 1757 (WO/71/65); Louisbourg, 24 August 1758 (WO/71/66).

119 Letter written on board the *Namure*, Gabarus Bay, 17 June 1758 (CKS, U1350/028/15).

Cut them of the King's Provision & chase them Shamefully away'.[120] Orders issued at Albany in the following February banned non-commissioned officers, soldiers or their wives from keeping a 'Sutling House or Booth where Liquor of any kind is sold'. Anyone disobeying was warned to 'expect the Consequences'.[121]

The presence of women and children with the battalions added a degree of domestic normality to army life. However, women could also prove a focus for rivalry and strife amongst the soldiery. As the case of Quartermaster Fraser has already demonstrated, such friction might end in violence. On other occasions women triggered disputes that were more farcical than tragic. For example, wrangling amongst wives at Niagara led to Sergeant Cameron, a 'brave fellow' of the 44th Foot, spending three months in jail on an unproven accusation that he had disparaged the garrison's commander, Lieutenant-Colonel William Eyre. Cameron's confinement stemmed from homely circumstances. Upon his arrival at Niagara, Eyre announced that he had heard Mrs Cameron was a very good woman, and wanted her to wash for him. However, Eyre soon changed his mind, as Mrs Cameron was in fact the worst laundress he had ever engaged. In consequence, Lieutenant Daniel Disney was sent to inform Sergeant Cameron that he must part with his wife. Cameron considered this 'a very hard Message, having lived with her Sixteen years & having a little Boy in the Regiment to take care of'. Later that day Cameron was confined on a charge of insolence, and Disney delivered another message from the furious Eyre, 'that the Colo was no Bishop or Pope, therefore could not take upon him to divorce the wife from the Husband, but he swore she never should come where he had anything of a command'. The hapless Cameron had been arrested after the appearance of an anonymous note reporting that 'a fellow who wears a serjeant's coat' had claimed eight or ten officers of the garrison intended to write to General Gage to have Major Beckwith and Lieutenant-Colonel Eyre 'broke' for turning his wife out of the garrison and confining him wrongfully. Cameron believed that Mary Colhoun, who had previously complained about his wife, wrote the mischievous message. According to another soldier's wife, Nancy Anderson, when Sergeant Cameron discovered his spouse in tears at the prospect of being ejected from the fort he had merely offered the innocent assurance that four or five officers would recommend her to General Gage's service instead. Cameron was cleared of any fault or misdemeanour and acquitted. The court members were plainly exasperated by the entire affair; they observed that in the interest

120 Orderly Book, Fort Stanwix, 11 November 1758 – 30 January 1759, in GD 125/34/7, fol. 4.

121 'Monypenny Orderly Book', in *BFTM* (June, 1971), p. 167.

of Sergeant Cameron the case could have been dealt with sooner by a Regimental Court Martial.[122]

Lads like Cameron's son provided a ready source of future recruits, so reinforcing the notion of the regiment as 'family'. Soldiers' sons were sometimes enlisted as drummer boys before reaching their teens. For example, Archibald Brunton was just ten years old when recruited by the 58th Foot at Quebec in May 1761. It is highly likely that this lad was the son of another drummer, Thomas Brunton: both served in Lieutenant-Colonel Howe's company in the following year.[123] Such children faced the same dangers as the soldiers in the ranks: Anstruther's casualties included William Thomas, who had been born at the fortress of St Philips on Minorca and was aged eleven upon his enlistment at Quebec in October 1759.[124] Like drummer John Fawcett of the 47th Foot, who was shot through the knee at Quebec, these youngsters had been 'born in the Army'.[125] Drummer boys were also recruited amongst the civilian population. John Hardman, a 'labourer' from County Cavan, was twelve years old when enlisted by the 22nd Foot in 1755; three years later drummer Hardman was wounded in the head at Louisbourg. Hardman's 32 years in the ranks had likewise embraced 'the whole of the american Rebellion', leaving him 'worn out in the service'.[126] Thomas Hall, a 'ribbon weaver' from Coventry, was just nine years old when enlisted in 1756. Hall had accompanied the Duke of Richmond's 72nd Foot to the siege of Havana, where he was wounded in the foot and arm. After eight years in the 72nd, Hall served another 24 in the 7th Foot before appearing at Chelsea in 1788. Besides the wounds he sustained as a teenager on Cuba, Hall suffered from the privations endured while held prisoner during the War of Independence and was also 'afflicted much with the Rheumatism'.[127]

Rights and resistance

Despite the draconian discipline of the British Army, soldiers were none the less quick to protest when they considered that their traditional 'rights'

122 See GCM, Oswego, 7 August 1760, in WO/71/46.

123 WO/25/435, fols 66–7; Muster of 58th Foot, Staten Island, 9 June 1762, in WO/12/6710, fol. 52.

124 Thomas died on 19 December 1762, while on passage from Havana (WO/25/435, fols 72–3).

125 When examined at Chelsea on 18 March 1760, Fawcett was aged 33 and had nineteen years of service (WO/120/4, p. 565).

126 WO/121/1, Board of 12 May 1787.

127 Of Hall's service, nineteen years had been spent as drum major and sergeant, suggesting that he began his army career as a drummer boy. Hall was aged 41 when discharged at Edinburgh Castle on 24 June 1788. See Chelsea Board of 14 July 1788, in WO/121/4 and WO/116/9.

had been flouted; for example, they proved notoriously reluctant to undertake extra fatigue duties without suitable compensation. Charles Morrison and John Johnstone of the 43rd Foot were both charged with disobeying orders and inciting a mutiny after they urged their comrades to refuse a wood-cutting detail unless they were paid for it.[128] John Anderson of the Royal Americans ran into trouble when he refused orders to clear rough ground at Saratoga, finding it unreasonable to do 'two Dutys in one day'.[129] Soldiers who considered that they were being pestered with unnecessary toil were apt to express their resentment through grumbling, and by grudging obedience: for example, when Lieutenant George Otter of the 4/60th ordered some men to make brooms with which to clean the guard tent, the response was distinctly half-hearted: the soldiers lamely claimed that they did not know how to make brooms, and proved so recalcitrant that Otter was obliged to call upon the services of his own servant.[130] Amherst subsequently sought to regulate the question of payment for extra duties: orders issued in the summer of 1759 fixed the daily rates of pay for soldiers employed as artificers and labourers on such works as the construction of storehouses, barracks and hospitals. Other tasks considered as 'the soldiers work & never paid' none the less earned each man a prized gill of rum.[131] As General Thomas Gage pointed out four years later, under the 'Custom of the Army' soldiers expected extra pay for all work carried out on behalf of 'the Publick'.[132]

Soldiers were also likely to protest when conditions of service became intolerable, or the 'contract' under which they had enlisted was breached. For example, inadequate rations at Oswego in the summer of 1755 prompted a mass demonstration by the men of Shirley's Regiment. Grenadier Patrick Carney was prominent among 'about two or three hundred soldiers' who gathered to demand 'their full allowance of Provisions'. Ensign Mountgarret, who was punched and stoned when he confronted the men on the parade, was told that 'they were going for their Right ... they were all of one Mind, and they would have it'. On the day following this 'riot', another grenadier, Ebit Roberts, had asked his comrades to sign a petition informing their officers that if the allowance

128 Both were sentenced to 1,000 lashes. GCM, Halifax, 13 February 1758, in WO/71/65.

129 Anderson was found guilty of mutiny and sentenced to 1,000 lashes. GCM, Fort Edward, 30 August 1757, in WO/71/66.

130 GCM, Lake George Camp, 21–2 August 1758, in WO/71/66.

131 Orders, Albany, 21 May 1759 (CKS, U1350/016/1, fol. 6). These orders were repeated at Albany on 1 June 1761, with the proviso that the men could not expect rum unless they were 'Employed in Wet Work' or the weather was severe enough to warrant an allowance (CKS, U1350/016/2).

132 Gage to Secretary-at-War Welbore Ellis, New York, 9 December 1763, in WO/1/5, fol. 322.

was not improved 'they propos'd to go off'.[133] Further insight into the concept of 'soldiers' rights' can be gained from the contents of an anonymous 'mutinous' letter addressed to Lieutenant-Colonel John Darby of the 17th Foot. Although received by Darby in the summer of 1759, the threatening note apparently voiced gripes that had surfaced a year earlier during the siege of Louisbourg; at that time the men had been 'very much discontented' with Darby's announcement that they were to lose one shilling and nine pence from their weekly pay to cover the cost of fresh provisions, spruce beer and washing. The letter demanded that Darby

> [firstly] Countermand the order, of the non commissioned officers carrying sticks to the Parade, and that no Officer is on any pretence to Strike a Man; if they Commit a Crime, the articles of War are to be put in Execution. 2d. That they are to be paid off their pay and arrears of pay 'till the Day the accts. are made up to. 3d That as Duty and fatigue is so hard ... the men can't get time to Cook their Victuals ... [however] any Duty of fatigue that is requisite to Carry on the Seige with vigor we are all able and Willing to Undergo without the least murmur, and that any Man that refuses any Necessary Duty or Fatigue all good Soldiers will allow to be punished to the Utmost severity ...

Darby was warned that if he did not immediately comply with these instructions the regiment would 'joyn together as one Man and take your life the first opportunity, as also the lives of some others'.[134]

Humble members of the rank and file did not hesitate to petition their commanders more formally over a range of grievances. Foreigners amongst the Royal Americans approached Lord Loudoun to intervene on their behalf against their colonel, the unscrupulous Jacques Prevost. The 29 subscribers and 'many more' of their comrades had been recruited by Prevost in Germany under the 'special agreement' that they would be paid *6d.* a day while on passage from Europe to America. However, at the end of the fifteen-week voyage, Prevost had not only reneged on his promise, 'but Threatened Several with Punishment when they talked to him about this pay'. Hearing that Prevost was now leaving America, the anxious petitioners begged Loudoun to secure them their 'Lawful ... and Righteous Demands'.[135] As a letter written to Loudoun in July 1757 by a private soldier drafted into the same regiment reveals, such appeals also

133 Carney and Roberts were both charged with mutiny. They received 700 and 500 lashes respectively. GCM, Oswego, 1–2 September 1755, in WO/71/42.

134 GCM, Fort Edward Camp, 20 June 1759, in WO/71/67.

135 See LO 5812: Petition of John Donner et al., New York, 22 April 1758.

played upon the paternal relationship between officers and men: emphasising that Loudoun was both 'Our Father as well as Commander in Cheif in North America', this man hoped and expected to receive the arrears he was owed.[136] It was a foolish officer who shrugged off such demands without giving them due consideration. That same month, men of Pepperrell's 51st Foot who had been drafted into the Royals lobbied Loudoun for the pay that was due to them before their capture at Oswego in 1756.[137] Although by no means satisfied with the details of these claims, Loudoun none the less authorised the transfer of funds to settle the accounts of men possessing certificates from their officers. The warrant stipulated that it was 'Just & equitable the same should be paid to Prevent discontent amongst his Majesty's Troops'.[138] Loudoun had little choice in the matter: as he explained to the Duke of Cumberland, had he ignored these men's demands 'they would probably have mutinied'.[139]

Particular resentment was felt by those soldiers who were denied their discharges despite having served beyond the term for which they had enlisted. Such was the case with John Ledby and Henry Sample of Gage's Light Infantry, who both deserted in the summer of 1762. In defence, Ledby claimed that he had been enlisted by Captain Quintin Kennedy in Pennsylvania on 20 December 1758, to serve for three years. Ledby had been unable to obtain a certificate of his enlistment at that time, or since, because of Kennedy's frequent absences from the regiment. Sample said that when he was enlisted Kennedy did not give him a certificate of his terms, but promised before his servant Charles Adams – the only other witness – that he would have his discharge in due time. When Adams left the Army, Sample had again applied for his certificate to Kennedy, 'who flew in a Passion and Confined him in the Guard at Ticonderoga'. Kennedy had released Sample the following day, promising on his 'word and honour' that he should be discharged when his term of enlistment expired: however, Kennedy was soon after captured by the Indians and Sample had not seen him since. Another man recruited by Kennedy in December 1758, Edward Stork, had enlisted for two years, or the duration of the 'Expedition against Canady'. Like the others, Stork had no certificate: on applying for his discharge, Captain George Le Hunt 'laughing told him, as he had no Certificate, he could do nothing for

136 Petition, Halifax, Nova Scotia, 10 July 1757 (LO 3924).

137 'The Petition of the Serjeants, Corporals and private Men of the Late Major General Sir William Pepperrell's Regiment', camp near Halifax, 31 July 1757 (LO 4008).

138 Loudoun to Deputy Paymaster-General William Johnston, Halifax, 7 August 1757 (LO 4137/8).

139 Letter begun aboard the *Winchelsea* at sea, 16 August, finished New York, 17 October 1757 (LO 4240).

him'.[140] James McLean, who was drafted into the 27th Foot from the 47th in the summer of 1763, went off that December. In defence, McLean said he had enlisted in 1755 at Philadelphia for three years: on that occasion he received a certificate signed by the recruiting officer but lost it with his knapsack during the amphibious assault at Gabarus Bay in 1758. At the time of his drafting into the Inniskilling Regiment, McLean had thrice applied to Major Ralph Spittal for his discharge, but to no avail; he subsequently absconded because of 'the good pretensions he had to his Discharge from his former Regiment'.[141] Another reluctant draft, Peter McLean, had been transferred from the 44th Foot to the 28th Foot in August 1763, despite having enlisted at Lancaster, Pennsylvania, in 1757, 'according to the general Proclamation at that time, to serve for the space of Three Years'. He had a certificate of his terms of enlistment from the recruiting officer 'which he lost, with all the rest of his things at the Battle of Niagara in the Woods'. When the regiment was reduced in 1761, McClean had applied for his discharge, only for Lieutenant-Colonel Beckwith to decree that the old and disabled men had to go first. At the next reduction, in August 1763, the irascible Beckwith bluntly told McClean that neither 'he, nor mankind should have their Discharge, who had not Certificates'.[142]

Even where a soldier did receive an enlistment certificate, and the precious scrap of paper had survived the hazards of campaign life, there was no guarantee that this would secure his discharge. Thomas Sherby of the 35th Foot, who was tried for desertion after leaving his regiment in August 1761, showed the court a certificate from Lieutenant Maurice Herbert dated 15 December 1756, proving that he had been enlisted for three years. Sergeants John Hutchison and Richard Smurphit of the 35th both testified to the authenticity of the certificate, and confirmed that Sherby was 'always looked upon as a man inlisted for three Years'. At Quebec, Sherby had repeatedly applied to Lieutenant-Colonel Fletcher and other officers for his discharge, without receiving a reply. Sherby finally resolved to put his case before Amherst himself; however, while on his way to see the General at Albany he met a Dutchman who dissuaded him from this course of action. Sherby worked for the Dutchman for some time, but was later turned in as a deserter. Despite his certificate, he was sentenced to 500 lashes.[143]

140 Both Ledby and Sample were found guilty and sentenced to 500 lashes each. Stork, who was also charged with robbery, was ordered to be shot at the head of the regiment; the others were pardoned. See GCM, Montreal, 31 July 1762, in WO/71/71.

141 Guilty, 1,000 lashes. GCM, Montreal, 4 April 1764, in WO/71/74.

142 McClean, who received a very good 'character' from his officers, was sentenced to 1,000 lashes, but Gage remitted the punishment (GCM, Montreal, 26 June 1764, in WO/71/74).

143 See GCM, Camp on Staten Island, 24 October 1761, in WO/71/71.

An overdue discharge likewise rankled with William Harris of the 1st Battalion of the Royal Americans as he garrisoned Detroit in 1762. A volunteer enlisted for four years, Harris had now been 'most unjustly Detained near seven' in what he regarded as 'a second Egyptian Bondage'. Addressing himself to his commanding officer, Henry Bouquet, the irate private did not mince his words. He wrote:

> it has always been my simple opinion that a Gentleman haveing true notions of honour would by no means Brake his promise, as in so doing he not only forfeits his honour, but Greatly Disapoints the poor person depending thereon, it is a great misfortune to poor soldiers that Gentlemen of good Rank in the army will Derogate so much as to make an hundred fair promises Without the least intention of Ever performing one of them.

Harris had received such 'false promises of Officers' since early July 1760, but with no more prospect of being discharged than if he had been a raw recruit. Hardships faced by soldiers in such remote 'Back Posts', combined with ill-treatment from their officers, were enough to make the men 'hate the service'; indeed, Harris would have absconded long ago were it not for Bouquet's promise, and the likelihood of giving a lead which others would imitate. However, Harris added, his patience was now exhausted; although obliged to winter at Detroit, he would expect his discharge with the spring.[144] The outbreak of 'Pontiac's War' in the summer of 1763 prolonged the service of many soldiers isolated in frontier posts, and claimed the lives of others. At the height of the conflict Bouquet reported a 'Spirit of discontent and desertion' among the Royal Americans at Fort Pitt: these men had demanded their discharges, but the 'necessity of the Service' prevented compliance.[145] When Lieutenant-Colonel Augustine Prevost of the 3/60th transferred his battalion from Havana to Florida in the following month he informed the Secretary-at-War that more than 150 men were now calling for the discharges to which they were entitled: however, as Prevost's position in occupying the former Spanish territory remained 'so critical', he was unable to meet their requests.[146]

There was also widespread bitterness at the unequal distribution of the fabulous wealth won at the costly siege of Havana. As James Miller observed, precious little of the city's booty – reputedly worth £4 million – was seen by the NCOs and private soldiers, 'owing to the two commanders in chief, sharing one third of the whole, between them!'; whether this

144 Letter of 23 November 1762, in Add. MSS 21,648.
145 Bouquet to Amherst, 26 August 1763, in Add. MSS 21,634, fol. 365.
146 Prevost to Secretary-at-War, Pensacola, 7 September 1763, in WO/1/19, fol. 271.

was 'consistent with equity . . . and whether after the most extraordinary fatigues, in such a climate, the blood of britons, should be lavished, to agrandise, individuals' were questions best left to posterity. According to Miller, when the Havana prize money was distributed, sergeants received just 22 dollars and privates a mere eleven – less than it had cost them to buy water during the siege. Lingering resentment later surfaced at Quebec, where the survivors of the 15th Foot were reviewed by Governor Murray at his farm. Murray ordered a pint of wine for each man of the depleted battalion and addressed himself to one of the grenadiers, 'of whom he used to take notice, with you B——r I did not know you, you look so black!' The sunburned veteran's reply gave voice to the prevailing mood of cynicism: 'we have been on black service, and have got very little white money for it!'[147]

Such simmering discontent soon boiled over in the most dramatic expression of 'soldiers' rights' that the 'American Army' had witnessed. With the coming of peace, the government decided to reverse the policy by which soldiers serving in America received rations gratis, instead stopping the men 4*d*. a day – *two-thirds* of the pay they actually pocketed after existing deductions – to cover the cost of provisions. This penny-pinching was more than the troops could stomach; from Florida to Canada the announcement triggered grumbling and open hostility.[148] In several posts, the officers believed that the new policy would place their men under extreme hardship, and were therefore reluctant to enforce it without further orders. At Quebec, the most important garrison on the continent, the announcement of the stoppage on 18 September sparked a spontaneous mass mutiny. That very evening, after roll-call, the garrison 'assembled to a man' to protest before Governor Murray's house. When some officers intervened and drew their swords, the soldiers ran to the barracks, collected their arms, and marched 'in good order, with drums beating' towards the St John's Gate. There they encountered Murray; having attempted in vain to assemble the pickets, he was accompanied by only a handful of officers and sergeants. Murray harangued the men, but they refused to listen and instead 'loudly declared their resolution to march to New York' and put their case to General Amherst himself. The mutineers proved well disciplined: although muskets were fired, and several officers manhandled, there was no killing, plundering, or even drunkenness. Through the 'urgent solicitations of the officers' the soldiers

147 'Memoirs of an Invalid', pp. 68–70; 77–8.

148 On this episode see P. E. Kopperman, 'The Stoppages Mutiny of 1763', in *WPHM*, LXIX (1986), 241–54. See now also P. Way, 'Rebellion of the Regulars: Working Soldiers and the Mutiny of 1763–1764', in *WMQ*, LVII (2000), 761–92. Prof. Way's detailed treatment appeared too late to be considered in the above analysis; however, our assessments of the mutiny's causes and significance are in broad agreement.

were finally persuaded to march to the grand parade, where Murray addressed them 'file by file'. Despite Murray's efforts to appease them, the men refused to submit to the stoppages. Sensing some 'glimpse of good humour', Murray ordered the men back to their barracks, where they should 'behave as soldiers ought, till their grievances were laid before the commander in chief'.[149] That night passed quietly, and next day Murray gathered his officers and NCOs, emphasising the 'necessity of reducing the Soldiers to obedience, or perishing in the attempt'. On the following day, Murray again faced the assembled garrison on the grand parade and demanded an explanation for such mutinous conduct. James Miller of the 15th Foot has left a vivid description of the scene:

> One of the 60th Regt, who was their commander, and spokesman, replied that they did not intend to mutiny, no men, were more attached to their King, and Country, or could have a greater regard for the Governor and all their Officers. But they consider'd it as the heighth of injustice, after having at the risk of their lives, conquer'd countries, in every climate, that now on a general peace, the reward is want and misery, which unavoidably must be the case, should four pence pr day be stopped from their pay, for Provisions, What is left to provide cloathing, proper for this severe climate? Better to die on a gibbet! than perish by inches.

Murray responded with 'good words', promising that the men would not be charged for their rations until the King's pleasure was known.[150] The governor was none the less determined to reassert his authority. Next morning, when the battalions paraded once again, Murray read them the *Articles of War*, stressed the seriousness of their behaviour, and 'declared his fixed resolution ... to oblige them to submit, or to die in the attempt'. According to an officer eye-witness, Murray went to the head of the 15th Foot's grenadier company, and promised to kill the first man who refused to obey his orders. The governor's firm stance proved effective. The grenadiers were ordered to march between two royal colours, in token of submission, which they did and 'returned with chearfulness, to their duty'; this example was followed by the rest of the men. The crisis now past, Murray declared that the garrison had 'recovered their character as good soldiers, and restored the battalions to their colours'.[151] Perhaps the

149 'Extract of a letter from an officer at Quebec, to his friend in Edinburgh', 12 November 1763, in *Scots Magazine, 1763* (Appendix), pp. 722–3.

150 'Memoirs of an Invalid', p. 81.

151 *Scots Magazine, 1763*, p. 723.

most striking aspect of the whole affair is the high degree of organisation and discipline demonstrated by the mutineers. Indeed, one commentator considered that the episode did honour to Governor Murray and the 'distressed soldiers' alike. The mutineers had dismissed all their superiors 'even to the sergeants and corporals, not desiring them to run any risk in their distressed cause, and sent them to assist the Governor in his critical Situation'.[152] The restraint shown by the mutineers, coupled with widespread recognition of the fundamental justice of their cause, probably explains why even the ring-leaders escaped punishment following the restoration of order.

Although obliged to bow to authority, the Quebec mutineers and those redcoats who voiced their discontent at other posts had not protested in vain. Faced with the crisis of a dangerous Indian war on the western frontier, Amherst took it upon himself to reduce the proposed stoppage to two pence half penny per ration: even this partial climb-down failed to mollify the garrisons of Nova Scotia. In December, Amherst's replacement as commander-in-chief, Thomas Gage, said that although the disturbances associated with the stoppages dispute had been quelled in Canada and elsewhere, the garrisons at Halifax and Louisbourg had persisted in their opposition despite the reduction.[153] It was not until May 1764 that Gage was able to report the submission of the hardliners at Louisbourg.[154]

The determined and well-organised reaction to the 1763 stoppages was an impressive demonstration of solidarity amongst the surviving soldiers of the 'American Army': the episode served notice that such veterans considered themselves entitled to a degree of respect, and were prepared to defy the Army's fearsome discipline to secure it. The mutineers' methods mirrored those characteristic of the labour disputes that regularly disturbed the peace of Georgian England. By employing mass demonstrations backed by the threat of violence, the irate redcoats adopted the same techniques as civilian workmen seeking to exert pressure upon their employers; indeed, it would be difficult to find a more clear-cut example of a phenomenon that Eric Hobsbawm has dubbed 'collective bargaining by riot'.[155]

Evidence examined in this chapter indicates that the prevailing perception of the British soldier in America during the Seven Years War

152 Intelligence dated Quebec, 28 September 1763, in ibid. According to this source, the mutineers chose a grenadier of the 47th Regiment, named Walker, as their 'commander'.

153 Gage to Welbore Ellis, New York, 9 December 1763, in WO/1/5, fol. 322.

154 Kopperman, 'Stoppages Mutiny', *WPHM* (1986), p. 252.

155 E. J. Hobsbawm, *Labouring Men* (2nd edn., London, 1968), pp. 5–10. For a discussion of the Georgian labour dispute, see J. Stevenson, *Popular Disturbances in England 1700–1870* (London, 1979).

requires considerable revision: rather than resembling mindless military marionettes jerking on the strings of an oppressive disciplinary regime, the redcoats retained a powerful sense of their own worth. As James Miller observed, although the Army in general was composed of 'Ignorant boys, who having enter'd into that line of life, at an early age, know no other', such men still possessed sufficient feelings 'to know when slandered, or treated with contempt'.[156]

[156] 'Memoirs of an Invalid', p. 134.

4

The environmental parameters of American compaigning

As James Fenimore Cooper observed in the opening sentence of his romantic classic *The Last of the Mohicans*, 'It was a feature peculiar to the colonial wars of North America, that the toils and dangers of the wilderness were to be encountered before the adverse hosts could meet.'[1] Although readers who venture beyond the novel's first pages have sometimes found the author's prose as laborious to negotiate as the terrain it describes, Cooper's verdict would surely have earned a wry nod of agreement from many a veteran of the 'American Army'. Such soldiers included Lieutenant Thomas Stirling of the Royal Highland Regiment. Just hours after a trio of Anglo-American armies converged on Montreal, Stirling penned a revealing letter to his brother back in Scotland. If this young officer felt any euphoria at the crowning triumph of British arms, it was clearly outweighed by relief at the apparent termination of an irksome and unglamorous war. He wrote:

> long may Peace reign here for sure god never intended any war should be carryed on by any other beside the natives for the soldiers are wrought like horses & the officers can acquire no honour in a Country where as the New England people says, every Tree is a fort and every man a Gen[era]ll.

It was Stirling's fervent hope that his regiment would be posted for home and then to Germany, 'for I am heartily tired of this Country as is every officer in it'.[2] Given these sentiments, it was perhaps fortunate that Stirling lacked the ability to divine the future. Far from returning to Europe that autumn, the Black Watch was destined to remain in America for a further seven years, serving through the costly Caribbean campaign of 1762, and subsequently playing a key role in quelling Pontiac's War. For Stirling himself the perils of the wilderness were to loom particularly large: in 1765 he led a detachment of Highlanders from Fort Pitt to Fort

1 James Fenimore Cooper, *The Last of the Mohicans* (first published 1826; Penguin Popular Classics edition, London, 1994, p. 11).

2 Thomas Stirling to William Stirling of Ardoch, Camp at Montreal, 9 September 1760 (GD 24/1/458/1).

Chartres in the Illinois – an exceptionally punishing round trip of 3,000 miles via the Ohio and Mississippi.[3]

Long before the capture of Montreal it was widely acknowledged that American campaigning made unusually heavy demands of both officers and men. Writing from the New York frontier in 1756, Captain Charles Lee of the 44th Foot told his sister that 'the severest work in Flanders is allow'd by those who have serv'd there to be a party of pleasure compar'd to this'.[4] That same year, Braddock's short-lived successor as commander-in-chief in North America reported that although the troops had been placed under 'stoppages' to cover the cost of their camp equipment, he hoped that this gear could be provided by the government instead, 'as the Service here, is in almost every respect of a more severe nature than what the British Troops are generally set upon'.[5] Similar sentiments were voiced by French soldiers. Volunteers from the *troupes de terre* who participated in a raid against Fort Bull, near Oswego, in March 1756 considered the fatigues endured to be far greater than those encountered during the notoriously arduous retreat from Bohemia during the War of the Austrian Succession.[6]

West Indian campaigning was likewise associated with extreme hardships. As Richard Gardiner of the Marines testified, the troops who conquered Guadeloupe in 1759 were 'exposed to Dangers they had never known, to Disorders they had never felt, to a Climate more fatal than the Enemy, and to a Method of fighting they had never seen'.[7] Thousands of officers and men of the 'American Army' campaigned in both of these theatres. For example, by 1762, Bragg's 28th Foot boasted some five years of American service, having fought at Louisbourg and Quebec before sailing for the West Indies. Reporting the regiment's exploits on Martinique, Lieutenant-Colonel Hunt Walsh observed that the change in climate had done nothing to diminish the spirit of his men. However, Walsh was now irate that promotion denied to such seasoned veterans

3 See Colonel David Stewart, *Sketches of the Character, Manners and Present State of the Highlanders of Scotland; with Details of the Military Service of the Highland Regiments* (2 vols, Edinburgh, 1822) I, 355 (note). Stirling's own detailed journal of this gruelling mission can be found in RH 4/22/2.

4 Lee to Miss Sydney Lee, Schenectady, 18 June 1756, in *NYHSC: Lee Papers*, I, 3.

5 William Shirley to Henry Fox, New York, 13 January 1756, in WO/1/4, fol. 33. It was in recognition of these extraordinary hardships that soldiers serving in North America during the Seven Years War were allowed their rations free of charge.

6 Montcalm to Madame la Marquise du Boulay, Quebec, 20 May 1756. See 'Montcalm's Correspondence', in *Report of the Public Archives [of Canada] For The Year 1929* (Ottawa, 1930), pp. 31–108; 43.

7 *An Account of the Expedition to the West Indies in 1759, by Major Richard Gardiner of the Marines* (Birmingham, 1762), p. 90. Two years later, the island's governor, Campbell Dalrymple, reported that his officers were 'exposed to numerous hardships & inconveniences they know nothing of in Europe' (Dalrymple to Secretary-at-War Charles Townshend, Basseterre, 4 August 1761, in WO/1/19, fol. 69).

as himself had gone to wealthy youngsters who were raising their own regiments back in England. To add insult to injury, Walsh continued, the pay of the 'American' officers failed to cover their expenses, or take account of 'the unhappy climate' and long spells 'confined to Transport ships' that they were obliged to endure.[8]

Amidst the mainland wilderness such difficulties were exacerbated by the savage nature of the guerrilla warfare that smouldered as a backdrop to the rare confrontations between rival forces of regulars. Whilst it would be misleading to suggest that the 'conventional' warfare of *ancien régime* Europe lacked episodes of brutality and wanton destruction, it was none the less appreciated that North American backwoods campaigning involved unusual risks.[9] The dangers inherent in such warfare were analysed in the *Annual Register* of 1763 during a discussion of Henry Bouquet's hard-fought Bushy Run campaign of that summer: those who had only experienced European campaigning, it argued, could 'Scarcely form an idea of what is to be done and endured in an American War'. When waged over the cultivated and inhabited countryside of Europe, war amounted to a contest for glory, rather than grim struggle between bloodthirsty foes. Across the Atlantic a very different situation prevailed:

> in an American campaign everything is terrible; the face of the country, the climate, the enemy. There is no refreshment for the healthy, nor relief for the sick. A vast unhospitable desert, unsafe and treacherous, surrounds them, where victories are not decisive, but defeats are ruinous; and Simple death is the least misfortune, which can happen to them. This forms a service truly critical, in which all the firmness of the body and the mind is put to the severest trial; and all the exertions of courage and address are called out.

It followed that although the events of these 'rude campaigns' lacked the dignity of a 'regular' war, they none the less remained 'more interesting to the heart, and more amusing to the imagination'.[10] Whether fabricated or genuine, stirring stories of endurance in the untamed wilderness and grisly tales of massacre at the hands of 'savages' certainly found an avid

8 Walsh to —— [General Philip Bragg?], Martinique, 31 January 1762, in WO/1/19, fol. 156.

9 For correctives to the enduring belief that European warfare during the 'Age of Reason' was essentially 'limited' and 'indecisive' see J. Black, *European Warfare, 1660–1815* (London, 1994), pp. 67–86; J. Childs, *Armies and Warfare in Europe, 1648–1789* (Manchester, 1982), in particular Chapters One and Four (pp. 1–27; 143–73); also A. Starkey, 'War and Culture, a Case Study: The Enlightenment and the Conduct of the British Army in America, 1755–1781', *War and Society*, VIII, 1 (May, 1990), 1–28; 1–5.

10 *Annual Register; or a view of the history, politicks, and literature of the year 1763*, pp. 28–9.

readership among the civilised inhabitants of London and New York.[11] This chapter, and that which follows, seeks to address some of those traits that combined to excite such curiosity, and which together rendered the experience of the 'American Army' so different from that of those British soldiers who served elsewhere.

Tackling America's terrain

In an age when polite society was demonstrating a growing awareness of the 'picturesque', and the formal gardens of country houses were being reshaped into realistic landscapes, it is unsurprising that some British officers should have been struck by the rugged grandeur of the American wilderness; but in contrast to the carefully crafted vistas of Lancelot 'Capability' Brown and his imitators, this was nature in the raw.[12] Hence, when Lieutenant John Grant of the Black Watch marched from Saratoga to Fort Edward in the summer of 1759, the path ran 'amidst splendid forests', while 'Nothing could be more wild or grand' than the virgin wilderness surrounding Fort Stanwix on the Mohawk River.[13] For Charles Lee of the 44th Foot, the sheer scale of 'Nature in every Article' made a deep impression as he surveyed the countryside about Schenectady: set beside the rivers and lakes of America, those of Europe were mere 'rivulets and brooks'.[14] The scenery encountered in the Caribbean could also earn the praise of men with a taste for natural beauty: when George Durant rode into the Guadeloupe countryside after the conquest of the island he found the 'Prospects most Noble & romantick'. Durant recorded viewing 'Hills whose tops reach'd the Clouds cover'd with Stately Woods of ten thousand different shades of Green'.[15]

It was one thing to admire such impressive landscapes, quite another to surmount them in the face of armed opposition. Describing the formidable terrain encountered during the brief Martinique operations of January 1759, one officer emphasised that even the Highlands of Scotland were dwarfed by the island's 'Woods, Mountains, Canes and continued

11 A particularly lurid specimen of the genre, written by Peter Williamson, a private soldier captured at Oswego in 1756, went through five editions in as many years. See *French and Indian Cruelty* (1st edn, York, 1757; 5th edn, Edinburgh, 1762).

12 For the increasing interest in 'sentimental scenery' in Britain, see Langford, *A Polite and Commercial People*, pp. 471–2.

13 'Journal of Grant', pp. 44–5.

14 Lee to Miss Sidney Lee, Schenectady, 18 June 1756, in *NYHSC: Lee Papers*, I, 3.

15 See 'George Durant's Journal', in *Army Records Society: Military Miscellany I*, p. 54.

Ravins'.[16] Guadeloupe presented an equally difficult theatre of operations. Upon the landing of Hopson's army the island's defenders had retired to a mountainous pass known as the *Dos d'Âne*, or 'Ass's Back'. As Richard Gardiner recalled, the steep approach route was 'interrupted by broken Rocks, and furrowed by a Variety of Gullies, which were extremely difficult to pass, and which rendered it very hazardous to make any Attempt to force it'. In consequence, the French had dubbed the position the '*Ne plus ultra* of the English Army' – and so it proved, obliging the baffled Barrington to transfer his operations elsewhere.[17]

For soldiers accustomed to the level roads, open countryside and winter quarters of the Low Countries, the interior of North America offered a prospect more daunting than dramatic. Confronted with the 'Trees, Swamps, and Thickets' of the Virginia backwoods, an officer with Braddock's expedition observed that 'the very Face of the Country is enough to Strike a Damp in the most resolute Mind'. As the column probed further into the wilderness, so this despondency deepened, prompting the same officer to a despairing admission: 'I cannot conceive how War can be made in such a Country.'[18] Some years after Braddock's army had been slaughtered on the banks of the Monongahela, Colonel John Forbes pondered the same puzzle. Forbes, who had served as quartermaster-general in Flanders, confessed that the more he thought about 'the natural surface of North America', the more he was 'embarrassed' by the problem of pursuing offensive operations against the French.[19] Forbes was soon grappling with this dilemma at first hand as he prepared to lead his own campaign against Fort Duquesne. Between Forbes's base at Carlisle and his objective on the Ohio lay 'an immense Forest . . . intersected by several ranges of Mountains, impenetrable almost to any thing humane save the Indians'. Weeks later, Forbes remained exasperated at 'those hellish woods'.[20] Winter was well advanced before Forbes's exhausted column finally occupied the fire-blackened ruins of the abandoned fort. Lieutenant-Colonel Henry Bouquet summarised both the fatigues of the campaign and the magnitude of the General's achievement:

> The obstacles which we had to surmount were immense, 200 miles of wild and unknown country to cross; obliged to open a road through woods, mountains, and swamps; to build forts along our lines of march for the security of our convoys; with

16 'Journal of an Officer', enclosed in Hopson to Pitt, Guadeloupe, 30 January 1759, in *Correspondence of Pitt*, II, 28.

17 Gardiner, *Expedition to the West Indies*, pp. 30–31.

18 Anon, *The Expedition of Major General Braddock To Virginia* . . . (London, 1755), pp. 13–14; 16.

19 Undated memorandum in Forbes's hand (summer 1757 to spring 1758), in RH 4/86/2.

20 Letters from Forbes at Carlisle to Pitt, 10 July, and to Bouquet, 9 August 1758, in *Writings of Forbes*, pp. 141; 171.

> an active and enterprising enemy in front of us, elated by his previous successes, and superior in this type of war. It was only with infinite trouble that we were able to transport provisions, artillery and munitions.[21]

Before his selection to head the expedition against Fort Duquesne, Forbes had served as adjutant-general at the New York Headquarters of Lord Loudoun; during his inglorious tenure as commander-in-chief Loudoun had grasped the fundamental importance of logistics for any effort to breach the natural defences shielding New France, and bequeathed an efficient commissariat to his successors. Adequate stockpiles of supplies – and a well-organised bateau and wagon service to transport them to troops operating hundreds of miles from the settlements – formed the mundane foundations upon which Britain's ultimate victory would be constructed.[22] Loudoun's initiatives had been prompted by the signal failure of his predecessor, William Shirley, to develop a reliable system of military supply and transport: such logistical inefficiency had undermined Shirley's own 1755 campaign against Niagara and contributed to the demoralisation of Oswego's garrison during the following winter.[23] Despite his failings, Shirley was none the less responsible for the advancement of an officer destined to play a key role in developing the Army's logistical capacity in America. A native of Nova Scotia, John Bradstreet had served in his province's resident regular unit, the 40th Foot, before gaining a captaincy in Pepperrell's 51st. Bradstreet's knowledge of local conditions bolstered a flair for wilderness warfare that was second only to his vaulting personal ambition. In the dismal summer of 1756 Bradstreet raised and led a corps of armed bateaumen who not only forwarded supplies to the starving defenders of Oswego, but also fought off a determined French and Indian effort to intercept their return journey. Bradstreet's versatility and drive subsequently won him the confidence of Loudoun and his successors, along with promotion to lieutenant-colonel and deputy quartermaster-general in America.[24]

21 Bouquet to the Duke of Portland, Fort Duquesne, 3 December 1758, in *Papers of Bouquet*, II, 620.

22 For the British Army's evolution of dependable transport and supply services in North America see K. L. Parker, 'Anglo-American Wilderness Campaigning 1754–64: Logistical and Tactical Developments' (unpublished PhD dissertation, Columbia University, 1970); also D. J. Beattie, 'The Adaptation of the British Army to Wilderness Warfare, 1755–1763', in *Adapting to Conditions: War and Society in the 18th Century*, ed. M. Ultee (Alabama, 1986), pp. 56–83.

23 Supply and transport under Shirley is addressed in T. Thayer, 'The Army Contractors for the Niagara Campaign, 1755–1756', in *WMQ* (1957), pp. 31–46.

24 On Bradstreet's chequered career see W. G. Godfrey, *Pursuit of Profit and Preferment in Colonial North America: John Bradstreet's Quest* (Waterloo, Ontario, 1982).

Loudoun's reforms and Bradstreet's remarkable talents made war in the wilderness possible; they did not make it easy. Blazing a trail through the North American wilderness always involved much back-breaking toil: crude roads were hewn through the forest; whaleboats and bateaux poled and rowed along rivers and lakes, or man-handled across the 'portages' between watercourses; provision barrels repeatedly loaded and unloaded from wagons and boats; and fortified supply dumps built to anchor the Army's methodical advances. Much of this fatigue fell to the provincials, but the redcoats bore their share: the consequences are reflected in the cases of disabled soldiers who sought pensions from Chelsea Hospital. Typical were the applications from veterans of the 27th Foot: Sergeant Joseph Shulton, a 44-year-old from Derby, was 'crushed by a batteau', whilst Armagh-born Robert Lucas, 37, suffered his injuries after being 'Disabled by the fall of a tree'. Another soldier of the Inniskilling Regiment to succumb to the rigours of American campaigning was John Kingsley: a 35-year-old weaver from Manchester, Kingsley appeared at Chelsea on 21 February 1761, having been 'Straind at Working at a Fort'.[25] Scientific analysis of skeletons excavated at the site of Fort William Henry – believed to be the remains of soldiers killed during the 'massacre' of 1757 – also testified to the hardships of army life: herniated discs in the vertebrae, and scars on the bones of the shoulders and limbs where muscles were torn away, all suggested that the men concerned had endured a demanding regime of manual labour.[26]

The expertise acquired in such gruelling and painstaking fashion was applied to striking effect in the 'British logistical triumph' of 1760, when three Anglo-American armies each succeeded in negotiating Canada's forests, lakes and rivers to rendezvous at Montreal.[27] But for all its celebrated synchronicity, even this final campaign against New France had teetered upon a logistical knife-edge. It was early August before the main army under Amherst had assembled its bateaux and provisions at Oswego. Operations had been hampered by unusually low water levels that obliged officers and men alike to drag boats over the shoals. In consequence, the troops had already undergone unprecedented 'Fatigue and Labour' before the descent upon Montreal even began.[28] The ensuing campaign was more finely balanced than the benefit of hindsight suggests: according to James Abercrombie of the Royal Highlanders, Murray's force from Quebec played a crucial role in distracting French attention from Amherst's advance: had the Oswego army encountered stiffer

25 WO/120/4, pp. 270–71 (Board of 18 March 1760); WO/116/5, fol. 59.
26 See D. R. Starbuck, 'Anatomy of a Massacre', *Archaeology*, XLVI (1993), 42–6.
27 See, Beattie, in *Adapting to Conditions*, pp. 81–2.
28 Dr Richard Huck to Loudoun, Oswego, 6 August 1760 (LO 6258).

opposition, 'the stopping us One month would have effectually frustrated our attempt, for want of Provisions'.[29]

Proof of the British Army's growing ability to penetrate the most arduous terrain was offered during the Cherokee Wars of 1760–61: in these campaigns redcoats scaled some of the loftiest mountain passes in the Appalachian range. Describing his second foray into Cherokee territory in the summer of 1760, Colonel Archibald Montgomery reported that he had never before seen 'so difficult and strong [a] country'.[30] Returning to the same area in the following year, Lieutenant-Colonel James Grant's command was forced to scale a path so narrow that the men had no option but to march in Indian file, '& if their feet had slipt, they were in Danger of falling Down a Precipice'. Eventually, the column breasted the Catouchee Mountain, 'One of the highest & perhaps the steepest in america'. In the event the expedition had succeeded in ravaging the Cherokee towns, although the men were so exhausted they could barely crawl, and even the allied Indians were 'knocked up'.[31] At the conclusion of the campaign Grant reported:

> the Officers and men I believe are most heartily tired of the Service ... the Fatigues and Hardships have been considerable, 33 days without Tents, heavy Rains frequently during that time, short allowance of Bread, long Marches, bad Roads, hard Duty, & what the men thought worse than all no Rum.[32]

According to Major Alexander Monypenny of the 22nd Foot, by the time these troops limped back to base they were 'all jaded and worn out'. On every march it was necessary to transport some 300 men on the pack-horses employed to carry provisions; about half of the troops 'had not a bit of shoe left'.[33]

Montgomery had initially depended upon the logistical support of a ponderous wagon train; when subsequently faced with terrain that was impenetrable to wheeled vehicles he had improvised pack-saddles for his draught horses. As his casualties mounted, Montgomery proved unable to transport both wounded and provisions and was obliged to turn back before breaking Cherokee resistance.[34] By contrast, Grant's reliance

29 Abercrombie to Loudoun, St Valerie, 17 October 1760 (LO 6270).
30 Montgomery to Amherst, Fort Prince George, 2 July 1760, in WO/34/47, fol. 17.
31 'Journal of the March & Operations of the Troops ... upon an Expedition from Fort Prince George against the Cherokees' (entries for 26/28 June 1761), in WO/34/40, fols 96–7.
32 Grant to Amherst, Fort Prince George, 10 July 1761, in WO/34/47, fol. 94.
33 Monypenny to Captain James Dalyell, Fort Prince George, 14 July 1761, in NAM MSS., 7905–48.
34 See Mante, *History of the Late War*, pp. 287; 292; also Corkran, *Cherokee Frontier*, pp. 211; 214.

upon a more flexible train of pack-horses allowed his column to remain in the field for long enough to fulfil its objectives. The techniques developed by the British Army during 1760–61 anticipated those that would be employed more than a century later by the Republic's foremost Indian fighter, General George Crook; however, despite the success of this 'innovation' against the Apache of the Southwest during the 1870s and 1880s, Crook's advocacy of pack-mules failed to sway his more orthodox colleagues.[35] Indeed, the United States regulars on the late nineteenth-century frontier proved notably reluctant to adapt conventional practice to local requirements – a charge that cannot be sustained against Britain's 'American Army' of the Seven Years War.

Climate, clothing and wildlife

The difficulty of the terrain encountered by the redcoats was only increased by the extremes of climate experienced in the Americas. On occasion, meteorological conditions manifested themselves with awesome violence: in August 1759, while marching from Albany to Oswego, the 2nd Battalion of the Royal Highland Regiment encountered 'a most terrible storm'. Rain, wind, thunder and lightning combined to produce a 'terrifick' scene that left the boldest men trembling. The storm sent trees toppling in every direction, and the adjutant was lucky to escape being crushed. Because of the constant threat of Indian ambush, the men were obliged to use their bonnets to cover the locks of their muskets and thus bareheaded 'bore the pelting of the pitiless storm'.[36]

The redcoats were often ill equipped for America's varied climate. In the West Indies and on the continent alike, humidity sapped the strength of soldiers clad in coarse woollen uniforms and burdened with cumbersome and constricting accoutrements.[37] In the backwoods of Virginia and Pennsylvania, the 'Heat of the Country' was such that the men of Braddock's expedition could scarcely carry their muskets.[38] In fact, Braddock had soon taken steps to lighten his redcoats' load. Orders issued at Alexandria on 8 April 1755 instructed the soldiers to leave shoulder

35 On Crook see R. M. Utley, 'Indian–United States Military Situation, 1848–1891', in *Handbook of North American Indians: Volume IV, History of Indian White Relations*, ed. W. E. Washburn (Washington, 1988), pp. 163–84; 172–3.

36 'Journal of John Grant', p. 46.

37 According to a meticulous survey conducted by Lieutenant Alexander Baillie of the 1/60th in 1762, the fully accoutred grenadier carried arms, ammunition, clothing, equipment and rations weighing some 65 lb 12 oz. See R. May and G. Embleton, *Wolfe's Army* (Reading, 1974; revised edn, 1997), p. 35.

38 *Expedition of Major-General Braddock*, p. 15.

Figure 2 Typical British infantryman on the eve of the Seven Years War. This 1753 engraving of *Corporal Jones loading musket* was executed by Lt William Baillie of the 13th Foot from his own drawing made while on recruiting duty in Worcester. It gives a good indication of the redcoat's appearance before the uniform and equipment modifications resulting from American campaigning. © Copyright The British Museum.

belts, waist belts and swords in store, and greatly reduced their spare kit. On the following day officers were ordered to supply the men with 'bladders' or discs of thin leather 'to put betwixt the Crown & lining of their Hatts to keep Them from the heat of the sun'.[39] Similarly, when the 17th Foot arrived in America from Ireland during the summer of 1757, the useless sidearms and heavy buff belts were swiftly jettisoned and stored at Albany.[40] Although contemporary pictorial evidence is sparse, written accounts indicate that British troops in America regularly dispensed with the pipeclay and powder of peacetime soldiering, resulting in a dramatic

39 See 'Halkett's Orderly Book', in *Braddock's Defeat*, p. 77.

40 Having dispensed with their belts, the men removed the slings from their muskets and fixed them onto their ammunition pouches instead, 'which eas'd the men much'. See Lt-Col. Arthur Morris to John Forbes, Fort Edward, 24 September 1757 (GD 45/2/21/3).

transformation of the redcoat's conventional appearance. In November 1757, John Knox recorded that a wood-cutting party returning to Annapolis Royal, Nova Scotia from an outlying fort bore little resemblance to British regulars: in contrast, they 'made as droll and grotesque an appearance as a detachment of Hungarian or Croatian irregulars'. These soldiers sported long beards, misshapen tricornes, and ragged, motley clothing; some wore brown or blue 'watch-coats'; others had only their thread-bare uniforms to cover them. While regretting this deterioration, Knox appreciated that it was inevitable for men obliged to discard the 'uniformity of the clean, smart soldier, and substitute, in his stead, the slovenly, undisciplined wood-hewer, sand-digger, and hod-carrier'.[41] On occasion, uniform modifications stemmed from official policy. An extreme example of this trend emerged in Abercomby's army on Lake George in the summer of 1758. At the instigation of the charismatic Brigadier-General Lord Howe, the brims of the men's tricorne hats and the long skirts of their uniform coats were both cropped short in keeping with the hair of their heads. Swords were replaced by handier tomahawks, and spare clothing was minimised to leave space for extra rations and ammunition.[42]

From 1759 onwards it became common for the regulars on both the continent and in the Caribbean to campaign in their waistcoats during the summer, with essential provisions rolled up in a blanket worn bandolier-fashion.[43] Other steps were taken to counter the debilitating heat of the tropics: the commanding officers of regiments assembled for Monckton's Martinique expedition were told to 'order the Lining to be riped out of the mens Cloaths, the Lapels to be taken off and Skirts cut Short'.[44] With their faded rust-coloured jackets, rolled blankets and slouched hats, by 1762 the redcoats of the 'American Army' would have looked more like the 'Johnny Rebs' of a century later than their contemporaries on duty across the Atlantic. During the Martinique operations John Grant of the Royal Highland regiment wryly noted this contrast in appearance between veterans of the American fighting and those troops recently sent from Europe. He observed that

41 *Knox's Journal*, I, 109.

42 See Huck to Loudoun, Albany, 29 May 1758 (LO 5837); also Pierre Puchot, *Memoirs on the Late War in North America Between France and England*, trans. M. Cardy, ed. B. L. Dunnigan (Youngstown, New York, 1994), p. 139.

43 Amherst recommended this 'Active Service' dress for both the troops bound for Martinique and the task-force sent to recapture St John's, Newfoundland. See Amherst to Monckton, New York, 9 November 1761, in CO/5/61, fol. 490; Amherst to Lt-Col. Amherst, New York, 13 August 1762, in Fyers, 'Loss and recapture of St John's Newfoundland', *JSAHR* (1932), p. 189.

44 Orders, Bridgetown, Barbados, 26 December 1761, in 'Hamilton Notebook' (NAM MSS 6707–11), pp. 211–12.

> the [officers of the] 76th who had lately arrived from the taking of Bellisle landed in white Spatterdashes, Gorgets & spontoons and sashes, and trusted their provisions to their servants. We older campaigners accustomed to backwoods expeditions took care to equip ourselves with haversacks containing our provisions and were ridiculed by the gay gentlemen for so doing.[45]

Regimental clothing was supposed to be replaced annually, although this represented the ideal rather than the reality. The neglected garrison of St John's, Newfoundland had not received any clothing for two years: when a consignment of new uniforms finally arrived in 1757, it proved insufficient to clothe all the men adequately.[46] Clothing was often delivered in less than pristine condition. For example, of items shipped over from Ireland for the 17th Foot, many of the men's breeches had been chewed by rats, and some of the shirts were 'Spoiled by carriage, having holes rub'd through them'.[47] American campaigning took a rapid toll of such shoddy garb. Reporting upon the condition of the 44th Foot in the autumn of 1756, Loudoun noted that the 'Regt is in Rags', although he conceded that these lean and tattered veterans looked like soldiers none the less.[48] Troops based in remote outposts could expect to fare far worse: by the summer of 1759, the men of Montgomery's Highlanders left at Fort Pitt following Forbes's expedition were in a deplorable condition. According to Captain James Robertson,

> The men have Scarcely a Stitch of Cloathes, their Coats were all in Raggs before the end of last Campaign, they had few or no hose then; their Plaids were extremely bad, and now numbers of them have none at all; so that they are oblige[d] to sleep at Night in the Raggs they ware all day whether wet or dry.[49]

As these descriptions indicate, British soldiers were poorly clad to face the rigours of the harsh continental winters. On occasion, extra clothing was issued to troops required to undertake operations in severe weather. For example, a detachment of some 1,200 men assembled on the New York frontier in February 1758 were each to receive a woollen cap and stockings, along with mittens and a flannel waistcoat, plus sufficient

45 'Journal of John Grant', p. 72.

46 R. Edwards to Barrington, on board the *Gosport*, Plymouth Sound, 21 March 1758 (WO/1/1, fol. 302).

47 Return of the clothing and camp necessaries of the 17th Foot, December 1757 (GD 45/2/38/11).

48 Loudoun to Cumberland, Albany, 2 October 1756, in *Military Affairs in North America*, p. 235.

49 Robertson to Maj.-Gen. John Stanwix, Pittsburgh, 6 August 1759, in *Papers of Bouquet*, III, 504.

coarse cloth to make a pair of leggings and socks.[50] Such generous provision was untypical: on a scout to Ticonderoga in March 1759, men of the Royal Regiment and 4/60th were obliged to cut up their blankets and wrap them around their frozen feet.[51]

For officers and men alike, the severity of the North American winters proved difficult to endure. In December 1757 the ageing Lieutenant-Colonel Arthur Morris of the 17th Foot begged permission to retire from the 'fatigues of a military Life, & a Climate I am not equal to', adding ruefully some days later that the cold was too much for his 'Minorca Constitution'.[52] In the New Year, Lieutenant-Colonel John Donaldson of the 55th Foot appended a heartfelt *post scriptum* to his account of recruiting in Connecticut: 'Its so confoundedly cold I can scarcely hold ye pen in my hand.'[53] The onset of winter could take the troops unawares: John Grant remembered how conditions in late November 1759 changed so suddenly that men marching to quarters in villages on the Hudson 'had their hair & body's frozen to the ground in their tents'.[54] For the fuel-starved British garrison of Quebec, that same winter proved particularly cruel. Governor Murray noted that between 17 and 24 December 1759, some 153 men had been 'frost-bit' while on sleighing parties in quest of firewood: Christmas Day itself was marked by the return of a party of 200 men, every one of whom had been 'frost-bit more or less'.[55] Sufferers in the garrison included Lieutenant John Knox of the 43rd Foot, whose cheeks and nose were frequently frozen 'as to be totally void of sensation'. James Miller of the 15th Foot was frost-bitten in the right foot while on guard duty, but 'by taking it in time, lost no bones'.[56] Other victims of that winter were less fortunate. Amherst reported how a detachment on the march from Crown Point to Ticonderoga 'suffer'd in an extraordinary manner from the intenseness of the cold'. No less than 166 men were frost-bitten; next day the surgeon was 'obliged to cut off above 100 Toes'.[57]

50 GD 45/2/21/16B.

51 Thomas Gage to Frederick Haldimand, Albany, 27 March 1759, in Add. MSS 21,662, fol. 24.

52 Morris to John Forbes, Albany, 13 and 19 December 1757 (GD 45/2/21/10–11).

53 GD 45/2/26/4: Letter from Albany, 28 January 1758.

54 'Journal of John Grant', p. 52. Two soldiers froze to death during the night of 2 December 1759 (*Journal of Amherst*, p. 196).

55 *General Murray's Journal of the Siege of Quebec, from 18 September, 1759 to 25 May, 1760*, ed. E. C. Kyte (Toronto, 1939), p. 15.

56 *Knox's Journal*, II, 295; 'Memoirs of an Invalid' (CKS, U1350/Z9A), pp. 32–3.

57 Amherst to Pitt, New York, 17 February 1760, in *Correspondence of Pitt*, II, 257–8. These men belonged to the 27th Foot (Gage to Haldimand, Albany, 11 February 1760, in Add. MSS 21,662, fol. 37). Of 55 discharged men of the 27th who hobbled along to Chelsea a year later, more than half had been maimed by frostbite. See WO/116/5, fol. 59, Board of 20 February 1761.

Throughout the Americas, the local wildlife added to the discomforts of soldiering. Describing the conditions he encountered in Nova Scotia in the early 1750s, Henry Grace of the 47th Foot warned that new arrivals were 'almost devoured' by insects: 'whoever goes to the Side of the Woods, cannot see twenty Yards before their faces in calm Weather, there are such Clouds of Muskitoes and black Flies'.[58] Arriving in the same district in 1757, Lieutenant Knox soon underwent assault from tormenting 'myriads of musketas'. These insects proved so 'immensely troublesome' that it was necessary to don long linen trousers and furnish hats with makeshift mosquito nets in an effort to keep the tiny assailants at bay. Employing jargon appropriate to the brutal guerrilla warfare of the province, Knox noted how neither 'that odious insect' the mosquito, nor its more diminutive 'pupil' the black fly, gave any 'quarter either by day or night'.[59]

Looking back on his Caribbean service in the ranks of the 4th Foot, 'Jonas' concluded: 'One may very properly say, that a man living in any of those islands, is never free from one sort of vermin or other troubling him.' Mosquitoes abounded in sheltered wooded and low-lying areas; besides their lethal role in transmitting malaria, these insects proved a frequent irritant, swarming so densely that sentries were obliged to fan themselves continually with a leafy branch. Once, when in pursuit of deserters, 'Jonas' encountered a rattle-snake measuring three yards in length with a girth to equal 'the small of a man's leg'. Toads, lizards, land-crabs, scorpions, cockroaches and ants all contributed to harass the soldier, but 'Jonas's' own personal *bête noirê* was the chigger. These 'Jiggers' proliferated amidst the sugar canes, but as 'Jonas' recalled, 'I need not have said where they were to be found, for they too soon found us.' Such fleas burrowed into the flesh of the feet, laying a 'bag' of eggs which had to be dug out with great care if it were not to burst and prove still more troublesome. Many of Guadeloupe's barefoot slaves had lost nearly all their toes to chiggers; Jonas witnessed the death of a soldier resulting from drastic surgery to remove 'a vast number' of these mites.[60]

Diet and disease

Like all troop concentrations before the enforced hygiene and mass medication of the twentieth century, the 'American Army' suffered from crippling levels of sickness. For example, of the 18,385 'effective' rank and

58 *Life and Sufferings of Grace*, p. 7.
59 *Knox's Journal*, I, 64; 158; 175; 319.
60 *A Soldier's Journal*, pp. 150–60.

file contained in 21 battalions and seven independent companies of regulars on the continent in the autumn of 1757, no less than 2,964 (16 per cent) were listed as sick. Certain battalions were particularly hard hit: of the 777 'effective' soldiers in Webb's 48th Foot – already 263 below the official establishment – some 424 (55 per cent) were on the sick list.[61] Although dysentery and typhus could wreak havoc in a crowded and filthy camp, a surprisingly persistent problem stemmed from scurvy. This ailment resulted from a deficiency of fresh meat and vegetables: it therefore proved the scourge of an army that usually neglected to supply either, and instead relied heavily upon a basic diet of salted pork and hard bread.[62] Scurvy is popularly viewed as the bane of the Georgian seafarer, yet the rations consumed by British soldiers in the Americas were frequently as bad as any issued on board a man-of-war, and were sometimes one and the same. For example, after storming Fort Louis, Guadeloupe in February 1759, the men of the 42nd dined upon ship's beef and bacon 'which had been in store since the former war and Biscuits full of maggots, so that after endeavouring to clear them of vermin we used to wet them and toast them'. Even the water was so putrid that the men could not drink it without holding their noses.[63] Rations provided on the mainland were often little better. Braddock's expedition was obliged to dine upon '*Indian* Corn, or mouldy Bisket' with 'rusty Salt Pork, or Beef'.[64] Examining supplies assembled for Forbes's 1758 expedition, Deputy Commissary of Stores Draper Simon Wood reported most of the pork to be 'extream bad'; indeed, 'some was entirely rotten & Stunk' while much of the flour consisted of meal, and some was not even worthy of that description.[65]

The Army's unbalanced diet made considerable inroads upon manpower. Returns compiled for ten regiments in October 1757 reveal 627 scurvy cases.[66] These 'Scorbutick men' had been sent to the thriving farmlands of New Jersey, where fresh provisions were available to aid their recovery. As this response demonstrates, the link between diet and disease was common knowledge within the 'American Army'. British soldiers sometimes took considerable risks to supplement their monotonous and ultimately lethal rations: orders issued at Albany in 1757 noted frequent robberies in the neighbourhood with 'sheep Fowl & Roots of all kinds

61 Since the previous month's return was compiled the regiment had lost 27 men dead and discharged another 26. See returns, 24 October 1757 (GD 45/2/13/3).

62 The soldier's weekly ration allowance consisted of seven pounds of beef or four pounds of pork; seven pounds of 'biscuit bread', or the same weight of flour; six ounces of butter; three pints of 'pease'; and half a pound of rice. See *Knox's Journal*, I, 48 (note).

63 'Journal of John Grant', pp. 35–6.

64 *Expedition of Major General Braddock*, p. 15.

65 Wood to Forbes, Carlisle, 9 June 1758, in RH 4/86/1.

66 These included 22 women. There were also another 69 listed as 'ill' plus 335 'recovering' (GD 45/2/36/1).

carried off in the Night'. For the future, guards would be posted on the targeted settlements with orders to fire on pilferers and arrest all soldiers strolling from camp after dark.[67] In August 1761 Gage's headquarters at Montreal was likewise inundated with complaints after soldiers toting swords, knives and pistols plundered local gardens and orchards to the terror of the inhabitants.[68] On occasion, opportunist foraging received official blessing. For example, in September 1758, when troops marching through Massachusetts halted near an apple orchard, Amherst sanctioned the despatch of scrumping squads from each platoon to gather fruit for their comrades.[69] A more systematic attempt to improve the Army's health was the practice of issuing 'spruce beer' whenever it could be manufactured. This beverage, which was brewed from molasses and boiled spruce boughs, was prized as an anti-scorbutic. On 2 August 1759, following the capture of Ticonderoga, Amherst noted with relief: 'our brewery things at last got up ... [and] will save several lives'.[70] With proper precautions, scurvy could be kept at bay. On the eve of his Quebec campaign James Wolfe praised the efforts of the officers at Halifax in providing fresh or frozen beef and spruce beer throughout the preceding winter, an 'excellent precaution' that had contributed to preserve these battalions from 'utter ruin'.[71]

At remote interior posts fresh provisions were all too rare: such isolated commands proved as vulnerable to scurvy as the crew of an ocean-going man-of-war. For example, by March 1759, the men of Fraser's Highlanders had spent four months in garrison at Fort Stanwix on the Mohawk River: they were now beginning to suffer from scurvy, 'having had no Vegetables, or scarcely any fresh Provisions during the Winter, or likely to have any for some Time'. Major Clephane had written to General Amherst, whose response was to request Colonel Fraser to send fresh men to relieve the sick. By the following February the garrison at Fort Ontario, Oswego was ailing with the scurvy. In a belated effort to combat the problem, Thomas Gage had ordered the Commissary-General, Robert Leake, to provide 'great Quantitys of Garden seeds' to be sent to Oswego and Niagara as soon as possible. Without delay, Colonel Haldimand at Fort Ontario was to construct a 'very large Garden, sufficient for the Service of all the troops'.[72] Leake also assembled all

67 Orders, Albany, 5 October 1757, in RH 4/86/1 (General Order Books of Loudoun's Commands).
68 'Brigade Order Books, 1 June, 1760 – 17 May, 1763', in *Hervey's Journals*, p. 151.
69 *Journal of Amherst*, p. 87.
70 Ibid., p. 149. For Amherst's account of the recipe for this brew, see ibid., p. 152 (note).
71 Wolfe to Pitt, *Neptune*, Halifax Harbour, 1 May 1759, in Willson, *Life and Letters of Wolfe*, p. 424.
72 Gage to Haldimand, Albany, 15 March 1759 and 11 February 1760, in Add. MSS 21,662, fols 22; 36.

the vinegar, onions and lime juice that could be collected for despatch to the 'Posts & Forts in the Lakes and Rivers'.[73] This tardy emphasis upon cure rather than prevention came too late for more than 280 men who died at these distant posts during that winter.[74] Once again, it was the beleaguered garrison of Quebec that suffered most heavily of all. Private Miller of the 15th Foot recalled that 'numbers fell Sick, and the scurvy made a dreadful havock among us'. In his journal for 9 March 1760, the city's governor noted that the illness was still on the increase, despite every effort to prevent it: orders had been given regarding the boiling and preparation of the salt pork, as it was impossible to obtain fresh provisions or vegetables.[75] According to Murray, on the eve of the battle of Sainte-Foy, the Quebec army had been 'melted down to Three Thousand fighting men, by a most Inveterate Scurvy'.[76] In the colourful words of one of these survivors, John Johnson of the 58th Foot, the redcoats who marched out to fight the French on 28 April amounted to 'a poor pitiful handful of have [half] Starved, Scorbutic Skeletons'.[77] The lessons of that grim winter did not go unheeded: in the following year the commanding officers of regiments destined for the attack upon Martinique were ordered to ensure that their men were supplied with vegetables, 'as it is so essential an Article to the preservation of their healths'.[78] Following the conquest of Canada, Britain's army of occupation in the St Lawrence Valley had lost little time in establishing a trade with the *habitants*: through fishing and fowling in their off-duty hours, many redcoats proved able to hoard their salted ration pork and then barter it for milk, eggs, alcohol or other goods. Such commerce raised opportunities for racketeering that did not go unexploited by business-minded and unscrupulous individuals: in 1762 William Pearce of the 4/60th was sentenced to death for stealing the King's provisions and then offering them to the locals for sale or exchange.[79] Trade of another kind helped to sustain those redcoats who manned remote stockades on the western frontier: such posts represented the very end of a hazardous logistical lifeline; from 1759 onwards their garrisons became increasingly dependent upon Indians for supplies of

73 Leake to Haldimand, Albany, 20 February 1760 (Add. MSS 21,728, fol. 44).

74 *Journal of Amherst*, p. 207.

75 *Murray's Journal of the Siege of Quebec*, p. 22.

76 Murray to Amherst, Quebec, 30 April 1760, in CO/5/58. On 24 October 1759, the rank and file fit for duty totalled 4,873, compared with 1,376 sick present or absent. By the following April the number of sick had risen to 2,898: there were now just 2,612 healthy private soldiers. There were also 347 sergeants and 184 drummers in the garrison, giving a total available manpower on 24 April of 3,143. This figure fell below the establishment by no less than 3,111 rank and file and six drummers. See CO/5/64, fols 90–91; 102–03.

77 'Memoirs of John Johnson', in *Siege of Quebec*, V, 120.

78 Orders, Bridgetown, Barbados, 21 December 1761, in 'Hamilton Notebook', p. 208.

79 Pearce was pardoned and three other men of the battalion were acquitted. See GCM, Montreal, 9 September 1762 (WO/71/71).

venison and corn. The British Army's Indian agents were employed to encourage participation in the trading system. In return for these essential foodstuffs, the tribes of the Ohio and Great Lakes were provided with coveted powder and shot.[80]

By the close of the Seven Years War other far-flung outposts had experienced a horticultural revolution. At Fort Ontario, Oswego, Major Alexander Duncan of the 55th Foot enclosed an extensive garden: enlisting the services of 'a sagacious old sergeant, who knew something of husbandry', the Major wrought a remarkable transformation: the garrison that had once proved a death-trap for so many redcoats now yielded bumper crops of produce. According to a daughter of the regiment, these vegetables 'throve beyond belief or example'. As a result the green-fingered redcoats of the 55th existed in a 'rough luxury' that permitted them to save much of their pay. Duncan's initiative was widely emulated; encouraged by a spirit of competition among rival military gardeners at Niagara, it ultimately spread to 'all the line of forts'.[81] The dietary dilemmas of the 'American Army' were not forgotten: during the Revolutionary War, British troops in America received regular issues of spruce beer, while all available space at Army posts was dedicated to the cultivation of vegetables.[82]

On the North American continent sickness maintained a slow but steady attrition. In the West Indies, by contrast, disease could ravage entire armies in a matter of months. Indeed, tropical illnesses – in particular malaria and yellow fever – wielded a major influence over the conduct of warfare in the Caribbean; their decisive role in baffling offensive expeditions was not lost upon defenders who aimed to resist long enough for nature to lend a hand against 'unseasoned' invaders. At no time were such infections more decisive than in the eighteenth century, when an upsurge in colonial trade saw the Caribbean become the 'crossroads of contagion' for an interchange of diseases between America, Europe and Africa.[83]

At the onset of the Seven Years War, the likely consequences for European armies and navies venturing into these biological killing fields were already notorious. Indeed, the 'American Army' included a handful of survivors of the disastrous West Indian campaign of 1740–42 which had foundered upon the costly siege of Carthagena: of the 14,000 Anglo-

[80] See M. N. McConnell, *A Country Between: The Upper Ohio Valley and Its Peoples, 1724–1774* (Lincoln, Nebraska, 1992), pp. 153–7.

[81] *Memoirs of an American Lady*, II, 74–7.

[82] R. A. Bowler, *Logistics and the Failure of the British Army in America 1775–1783* (Princeton, 1975), p. 8.

[83] See J. R. McNeill, 'The Ecological Basis of Warfare in the Caribbean, 1700–1804', in *Adapting to Conditions*, pp. 26–42; 30.

American troops involved, 10,000 lost their lives, with fewer than one in ten of these deaths resulting from combat.[84] Such veterans knew only too well that unacclimatised troops who were forced to endure the 'sickly season' could expect to pay a heavy price in dead and disabled. Given the high mortality sustained by regiments posted to the Caribbean, drastic measures were required to recruit the units forming the island garrisons. For example, fourteen convicts held in the Woodstreet Compter while awaiting transportation were pardoned after they agreed to enlist in the 49th Foot at Jamaica or the 38th on Antigua.[85] It was also common for soldiers convicted of desertion to be offered a reprieve upon enlisting with these regiments. However, the perils of Caribbean service were so infamous that some soldiers presented with this unenviable choice preferred to submit to their original punishment. For example, two men of the Earl of Loudoun's Regiment sentenced to 500 and 1,000 lashes for desertion were pardoned on condition of serving with Walsh's 49th Foot: both opted to 'kiss the cat' instead.[86] Lower physical standards than were customary for the Army were likewise considered acceptable for the West Indies garrisons. In 1757, when Colonel Walsh rejected recruits sent to Jamaica from England, he received instructions from the Duke of Cumberland to be less choosy in the future and instead 'entertain all Recruits, which your Officer shall send over, of whatever Country within the King's Dominions or Size they may be, provided they are able bodied and fit for the Service'.[87]

Private soldiers posted to the tropics had no choice in the matter; for officers prepared to shirk their duty absenteeism offered an escape route. In November 1761, when a detachment was mustered from the Guadeloupe garrison to join Monckton's Martinique expedition, the size of the force was limited to 350 men because there were insufficient officers to command it. As Guadeloupe's governor Campbell Dalrymple explained to the Secretary-at-War, 'I could send more men, if I had more officers.' Dalrymple had even been obliged to borrow a captain from one of the independent companies to accompany the contingent from the King's Own; that regiment had 'a Lieut-Col & five Captains in England', while the sole remaining captain was unfit for service. In fact,

84 For a detailed account of these operations, see Harding, *Amphibious Warfare in the Eighteenth Century*.

85 Barrington to the Earl of Holderness, 11 October 1757, in WO/4/54, p. 538. Of the limited number of felons recruited during the American War of Independence, many were sent to such unhealthy destinations. See S. Conway, 'The Recruitment of Criminals into the British Army, 1775–81', *Bulletin of the Institute of Historical Research*, LVIII (1985), 46–58; 46; 52–4.

86 Henry Fox to the Judge Advocate General, 2 September 1755, in WO/4/50, p. 423.

87 Barrington to Walsh, 5 February 1757, in WO/4/53, p. 173.

as Dalrymple informed Pitt, no less than 40 of the Guadeloupe officers were currently away from their units.[88]

However reprehensible, such truancy was at least understandable in the light of recent events. On the 1759 expedition to the West Indies, disease devastated the troops before they even reached their first objective of Martinique. By the time the battalions left the rendezvous at Barbados on 13 January they had already been reduced by a third to some 5,000 men. Captain Gardiner of the Marines explained: 'The Troops unaccustomed to the Climate, suffered greatly from *Fevers*, from the *Flux*, the Scurvy from the Use of Salt *Provisions*, and from an accidental *Evil*, the *Small-Pox*, which broke out amongst the *Transports*'.[89] Once established on Guadeloupe, the fever cases rose steadily. Hopson admitted that the 'great Number of sick' had proved so embarrassing that he was unsure how to act for the best; a month later the army had been reduced to 2,796 men fit for duty, a circumstance that Barrington considered to be a 'very melancholy Consideration'.[90] For those redcoats left behind in garrison this ordeal by illness continued until the territory was restored to France at the peace of 1763. In the autumn of 1759, Guadeloupe's governor, Byam Crump, tallied the death of eight officers and 577 men since Barrington's departure on 25 June, a mortality exacerbated by 'very sultry weather' and a lack of suitable lodgings for the sick.[91] Despite Crump's best efforts, the garrison continued to sicken and die: on joining the King's Own as a draft in May, 1760, 'Jonas' heard that the regiment had 'buried ... near three hundred men in the space of a year'.[92]

In 1762, when the conquerors of Martinique learned that Spain had now entered the war on behalf of France, the news was therefore greeted with foreboding by the army physician, Doctor Richard Huck. He remarked: 'A Spanish war gives me great concern; I am afraid we shall broil long in the Torrid Zone.'[93] Huck's gloomy forecast proved all too accurate: by May, the 11,356 'effective' rank and file on Martinique already included 2,209 (19 per cent) sick.[94] The subsequent Havana

88 Letters from headquarters at Basseterre, Guadeloupe, dated 18 November (WO/1/19, fol. 95) and 16 November 1761 (*Correspondence of Pitt*, II, 482).

89 Gardiner, *Expedition to the West Indies*, p. 4.

90 Hopson to Pitt, Basseterre, Guadeloupe, 30 January 1759, *Correspondence of Pitt*, II, 24–5; General Barrington to Pitt, Basseterre, 2 March, in ibid., 46.

91 Crump to Secretary-at-War Barrington, Guadeloupe, 4 October 1759, in WO/1/19, fols 32–3.

92 *A Soldier's Journal*, p. 68.

93 Huck to Captain Dalyell, Fort Royal, Martinique, 14 February 1762, in NAM MSS 7905–48.

94 Returns, 7 May 1762 (WO/17/1489/18). Writing six months later, and basing his prognosis on the intervening period, the director of the hospital on Martinique, Doctor William Russell, considered that the number of sick on the island and its dependencies would always average 450 to 500 men at any given time. See Russell to Governor William Rufane, St Peter's, Martinique, 19 October 1762 (WO/1/19, fol. 204).

operations sounded the death knell of the veteran 'American Army'. By the autumn, just 1,039 men remained fit for action under Albemarle: this corresponded with the rank and file strength of a single battalion at the original establishment. In some regiments, the number of healthy men was scarcely sufficient to fill a platoon. For example, although the ten companies of Talbot's 43rd Foot numbered 352 'effectives' – a figure already 248 short of establishment – no less than 327 (93 per cent) were on the sick list. Another veteran battalion of the 'American Army', the 48th Foot, was in little better condition: of 368 'effective' privates and corporals, just 28 (8 per cent) were 'fit for duty'.[95] When Captain Henry Moore of the 48th mustered his company on 11 December he was the only officer still standing: besides one sergeant and one drummer, just four privates remained fit for action.[96]

Medical care

The cataclysm at Havana highlighted the limitations of contemporary medical knowledge: despite the advocacy of preventive medicine by such eminent military physicians as Sir John Pringle, it would be more than a century before the science of bacteriology made it possible to identify the causes of the fatal infectious diseases that had swept through the 'American Army'.[97] Although increasing research was devoted to preserving the health of Britain's servicemen in the course of the eighteenth century, during the 'Great War for Empire' casualties on the mainland and in the Caribbean alike were only compounded by the inadequacy of the Army's medical provision. By the 1750s, medical care in each theatre of operations centred upon an itinerant 'general' hospital comprising a staff of experienced physicians and surgeons, backed by apothecaries, mates, nurses and orderlies. These personnel manned facilities that sometimes acquired a semi-permanent status: for example, the general hospital at Albany functioned from 1756 to 1760. Such rear-echelon establishments offered well-qualified staff and a reasonable level of care. However, most soldiers wounded or taken sick in the field were initially obliged to rely

95 Returns, 24 October 1762 (WO/17/1489/21).

96 Of the remaining rank and file on the muster, there were 24 sick plus three invalids recommended to Chelsea. See 'Order Book of Henry Moore'.

97 Pringle's influential *Observations on the Diseases of the Army* was first published in 1752. For the growing role of the Georgian armed services in testing the techniques of preventive medicine, see 'Swords and Ploughshares: The Armed Forces, Medicine and Public Health in the Late Eighteenth Century', in P. Mathias, *The Transformation of England: Essays in the Economic and Social History of England in the Eighteenth Century* (London, 1979), pp. 265–85.

upon the far more rudimentary aid provided at regimental level, whereby each battalion of infantry mustered a surgeon and his mate.[98] In the opinion of many military men, the paltry pay offered for such staff posts ensured that only the ignorant and lazy applied; inexperienced candidates often secured their positions through '*interest and mis-applied recommendation*'.[99] By no means all regimental surgeons conformed to the stereotype of drunken sawbones. Richard Huck, physician to the Army in America during the Seven Years War, began an outstanding career when he became surgeon to Lord Sempill's Regiment, serving with that unit in Scotland and Flanders before securing the degree of Doctor of Medicine and joining the 33rd Foot at Minorca.[100]

Even those regimental surgeons who demonstrated a zeal for the service were hampered by the inefficiency of medical supply for units in the field. In theory, provision was generous: stoppages from the troops furnished 'medicine money' of about £80 a year to cater for the needs of each battalion; regiments embarking upon foreign service also received a pair of 'chests of good and wholesome medicines as well Internal as External', along with a set of surgical instruments. Such stores were supposed to be replenished from the general hospital, but centralised stocks were not inexhaustible. Regiments deprived of their original allocation of medicines through enemy action sometimes requested replacements from Britain itself. For example, Webb's 48th Foot lost its medicine chests at the Monongahela in July 1755, although it was not until March 1757 that orders were issued for the despatch of substitutes.[101] Medical supply for far-flung units remained a problem throughout the war: in the winter of 1762, the surgeon responsible for two companies of the 1/60th in garrison at Niagara called for medicine chests to be renewed automatically on an annual basis, at the same time as units theoretically received their new clothing.[102] Those medical supplies that did reach the battalions in the field left much to be desired. Thomas Wilkins, the surgeon of the 35th Foot, lost all of his kit at the fall of Fort William Henry, being left '[not] so much as a Lancett'. Unable to acquire suitable medicines or instruments of any kind in America, Wilkins therefore applied to Barrington for replacements; however, he stipulated 'Good Instruments, as those sent out to

98 For a general discussion see N. Cantlie, *A History of the Army Medical Department* (2 vols, Edinburgh, 1974), I, 102–38; also P. E. Kopperman, 'Medical Services in the British Army, 1742–1783', in *Journal of the History of Medicine and Allied Science*, XXXIV (1979), 428–55.

99 Hamilton, *Regimental Surgeon*, I (preface), iii.

100 Anon, *A Short Account of the Late ... Dr Richard Huck Saunders, Physician, ...* (Edinburgh, 1786), pp. 8–9.

101 Barrington to the Apothecary-General, 16 March 1757, in WO/4/53, p. 363.

102 Dr James Stevenson to Bouquet, Niagara, 7 December 1762, in Add. MSS 21,648, fol. 468.

regimental Surgeons are quite bad, not fitt for use, so much soe, that I have known them fail frequently in an Operation'. Wilkins added that many of the medicines despatched in the regimental chests were 'of little use in this part of the World' and hoped that more useful alternatives could be substituted.[103]

Such provision was not calculated to meet the heavy demands of American campaigning. Men wounded far from the major hospital facilities were lucky to receive the most basic care: those casualties who escaped from Braddock's defeat had to wait four days before their injuries were even dressed; by then the hot weather had 'Ca[u]sed a great many magets in the mens wounds'. It was only on 22 July – nearly two weeks after the engagement – that the wounded received hospital treatment at Fort Cumberland.[104] A medical service which had functioned smoothly in Flanders rapidly buckled beneath the strain imposed by epidemic tropical illness. The defects of hospital provision were soon revealed during the West Indian campaign of 1759. By Guadeloupe's fall the hospital supplies sent out with Hopson had long since been consumed, and two of the regimental surgeon's mates were themselves dead. Crump believed that the high mortality suffered by the troops stemmed partly from the inexperience of the British surgeons in treating such disorders, a failing which had obliged him to place the hospitals under the regulation of a local French physician.[105] Although Jeffery Amherst praised the 'diligent care of the surgeons of the Hospital' at New York who dealt with the sick arriving from the West Indies in June 1762, the director of the hospital plainly foresaw problems: he had requested eight or ten surgeon's mates to be sent over from England, as few suitably qualified men could be found in America. Later that summer the arrival of the first brigade of Havana survivors swamped the medical facilities: not only was Amherst obliged to convert the barracks at New York, Elizabethtown and Amboy into hospitals, but he had been forced to seek assistance from the local civilian surgeons.[106]

Accounts left by survivors of the Caribbean operations of 1762 suggest that attention from the Army's overworked surgeons was desultory: the seriously wounded or sick were simply left to recover or die. For example, James Miller of the 15th Foot was grazed in the neck by a musket-ball at the storming of Martinique's Morne Garnier. Although superficial, Miller's wound provoked a swelling that prevented him from even

103 Wilkins to Barrington, Albany, 14 September 1757 (WO/1/973, pp. 1,191–2).
104 'Journal of Cholmley's Batman', in *Braddock's Defeat*, pp. 32; 34.
105 Crump to Barrington, Guadeloupe, 4 October 1759 (WO/1/19, fols 32–3).
106 Amherst to Charles Townshend, New York, 20 July and 23 September 1762, in WO/1/5, fols 240; 251.

swallowing water. The surgeon responded by sending Miller on board a hospital ship, where he 'remain'd in the same deplorable state three days'. Finally, when all hope of life was over, a 'Violent perspiration' caused the swelling to subside and permitted Miller to rejoin his unit.[107] Much of Miller's experience was shared by Robert Kirk of Montgomery's Highlanders, who contracted a fever during the campaign and left a harrowing account of hospital conditions:

> I was sent with a number ... on board the hospital ship, for the recovery of my health, where for want of fresh air and room to stir, they almost all died; the living were scarce sufficient to bury the dead ... you might see the corps thrown overboard by half dozens in a day, so that the sea was covered in dead bodies, for the Sharks (of which there were great plenty), to prey upon.

Having survived the hazards of the hospital ship and the subsequent voyage to New York, Kirk was billeted upon the Quakers who inhabited Long Island. Kirk, whose 'disorder was of the putrid kind, attended with a terrible swelling', was lucky enough to lodge with 'a very humane woman ... who took great care of me, [and] nourished me with everything that was salutary'.[108] Neither Kirk nor Miller had received anything more than perfunctory treatment at the hands of trained medical men. Other soldiers may have considered them fortunate in this respect: when John Grant of the Black Watch contracted a fever at Guadeloupe in 1759 he believed that he had survived despite rather than because of the attentions of the Royal Navy surgeons; these 'bled us profusley [and] would have killed us but luckily their ships were order'd of and we were saved'.[109]

As such testimonies indicate, the lethal disease environment of the Caribbean circumscribed the activities of the 'American Army' to a far greater degree than the physical barriers posed by the continent's mountains, lakes and forests. Indeed, many of those redcoats who succumbed to 'yellow jack' or malaria in 1762 had already sweated, strained and cursed as they toiled to surmount such hazards during repeated mainland campaigns. The skills necessary to negotiate the wilderness had not been acquired easily; British soldiers arrived in America geared to the conditions of Europe, and their process of adaptation had proved irksome and protracted. The redcoats' capacity to wage war on enemies shielded by

107 'Memoirs of an Invalid', pp. 56–7.

108 *The Memoirs and Adventures of Robert Kirk, Late of the Royal Highland Regiment, Written by Himself* (Limerick, 1770), pp. 73–4.

109 'Journal of John Grant', p. 37.

daunting natural defences none the less represented a remarkable achievement by the standards of the age, and should not be underestimated. As the weary Lieutenant Stirling of the Black Watch had observed following the conquest of Canada, God surely never intended Europeans to fight their battles across such a punishing landscape; yet as Stirling knew all too well, the British Army had ultimately demonstrated its ability to do just that.

5

The 'American Army' and Native Americans

In the early hours of 8 August 1759, some six miles downstream from the beleaguered city of Quebec, two alien cultures came face to face. The Honourable George Townshend, heir to a viscountcy, Member of Parliament for Norfolk, graduate of St John's College, Cambridge, and now Brigadier-General in the army of His Britannic Majesty King George the Second, found himself contemplating a captive Indian warrior. Townshend reported that this Indian had swum the ford below the Montmorency Falls 'with an Intention as we supposed to Scalp a Centry'. The brave had instead emerged from the river to find himself gazing into the muzzle of a vigilant redcoat's musket, and was dragged dripping before the aristocratic Brigadier. Townshend described the prisoner as 'a very savage looking brute & naked all too an arse Clout'. Efforts to communicate proved futile, even though 'there was several in the Camp that spoke Indian Language'. Plainly intrigued by this chance encounter, Townshend concluded his journal entry with a comment suggestive of wild beasts rather than fellow men: 'Most nights we hear the Indians Hollow in the Woods all about us'.[1]

Other sources provide a sequel to Townshend's anecdote. A French journal identifies the Indian as an Ottawa from beyond the Great Lakes, and tells how he was subsequently clapped in irons aboard a British ship of the line. It had been intended to send him home as a gift for King George, but one night, while his guards slept, he slipped his chains and, 'flinging himself out of a port-hole into the water, abandoned himself to the current'. Sentries on deck opened fire, and boats were launched to recover him, but to no avail.[2] Some idea of this evasive Indian's likely appearance can be gained from a remarkable series of water-colours that Townshend executed during the St Lawrence expedition. Already a noted political caricaturist, Townshend had found time to practise his skills

[1] 'The Townshend Papers' in *Siege of Quebec*, V, 191–281; 257. This Indian was more talkative than Townshend suggests, having 'confessed that his intention was to surprise two or three centries, and carry back their scalps, in order to recover his credit with Monsieur Montcalm, who had punished him for some misdemeanor' (*Knox's Journal*, II, 21).

[2] See 'Journal of the siege of Quebec', in *Northcliffe Collection*, pp. 222–66; *Knox's Journals*, II, 40.

Figure 3 These vivid sketches of Native Americans were made by Brigadier-General George Townshend during the 1759 Quebec campaign. *An Indian War Chief compleatly equipped with a scalp in his hand* bears a strong resemblance to the marble Indian warriors supporting the sarcophagus of the memorial to Townshend's brother Roger (killed at Ticonderoga in 1759) in the South Aisle of Westminster Abbey; although positive proof is lacking, a link seems likely between Townshend's paintings and Robert Adam's design for the monument. By courtesy of the National Portrait Gallery, London.

on the unusual profile of his brave but sickly young commander.[3] Townshend also sketched the hostile warriors who harried Wolfe's outposts. The surviving images represent the only known eyewitness impressions of North American Indians made by a British soldier during the Seven Years War.[4]

3 Examples are reproduced in C. Lloyd, *The Capture of Quebec* (London, 1959), pp. 55; 105.

4 For example, see Fig. 3. Life drawings of North American Indians remained 'extremely rare in England at this date'. See E. Harris, *The Townshend Album* (London, 1974), p. 25.

Townshend returned from America with an abiding interest in the Indians he had seen there. According to the poet Thomas Gray, whose own *Elegy* was destined to become bound up with the legends surrounding Wolfe's final campaign, Townshend's mementoes included an eleven-year-old Indian boy. Townshend was in the habit of introducing this youth as an after-dinner diversion for his guests. On one such occasion events took an alarming turn when the General produced a chest full of Indian weapons and other curiosities. At this,

> the Boy got to the box & found a scalp, wch he knew by the hair belong'd to one of his own nation ... grew into a sudden fury ... & catching up one of the scalping-knives made at his Master with intention to murther him, who in his surprise hardly knew how to avoid him, & by laying open his breast, making signs, & with a few words of French Jargon, that the Boy understood, at last with much difficulty pacified him.[5]

Although enacted amidst the peaceful surroundings of a mansion in rural England, the mayhem described by Gray none the less reflected something of the wider experience of British soldiers who met Native Americans on their own ground. These contacts occurred at the very period when such *philosophes* as Jean-Jacques Rousseau were debating the concept of the 'noble savage'.[6] Yet the idealised *bon sauvage* of the Parisien *salons* did not always resemble the reality found within the woods of America: on a frontier fraught with the potential for cultural misunderstandings, the very 'savagery' that fascinated so many Europeans could manifest itself in unpredictable and shocking fashion. This chapter examines the redcoats' varied exposure to Native American culture and considers the impact of such contact upon the outlook and conduct of the 'American Army'.

Fraternisation and segregation

In the course of their rambling American campaigns British soldiers encountered a broad cross-section of humanity. Within a period of months, a soldier like John Grant could come face to face with both the institutionalised cruelty of West Indian slavery ('unlimited power being in the hands of the masters') and sample the rude 'Frolics' of the Dutch 'boors' settled around Albany ('lots of food – fat mistress – uncoath sort

5 Gray to Dr Thomas Wharton, London, 23 January 1760, in *Correspondence of Thomas Gray*, eds P. Toynbee and L. Whibley (3 vols, Oxford, 1935), II, 657.

6 See P. J. Marshall and G. Williams, *The Great Map of Mankind: British Perceptions of the World in the Age of Enlightenment* (London, 1982), in particular Chapter Seven: 'Savages Noble and Ignoble: Concepts of the North American Indian' (pp. 187–226).

of dancing – old folks smoked – cider the chief drink').[7] Whether white, black or Creole, such diverse inhabitants were themselves transplants or the descendants of immigrants originating in regions remote from the Americas; while these peoples attracted their share of comment, it was the aborigines of the mainland who left a particularly deep impression upon the redcoats.

The climactic bout of the struggle between Britain and France for mastery of North America represented a crucial era for these culturally diverse tribes.[8] By the 1750s the lifestyles of most of the eastern woodland Indians were slowly but inexorably changing as their communities became increasingly dependent upon European trade goods: those tribes in regular contact with the colonists had no illusions about the threat that the whites posed to their traditional existence. Old World diseases had ravaged New World communities that lacked immunity, whilst alcoholism was eroding the values upon which tribal society was based.[9] Many nations had also sustained severe losses in wars waged by the Europeans: some had been virtually exterminated during bitter struggles of resistance; others suffered through their involvement in the smouldering conflict between the rival colonial powers. The butcher's bill had been lengthened by the European policy of supplying allied Indians with firearms. This innovation had revolutionized the whole nature of intertribal warfare as the ritualised brawls of the pre-contact era gave way to more murderous affairs. Heavy casualties prompted calls for further combats to avenge the slain, resulting in a vicious circle of escalating violence.[10]

Despite such threats to their societies, in the mid-eighteenth century those tribes that ringed the English and French settlements in North America still retained considerable power. Nations such as the Iroquois, ranged between New York and Canada, could exploit their strategic locations to obtain favourable treatment from French and English alike. It was a diplomatic balancing act that required great skill – and the continuing presence of both European protagonists. Should one of those powers be eliminated from the picture, as occurred after the British conquest of Canada, that equilibrium would disappear – and with it the crucial bargaining power of the tribes.

Both France and Britain courted Indians because of their value as military allies. France's ability to attract large numbers of such warriors during the opening phase of the Seven Years War was a favourite topic of

7 'Journal of John Grant', pp. 42; 53–4.

8 See Jennings, *Empire of Fortune*; White, *Middle Ground*; and McConnell, *A Country Between*.

9 P. C. Mancall, *Deadly Medicine: Indians and Alcohol in Early America* (Ithaca, New York, 1995).

10 D. K. Richter, 'War and Culture: The Iroquois Experience', *WMQ*, XL (1983), 528–59; 537–8.

debate for envious Anglo-American writers. For example, a contributor to one London journal in 1755 stressed the French aptitude for mingling with the Indians on their own terms: young Canadian fur trappers actually lived among the natives, moulding 'themselves to the Indian ways, as scarce to be distinguished'. Intermarriage likewise helped endear the French to the Indians, who were 'very true to them'.[11] Captain Pierre Pouchot of the *troupes de terre* agreed that the Indians generally preferred his nation 'because of their easy-going attitude towards life & their cheerfulness'. However, the canny Pouchot – who negotiated with many tribes during his sojourns as commandant at Niagara – remained well aware that these peoples possessed their own agendas. He observed: 'they understand very well the advantage of adhering to the stronger side, for, although some of them are genuinely fond of us, they only like Europeans in relation to their own self-interest'.[12]

For British soldiers sent to fight in North America, allied Indians invariably proved an object of great curiosity. In the autumn of 1756 the 'Indian camp' at Fort Edward was a popular attraction for the regular troops; its lure provided a convincing alibi for John Stephens of the 48th Foot, who was acquitted on a charge of suspected robbery and desertion after he explained that at the time of the alleged crime he had gone off 'to see the Indians dance'.[13] The crowd-pulling novelty of such sights was emphasised by an officer with Braddock's expedition who witnessed the dances performed by the General's Indian scouts. Spectators ringed the dancing area 'as at a Cricket-match in *England*', although the entertainment proved less homely: to the 'rough Musick' of drums made from brass kettles covered in deer skins, and an equally 'terrible and savage' singing, 'horrid Figures rushed into the Ring', bringing to mind 'all the Descriptions of the Fawns and Satyrs of the *Latin* Poets'.[14] A young midshipman on the same expedition reported that the customs and manners of the Indians were 'hardly to be described'. He did note, however, the Indians' tufted scalp locks, strangely cut ears, and liberal use of red, yellow and black paint.[15] In the following year, Captain Charles Lee praised the tall and slender Mohawks in a lively letter to his sister at Bath. Lee wrote: 'I assure you that if you were to see the young Warriors dress'd out and arm'd you would never allow that there was such a thing as gentility amongst our finest gentlemen at St James's!'.[16]

11 *London Magazine, 1755* (June), p. 285.
12 *Pouchot's Memoirs*, p. 105.
13 GCM, Fort Edward, 10 October 1756, in WO/71/44.
14 *Expedition of Major General Braddock*, pp. 18–20.
15 'A Journal of the Proceedings of the Seamen', in *The History of an Expedition Against Fort Duquesne, in 1755; Under Major-General Edward Braddock . . .*, ed. W. Sargent (Philadelphia, 1855), p. 374.
16 Lee to Miss Sidney Lee, Schenectady, 18 June 1756, in *NYHSC: Lee Papers*, I, 4–5.

Fraternisation between white troops and allied Indians was swiftly discouraged as a likely source of discord. For all their cultural differences, soldiers and Indians shared a love of strong drink, but liberal quantities of New England rum sometimes acted as a catalyst for ugly incidents. Orders read to Halkett's 44th Foot threatened harsh penalties to soldiers or camp followers who supplied Braddock's Indian allies with 'strong Liquors'.[17] In 1758, a drinking bout involving rangers and Iroquois warriors led to 'handy-cuffs'. In the ensuing brawl several Indians sustained a 'drubbing', although there were no serious injuries.[18] Such misunderstandings stemming from linguistic and cultural disparities prompted repeated attempts to segregate the races. In June 1758, when Bouquet was encamped at Raystown awaiting Forbes's advance on Fort Duquesne, his regulars and provincials were warned against going to the Indians' camp, or having 'any Dealings with them'.[19] These orders proved easier to issue than enforce: in the following month two sentries were placed on the Indian camp 'to prevent the Soldiers going amongst them'.[20] That November, Major Clephane of Fraser's Highlanders likewise gave orders at Fort Stanwix 'that no Person Dare to Molest or anyway's Disturb the Indians, that are now here or may Come, and that no soldier go into their Huts at any time, or upon any Pretence whatever'. In the following April the Major was obliged to issue a further edict forbidding his Highlanders from interfering with the 'Indians or Squa's'.[21]

As these orders indicate, British officers spared no efforts to defuse episodes of interracial friction and maintain cordial relations with their Indian allies. For example, Major-General Abercromby took swift action after learning of a fracas between redcoats and Mohawks in 1758. According to Lieutenant-Colonel Andrew Rollo of the 22nd Foot, a young warrior who sought entrance to Fort Hunter to pay his compliments to the commandant was felled by the sentry; on leaving, the warrior was pelted with snowballs and a 'pis pot'. When the same man later tried to prevent two soldiers from entering the 'Indian fort' he was again attacked. Without even hearing the soldiers' side of the story, Abercromby gave immediate orders to relieve the garrison and employed Sir William Johnson to assure the injured parties that they would 'have all manner of satisfaction'. In consequence of the incident Abercromby

17 See 'Halkett's Orderly Book', in *Braddock's Defeat*, p. 92.

18 Abercomby to Johnson, Camp at Lake George, 26 September 1758, in *The Papers of Sir William Johnson*, eds J. Sullivan and A. C. Flick (14 vols, Albany, 1921–65), III, 16; Johnson to Abercromby, Fort Johnson, 30 September 1758, in ibid., 17–18.

19 'Bouquet Orderly Book' (17 June to 15 September 1758), in *Papers of Bouquet*, II, 656–90; 659.

20 ibid., 664.

21 See GD 125/34/7, fol. 5; GD 125/34/4, fol. 26.

had ordered all the British posts to 'treat our Indians civilly & to give them provisions to carry them home upon returning from hunting & scouting'.[22] As late as 1761, when the defeat of New France had reduced the immediate necessity for Indian allies, Lieutenant-Colonel Henry Bouquet of the Royal Americans sided with tribesmen who complained of abuse from the garrison of Venango: any soldier or sutler who injured an Indian 'by words or deeds' could expect rigorous punishment.[23] Bouquet's stance reflected ample experience of frontier diplomacy; when Jeffery Amherst interfered with such policies by ending the established practice of making gifts to frontier tribes, he unwittingly contributed to the eruption of 'Pontiac's War' soon after.[24]

Among the tribes: captives, deserters and renegades

George Townshend's Indian sketches undoubtedly highlight the perceived 'savagery' of their subjects: a similar emphasis characterises the Indians depicted upon the carved powder horns carried by the provincial troops; for example, that engraved for Edward Courtney at Fort Edward in 1757 features 'intense, ideologically charged imagery' of two 'naked' Indians aiming muskets from behind trees.[25] As such rare contemporary visual evidence suggests, for the majority of soldiers Canada's Indian allies remained shadowy and sinister figures, glimpsed only fleetingly amidst the fear and confusion of a forest fire-fight. But while most British soldiers were afforded a superficial impression of Indians, others experienced tribal life at far closer quarters. Redcoats captured by hostile nations, and deserters seeking refuge in 'neutral' tribal villages, were well placed to acquire a deeper understanding of the woodland Indians and their ways.

Camp-fire gossip highlighted the horrors awaiting the soldier who fell into Indian hands. On occasion these terrors were real enough. In the wake of Braddock's defeat, the teenaged captive James Smith watched from the ramparts of Fort Duquesne as the victorious Indian allies of the French began to torture several prisoners on an island in the Ohio.[26]

22 Abercomby to Loudoun, Albany, 16 January 1758 (LO 5413).

23 Bouquet to the commanding officer at Venango, Fort Pitt, 13 October 1761 (BL Add. MSS 21,653, fol. 85).

24 White, *Middle Ground*, pp. 256–68.

25 W. H. Guthman, *Drums A'beating, Trumpets Sounding. Artistically Carved Powder Horns in the Provincial Manner 1746–1781* (Hartford, Connecticut, 1993), pp. 101–2.

26 *An Account of the Remarkable Occurences in the Life and Travels of Col. James Smith During his Captivity with the Indians, in the Years 1755, '56, '57, '58 and '59 ... Written by Himself* (Lexington, Kentucky, 1799), p. 9.

Reporting Wolfe's withdrawal from Montmorency in July 1759, John Johnson of the 58th Foot regretted that the wounded had to be abandoned 'to the mercy of those barbarous Cannibals ... who massacred and Scalped them in our own Sight'.[27] Despite Johnson's testimony, some British soldiers captured by the Indians on that same day fared very differently. On 5 September 1759, Brigadier Townshend reported the escape of a soldier who, with another grenadier, had been 'treated very well' by their Indian captors; in fact, they 'gave them the best of everything they had'.[28] Indeed, when discussing the issue of captivity, it is necessary to appreciate the wide diversity of fates that could befall the individual taken prisoner by Indians. Attitudes to captives were governed by a variety of factors, the most important of which were age and sex: a child was more likely to be assimilated into tribal society than an adult, while men ran a far greater risk of maltreatment than women.[29] The temperaments of individuals could also prove significant, as Thomas Brown of Rogers's Rangers discovered after being captured near Ticonderoga in 1757. The seventeen-year-old New Englander was eventually taken to a tribal village 'about 200 miles from the Ohio'; on his third night there, one Indian attempted to push Brown into the camp fire and repeatedly butted and punched him. The exasperated Brown finally retaliated with a blow that sent his assailant sprawling: at this act of defiance all the other Indians laughed and called him '*a good Fellow*'.[30]

A male captive's destiny was essentially a matter of luck. Many tribes divided prisoners into distinct categories according to a 'last Doom of Life or Death'. This process separated the captives into two groups: those to be sacrificed to assuage communal grief and vengeance; and others spared for adoption or enslavement. Referring to the customs of the Iroquois, Cadwallader Colden described how captives were 'presented to those that have lost any Relation in that or any former Enterprize. If the Captives be accepted, there is an End to their Sorrow from that moment ... but if otherwise, they die in Torments, to satiate the Revenge of those that refuse them.'[31]

27 'Memoirs of John Johnson', in *Siege of Quebec*, V, 81–2.

28 See 'The Townshend Papers' in ibid., 265. This escaped prisoner was a soldier in the Royal Americans (see 'Journal of the Sergeant-Major of Hopson's Grenadiers' in ibid., 8).

29 J. Namias, *White Captives: Gender and Ethnicity on the American Frontier* (Chapel Hill, North Carolina, 1993), pp. 3–4. See also I. K. Steele, 'Surrendering Rites: Prisoners on Colonial North American Frontiers', in *Hanoverian Britain and Empire. Essays in Memory of Philip Lawson*, eds S. Taylor, R. Connors and C. Jones (Woodbridge, Suffolk, 1998), pp. 137–57; 138–43.

30 *A Plain Narrative of the Uncommon Sufferings, and Remarkable Deliverance of Thomas Brown* ... (Boston, 1760), p. 20.

31 Colden, *History of the Five Indian Nations of Canada* ... (3rd edn, 2 vols, London, 1755), I, 9–10. For rituals surrounding the fate of captives amongst the Iroquois at a slightly earlier date see *Journal of a Voyage to North America ... by Pierre Francois Xavier de Charlevoix* (2 vols, London, 1761), I, 368–77.

These stark extremes colour the story of Robert Kirk of Montgomery's Highlanders, who was made prisoner by the Shawnees during Major Grant's botched night attack on Fort Duquesne in September 1758. Kirk was pursued by four Indians who wounded him in the leg with buck-shot. 'I was immediately taken,' he recalled, 'but the Indian who laid hold of me would not allow the rest to scalp me, tho' they proposed to do so; in short he befriended me greatly.' After his wound was dressed with 'great care', Kirk was stripped of his uniform and clad instead in 'an old Indian blanket and britch-clout'. On the fifth day of his captivity, Kirk and eight other prisoners were brought before a great throng of Indians:

> we were unbound, scourg'd, and tortur'd the whole day ... As night approached we were carried into a council of the gravest Indians, and were by them ordered to be severally tied to posts, where there were all kinds of Pine-firr in heaps ready to be burnt. I here summoned all the fortitude I was master of, in order to resign myself to the will of providence. But I was not much longer in suspence, for the Indian who had taken me prisoner, accompanied by one of their chiefs, came and told me in English, which he could speak brokenly, that I was not to be burnt; that I was for the future to be to him as a brother, his father being my father, and all his friends my friends. I was sometime before I collected myself so much as to understand him, being quite ignorant of their method of adoption ...'

Luckily for Kirk, the brave who captured him had lost his own brother fighting the Cherokees four months before, and viewed the bemused redcoat as a divinely ordained replacement. Other prisoners were less fortunate: Kirk was taken by his 'brother' to view the war-dance, 'and to my unspeakable grief and terror saw five out of the nine burned in the most cruel manner'.[32] Kirk was subsequently dressed in fine Indian clothing, had his hair cropped 'after the Indian form', and was painted and greased.[33] However, he absolutely refused to allow his 'brother' to cut his ears to receive the elaborate metal decorations beloved by many tribes.[34] Next, he was equipped with a gun and ammunition, along with tomahawk and scalping knife. Besides these material possessions, Kirk found that he

32 *Kirk's Memoirs*, pp. 7–9.

33 Indians swiftly changed the appearance of prisoners to comply with tribal notions: British troops following Indians who captured Presque Isle in 1763 found 'several of their Camps where they had trimmed and cut our Soldiers Hair'. See letter from Detroit, 8 August 1763 in *Pennsylvania Gazette* (no. 1811), 8 September 1763.

34 The Virginian soldier Henry Timberlake noted that the Cherokees' 'ears are slit and stretched to an enormous size ... and are adorned with silver pendents and rings' - a custom originating with the 'Shawnese, or other northern nations'. See *The Memoirs of Lieutenant Henry Timberlake* ... (London, 1765), pp. 49–50.

had also inherited a wife, 'a fine boy who my brother told me was my son', and his own personal corn field. Clearly making the best of his situation, Kirk concentrated upon 'providing meat for my spouse and son, that being all required of me, it being her part to find the bread and other domestic necessaries'. To this end, Kirk joined a Shawnee hunting party along the Ohio, penetrating 500 miles into the virgin territory beyond Fort Duquesne. Kirk proved himself to be an enthusiastic and effective trapper, trading furs and skins with the French. With the proceeds, he bought himself a rifle and two new blankets, 'one of which I sent as a present to my adopted spouse, which was received as a great mark of my love and affection'. For several months Kirk ranged far and wide by land and canoe, hunting muskrat, bear and beaver; with the onset of winter the party donned snow-shoes to pursue the elk. In the spring of 1759 Kirk volunteered his services when a raiding party of 40 warriors was mustered to fight the Cherokees. Crossing the Ohio, Kirk participated in a war dance, 'having our faces black'd, in token of the destruction and immediate death which we meant to give our enemies'. Penetrating to enemy territory, the Shawnee raiding party dispersed to forage: Kirk used this opportunity to slip away in the company of another white captive. The pair finally reached Fort Cumberland on 20 June 1759, some 22 days after leaving the Shawnees.[35]

Kirk had not seen the last of his Indian 'family'. Five years later, while serving in the Royal Highland Regiment during Bouquet's Muskingum campaign, Kirk was reunited with his Shawnee 'brother'. At the peace congress Kirk's Indian friends were overjoyed to see him alive and well: having skirmished with the Cherokees on the day that Kirk escaped, they presumed that he had been captured. Kirk was invited to the Indian camp and 'used with the greatest hospitality'. The Shawnees pleaded with Kirk to return to his 'family': 'They laid several schemes in order to get me home, as they called it, but I knew too much of their maxims, ever to live amongst them with my own choice, so I constantly defeated their purposes.' Despite such views, Kirk retained a deep affection for his devoted 'brother'. He recalled: 'I believe I shall always have a regard for him, as his friendship was the most sincere I ever met in all my life and if it is ever in my power I will requite his kindness.'[36]

Although some prisoners received favourable treatment following formal adoption, others endured a miserable existence as slaves. Such proved the fate of Henry Grace of Lascelles's 47th Foot, who was seized by the Micmacs of Nova Scotia during the smouldering conflict of the early 1750s. Grace's captors dragged him through the woods to their

35 *Kirk's Memoirs*, pp. 10–14; 36–8.
36 Ibid., pp. 84–8.

village, where an intimidating reception awaited him. The Indians raised 'a most dreadful horrible Noise' and prepared to greet their terrified captive. Grace wrote:

> I was ignorant what these Barbarians were going to do to me, but they soon shewed me. I was to run between two Rows of them, some beating me with Sticks, and some with their Hands, while others flung any Thing they could lay their Hands on; I ran till I came to the Chief Man's Wiggwam.

Eventually, Grace was given Indian clothing and a tomahawk with which to cut fire-wood. Continually bullied and threatened with scalping, the young redcoat joined the Indian women in the toil of dragging provisions from the district's French forts. Grace remained with the Micmacs while they bickered with the garrison of Fort Lawrence. At one point there were a dozen British prisoners at the village, belonging to Hopson's 40th and Warburton's 45th regiments. Three of these captives were unceremoniously tomahawked when they became too weak to haul supplies through the snow. After fourteen months, Grace's 'family' sold him and five other prisoners to the St John's Indians. This change of masters brought no respite for the long-suffering Grace who maintained that all Indians possessed 'the same cruel Temper'.[37]

During a rambling hunting trip to the 'upper Countries' Grace encountered several Indian nations, and on arrival at each new tribal territory was obliged to run the gauntlet to make him 'free of the Country'.[38] These regular drubbings were almost the least of Grace's problems. Twice, when provisions were running low, his captors prepared to eat him. On the first occasion Grace was reprieved when he killed a deer; on the second, the Indians had tied him to a tree and were already heaping up the fire-wood when curious Cherokees intervened and provided meat from their own stores. While in the territory of the Chickasaws, Grace was forcibly tattooed according to the fashion favoured by that tribe: his right arm was tied to a fallen tree, then pricked with thorns and rubbed with paint until it became swollen to the size of his leg. Years later, when he was back home in Basingstoke, Grace wrote bitterly: 'I feel the ill Effects of it to this Hour.'

Sometime in 1757, Grace was bought from the Indians by a French officer for 'four hundred Livres and a Cask of Rum'. As a servant, Grace was due to receive his freedom after four and a half years. In 1759, as the British tightened their grip on Canada, Grace made an unsuccessful bid to join Wolfe's troops besieging Quebec. Eventually meeting

[37] *Life and Sufferings of Grace*, pp. 11; 13; 25–6.

[38] Ibid., p. 31. Grace ran the gauntlet for the Abenakis, Iroquois, Choctaws, Chickasaws and Cherokees. See ibid., pp. 30–31; 35; 37; 41–2.

Amherst's army in 1760, Grace was reunited with his old company at Quebec after an absence of a decade. He was discharged from the army at the peace of 1763, 'with the Loss of ten Years' Pay and Cloathing, and ... no Pension, though it has been granted to many who had not gone through anything like the Miseries I suffered'.[39] Grace's book was published to ease his financial plight, and a recent discussion of captivity narratives dismisses his account as deliberately sensationalised 'anti-Indian propaganda'.[40] However, there is no reason to believe that this bleak tale was exaggerated in any significant sense: just as Kirk reported the kindnesses bestowed by his captors, so Grace emphasised the very different treatment that he received.

Despite their diverging experiences, both Grace and Kirk turned their backs on tribal society. Other soldier-prisoners proved more reluctant to return to 'civilisation': they formed part of a wider phenomenon that James Axtell has dubbed the 'white Indians'.[41] According to a French prisoner interrogated in June 1757, English captives brought to Fort Duquesne and adopted by the Indians became 'so well satisfied and pleased' with their new lifestyle that they preferred to remain with their captors. Like the Frenchmen who lived among the tribes, these young adoptees often became more 'boisterous in their behaviour and loose in their morals' than the Indians themselves.[42] Such wholesale rejection of European values proved incomprehensible to senior British Army officers. In January 1760, Major-General John Stanwix reported how, in consequence of treaties, the Indians were now surrendering their prisoners. These included a lieutenant and sergeant of Montgomery's Highlanders who had returned from Detroit with assurances that more of their comrades were following. However, Stanwix added, 'what Surprizes me most, is that a great many of Our Prisoners absolutely refuse to leave the Indians, and a good many [are] gone back to them after being very formally delivered up here'. Amherst agreed that this behaviour was 'very extraordinary'; he could only account for it because the 'Savages' lived 'an idle and unconstrained life'.[43]

39 Ibid., pp. 51; 54.

40 See K. Z. Derounian-Stodola and J. A. Levernier, *The Indian Captivity Narrative, 1550–1900* (New York, 1993), p. 68. These authors doubt the basic veracity of Grace's story, noting for example, that he 'claimed' to have been captured by Indians (ibid., p. 166). Yet the surviving muster of Captain William Drake Spike's company of the 47th Foot, dated at Quebec, 17 November 1760, shows that 'Henry Grace' did indeed rejoin the battalion where and when he stated, being 'Recruited' on 5 November. See WO/12/5871 (Part One), fol. 20.

41 J. Axtell, 'The White Indians of Colonial America', *WMQ*, XXXII (1975), 55–88.

42 Examination of Michael La Chaurignerie, 26 October 1757 (LO 4706).

43 Stanwix to Amherst, 'Fort Pittsburgh', 26 January 1760 (CO/5/57, fol. 450); Amherst to Stanwix, New York, 15 February 1760, in ibid., fol. 452.

Tribal villages clearly held attractions for disgruntled soldiers. In May 1756 Sir William Johnson was worried that the 'great numbers' of deserters from Oswego amongst the 'Delawares and Susquehanna Indians' were undermining his diplomatic efforts by spreading lies to 'justify their quitting the Service and ingratiate themselves with the Indians'.[44] Five years later at Montreal, Major-General Thomas Gage resolved 'to take up all white Men of ours' who were living with the Indians 'wherever they can be got'. Johnson was informed that Gage intended to despatch such suspects to Quebec, where they would be sent on board the first man-of-war to arrive.[45] Amherst was sceptical of claims that some of these men were prisoners originally belonging to Shirley's and Pepperrell's regiments, for, 'if they are not Deserters they have stayed voluntarily amongst the Indians, or Canadians'.[46] At the termination of Pontiac's War further efforts were made to retrieve those 'white Indians' remaining with the tribes. Colonel John Bradstreet's peace terms with the Western Indians in 1764 included the following article: 'You must deliver up all prisoners and deserters that you have, as soon as possible. Should any white people desert to you, you are to send them ... prisoners to the post or settlement, nearest to you'.[47]

Just as prisoners with the Indians encountered treatment ranging from genuine kindness to wanton cruelty, so the experience of those soldiers who elected to live among the tribes varied dramatically. According to Major John Wilkins, the British commandant at Fort Niagara in 1762, deserters from the 60th and 80th regiments and Queen's Royal American Rangers were living with the Senecas 'in a miserable way, strip'd off everything, & slaves to the Savages, who watch them close & prevent their leaving the place they are in'. As most of these deserters regretted their action and begged for a pardon, Wilkins had decided to send Jean Baptiste de Couagne, the 'Intendant of Indian Affairs', to negotiate their release. De Couagne duly returned from the 'Six Nations' with fourteen deserters escorted by twenty 'trusty Indians'. The Major hoped this doleful parade would create a suitable impression, and 'prevent Idle men from making attempts to leave the best garrison for a soldier I ever saw'.[48] A subsequent court of inquiry revealed that these deserters were motivated by factors that owed more to the traditional tribulations of army life than any deep-

44 Sir William Johnson to the Lords of Trade, Fort Johnson, 28 May 1756, in *NYCD*, VII, 88.
45 Daniel Claus to Johnson, Montreal, 9 April 1761, in *Johnson Papers*, III, 377.
46 Amherst to Gage, Albany, 13 June 1761, in WO/34/7, fol. 39.
47 Mante, *History of the Late War*, p. 520.
48 Major Wilkins to Amherst, Niagara, 8 November 1762, in WO/34/22, fol. 90; same to same, Niagara, 7 December 1762, in ibid., fol. 95; also, De Couagne to Sir William Johnson, Niagara, 6 December 1762, in *Johnson Papers*, III, 957–8.

seated desire to sample tribal culture: Benjamin Murray and Samuel Brickerton of the Royal Americans and Dawson Brown of the 80th had all been drunk when they decamped; seven men of the Rangers were angry at failing to secure their enlistment bounties and subsequent pay; while three New Jersey provincials wanted both money and clothes.[49] Despite the discouraging experience of these repentant runaways, Iroquois villages continued to lure members of the isolated Niagara garrison: in the spring of 1764 Lieutenant-Colonel William Browning sent two men of the 80th – one of whom spoke 'Indian' – to the Seneca 'castle' in an effort to recover three of their fugitive comrades.[50]

The 'American Army' included men capable of moving easily between the worlds of the Indian and white man. Robert Taylor, a former soldier, had plainly become familiar with native society before he broke out of the Provost's lock-up at Montreal in August 1760 to escape a charge of desertion. A description of Taylor circulated after the gaol-break noted that he spoke 'French and Indian'.[51] Another soldier who demonstrated an ability to cross cultural boundaries was David Owens. Once a corporal in Captain John McClean's New York Independent Company, Owens was a deserter who had spent time amongst the Shawnees and Delawares. In the summer of 1764 Owens surfaced at Philadelphia in possession of five fresh scalps. According to information supplied to Johnson, Owens had gone out hunting with his 'Indian Wife & Several of her Relations', most of whom he killed and scalped as they slept. Johnson believed that Owens had committed this barbaric act to make his peace with the English rather than from any dislike of the Indians, or their 'principles'.[52] Whatever his shady background, Owens's knowledge of the Delaware tongue not only saved him from retribution but secured his employment as an interpreter on Bouquet's Muskingum expedition of 1764.[53]

The existence of cultural go-betweens like Owens only complicated the task facing those officers obliged to stem desertion within the 'American Army'. Records of the General Courts Martial reveal that the proximity of the wilderness, and the presence of Indians, created a unique 'grey area' of military justice, where the sentence meted out to the soldier charged with desertion depended largely upon the willingness of the judges to believe a

49 Court of Enquiry, Niagara, 4 December 1762 (WO/34/22, fols 97–9).

50 Browning to Johnson, Niagara, 23 May 1764, in *Johnson Papers*, XI, 196.

51 'Brigade Order Books', in *Hervey's Journals*, p. 152.

52 John Penn to Johnson, Philadelphia, 9 June 1764, in *Johnson Papers*, XI, 224–5; Johnson to Penn, 'Burnetfeild', 18 June 1764 (ibid., 241).

53 See 'Minutes: Conference With Delaware Chiefs', 11 November 1764, in *Papers of Bouquet*, VI, 693. Michael McConnell emphasises the role of army deserters as 'brokers' within frontier society. See *A Country Between*, pp. 157–8.

redcoat's version of events. Unlike the standard excuse of drunkenness, a defence featuring the well-known hazards of the forest and Indians stood some chance of success. Circumstantial stories of Indian captivity, particularly those lacking any independent corroboration, were unlikely to be swallowed. A trio of Germans from the 3rd Battalion of the Royal Americans who went missing from Quebec on the same day in November 1759 received short shrift: *all* claimed to have been captured by three Indians while going to buy greens from a house near the General Hospital. A more plausible defence earned an acquittal for Matthew Jackson, a private in the 80th Regiment who had gone missing while in camp at Lake George in June 1759. Jackson told how 'he with another man, whose name is Roger Clark, being one evening after Sunsett down at the Spring below the Hill on which the Regt was Encamped, they were surprised by six Indians, who made them prisoners'. Clark advised Jackson 'to tell the Indians that they were about to Desert, to prevent their killing them'. Jackson's defence was bolstered by the fact that he had left 'all his necessaries and arms' behind, and was due to receive a month's pay on the following morning. A similar finding was returned upon William Macqueed of the Royal Americans, who claimed to have been abducted by Indians near Fort Edward in the summer of 1757. On the evening of 8 July, Macqueed was 'taken with a Griping' and went to the riverside to 'ease himself'. It was while in this vulnerable position that 'Two Indians jumped up from behind a Log and took him prisoner, and held a Tommahawk up to him which he imagined was a threat they would kill him if he cried out'. Binding Macqueed's hands, these Indians carried him off, meeting next morning with a larger war-party. Macqueed was left with three warriors, two of whom went to hunt. As the old man who remained was soon preoccupied with the task of converting Macqueed's waistcoat into a pair of leggings, the soldier decided to run for it. The Indian 'fired upon him and set up the Holla' which was answered from the swamps, but Macqueed managed to get clear and was eventually picked up at Stillwater.[54]

Mercy was unlikely to be extended to a soldier suspected of lingering with his captors. Henry Hamilton of the 48th Foot had left Wolfe's army in mid-summer 1759, as the siege of Quebec became mired in a frustrating stalemate. When Hamilton was finally brought to trial two years later, an officer's servant testified that he had spotted him in the French camp at Beauport, 'at which time the Prisoner wore a White Coat, & told him he had Deserted'. The same man later saw Hamilton with the Abenaki

54 GCMs, Quebec, 26 October 1760 and Montreal, 1 April 1761 (WO/71/68); and Fort Edward, 18 July 1757, in WO/71/65. Like Jackson of the 80th, Macqueed's defence was aided by the fact that he had left his 'necessaries' in his tent.

Indians at St Francis. By his own account, Hamilton had been out plundering when he was captured by a group of Canadians. Escaping from these irregulars, and seeking to return to his unit, Hamilton was 'taken by a party of Savages' who 'took him to hunt for about four months'. Hamilton returned from the trip with beaver pelts to sell at Trois Rivières. He later slipped away from the Indians, only to be picked up by a French patrol and sent a prisoner to Montreal. There, 'an Indian got him out of jail, and took him to St Francis where he continued hunting with the Indians 'till about July 1760, when he, and two other Englishmen, made their escape to New England'. Hamilton's judges remained unconvinced. He was found guilty and sentenced to death.[55]

The ambiguous nature of Hamilton's relationship with the Abenaki, as revealed in his own evidence, can only have helped to place the hangman's noose around his neck. Some soldiers forged stronger links with their Indian captors, and actually fought alongside them against their former comrades. Evidence for a renegade soldier emerges from a military investigation into the loss of the outpost of Presque Isle during Pontiac's War. The commander of the small garrison of Royal Americans, Ensign John Christie, told the inquiry how the blockhouse was besieged in June by about 200 warriors from four different nations. These Indians constructed several breastworks of logs, and began 'digging a passage through the earth to get at the body of the Block House'. Such methods owed more to European military engineering than to traditional tribal methods of warfare, and suggest that the Indians were advised by a white man with a knowledge of conventional siegecraft. In fact, Christie soon discovered that a renegade was present with the Indians. With his men 'fatigued to the greatest Extremity', and fearing that the Indians would incinerate the blockhouse, the young officer decided to seek terms:

> He ask'd them in English if any amongst them understood that Language. They answer'd there was one, an Englishman who had been a prisoner for seven years and fighting then against him [Christie], they desir'd to cease firing and he should speak with him.

Christie and his men agreed to capitulate on condition they would be free to go. However, when the fort surrendered the garrison was seized and 'brought [as] Prisoners to the Villages around the Detroit'.[56] Although

55 GCM, Crown Point, 24 July 1761, in WO/71/68.

56 'A Court of Enquiry held by Order of Major Gladwin to enquire into the Particulars of the loss of the Post at Presqueisle, Detroit, July 9th, 1763' (WO/34/49, fol. 213). See also Peckham, *Pontiac and the Indian Uprising*, pp. 168–70. Although there is no specific evidence to confirm that this renegade had actually served as a soldier, the circumstances of Presque Isle's capture certainly suggest specialised military knowledge.

originally held by the Indians against his will, the Englishman mentioned by Christie had since been assimilated into the tribe – in this case the Hurons or Wyandots – to such a degree that his loyalty now lay with them.

Unimpeachable evidence for a military prisoner siding with his Indian captors emerges from a court martial held at Montreal in April 1761. Jonathan Barns, a former provincial private, was charged with 'being a Traytor to his Country and being in Arms against it'.[57] The case against Barns stemmed from the sequel to Robert Rogers's raid on the Abenaki village of St Francis in the autumn of 1759. Rogers's mixed force of rangers, Indians and regular volunteers succeeded in destroying the mission village, but, faced with the twin problems of vengeful pursuers and dwindling rations, was obliged to divide in an effort to reach friendly territory. The prosecution alleged that Barns had aided the Abenakis as they hounded Rogers's exhausted men.

Barns was only apprehended in March 1761 after he accompanied some Indians to Oswegatchie as an interpreter. Several soldiers recognised him as the perpetrator of 'crueltys against some of Major Rogers's party'. Private James Brown of Gage's Light Infantry testified that Barns and another Englishmen had led Indians to the hut in which he and two rangers were sheltering. Stripped and taken to a small stockade, Brown subsequently witnessed Barns and the Indians leave in pursuit of a further small party of Anglo-American fugitives. This hunt prove successful: a sergeant and two others were captured and slain in revenge for an Indian boy that the famished trio had killed and eaten. Brown added that 'the first man he saw enter the Place they were in was the Prisoner with a Scalp in his hand, who took up a stick and struck a man of Rogers' party', only desisting when some squaws intervened.[58] Barns told Brown that the 'Indians were too mild to him, & behaved very insolently and cruelly to him'. Another witness, Sergeant Josiah Malone of Rogers' Rangers, said that Barns had told him

> that if it had not been for the Squaws his scalp might have been off too, saying that he, the Prisoner, had stab'd one of the English Prisoners with his Knife, and taken off his scalp; and that the Indians would trust him now to go, where before this Action they would not have done.

In June 1760 the pair met once again in the hospital at Montreal, where Barns asked the sergeant's pardon for such callous treatment. Urged to

57 See GCM, Montreal, 1–4 April 1761, in WO/71/68.

58 Among the woodland tribes, women exerted particular influence over the treatment of prisoners. See Namias, *White Captives*, p. 4.

return to his white friends, Barns had replied: 'He could not, as he had done such things, that he durst not go home.' Exactly what had put Barns so literally beyond the pale emerged after the court had found him guilty as charged. At the gallows, with all prospect of mercy now gone, Barns decided to unburden his conscience to the clergyman in attendance, the ever-diligent John Ogilvie of the Royal Americans. When set beside this last confession, the court martial evidence was tame fare. Barns admitted being out with a party of Indians in the autumn of 1759 when they captured one of Rogers's men near Crown Point. Arriving at Isle au Noix, these Indians soon decided to 'Sacrifice' this prisoner, who was 'tortured in a most barbarous Manner' while French soldiers from the nearby encampment looked on. Barns swore 'as a dying man' that he had 'assisted in this shocking Murder'.[59]

The 'American Army' and the laws of war

From his New York headquarters an outraged Amherst reported these revelations to William Pitt. The General was not merely concerned with the brutal nature of Barns's deeds, heinous as these were: what really interested Amherst was the fact that they were apparently committed under circumstances reflecting 'no great Credit to Monsieur Bourlemaque and the French Regulars'.[60] Although Canada had long since fallen to British arms, Amherst sought a further, moral, victory over his old rivals by documenting French complicity in what a later age would describe as 'war crimes'.

Gallic 'perfidy' – frequently in tandem with Indian 'savagery' – had long furnished a favourite theme for Anglo-American commentators, particularly as France was popularly regarded as the very fountainhead of civility. In the summer of 1756, Charles Lee of the 44th Foot considered that whilst the Indians had some justification for their behaviour, being 'bred up in these bloody notions', the French could offer no such excuse. He wrote:

> it is certain that these patterns of generosity and humanity (as They are pleas'd to style themselves) commit more murders and butcheries upon men, women and children with their own hands than do their savage Allies.[61]

59 See Ogilvie's note of 'The Substance of Jonathan Burns's Confession, a few Minutes before his Execution on the 7th of April last' (WO/34/5, fol. 196).

60 Amherst to Pitt, New York, 4 May 1761, in *Correspondence of Pitt*, II, 426. Although Amherst mentioned no names, he told Pitt that his last letters from Canada were dated 9 April. As Barns's sentence had been confirmed on 6 April, and put into execution on the following day, it is highly likely that Amherst was referring to this trial.

61 Lee to Miss Sidney Lee, Schenectady, 18 June 1756, in *NYHSC: Lee Papers*, I, 3.

Such conduct aroused condemnation because it flouted the accepted standards of European warfare. Although the wars of mid-eighteenth-century Europe did not lack their atrocities, armies were typically prepared to observe certain internationally recognised 'laws of war' intended to prevent unnecessary bloodshed.[62] The customs embraced in this loose body of thought theoretically extended protection to non-combatants and promoted the humane treatment of wounded and prisoners; they also recognised specified 'honours of war'. For example, a garrison which only surrendered after a gallant defence might be permitted to march forth – ideally via a breach in the fortifications if that proved 'practicable' – with muskets shouldered, drums beating, and colours flying. Such codes exerted a powerful hold over professional soldiers; a striking demonstration of their importance was given at Montreal in the summer of 1760, when the Chevalier de Lévis protested at Amherst's refusal of the 'honours of war' to the French regulars. Lévis petitioned Vaudreuil to terminate ongoing surrender negotiations and instead allow the troops to defend Montreal until the British were obliged to employ artillery, for ''Twoud be a thing unheard of to submit to conditions so severe and so humiliating for the troops without having been cannonaded.' Even should Vaudreuil feel obliged to capitulate, Lévis desired permission to retire with his regulars to St Helen's island, there to sustain in their own name 'the honor of the King's arms'.[63]

For all their obsession with etiquette, the 'laws of war' none the less sanctioned behaviour that an Indian warrior would have considered excessive. Indeed, on 27 March 1756, when a mixed force of 362 French regulars, Canadians and mission Indians captured Fort Bull on the Oneida Carrying Place, all save a handful of the garrison were butchered. The French commander, Lieutenant Joseph-Gaspard Chaussegros de Lery, had offered quarter to the fort's commandant and his garrison if they surrendered: when this summons was greeted with a volley of musket-balls and grenades, an assault was launched. Within an hour the main gate was hacked to pieces, at which 'the entire detachment rushed into the fort with a cry of *Vive le Roi*, and put everyone to the sword they could lay hands on'. Of the 60-strong garrison, just one woman and a 'few soldiers' escaped 'the fury' of the French troops.[64] Although Lery's force included

62 Geoffrey Parker observes that 'most of the modern conventions concerning restraint in war appeared in Europe between 1550 and 1700, both in theory and, rather more slowly, in practice'. See *The Laws of War. Constraints on Warfare in the Western World*, eds M. Howard, G. J. Andreopoulos and M. R. Shulman (New Haven, 1994), p. 41.

63 'Protest of the Chevalier de Lévis . . .', in *NYCD*, X, 1,106.

64 'Journal of Occurences in Canada from October, 1755, to June, 1756', in ibid., 403–5. Montcalm reported frankly that the garrison 'was put to the edge of the sword', with just three prisoners taken. See letter to Madame la Marquise du Boulay, Quebec, 20 May 1756, in 'Montcalm's Correspondence' (*Report of the Public Archives for 1929*), p. 43.

more than 100 Indians, only six of these warriors participated in the storm: the killing was the work of white men. As the attackers lost just two slain and five wounded, the carnage inside the stockade clearly qualified as a genuine 'massacre'.

European interpretations of the 'laws of war' meant little to Indian warriors who had been raised to observe a very different code. Among the woodland tribes martial prowess was an attribute to be paraded before admiring relatives: it consequently required such concrete proofs as captives, scalps and loot rather than the token possession of some empty fort. Indians were naturally incredulous when their European allies permitted vanquished foes to depart unscathed to fight another day: such cultural differences proved an increasing source of friction between Montcalm and his tribal allies. In Indian eyes, enemies were to be 'consumed', both metaphorically and, on occasion, literally. After James Dalyell's sortie from Detroit was rebuffed by Pontiac's warriors in July 1763, British captives witnessed the victorious tribesmen roasting the gallant Captain's heart before eating it.[65]

Early notice of the dichotomy between the European and Indian attitudes towards the 'laws of war' was served following the capture of Baron Dieskau at the Battle of Lake George in 1755. William Johnson's Mohawk allies had lost three of their chiefs and many other warriors during the day's fighting: they accordingly viewed the Baron as a suitably prestigious object of vengeance. Convalescing from his wounds, Dieskau reported that but for Johnson's efforts he would have 'been assuredly burned at a slow fire by the Iroquois'.[66] Having saved the Baron's skin, Johnson proved equally keen to spare the vanquished veteran's feelings: provincials escorting Dieskau to Albany were to ensure that the General was treated with all possible courtesy. Johnson told their officer: 'dont let any one Croud about him to indulge their impertinent and ill mannered Curiosity'. Indeed, the Baron was to be accorded the respect due to 'a Man of Quality, a Soldier & a Gentleman'.[67] This scrupulous care continued when the invalided Dieskau finally arrived as a prisoner in England. On learning that Dieskau intended to visit Bath in the hope that the spa's famous waters would ease his wounds, Lord Barrington obtained the sum of 100 guineas for his immediate use. He added: 'an officer of the

65 'Rutherfurd's Captivity Narrative', in *Siege of Detroit*, p. 264. The Indians were paying Dalyell a back-handed compliment: by devouring his heart they hoped to imbibe his bravery. For cannibalism as a means of absorbing an enemy's strength see G. M. Sayre, *Les Sauvages Americains. Representations of Native Americans in French and English Colonial Literature* (Chapel Hill, 1997), p. 298.

66 Dieskau to Count d'Argenson, New York, 22 June 1756, in *NYCD*, X, 422–3.

67 Johnson to William Cockcroft and Captain Hubert Marshall, Camp at Lake George, 16 September 1755, in *Johnson Papers*, II, pp. 44; 45–6.

Rank and Merit of Baron Dieskau has a Claim to every Civility and assistance and not the less for his being wounded and a Prisoner'.[68]

Johnson enjoyed an unusually close relationship with the Mohawks, and possessed a unique ability to influence their behaviour, yet there were limits to even his authority: although the high-ranking Dieskau was preserved from a grisly fate, other less illustrious captives were distributed as replacements for slain warriors.[69] Unlike the British, the French drew their Indian allies from many different nations and in consequence experienced greater difficulty in controlling them. Montcalm's victory at Oswego in the summer of 1756 gave warning of potential problems: as one of the garrison's officers recalled, the Indians 'murther'd several of our Soldiers, as they stood on the Parade, and Scalped all our sick in the Hospital'.[70] Reporting the victory, a French officer admitted that the Indians had 'supped full of horrors': they had 'massacred more than 100 persons who were included in the capitulation, without our being able to prevent them or having the right of remonstrating with them'.[71]

Events at Oswego excited relatively little comment amongst Anglo-American journalists: the garrison were carried off to Canada before their tale could spread. It required the more notorious slaughter at Fort William Henry in 1757 to grant the British the unequivocal propaganda victory they had been seeking. Early newspaper coverage of the incident had ranged from the hysterical to the surprisingly restrained.[72] However, it was the full-blown 'massacre' account that soon became the 'official' version of the episode; for example, in his popular history of the war, John Entick catalogued alleged atrocities in gruesome detail and inflated the casualties to '1300 men, besides women, children and other attendants'.[73] Regardless of the true scale of the losses, the events at Fort William Henry were viewed by the Anglo-Americans as a blatant breach of the laws of war. The opportunity was too good to miss: the *London Magazine* employed the most lurid account of the episode to preface a broadside against the French which reminded readers of previous atrocities:

> The report of such cruelty and barbarity could hardly be believed, were we not assured of the horrible massacre of several hundreds

68 Barrington to the Mayor of Bath, 28 April 1757, in WO/4/54, p. 3.

69 See Steele, *Betrayals*, p. 54.

70 'Journal of the Siege of Oswego', in *Military History of Great Britain for 1756, 1757*, p. 42.

71 'Letter from an Officer, Camp at Chouaguen [Oswego], 22nd August, 1756', in *NYCD*, X, 456.

72 Contrast, for example, the bloodthirsty but circumstantial description in the *Gentleman's Magazine, 1757* (October), pp. 475–6, with the more restrained and balanced version printed alongside it ('Letter from New-York, Aug. 24', in ibid., p. 476).

73 Entick, *General History*, II, 401. In reality, the carnage was far less extensive: see Steele, *Betrayals*, p. 144.

> of general Braddock's wounded men; of whom we hear not of one that survived the carnage; were we not also assured of the murder of all the sick and wounded of the garrison at Oswego, notwithstanding the previous capitulation. . . . To what a pitch of perfidy and cruelty is the French nation arrived! [74]

Real and imagined French contraventions of the laws of war allowed the Anglo-Americans to occupy the moral high ground throughout the journalistic wrangling that provided a printed refrain to the armed conflict; it was a commanding position they proved reluctant to relinquish during the remainder of the war. In coming years no opportunity was neglected to contrast Gallic cruelty with British humanity. Upon his arrival before Quebec in June 1759, James Wolfe proclaimed that all Canadians remaining neutral in the coming struggle would go unmolested, even though the 'unparalleled barbarities' of the French against English settlements in America justified the harshest revenge. As Wolfe explained, 'Britons breathe higher sentiments of humanity, and listen to the merciful dictates of the Christian religion.' [75] Following the capture of Frontenac, Abercromby reported the 'good Treatment & civil usage' encountered by the garrison at the hands of Bradstreet's command, even though that force included 'Sundry Indians': in fact, the incident was 'an evident Proof' that such warriors *could* be restrained.[76] As this report indicates, for all their efforts to dominate the propaganda war by protesting at France's use of tribal allies, British commanders had never hesitated to employ Indian warriors when they could recruit them. Hence, when Wolfe remonstrated with Vaudreuil over the French use of Indians during the siege of Quebec, he received a blunt response: both sides had always sought to attract the greatest number of Indians to their cause, and the cruelties that inevitably resulted were viewed by French soldiers as 'the fortunes of war'.[77]

By its very nature wilderness warfare was an unusually ruthless business: inconvenient prisoners and the badly wounded were apt to be tomahawked and scalped, while deliberate acts of ferocity were employed to intimidate the opposition. Even for men accustomed to witnessing their comrades' backs corrugated by the lash, such sights could prove unsettling.[78] In January 1759, when the 43rd Foot was in garrison at Fort

74 *London Magazine, 1757* (October), p. 495.

75 *Knox's Journal*, I, 388.

76 Maj.-Gen. Abercromby to Col. Peter Schyler, camp at Lake George, 1 October 1758, in CO/5/50, fol. 385.

77 Vaudreuil to Wolfe, Head Quarters, 5 August 1759, in *Northcliffe Collection*, pp. 137–8.

78 See P. Way, 'The Cutting Edge of Culture: British soldiers encounter Native Americans in the French and Indian war', in *Empire and others: British encounters with indigenous peoples, 1600–1850*, eds M. Daunton and R. Halpern (London, 1999), pp. 123–48; 131–5.

Cumberland, Nova Scotia, a party of eleven redcoats and rangers failed to return from a wood-cutting expedition. The next day, a patrol was despatched and returned with the bodies of five of the missing men. According to Lieutenant John Knox, 'these poor creatures' had apparently been shot and then scalped while still alive:

> their hands, respectively, were clasped together under their polls, and their limbs were horridly distorted, truly expressive of the agonies in which they died: in this manner they froze, not unlike figures, or statues, which are variously displayed on pedestals in the gardens of the curious.

The naked body of one of the rangers was daubed in blood with some 'hieroglyphic characters', evidence that 'great deliberation was used in this barbarous dirty work'. The shocking spectacle had a profound effect upon the garrison: when the victims of the ambush were buried next day, Knox reported the men to be 'greatly irritated at the inhuman lot of their friends' and impatient for revenge at the first opportunity.[79]

As Knox's accounts suggests, such behaviour only hardened those men it sought to demoralise. The brutalisation that inevitably resulted was encouraged by official policy. During Braddock's expedition, orders were issued promising a £5 bounty to any soldier or 'follower of the Army' who brought an Indian scalp into camp.[80] In July 1759, during the siege of Quebec, Wolfe sanctioned scalping where the enemy were 'Indians, or Canadians dressed like Indians'.[81] Brigadier Townshend reported on 11 August how 'The General gave it out in orders that if any soldier choos'd to go out in the Woods and lay in Ambush for the Indians and bring in an Indian Scalp [he] should have 5 Guineas reward.'[82] Such generous payments offered a tempting incentive to soldiers who were paid just 8*d*. per day before stoppages, and may go some way to explain the viciousness of that summer's skirmishing.

George Townshend was not alone in deploring this 'War of the worst Shape'.[83] For a young subaltern of Fraser's Highlanders the suspension of

79 *Knox's Journal*, I, 289–91.

80 'Halkett's Orderly Book', in *Braddock's Defeat*, p. 113. Similar bounties were offered for Indian or French prisoners or scalps in May 1756, when Shirley sought to raise a company of Stockbridge Indians and three companies of New England rangers. See Pargellis, *Lord Loudoun*, pp. 301 (note); 302. By the mid-eighteenth century the English colonies already had a long tradition of such payments. See J. Axtell, *The European and the Indian: Essays in the Ethnohistory of Colonial North America* (paper edn, New York, 1982), pp. 207–41.

81 *Knox's Journal*, I, 483.

82 'The Townshend Papers', in *Siege of Quebec*, V, 258.

83 Townshend to Charlotte Lady Ferrers, 6 September 1759, in *HMC: Townshend Manuscripts*, p. 309.

accepted codes of conduct also proved hard to stomach. It was with considerable anger that Malcolm Fraser reported an incident on 9 July after a party of rangers operating on the south side of the St Lawrence captured a Canadian *habitant*. The prisoner's two young sons persisted in following the raiders, repeatedly shouting out in their distress; both were 'murdered by those worse than savage Rangers, for fear, as they pretend, they should be discovered by the noise of the children'. Fraser blamed these killings upon 'that cowardice and barbarity which seems so natural to a native of America, whether of Indian or European extraction'. Within weeks, Fraser discovered that 'Americans' did not maintain a monopoly upon inhumanity. On 23 August, Fraser's detachment joined a body of light infantry and rangers under the command of Captain Alexander Montgomery of the 43rd Foot. In an ensuing skirmish a number of prisoners were taken: on Montgomery's orders these captives were 'butchered in a most inhuman and cruel manner', including two men to whom Fraser had personally promised quarter.[84] One of the Light Infantrymen involved in the episode was less squeamish, casually noting in his journal how he and his comrades 'kill'd and Sculp'd the whole party, Returning about three O'clock in the afternoon to Camp with their Sculps.'[85]

Whilst sanctioning the slaughter of enemy irregulars, British commanders in America went to considerable lengths to protect non-combatants. Orders issued to Wolfe's army before Quebec threatened death to anyone offering violence to a woman.[86] Similarly, before landing on Martinique in 1762 the troops were warned that plundering, marauding, and the 'inhumanity of offering violence to Women and Children' were all capital offences.[87] Evidence of official action to limit brutalities comes from an incident during the siege of Havana. Corporal Johnson Knipe of the 48th Foot was charged with robbing and 'barbarously using' a Spanish woman. Robert McCullough, a corporal in the 90th Regiment, said that while on the march he had gone into a roadside house along with Knipe and some others. A woman was sitting inside with a young child on her lap, and when the redcoats demanded water she sent for it. McCullough described what happened next:

> [Knipe] went up to her, and seizing both Ears at once with his hands forcibly pulled from them her Earings which from her

84 'The Capture of Quebec. A Manuscript Journal Relating to the Operations Before Quebec From 8th May, 1759, to 17th May, 1760, Kept by Colonel Malcolm Fraser. Then Lieutenant in the 78th Foot (Fraser's Highlanders)', ed. Brig. R. Alexander, *JSAHR*, XVIII (1939), 135–68; 142; 148.

85 'Journal of Richard Humphrys', p. 45. According to Knox, the victims were a local priest and some 30 of his flock; these Canadians were treated with such cruelty because they had 'disguised themselves as Indians' (*Knox's Journal*, II, 45).

86 *Knox's Journal*, I, 400.

87 Orders, 7 January 1762, in 'Hamilton Note Book', p. 237.

> violent Screaming seemed to give her great Pain, and which all that were in the House condemned instantly as a most barbarous action, that the Prisoner with the others very soon after this quitted the House, and upon the Witnesses upbraiding the Prisoner with the Barbarity of the action, He the Prisoner presented his Piece at him, and swore that he was no Soldier, who would not do that, or much worse.

In court, Knipe claimed rather lamely that the earrings were a present from the woman. He was sentenced to 1,000 lashes and reduced to private.[88]

Although British commanders usually took pains to prevent their soldiers and tribal allies from harming civilians, the failure of Indians to subscribe to the recognised European codes of warfare meant that attitudes towards Native American non-combatants were more ambivalent. Robert Rogers's destruction of the Abenaki mission village of St Francis illustrates the point. Traditional narrative historians glorified Rogers's raid as an epic of frontier hardihood; by contrast, a new generation of scholars has condemned the episode as a colonial Sand Creek or My Lai.[89] In ordering Rogers to destroy St Francis, Amherst had told him to 'Remember the barbarities that had been committed by the enemy's Indian scoundrels on every occasion, where they had an opportunity of Shewing their infamous cruelties on the king's subjects.' Amherst added: 'Take your revenge, but don't forget that tho' those villains have dastardly and promiscuously murdered the women and children of all ages, it is my orders that no women or children are killed or hurt.' The General was therefore perplexed to learn from Captain Cadillac of the regiment of Berry, who proposed an exchange of prisoners on 2 November 1759, that Rogers had 'burnt the settlement at St Francis, killed some Indians, women and children'. Amherst observed: 'I fancy he is mistaken about the women & children.'[90] According to Robert Kirk, who served as a volunteer on the St Francis raid, whoever was in error, it was not Cadillac. Indeed, Kirk's *Memoirs* describe an indiscriminate massacre. When Major Rogers gave the signal, Kirk recalled, 'we were to fire the town at once and kill everyone without mercy'. St Francis was soon ablaze, and 'the carnage terrible'. Few of the villagers escaped: 'those whom the flames did not devour were either shot or tomahawk'd ... thus the inhumanity of these

88 GCM, 'headquarters near Cajamar [Coximar]', Cuba, 28 June 1762, in WO/71/71. It is perhaps significant that the 48th had served in America since 1755, while the 90th arrived in the Caribbean from Europe just months before this incident.

89 The doyen of the 'old school' approach was Francis Parkman, who recounted Rogers's raid in his *Montcalm and Wolfe* (II, 263–9). For an example of the more recent 'ethnohistorical' perspective, see Jennings, *Empire of Fortune*, p. 200.

90 *Rogers' Journals*, p. 145; *Journal of Amherst*, p. 186.

Savages was rewarded with a calamity, dreadful indeed, but justly deserved'. It was, Kirk concluded, 'the bloodiest scene in all America, our revenge being completed'.[91]

Such ruthless methods had been employed against Indians since Englishmen first settled in America: John E. Ferling has argued that the uncompromising ferocity of these early contacts set the tone for subsequent bouts of warfare during the colonial era, thereby creating a veritable 'wilderness of miseries'.[92] The brutal traditions of New World warfare were increasingly reflected in the British Army's conduct of operations against Indians waging wars of resistance between 1760 and 1764: in addition, the frontier ethos of 'total war' was echoed by the use of methods traditionally reserved for 'rebels' beyond the protection of the laws of war. Much the same techniques employed to crush support for the Scottish Jacobites in 1746 were used against the Cherokee Indians in 1760–61. Just as 'Butcher' Cumberland's men had ravaged Highland communities, so the expeditions against the Cherokee targeted not only hostile 'gun men', but Indian society in its entirety.[93] The scorched-earth tactics employed by Grant in 1761 left 5,000 men, women and children with the grim choice of submission or starvation.[94]

The campaigns against the Cherokees also witnessed an apparent hardening of attitudes towards Indian non-combatants. Whereas Montgomery's men in 1760 had been ordered to spare the lives of women and children, by the following year more ruthless measures were being advocated: heading a detachment to surprise the town of Tasse on 10 June, Captain Christopher French of the 22nd Foot was instructed to 'put every soul to Death'.[95] The same campaign highlighted the Army's inability to safeguard captives from the vengeance of allied Indians. Grant himself reported how on 13 June 'a poor miserable Old Squaw was brought in from Tassee' and put to Death in the Indian Camp by one of

[91] *Kirk's Memoirs*, pp. 44–5. See also *Rogers' Journals*, p. 147; C. G. Calloway, *The Western Abenakis of Vermont, 1600–1800. War, Migration, and the Survival of an Indian People* (Norman, Oklahoma, 1990), p. 178. Interestingly enough, the raid was portrayed as an uncompromising, albeit well-merited, massacre in King Vidor's 1939 film *Northwest Passage*. The role of Rogers was played by a convincing Spencer Tracy. See R. Durgnot and S. Simmon, *King Vidor, American* (Berkeley, California, 1988), p. 193.

[92] See J. E. Ferling, *A Wilderness of Miseries: War and Warriors in Early America* (Westport, Connecticut, 1980), passim. For a discussion of alternatives to Ferling's 'total war' thesis see Higginbotham, 'The Early American Way of War', *WMQ*, (1987), pp. 232–5.

[93] See B. Lenman, *The Jacobite Clans of the Great Glen, 1650–1784* (London, 1984), p. 196. For the British Army in the Scottish Highlands in 1746, see J. Prebble, *Culloden* (London, 1961), pp. 174–229.

[94] Amherst to Johnson, New York, 16 August 1761, in *Johnson Papers*, III, pp. 516–17.

[95] Mante, *History of the Late War*, pp. 288–9; 'Journal of an Expedition to South Carolina, by Captain Christopher French', in *Journal of Cherokee Studies* (1977, 2), 275–301; 284. As Tasse was deserted, the order was not enforced.

the Catabaws'. Three days later another 'poor Old Squaw' was killed by the Catawbas, and on 27 June Indian allies slew an elderly Cherokee man.[96] Grant's comments suggest sympathy for these pathetic victims, but also indicate an unwillingness to protect them. Ironically, by failing to curb the activities of its own tribal allies the British Army was guilty of much the same transgressions that had previously led it to deny French regular troops the coveted honours of war.

By 1763, when a widespread tribal war of resistance looked set to tarnish his laurels as conqueror of Canada, Amherst had no qualms about adopting the harshest measures towards Indians. At New York, Amherst received a depressing succession of reports detailing the loss of isolated garrisons, and the grisly fate of trusted subordinates. It was in a mood of rage and exasperation that Amherst wrote to Bouquet in July, ordering that all hostile Indians should be slain without mercy, as 'no punishment we can Inflict is Adequate to the Crimes of those Inhumane Villains'. Within weeks Amherst wished 'there was not an Indian settlement within a Thousand miles of our Country, for they are only fit to live with the Inhabitants of the Woods, being more nearly allied to the Brute than the Human Creation'.[97] The crisis triggered by Pontiac's War led British officers to consider responses that were barbaric even by the savage standards of the wilderness. Bouquet proposed that the Indian 'vermin' should be hunted down with dogs, and connived with Amherst in a scheme to deliberately infect the tribes with smallpox. Indeed, Amherst was willing to try any method that would 'extirpate this execrable race'.[98] The language employed by Amherst and his officers in 1763 branded Indians as 'subhuman', and therefore utterly beyond the scope of the 'laws of war'; it thus once more mirrored the attitudes of the first English colonists in their conflicts with the coastal tribes of Virginia and Massachusetts a century and a half before.[99] In this grim sense, the brutal ethos of the American frontier left its imprint upon the British Army.

Pontiac's War represented a low point in relations between British soldiers and Indians: the notorious responses it evoked should not be taken as

96 'Journal of the march against the Cherokees', in WO/34/40, fols 96–7.

97 Letters from New York, 16 July and 7 August 1763 (WO/34/41, fols 113; 117).

98 Add. MSS 21,634, fols 241; 243; 321. See B. Knollenberg, 'General Amherst and Germ Warfare', *Mississippi Valley Historical Review*, XLI (December, 1954), 489–94, and D. H. Kent's letter on the same subject in ibid. (March, 1955), 762–63; also McConnell, *A Country Between*, pp. 194–6.

99 It has been suggested that the Jacobean settlers used the same pretexts to justify their extermination of the American Indians that other Englishmen had recently employed in Ireland - that such enemies were 'savage', 'barbarous' and 'dehumanised'. See F. Jennings, *The Invasion of America: Indians, Colonialism, and the Cant of Conquest* (paper edn, New York, 1976), pp. 45–6; also H. E. Selesky, 'Colonial America', in *The Laws of War*, pp. 59–85; 60–62.

typical. As has been seen, Bouquet himself had previously demonstrated respect and sympathy for native peoples. Even Amherst, who was plainly uncomfortable with many aspects of tribal culture, could reveal attitudes at striking variance with those which have since branded him an 'Indian hater'. An example is provided by the General's personal record of a scene he witnessed in July 1760:

> I encamped at the three Rivers where I found an Indian with his Squaw, two children, a dog, a small canoe, Gun & fishing rod. He made us understand he was an Onondaga & pointed round the compass to show what belonged to him. I gave them some victuals & the little child eat salt Pork abundantly & then sucked. The young lady was greased all over by eating out of a kettle ... The father & mother appeared vastly fond of the little child & always gave it some of everything we gave them.[100]

The gulf between Amherst's sympathetic portrait of the Onondaga family and his 'genocidal' policies of 1763 underlines the danger of employing glib generalisations to characterise contacts between redcoats and Native Americans. As the evidence examined above suggests, such relationships could prove ambivalent; but even those men who were shocked and baffled by the wild extremes of cruelty and kindness they encountered among the tribes might occasionally sense that such 'savage' peoples possessed a dignity and integrity that was often lacking in the 'civilised' world of the Anglo-Americans.

This chapter has argued that most British soldiers gained only a superficial knowledge of Indian culture. Yet there remained another, broader sense in which America's tribal societies stamped their mark upon the King's regiments. During its mainland campaigns the British Army had dabbled with traditional Indian techniques and artefacts in an effort to ease its path through the wilderness: for example, in February 1759, the regulars at Fort Stanwix received Indian-style leggings and moccasins for distribution to scouting parties using snow-shoes.[101] Lists of equipment lost when Bouquet's redcoats discarded their packs to charge the Indians during the first phase of the fighting at Bushy Run reveal further evidence of native influence: besides regulation items of kit, the Royal Highland Regiment was missing some 30 pairs of 'leggans', while Montgomery's Highlanders sought compensation for 23 lost 'tomplines' – Indian straps used for carrying heavy loads.[102] During the gruelling Cherokee campaign

100 *Journal of Amherst*, p. 217.
101 Orderly Book, Fort Stanwix, 1 February to 9 April 1759, in GD 125/34/4, fol. 7.
102 WO/34/40, fols 340–41. See also G. S. Zaboly, 'The Use of Tumplines in the French and Indian War', in *Military Collector and Historian*, XLVI, 3 (Fall 1994), pp. 109–13.

of 1761, when only officers slept under canvas, Grant's footsore soldiers proved adept at constructing 'wigwams' for themselves.[103] As will be demonstrated in the next two chapters, by the culminating Caribbean operations of the Seven Years War this shared experience of the wilderness and an awareness of its tribal peoples would influence both the self-image of those redcoats who formed the 'American Army' and their tactics on the battlefield.

[103] See 'Journal of Christopher French', in *Journal of Cherokee Studies* (1977), pp. 281; 284.

6

Irregular warfare in the Americas

At the onset of the '*Annus Mirabilis*', four companies of Fraser's Highlanders manned Fort Stanwix in the Mohawk Valley. The bastioned strong point bolstered the northern frontier of New York, a province that now shivered in the grip of winter. Military activity had dwindled with the temperature and was restricted to the despatch of routine patrols and escorts. Inactivity bred boredom among the Highlanders, a problem reflected in the orders issued by the fort's commandant, Major James Clephane: on 8 January 1759, he ruled that 'No Snow balls were to be thrown in the Fort by any person whatever.' Ten days later the sergeants and corporals were ordered to prevent gambling among the men in the barracks and guard room, 'by which there is a Good Deal of Money Loss'd & Gaind'. For the Major, such minor irritants proved an unwelcome distraction from his task of safeguarding the fort from French and Indian assault. On 25 January he warned: 'If the Enemy is to make any attack here it will Certainly be soon or much about this time.' In consequence, he trusted that the garrison would 'be always alert & ready to do our Duty to our King and Country and to preserve the good Character we have already Gain'd'. Despite such appeals, the mundane routine of garrison life continued to erode regimental discipline. By the end of the month, drunkenness had become a serious problem, as the men began to 'Debauch themselves by Drinking a Great Deal too Much of that Pernicious & hurtful Licquor New England Rum'.[1]

The weeks passed quietly enough until 27 February, when the guard was strengthened, and the entire garrison ordered under arms; this alarm proved false, but within days the need for continuing vigilance was underlined in brutal fashion. Shortly before noon on 1 March, a corporal and four men guarding cattle within 300 paces of the fort were ambushed by a party believed to consist of 30 Indians. The privates, 'who were sitting upon a logg by a fire' were all killed by the 'first fire of the Enemy'. The corporal escaped this opening salvo but proved unable to retrieve his musket, which was trapped beneath a comrade's body. As the corporal headed for the fort the Indians fired several shots at him, and attempted to

1 Orderly Book, Fort Stanwix, 11 November 1758 to 31 January 1759, in GD 125/34/7, fols 34; 38–9; 45.

intercept his retreat. With the garrison alarmed, Captain Henry Wendell and a handful of his rangers sallied out, but before they reached the ambush scene the raiders had already decamped, taking four scalps and five muskets with them. A pursuit was organised, but the hostiles escaped unscathed.[2] In due course the incident was reported to William Pitt by the meticulous General Amherst, who noted rather testily that the sufferers had only themselves to blame, having straggled into the woods contrary to orders.[3]

Although a minor episode in the 'Great War for the Empire', the grim fate of the corporal's guard none the less exemplified the underlying harshness of warfare in the North American wilderness. Such incidents also serve to qualify the views of those historians who have followed in the footsteps of Lawrence Henry Gipson by arguing that the Seven Years War in North America amounted to 'a European conflict in a New World setting'.[4] Whilst it is certainly true that the war witnessed the first significant commitment of European regulars to the North American continent, and that several key campaigns involved sieges and battlefield confrontations employing Old World methods, such techniques by no means ousted the *petite guerre* of raid and ambush that represented America's indigenous brand of warfare; indeed, the brief bouts of 'regular' warfare were invariably waged against a broader canvas of low-intensity 'irregular' conflict. If, as I. K. Steele has recently stated, 'the Europeans came and imposed their kind of warfare on the wilderness',[5] they only did so by acknowledging and embracing the particular requirements of North American campaigning: for example, the armies sent against Canada in 1759 and 1760 were shielded by hundreds of light infantry, rangers and allied Indians employed to counter the French irregulars.

When discussing the extent to which warfare in America conformed to Old World models it is important to remember that this theatre lacked features typical of the European battlefield: unlike their fellows at Minden and Warburg, the redcoats of the 'American Army' were rarely obliged to watch as their comrades were dismembered by round shot or shredded by canister issuing from the mouths of massed batteries of cannon. America likewise remained innocent of the wheeling squadrons of hussars, dragoons and cuirassiers whose sabres and broadswords could swiftly transform a shaken infantry battalion into a bloody shambles.

2 GD 125/34/4 (Orderly Book, Fort Stanwix, 1 February to 9 April 1759), fols 8–9.

3 Letter dated New York, 29 March 1759, in *Correspondence of Pitt*, II, 78–9.

4 Gipson, *British Empire Before the American Revolution*, VII, x. The eventual triumph of regular methods in America is likewise emphasised in H. H. Peckham, *The Colonial Wars, 1689–1762* (Chicago, 1964); Leach, *Arms for Empire*; and Steele, *Warpaths*.

5 Ibid., p. 221.

It is also necessary to exercise caution in catergorising North American warfare on geographical lines: this approach draws a distinction between the 'conventional military struggle' of the 'northern theatre' (identified as the Hudson, St Lawrence and Mohawk river valleys, and the coast of Acadia and Cape Breton) and the guerrilla warfare of the 'western theatre' (the Ohio Valley and the Appalachian frontier of Virginia and Pennsylvania).[6] In reality, the cleavage between regular and irregular warfare was never that precise. It was not merely in the interior wilderness that the British Army encountered guerrilla opposition. Anglo-American armies also faced large numbers of irregulars in the 'northern theatre', a factor which explains the concerted efforts to evolve troops capable of meeting such opponents on their own terms: Wolfe's short and sharp 'conventional' victory on the Plains of Abraham only followed upon months of 'unconventional' skirmishing in which redcoats and rangers had clashed frequently with Indians and Canadian militia. Hence, one participant in the battle of 13 September could describe the encounter as 'the first regular engagement that ever was fought in North America'.[7] Conversely, 'regular' methods of warfare were sometimes found in the forests of the far-flung 'western theatre': the Vaubanesque bastions of Fort Niagara were invested using standard European siege techniques, while the French force that attempted to relieve Pouchot's garrison was rebuffed at La Belle Famille in a 'conventional' fire-fight.

Between 1755 and 1763, the officers and men of the 'American Army' soldiered under a wide variety of conditions: they encountered French regulars arrayed on open ground or ensconced behind field-works; skirmished through woods and scrub with Indians and militia; sapped forward methodically with pick and shovel against permanent fortifications; and developed considerable expertise in the amphibious operations that form such a striking feature of Britain's war effort in the Americas. The mixture of regular and irregular warfare which characterised these campaigns demanded diverse combat skills; the resulting fusion of Old and New World techniques created troops capable of fighting in both the conventional fashion of Flanders and in a more flexible manner that owed little to the traditions of Dettingen and Fontenoy. In the summer of 1760, the regulars and provincials that Amherst led against Canada 'were instructed in the regular and irregular ... method of fighting ... in fine, they were trained up in every particular that prudence, with experience, could dictate, to render the troops expert in an open or covered country'.[8] By

6 See M. C. Ward, '"The European Method of Warring Is Not Practiced Here": The Failure of British Military Policy in the Ohio Valley, 1755–1759', in *War in History*, IV, 3 (July 1997), 247–63; 248.

7 'Journal of Malcolm Fraser', *JSAHR* (1939) p. 157.

8 *Knox's Journal*, II, 529.

the onset of the Martinique operations of 1762, the veterans of the 'American Army' possessed an outlook and tactical ethos that set them apart from those redcoats sent to the Caribbean from Europe: these differences helped to fuel a debate over the relative merits of 'American' and 'German' tactics which flared afresh in the wake of the Revolutionary War of 1775 to 1783; it was the eventual reconciliation of these rival camps that furnished the foundations for a spectacular renaissance of the British Army during the victorious climax of the 'Second Hundred Years War' against France. The following pair of chapters examine the redcoats' experience of combat during the American operations of the Seven Years War, and consider the extent to which these same campaigns influenced the evolution of a distinctive tactical doctrine within the British Army.

The bush-fighting challenge

In the woods and scrub of the continental wilderness and amidst the jungle and cane fields of the Caribbean, British soldiers encountered a mode of warfare that was both unfamiliar and disconcerting. Such guerrilla tactics made a profound impression on troops whose peacetime training catered exclusively for the ritualistic combats characteristic of the open European battlefield. During the first half of the eighteenth century this 'conventional' warfare had itself undergone significant changes as the increasing efficiency of infantry and artillery was matched by a corresponding decline in the importance of cavalry. By the onset of the War of the Spanish Succession, the clumsy combinations of pike and matchlock which had dominated infantry tactics for the previous two centuries had been rendered obsolete by the emergence of the flintlock musket and socket bayonet. This union of firepower and cold steel revolutionised warfare: uniformity of armament simplified drill, enhanced the scope for manoeuvre, and rendered infantry less vulnerable to prowling cavalry.[9] The tactical flexibility of the infantry was enhanced further by the revival of the cadenced marching last practised by the hoplites and legionaries of the classical world. Here, as in many other aspects of military science, the lead came from the Prussia of Frederick the Great. Before the adoption of cadenced marching, troops had manoeuvred in open-order columns, only closing their file intervals prior to the linear confrontation; stepping forward in unison to the sound of fife and drum, the infantry now proved

[9] For a discussion of these developments see J. Black, *European Warfare*, pp. 38–66. A detailed analysis of tactical trends in France and Prussia is provided by B. Nosworthy, *The Anatomy of Victory. Battle Tactics 1689–1763* (New York, 1992).

capable of swift and coherent movement in close order.[10] In France, where great faith was placed in that nation's supposed penchant for the bayonet, the years immediately before the onset of the Seven Years War had seen much wrangling over the relative merits of column and line as attack formations.[11] Elsewhere, the line – typically consisting of three ranks ranged elbow to elbow – reigned supreme because it maximised the available musketry. The firepower generated by such formations had itself been amplified by recent developments: time saved by priming and loading from the same paper cartridge, and growth in use of the sturdy metal ramrod, had increased the average rate of fire from two to three rounds per minute. Unlike its old enemy, Britain had never doubted the superiority of fire over steel. Marlborough's great victories had implanted faith in the British Army's mastery of the era's international tactical system based upon the use of designated fire-units; on the eve of the Seven Years War the typical British battalion of ten companies was divided into eighteen of these 'platoons'. Such units, which cut across company structure, were numbered and grouped into three 'firings' involving platoons drawn from different sections of the line; volleys were delivered by the combined 'firings' or individual platoons in a variety of sequences aimed at maintaining a rippling barrage along the battalion's frontage. The object was to generate a virtually continuous fire, while always husbanding an adequate reserve of loaded muskets.[12] So ran the theory: what actually occurred on the battlefield rarely resembled the carefully choreographed movements of the drill-square, still less the serried ranks depicted in the canvases decorating the walls of Versailles and St James's.[13] Amongst the smoke, noise, fear and confusion of combat, the artificial bonds of discipline often waged a losing battle with the stronger instincts of self-preservation. Describing the infantry fire-fight at Dettingen in 1743, the young James Wolfe reported 'begging and ordering the men not to fire at too great a distance'. Such pleading was in vain, and Wolfe's men discharged their muskets prematurely. What followed proved equally unorthodox:

> As soon as the French saw we presented they all fell down, and when we had fired they all got up, and marched close to us in

10 Marching to cadence surfaced within the Prussian Army during the 1730s, forming a key prerequisite for Frederick the Great's famous 'oblique order' of attack. See D. E. Showalter, *The Wars of Frederick the Great* (Harlow, 1996), pp. 109–10.

11 Nosworthy, *Anatomy of Victory*, p. 202.

12 A discussion of British platoon fire systems, with clear explanatory diagrams, can be found in Houlding, *Fit for Service*, pp. 318–21.

13 Campbell Dalrymple remarked in 1761: 'The present method of firing by platoons is pretty, but not to be executed in action' (*Military Essay*, p. 51). For a fine evocation of the realities of 'conventional' combat in this period see C. Duffy, *The Military Experience in the Age of Reason* (London, 1987), pp. 189–267.

> tolerable good order, and gave us a brisk fire, which put us into some disorder and made us give way a little . . . However, we soon rallied again, and attacked them with great fury, which gained us a complete victory, and forced the enemy to retire in great haste.[14]

According to Lieutenant-Colonel Charles Russell of the 1st Regiment of Guards, rather than conform to the strict discipline of 'Hide Park firing', the British infantry had made a 'running fire of their own accord'. Commenting upon this outbreak of what a later age would describe as 'independent fire', the redcoats' commander, Lord John Stair, observed that 'he had seen many a battle and never saw the infantry engage in any other manner'.[15]

If the British Army's fire discipline could degenerate so dramatically when confronted by 'conventional' foes on the unobstructed plains of Germany, it is unsurprising that 'regular' methods should prove even less effective under 'irregular' conditions. Early notice of the likely problems had been served upon those unfortunate redcoats obliged to counter the runaway slaves, or 'Maroons', of Jamaica during a guerrilla war that festered through the 1720s and 1730s. Well armed with muskets and machetes, the Maroons proved skilful and ruthless opponents who avoided conventional confrontations; instead, 'surprise and ambush were the chief principles of their warfare'.[16] From their mountainous strongholds, or 'cockpits', the Maroons defied Jamaica's militiamen and the regulars sent to stiffen them. As the island's governor Edward Trelawny reported in 1738,

> The service here is not like that in Flanders or any part of Europe. Here the greatest difficulty is not to beat, but to see the enemy. The men are forced to march up the currents of rivers over steep mountains and precipices without a track, through such thick woods that they are obliged to cut their way almost every step . . . In short, nothing can be done in strict conformity to usual military preparations, and according to a regular manner, bush-fighting as they call it being a thing peculiar by itself.[17]

14 Wolfe to his father, Höchst, 4 July (New Style), 1743, in Willson, *Life and Letters of Wolfe*, p. 37.

15 Russell to his wife, 'camp near Bibrick', 6–7 August 1743 (Old Style), in *Historical Manuscripts Commission: Mrs Frankland-Russell-Astley Manuscripts* (London, 1900), p. 278.

16 R. C. Dallas, *The History of the Maroons* (2 vols, London, 1803; reprinted London, 1968), I, 39.

17 Cited in M. Craton, *Testing the Chains. Resistance to Slavery in the British West Indies* (London, 1982), p. 83.

Although the British authorities gained some successes by employing 'rangers' and black and Indian auxiliaries, peace was only restored through treaties that recognised the autonomy of the Maroon communities.[18]

Relatively few regular soldiers fought on Jamaica; fewer still lived to tell the tale, and it is unlikely that the skirmishes on that remote island exerted any significant impact on opinion within the British Army. By contrast, many of the British officers who saw service in North America in the 1750s and 1760s were already familiar with both the theory and practice of the 'irregular' warfare conducted in Europe. Veterans of the War of the Austrian Succession had observed the 'croats', 'hussars' and 'pandours' of their Austrian allies, and also fought against the light troops of the French. Treatises by European officers, which reflected their knowledge of the 'little war' as waged from Bohemia to the Balkans, were also in circulation. It has been argued that British veterans of European campaigning drew upon their knowledge of irregular warfare on that continent to help overcome the problems they later encountered in the North American wilderness.[19] While a seasoned soldier was clearly more useful than a raw recruit, the experience of flushing French skirmishers from a thicket in Flanders, or ravaging the homes of dispirited Scottish Highlanders, scarcely prepared a soldier for the hazards lurking within the woods of America. For example, James Grant had served as a captain in the Royal Regiment at the bloody battle of Fontenoy in 1745.[20] Arriving in America as a major in Montgomery's Highlanders, Grant was regarded as a brave and competent officer, 'suitable for all purposes'.[21] Despite this fine record, Grant was clearly out of his depth when he led a night attack upon Fort Duquesne in September 1758. Although Grant's command reached the vicinity of the fort undetected, he rapidly lost control of the ensuing bush-fight with the French and Indians and was defeated with heavy losses. The

18 For the British Army's development of 'counter-insurgency tactics' during the Maroon wars, see A. Guy, 'King George's Army, 1715–1750', in *1745. Charles Edward Stuart and the Jacobites*, ed. R. G. Woosnam-Savage (Edinburgh, 1995) pp. 41–56; 51–2. Scholarly accounts of the struggle are provided by Craton, *Testing the Chains* (pp. 61–96), and G. Metcalf, *Royal Government and Political Conflict in Jamaica 1729–1783* (London, 1965), pp. 33–79.

19 P. E. Russell, 'Redcoats in the Wilderness: British Officers and Irregular Warfare in Europe and America, 1740–1760', *WMQ*, XXXV (1978), 629–52.

20 P. D. Nelson, *General James Grant: Scottish Soldier and Royal Governor of East Florida* (Gainesville, Florida, 1993), p. 9.

21 Bouquet to Forbes, Fort Loudoun, 16 June 1758, in *Papers of Bouquet*, II, 97.

Major's commanding officer, Brigadier-General Forbes, could only conclude that his friend's thirst for fame had 'brought on his own perdition'.[22]

While perfectly willing to use European techniques where applicable, Forbes himself remained well aware that wilderness warfare demanded very different methods from those familiar on the other side of the Atlantic. In his opinion, it was necessary to 'comply and learn the Art of Warr, from Ennemy Indians or anything else who have seen the Country and Warr carried on in itt'.[23] Put bluntly, war in the forests of America was a very different business from war in Europe. Such sentiments were endorsed by Henry Bouquet, a Swiss-born mercenary with ample experience of soldiering on both continents. Bouquet had no doubts about which theatre was the more dangerous. After reviewing the various irregular units employed by the Prussians, Austrians and French in Europe, Bouquet remarked that 'the light troops wanted in America must be trained upon different principles'. The reason Bouquet gave was simple: 'The enemies we have to deal with are infinitely more active and dangerous than the Hussars and Pandours.'[24]

The truth of this verdict had been made brutally clear to those redcoats who marched to defeat at the Monongahela. In the short time available, Braddock had endeavoured to prepare his regulars for local conditions. Besides his initiatives to modify clothing and discard surplus kit, the general also gave orders for the complex regulation platoon-fire system to be simplified by using the administrative company as the basis for the tactical fire-unit, so allowing the men to remain under the immediate command of their own familiar officers and NCOs.[25] Braddock's personal instructions from Cumberland had emphasised the need for 'strict discipline' and constant care to prevent the troops being thrown into a panic by the 'savages, whom the French will certainly employ to frighten

22 Forbes to Bouquet, Raystown, 23 September 1758, in *Writings of Forbes*, p. 220. For Grant's own lengthy account of this confused fight see Grant to Forbes, no date, in *Papers of Bouquet*, II, 499–504.

23 Forbes to Bouquet, Philadelphia, 27 June 1758, in *Writings of Forbes*, p. 125.

24 'Reflections on the War with the Savages of North America', in Smith, *Expedition Against the Ohio Indians*, p. 44. The author of these important 'Reflections' is not identified as Bouquet in Smith's book. However, in the introduction to his work, Smith remarks that these 'military papers' were 'composed upon the experience' of the battle of Bushy Run by 'an officer long employed in the service he describes' (ibid., p. xii). The 'Reflections' advocate the development of tactics closely based upon those Bouquet employed at Bushy Run. In a letter to Sir William Johnson in January 1766, Smith said that his volume was prepared using 'some papers' that Bouquet had given him. See *Johnson Papers*, V, 10.

25 See 'Orme's Journal' in *History of an Expedition Against Fort Duquesne*, p. 293.

them';[26] the Duke's advice was heeded so well that efforts to disrupt the advance to Fort Duquesne were repeatedly thwarted.[27]

This fine record of vigilance was only blotted on the hot afternoon of 9 July 1755, after Braddock's column began the final approach march to its objective. The outcome of that bloody day was to prompt considerable debate on both sides of the Atlantic as military officers and civilian commentators pondered the causes and consequences of the disaster. In the immediate wake of the fiasco, the humble redcoats of the 44th and 48th regiments proved convenient scapegoats. An official inquiry recorded that although the main body had marched to the support of the advance-guard in good order, when instructed to halt and form a line of battle it had fallen into confusion. After this,

> all the endeavours of the Officers could not get them into any Regular form and being by this time within reach of the Enemy's fire, they appeared struck with a Panick, and tho' some seemed willing to Obey, When ordered to form, others Crouded upon them broke their order and prevented it; and [in] this irregular manner they expunded a great part of their ammunition.

The inquiry blamed this 'Bad Behaviour' on four factors: demoralisation stemming from hard duty and scarce provisions; the provincials' discouraging verdict that if the redcoats 'Engaged the Indians in their European manner of fighting they would be Beat'; a dearth of allied Indians or other irregulars to warn of the enemy's approach; and lastly, the 'Novelty of an Invisible Enemy and the nature of the Country which was entirely a forest'. This laconic analysis was the work of Lieutenant-Colonel Gage and Colonel Dunbar, respectively the commander of the advance-guard that had failed to secure a crucial height, and the officer responsible for the over-hasty withdrawal of the survivors to Philadelphia; as such, neither was in a strong position to apportion blame to others.[28] Indeed, news of the débâcle had scarcely crossed the Atlantic before some British pundits were already hinting that the set-back owed 'more to presumption and want of conduct in the officers, than to cowardice in the private men'.[29] Another correspondent accused Braddock of 'shameful neglect', by failing

26 'A letter written by Colonel Napier and sent to General Braddock by Order of the Duke of Cumberland', London, 25 November 1754, in ibid., p. 396.

27 For example, on 25 June Captain Orme reported: 'Some French and Indians endeavoured to reconnoitre the camp, but wherever they advanced, they were discovered and fired upon by the advanced Centinels' ('Orme's Journal', in ibid., p. 342).

28 'Inquiry into the Behaviour of the Troops at the Monongahela', Albany, 21 November 1755, in WO/34/73, fols 45–6.

29 *Gentleman's Magazine*, 1755 (August), p. 380.

to scour the woods with his flanking parties.[30] This interpretation, which shifts culpability for the disaster from the lowest ranks to the highest, has found support among modern historians. Stanley Pargellis considered that the 'fault lay in the quality of the leadership, not in the quality of the men'. Pargellis blamed Braddock and his staff for failing to observe the recognised European formations, thereby allowing the army to become confused and susceptible to panic. According to this theory, Braddock's blundering, rather than his soldiers' innocence of wilderness warfare, was the primary cause of the British defeat.[31] Whilst it is true that Braddock relaxed his march discipline at the very time it was most needed, a conclusion that blames his defeat on poor generalship surely underestimates the sheer novelty of the situation faced by his men. Indeed, to one contemporary French writer, it was the redcoats' ignorance of 'Indian' warfare that made their defeat inevitable. He observed that the British had attempted to fight using European tactics that were 'good for nothing in this country', forming up in a 'battle array' that provided a perfect target for men who were themselves concealed behind trees.[32] Another French commentator, that astute professional soldier Pierre Pouchot, considered that the bravery and discipline of Braddock's men had counted for little owing to 'an inability to direct fire & ignorance of the nature of the enemy they were engaging'.[33] Surrounded by woods that echoed with the blood-curdling whoops of the dreaded Indians, and subjected to the murderous fire of an unseen enemy, the truly surprising aspect of the affair is not that Braddock's redcoats bolted, but that they stood their ground for some three hours before doing so.

For the purposes of this chapter, exactly what happened on the day of Braddock's downfall, and why, is of less significance than the massacre's impact on opinion in the British Army. The shambles on the Monongahela provided a bloody benchmark against which all subsequent encounters with the Indians were measured. Braddock's defeat, and the grisly fate of the wounded abandoned on the battlefield, also instilled a lingering fear of Indians. Like the Jacobite clansmen whose broadswords had butchered British battalions at Prestonpans a decade before, the woodland warriors became the bogey-men of camp-fire gossip. This legacy was not easily

30 'Some Remarks on the late Engagement near Fort du Quesne ...', in *London Magazine, 1755* (September), pp. 403–4.

31 S. Pargellis, 'Braddock's Defeat', *American Historical Review*, XLI (January 1936), 253–69. R. L. Yaple felt that Braddock was unlucky rather than incompetent, and shifted the chief blame for the disaster onto Gage for neglecting to secure the crucial high ground. See R. L. Yaple, 'Braddock's Defeat: The Theories and a Reconsideration', in *JSAHR*, XLVI (1968), 194–201.

32 'Journal of the Operations of the Army', in *NYCD*, X, 337–8.

33 *Pouchot's Memoirs*, p. 83. Although not present at Braddock's Defeat, Pouchot based his analysis upon the accounts of 'Canadian officers who were there' (ibid., p. 80).

overcome: the proverbial savagery of the Indians, coupled with the forbidding gloom of the heavily wooded wilderness, haunted the British Army long after 1755.[34]

Back in England, the distinctive Indian war whoop was widely seen as a major cause of the British regulars' unease in the American wilderness. One description of the combat at La Belle Famille in 1759 told how the 'engagement began by a violent and horrible scream of the enemy's savages ... It was this scream, perhaps the most horrid sound that can be imagined, which is said to have struck a panic into the troops of general Braddock.'[35] In December 1758, an English commentator argued that operations against Canada should proceed via the St Lawrence river rather than by way of the lakes and forests that divided the English and French colonies, because 'our regulars do not fight well in woods; the Indian yell is horrid to their ears, and soon throws them into confusion'.[36] This aural phenomenon aroused such interest that Samuel Johnson, who considered it strange that the 'savage clamours of naked Barbarians should thus terrify troops disciplined to war', jokingly proposed a remedy in his satirical newspaper column. Johnson recommended that the noise generated by 'a proper mixture of asses, bulls, turkeys, geese and tragedians' might serve to inure British soldiers to the 'howl of America'.[37] Such banter was all very well for the coffee houses of Covent Garden, but to men serving in America the 'infernal clamours' of the Indians were hardly a laughing matter.[38] The sheer spine-tingling terror inspired by these shrieks is well conveyed in the words of one Monongahela survivor. Weeks after the massacre, Lieutenant Matthew Leslie of the 44th Foot wrote: 'The yell of the Indians is fresh on my ear, and the terrific sound will haunt me to the hour of my dissolution'.[39]

The flavour of backwoods campaigning is evoked in the detailed journal of John Knox of the 43rd Foot. Knox's account of a skirmish with Acadian irregulars near Annapolis Royal, Nova Scotia, in December 1757, admirably conveys the physical and mental shock of 'American' warfare. Fresh from garrison duty in Ireland, Knox was among the officers sent with 130 men to recover a captured wood-cutting detail. Poor weather forced the redcoats to turn back, but on their homeward march they were ambushed at a river crossing. Here, in Knox's words, the British

34 John Shy believes that British regulars never did overcome their fear of the wilderness. See *Toward Lexington*, p. 127.

35 *Annual Register, 1759*, p. 34.

36 William Beckford to William Pitt, Fonthill, 18 December 1758, in *The Correspondence of the Earl of Chatham* (4 vols, London, 1838), I, 377–8.

37 'The Idler, no. 8', in *London Magazine, 1758* (June), pp. 288–9.

38 *Accurate and Authentic Journal of the Siege of Quebec*, p. 23.

39 Leslie to a merchant of Philadelphia, 30 July 1755, given in Kopperman, *Braddock at the Monongahela*, p. 204.

met with 'a dreadful shower of ball and buck-shot, seconded by as horrid a yell as ever I heard'. The party's commanding officer was killed instantly, and with the advance-guard isolated on the far bank, the rest recoiled in confusion. Rallied by their officers, the redcoats crossed the river in the teeth of heavy fire, forcing the enemy to withdraw. The column eventually returned to base, 'much harassed' and with the loss of 24 men. In a thoughtful passage Knox conceded that under the circumstances most of his redcoats had behaved well:

> some, it is true, were restless and foolish, but they were young, strangers to woods and bush-fighting, and, as this was their first bleeding, every allowance ought to be made for inexperienced soldiers, especially when obliged to act out of their proper sphere.

Knox none the less remained troubled by the psychological effect of the fight on his soldiers, who now seemed 'fully convinced that they were by no means a match for the rabble in the woods'.[40]

The consternation of Knox's men was shared by other British regulars obliged to fight in the jungle and cane fields of the Caribbean. As one officer recalled, when Hopson's expeditionary force landed on Martinique in January 1759, the enemy emerged 'thro' Woods and Ravins in great Numbers in an irregular Manner, [and] began from all Quarters to fire upon our Advanced Posts, from Woods and Canes'. Troops advanced to counter-attack were 'fired at from all Corners always under Cover of Woods, canes & ca'. Having cleared the bushes of their defenders, the grenadier companies were soon ordered to retire, 'as they could not see the Enemy that fired at them'.[41] Army paymaster George Durant reported that the British troops could not advance '10 paces without considerable loss'. Durant added:

> nor did our firing in Platoons do much Execution, as the Enemy were not only hid & secured by large Trees, thick Bushes & Plantations of Cane but had also thrown up Entrenchments which were imperceptable to us & [were only] with some loss & the utmost Difficulty forced.[42]

Brigadier-General George Haldane testified that Martinique's numerous defenders, who were 'chiefly Mulattoes', fought 'in an irregular Indian

40 *Knox's Journal*, I, 117–27. See also reports to Lt-Col. Demetrius James of the 43rd Foot from Captain Richard Maitland and George Montgomery, volunteer, December 1757 (LO 4962; 4963).

41 'Journal of an Officer', enclosed in Hopson to Pitt, Basseterre, Guadeloupe, 30 January 1759, in *Correspondence of Pitt*, II, 27–9.

42 'George Durant's Journal', in *Army Records Society: Military Miscellany I*, p. 32.

manner'; as it was futile to respond in a 'regular way', Hopson sent out the Highlanders of the 42nd Regiment to skirmish with these militiamen – a gambit that gained sufficient breathing space to permit the construction of defensive redoubts.[43] The discomfiture of the redcoats was all the more galling given the inexperience of their opponents: according to a French officer at Martinique, the island's militia had been 'entirely ignorant' of the arts of war, knowing 'nothing more than how to run up to the enemy, and fire away'. Such improvised tactics were clearly effective: a British deserter reported that his comrades grew discouraged because 'they saw no enemy to fight with, and yet bullets were flying about them, from every leaf and bough they came near; that the country was full of ambuscades; and that, if they proceeded further, they must all be cut to pieces'.[44] Richard Gardiner of the Marines believed the Army's withdrawal from Martinique had been dishonourably hasty, as there were 'no regular Battalions drawn out in array against them, but lurking Negroes here and there dispersed and scudding from Tree to Tree and Bush to Bush'. Similar opposition had been encountered when operations were transferred to Guadeloupe. Despite their losses from the 'concealed Fires' of 'armed Negroes that could not be discovered', the troops had responded with resolution: 'On such Occasions they preserved their Ranks inflexibly, or rushed with Bayonets fixed among the Trees and Bushes till they had scoured them thoroughly'.[45]

In their descriptions of the West Indian campaigns of 1759, British soldiers employed vocabulary that echoed that of their comrades fighting in the mainland forests; but for all these surface similarities the 'irregulars' of the North American wilderness represented a far deadlier foe than the amateur militias defending Martinique and Guadeloupe. Between 1755 and 1763 the British Army encountered Indians operating in conjunction with Franco-Canadian forces and also fought warriors who were waging their own tribal wars of resistance without European allies. War parties sent against the Anglo-Americans during the contest for Canada typically fielded varying proportions of Indians, mixed-race or heavily 'indianised' *coureurs de bois*, militia and regular soldiers, often led by seasoned officers of the *compagnies franches de la marine*. The Indians were expert guerrilla fighters; many of the white men who served alongside them were scarcely less skilled in waging the savage war of the backwoods. Some Canadians became so immersed in tribal culture that it was difficult to distinguish them from the Indians. For example, at Quebec in July 1759,

43 'Journal of Brigadier-General George Haldane' (entry for 17 January 1759), cited in J. Fortescue, 'Guadeloupe, 1759', *Blackwood's Magazine*, CCXXXIV (October, 1933), 552–66; 558.

44 'Journal of a French Officer at Martinico', in *London Magazine*, 1759 (July), pp. 362–3.

45 Gardiner, *Expedition to the West Indies*, pp. 10; 90–1.

John Knox recorded the capture of an 'Indian' who was 'quite naked, painted red and blue, with bunches of painted feathers fastened to his head'; it transpired that the prisoner was in fact a disguised Canadian, 'a practice not uncommon among the natives of this country, when detached on any enterprise with the savages'.[46]

To Knox, the Indians and other irregulars who harassed his men were 'skulking wretches', 'bloodhounds', or 'monsters of butchery'.[47] Similar language was used by other British soldiers, and stemmed from resentment at the Indians' mode of warfare, which was regarded as cowardly by 'conventional' standards. During the siege of Quebec, Wolfe warned his redcoats to be wary of sniping 'by rascals who dare not shew themselves'.[48] Rather than fight in the open like Englishmen, the Indians invariably 'skulked' in their woods and bushes. Robert Rogers, the noted New Hampshire ranger, observed that the Indians launched their attacks 'in as many different ways as there are occasions on which they make them, but generally in a very secret, skulking, underhand manner'.[49] An excellent description of these tactics is provided in the memoirs of John Johnson of the 58th Foot, who complained that the 'skulking parties of Canadians and Indians' menacing Quebec in the winter of 1759–60 would never dare to face the British in an 'open plain'. Instead, Johnson observed indignantly:

> at our approach they would always betake themselves within the skirts of the wood and lie concealed behind the trees and bushes till we were within their reach, and then suddenly fire upon us, and rush out upon us before we would be ready to receive them, and very often would beset us round about, and do us considerable damage.[50]

These tactics, which seemed so unsporting to British soldiers, were calculated to inflict maximum damage at minimum cost. As the Jesuit priest Pierre de Charlevoix explained after visiting the Iroquois during the 1720s, in Indian eyes 'a victory bought with blood is no victory', while chiefs gained most glory by bringing back their warriors in 'whole skins'.[51] James Smith, who spent four years with the Indians after being captured by the Delawares in 1755, agreed that the natives never attacked 'without what appeared to them the sure prospect of victory, and that with the loss of few men'. Smith added that the Indians disliked fighting at close

46 *Knox's Journal*, I, 428–9.
47 Ibid., 134; 290; 300.
48 Ibid., 384.
49 Robert Rogers, *A Concise Account of North America* (London, 1765), p. 229.
50 'Memoirs of John Johnson', in *Siege of Quebec*, V, 117.
51 Charlevoix, *Journal of a Voyage to North America*, I, 360.

quarters, noting that 'they will not stand cutting, like the Highlanders or other British troops'. However, this aversion to cold steel stemmed from compliance with their approved method of warfare rather than cowardice: as Smith pointed out, if hopelessly surrounded, Indians would fight to the last man without seeking quarter.[52]

The apparently haphazard skirmishing tactics employed by the Indians led many European soldiers to assume that they were no more than an armed rabble. This view stemmed from the fact that the Indians were usually encountered in small raiding parties rather than the large formations familiar from the battlefields of Flanders. Such failure to conform to European concepts of military organisation has been taken as an indication that the Indians were therefore 'virtually without discipline in their fighting methods'.[53] However, the evidence of eighteenth-century writers with experience of American wilderness warfare indicates that the Indians followed well-proven military techniques of their own. Henry Bouquet identified three 'invariable' maxims governing the Indian approach to warfare: first, attempt to surround the enemy; second, 'fight scattered, and never in a compact body'; and finally, never meet an attack, 'but immediately give way and return to the charge'.[54] In larger-scale confrontations, Indians sometimes employed the traditional techniques of communal hunting to drive opponents within a half-moon of musketry; when the jaws of this trap closed, the enemy was caught inside 'a circle of fire, which, like an artificial horizon, follows him everywhere'.[55]

James Smith also recognised the underlying element of control in Indian warfare, remarking that those British officers who dubbed the Indians 'undisciplined savages' were badly mistaken, as the Indians in fact possessed 'all the essentials of discipline' and were under 'good command'.[56] Writing some 30 years earlier, Robert Rogers described how one Indian commander was assigned to each group of ten warriors.

52 *Life and Travels of Smith*, p. 87.

53 J. K. Mahon, 'Anglo-American Methods of Indian Warfare, 1676–1794', in *MVHR*, XLV (September 1958), 254–75; p. 257.

54 Smith, *Expedition Against the Ohio Indians*, p. 46.

55 See L. V. Eid, '"A Kind of Running Fight": Indian Battlefield Tactics in the Late Eighteenth Century', *WPHM*, LXXI (1988), 147–71; Smith, *Expedition Against the Ohio Indians*, p. 45.

56 *Life and Travels of Smith*, p. 83. James Smith reiterated his ideas on Indian warfare when he published *A Treatise on the Mode and Manner of Indian War* ... (Paris, Kentucky, 1812). For a modern overview that emphasises the effectiveness of 'Indian' tactics, see A. Starkey, *European–Native American Warfare, 1675–1815* (London, 1998). Leroy V. Eid observes that 'while hostile Indians, generally in very small groups, usually followed the "skulking" pattern, at certain decisive times the Indians were able to coalesce into impressively large and successful armies that could perform well in large-scale conflicts'. See '"National" War Among Indians of Northeastern North America', in *Canadian Review of American Studies*, XVI (1985), 125–54; p. 129.

When 100 or more Indians were assembled, a general was 'appointed over the others, not properly to command, but to give his opinion and advice'. Each morning this commander harangued the warriors, suggesting a plan for that day. While such an officer lacked the power to reward or punish warriors, he was rarely opposed. Rogers added that the Indians' chief commander was required to be 'fortunate, brave and disinterested'. In Rogers's opinion, it was hardly surprising that warriors were willing to follow a man 'in whom they firmly believe that all these qualifications are united'.[57]

Writers such as Smith and Rogers were obliged to describe the Indians' distinctive mode of warfare by resorting to vocabulary that could be understood by their English-speaking audience. However incongruous such terms as 'officer', 'commander' and 'company' might sound when applied to the Iroquois or Shawnees, it is clear that the woodland Indians did possess a 'discipline' of their own. Even James Wolfe, who generally expressed a very low opinion of Indians, was impressed by the tactical awareness of hostile war parties in July 1759, during the Quebec campaign. On one occasion he noted how the Indians mauled a company of rangers, then executed an adroit withdrawal under covering fire. Wolfe's professional interest overcame his prejudices when he reported the 'Admirable management of those savages in their Retreat, favoured by the fire of the rest from the Bank of the River'.[58]

Given the importance of martial prestige within the culture of the woodland Indians, it is unsurprising that individual warriors should have prided themselves on mastering the skills of war and the chase. Those whites possessing close knowledge of the Indians were unanimous in praising their dexterity with a variety of weapons. On their introduction to firearms more than a century before, the Indians had quickly learned to employ the smooth-bore musket with an accuracy that surprised the Europeans. Constant practice of aiming at individual targets allowed the Indians to maximise the performance of this basic weapon.[59] Indeed, archaeological evidence indicates that the Iroquois were making considerable use of Dutch-manufactured flintlocks as early as the 1630s – a clear half century before these weapons began to replace the inferior matchlock within the armies of Europe.[60] Contemporary accounts also

57 Rogers, *Concise Account*, pp. 228–31.

58 B. Willson, 'Fresh Light on the Quebec Campaign – From the Missing Journal of General Wolfe', in *The Nineteenth Century And After*, CCCXVII (March 1910), 445–60; 451; 452.

59 P. Malone, *The Skulking Way of War: Technology and Tactics Among the New England Indians* (Baltimore, 1993), pp. 67–87.

60 J. P. Puype, 'Dutch Firearms from Seventeenth Century Indian Sites', in *The Arsenal of the World. The Dutch Arms Trade in the Seventeenth Century*, eds J. P. Puype and M. van der Hoeven (Amsterdam, 1996), pp. 52–61.

indicate that Indians employed rifles. While slower to load than the musket, the grooved rifle was well suited to hunting and skirmishing where precision and range were more important than rate of fire. For example, a midshipman who accompanied Braddock's expedition noted that the General's native allies were 'very dexterous with a rifle barrelled gun'.[61] During the campaign against the Cherokees in June 1760, one of Montgomery's men reported how the Indians 'had vastly the advantage of us with their rifle barreled guns, which did execution at a much greater distance than our musket'.[62] Indians were likewise celebrated for their murderous use of the hatchet or tomahawk, 'which they throw with great certainty for a considerable distance and seldom miss'.[63]

Drawn from diverse cultural backgrounds, the Indians encountered by the British Army varied greatly in appearance: by no means all conformed to the stereotypical image of the painted 'savage'. For example, warriors who captured Sergeant Robert Beckett of the 28th Foot near Fort Cumberland, Nova Scotia in November 1757, made a more prosaic sight. These Indians – presumably local Micmacs – were clad in blankets fastened around the middle with belts or strings. Of the nine, seven wore 'Mauchassins' while the other two were 'quite barefoot'; for headgear, three 'had hatts on Slouchd, and the rest wore Caps, either of Cotton or Worsted he cant say which, but that they were very coarse'. They carried muskets with blackened barrels; Beckett also noticed three or four tomahawks among them.[64] A more common perception of the Indian was reflected in Bouquet's description of the 'typical' warrior of the Ohio Valley: smeared with bears' grease to make him 'as slippery as the antient gladiators', daubed with paint and shaven-headed save for a central tuft, he often went 'naked' or clad in little more than breech-clout, leggings and moccasins. Simply equipped with a light musket or rifle, powder-horn, shot-pouch, tomahawk and scalping knife, the North American Indian was a wily and intimidating adversary when encountered in his forest home – one who retained the potential to strike panic into the 'bravest and best disciplined troops'.[65]

61 See 'A Journal of the Proceedings of the Seamen', in *History of an Expedition Against Fort Duquesne*, p. 374.

62 Letter published in the *South Carolina Gazette*, 12–19 July 1760, cited in T. Hatley, *The Dividing Paths: Cherokees and South Carolinians Through the Era of Revolution* (New York, 1993), p. 131. See also Montgomery to Amherst, Camp at Fort Prince George, 2 July 1760, in WO/34/47, fol. 17.

63 'Memoirs of John Johnson', in *Siege of Quebec*, V, 166. Despite the widespread adoption of firearms by Indians at this period, some western nations also used more traditional weapons: Indians who ambushed a group of carpenters in the woods near Fort Edward in July 1757 were identified as Ottawas by arrows left at the scene. See *NYHSC: The Montresor Journals* (New York, 1882), p. 22.

64 GCM, Fort Cumberland, 28 November 1757, in WO/71/65.

65 Smith, *Expedition Against the Ohio Indians*, pp. 38–41.

The British Army's response (i): Allied Indians and rangers

It is significant that this respectful verdict was delivered after Bouquet had reaped laurels for repelling the Ohio tribes at Bushy Run, and brought many of the remaining hostiles to the peace table through his virtually bloodless Muskingum expedition of 1764. However, not all British officers shared Bouquet's high opinion of the woodland Indian's martial qualities. Contempt for the Indian was particularly marked among those soldiers who had not experienced the early years of Anglo-American defeat. Regular officers fed on lurid tales of Braddock's massacre and other disasters initially found the Indian allies of the French to be far less formidable than such anecdotes suggested; this attitude emerges clearly from the comments of officers engaged in the siege of Louisbourg in 1758. Captain William Amherst wrote in scathing terms of an early brush with the Micmacs:

> The cowardice of these Barbarians is so great, & their little arts in War so easily prevented from taking place, that it is astonishing they should ever have had an advantage over us, as in Mr Braddock's affair. Their whole dependance is upon a tree, or a bush, you have nothing to do, but to advance, & they will fly, they never stand an open fire, or an attack.[66]

Later in the campaign, James Wolfe gave vent to a typically fiery outburst when he contrasted the 'horrible Stories' told in England about the Indians with those actually encountered on Cape Breton. Wolfe characterised these Micmacs as 'the most contemptible bloody cowardly Scoundrels, in the Creation'.[67]

Despite such comments, officers like Wolfe none the less appreciated that troops trained and equipped on European lines were disadvantaged in the wilderness. Writing from Halifax, Nova Scotia, in May 1758, Wolfe feared that the battalions in America would be 'cut off one after another unless they fall into some method more suited to the country and to the kind of enemy they have to deal with': he believed that the redcoats' uniforms, arms and accoutrements were all inappropriate for local conditions.[68] Wolfe's misgivings proved well founded; for example, in February 1758 men of the 22nd Foot in garrison at Fort Herkimer on

66 'William Amherst's Journal', in CKS, U1350/0100/1 (entry for 18 June 1758).

67 Wolfe to Charles, 3rd Duke of Richmond, Isle Royale, 28 July 1758, in 'Some Unpublished Wolfe Letters', *JSAHR* (1975), p. 84.

68 Wolfe to Lord George Sackville, in *HMC: Stopford–Sackville Manuscripts* (2 vols, London, 1910), II, 261.

the Mohawk River could only watch in helpless horror as four youths and a girl were 'miserably Butchered' by Indian raiders. Recording the incident in his diary, Captain Philip Townsend explained that 'there was no possibility of assisting them as we had no Snow shoes and ye snow was att Least three foot Deep'.[69] That same month, Major-General Abercromby had warned that troops attempting to fight without snow-shoes would find themselves 'on a worse footing with Indians & Canadians than in the thickest woods of America'.[70] But warfare in America posed a dilemma: once the redcoat had overcome the difficulties of terrain and climate, and survived the attentions of the enemy's irregulars, he still needed all his traditional training to tackle the disciplined battalions of Old France. Too drastic a transformation of the British Army would damage this primary role. The solution adopted was a compromise: Britain would employ limited numbers of 'light' troops to screen the solid core of the army as it negotiated the wilderness, so preserving the redcoats for the set-piece fire-fights in which they specialised.

Initially, much emphasis was placed upon recruiting Indian allies to counter those tribes who supported the French. One Anglo-American soldier with strong personal reasons for canvassing such assistance was George Washington. As an aide-de-camp to Braddock, Washington had witnessed the rout at the Monongahela; in the following year, when commanding a battalion of Virginia provincials, he maintained that 500 Indians would prove more troublesome on the frontier than ten times as many regulars. Washington warned that 'the cunning and vigilance of Indians in the woods are no more to be conceived, than they are to be equalled by our people. Indians are only match for Indians; and without these, we shall ever fight upon unequal Terms'.[71] Another rising young soldier, Louis Antoine de Bougainville, tempered his frequent complaints about the unreliability of France's Indian allies with the frank admission that 'in the woods of America one can no more do without them than without cavalry in open country'.[72]

From their earliest days in America the English colonists had appreciated the military value of native allies. Back in 1637, the fledgling colony of Massachusetts Bay employed Narragansett Indians to help annihilate the troublesome Pequots at the Mystic River. Allied Indians had also played a decisive role 40 years later when the very existence of New England was threatened by the determined revolt known as King Philip's War: on that occasion it required the scouting skills of Indians

69 'Diary of Philip Townsend', NAM MSS 8001–30.

70 Abercromby to John Forbes, Albany, 26 February 1758 (RH 4/86/1).

71 Washington to John Robinson, Winchester, 7 April 1756, in *Writings of Washington*, I, 304–05.

72 *Adventure in the Wilderness*, p. 149.

to lead the colonists to their Wampanoag rival. In the 1740s Mohawk warriors had provided a grimly effective antidote to the pro-French Micmacs.[73] Indians could also furnish the colonists with valuable aid against their European competitors. Cherokees, Chickasaws and Creeks joined Georgia's 1740 expedition against the stronghold of St Augustine in Spanish Florida; that venture ended in ignominious retreat, but two years later the Creeks returned to help baffle a Bourbon riposte against Savannah at the Battle of the Bloody Swamp.[74]

During the final confrontation with New France it was only from the summer of 1758 that the British Army was able to employ significant numbers of allied warriors. Most of the Indians who operated alongside the redcoats fought as loosely affiliated groups, usually under the tenuous control of white 'Indian officers'. By contrast, the 'domesticated' Mohegans of Connecticut and Mahicans of Massachusetts served in formally structured and regulated companies with their own native leaders.[75] The first of these Indian companies was raised amongst the Stockbridge Mahicans by William Shirley in May 1756: it had a theoretical establishment of 50 men commanded by a captain, Jacob Cheeksaunkun, aided by his son and lieutenant, Jacob Naunauphtaunk, and an ensign, Solomon Uhauamuaumut.[76] Unlike other Indians, who fought in exchange for gifts, these warriors received specified rates of pay. Such services did not come cheap: William Johnson's accounts for 1 August 1756 reveal that a total of £98 and sixteen shillings was paid to fifteen Stockbridge Indians for their efforts during the previous two months.[77] The employment of Indian allies, particularly those of the more casual variety, posed numerous problems. Forbes voiced the frustration of many European officers when he complained that the powerful contingent of Cherokees who joined his drive against Fort Duquesne were 'capable of being led away upon any Caprice or whime that seizes them'.[78]

73 The Mohawks already boasted a fearsome reputation as predatory raiders throughout the north-east. See W. S. Hadlock, 'War Among the Northeastern Woodland Indians', in *American Anthropologist* (New Series), XLIX (1947), 204–21; 217.

74 Anon, *An Impartial Account of the Late Expedition against St Augustine under General Oglethorpe* (London, 1742), pp. 22; 43–4.

75 Despite the similarity of their names, the Mohegons and Mahicans represent two distinct groups of the Algonquian peoples. To further confuse the issue, both tribes are sometimes dubbed 'Mohicans', a term apparently coined in 1826 with the appearance of James Fenimore Cooper's historical novel. See T. J. Brasser, 'Mahican', in *Handbook of North American Indians: North East*, pp. 198–212.

76 Pargellis, *Lord Loudoun*, p. 301. Jacob senior and junior both became known to the British by the 'surname' of 'Jacobs'.

77 *Johnson Papers*, II, 631.

78 Forbes to Pitt, Philadelphia, 1 May 1758, in *Writings of Forbes*, p. 78.

Officers frequently viewed their Indian allies as unreliable and slothful, more interested in making inroads upon the Army's provisions than war against the French. On occasion, Indians were accused of standing idle while British regulars got on with the fighting: such carping ignored the fact that the mere presence of Indians alongside British troops could serve to intimidate the opposition. For example, although the 400 Iroquois with Abercromby in July 1758 remained as onlookers during the murderous assault upon Ticonderoga, they none the less discouraged the French from issuing forth from their abatis to complete the rout of the shattered Anglo-Americans.[79]

In subsequent years the British Army's attitude to Indian allies remained ambivalent: Gage complained that the Indian companies led by the 'two Jacobs' had been of 'little service' during the 1758 campaign; owing to 'the Disturbance their Crew made in the Camp', he never wanted to see them again. But for all his criticisms, Gage was keen that the elder Jacob should muster his company in good time for the coming summer offensive.[80] Like Gage, Amherst doubted the value of Indian allies; in common with his subordinate he remained reluctant to lose their services altogether. Justifying his decision to retain the Jacobs's companies in 1759, he explained:

> they are a pack of lazy rum-drinking people and little good, but if ever they are of use to us it will be when we can act offensively: the French are more afraid of them than they need be, numbers will encrease their Terror and may have a good Effect.[81]

Until the events of 'Pontiac's War' transformed his dislike of Indians into undisguised hatred, Amherst proved willing to use such auxiliaries: when James Grant was preparing to lead a punitive column into Cherokee territory, some of the Mohawk and Stockbridge warriors incorporated within the 'Indian Corps' formed for the expedition were sent south by the General himself.[82]

The dearth of Indian allies in the opening phase of the struggle had prompted the British Army to explore alternative methods of recruiting skirmishers. In the summer of 1756, Lord Loudoun turned to locally raised 'rangers', although he envisaged this as merely a temporary

79 See 'M. de Montcalm's Report of the Battle of Ticonderoga', in *NYCD*, X, 740.

80 Gage to Haldimand, Albany, 19 February and 15 March 1759, in Add. MSS 21,662, fols 13; 22.

81 Amherst to Pitt, 28 February 1759, in *Correspondence of Pitt*, II, 44.

82 Amherst to Barrington, New York, 9 December 1760, in WO/1/5, fol. 147. This formation also included Chickasaws and Catawbas from the south-east.

measure 'till I can make some of our own people fit for that Service'.[83] A limited number of redcoats did gain a closer acquaintance with wilderness warfare by serving as volunteers alongside the Indians or rangers. Such soldiers included Lieutenant Quintin Kennedy of the 44th Foot. In August 1756, this young veteran of Braddock's defeat led 40 regulars and Mohawks from Fort Edward, bound for Canada on a 'scalping party'.[84] After six weeks in the wilderness, Kennedy's patrol returned with two prisoners and valuable intelligence. The raid had proved both gruelling and hazardous. For five days the detachment was dogged by a large body of Indians: forced to jettison their provisions, Kennedy's men were so famished that they contemplated eating one of their captives. When the party finally arrived back at Fort Edward they were barely alive. Loudoun had never seen 'People so thoroughly wore out'.[85] The fame of Kennedy's exploits soon spanned the Atlantic. One journal informed its readers:

> Lieut. Kennedy has married an Indian squaw, whose tribe has made him a king. Gen Abercrombie gave him a party of highlanders joined with a party of Indians to go a-Scalping, in which he had some success. He has learned the language, paints [himself] and dresses like an Indian, and it is thought will be of service by his new alliance. His wife goes with him, and carries his provisions on her back.[86]

But there were never enough men like Quintin Kennedy: far from being phased out, as Loudoun had anticipated, the rangers accordingly underwent a steady expansion during the course of the war with France. By 1759, the armies under Amherst at Lake George and Wolfe before Quebec each fielded six companies of these troops – a theoretical total of some 1,200 men.[87] The only such unit to be taken on to the official establishment and appear in the *Army List* was the 'Corps of Rangers in North America' formed in September 1761 under Major-Commandant Joseph Gorham.[88] The exact status of the rangers used in the campaigns against New France remains vague; although clearly distinct from redcoats and provincials alike, those in Crown pay were sometimes regarded as

83 Loudoun to Cumberland, Albany, 20 August 1756, in *Military Affairs in North America*, p. 224.
84 See *London Gazette*, no. 9505 (23 to 26 August 1755); *Hervey's Journals*, pp. 40–41.
85 Loudoun to Cumberland, Albany, 3 October 1756, in *Military Affairs in North America*, p. 242.
86 *Scots Magazine, 1756* (November), p. 559.
87 *Rogers' Journals*, p. 138; *Knox's Journal*, I, 333.
88 See *Army List*, 1762.

'independent' companies of regulars.[89] Like the Indian companies they usually served with, such troops could prove expensive. For example, in early 1757 the pay for privates under the command of Robert Rogers was set at two shillings and sixpence New York currency per day; this equated to a daily rate of one shilling and five-and-a-half pence sterling – more than double the wage received by the redcoat.[90]

The rangers have always been associated with their most famous officer, Major Robert Rogers. In fact, Rogers was following in a well-established tradition, as John Gorham's ranging company had operated in Nova Scotia since 1744.[91] However, it was the companies led by Rogers himself that captured public imagination at the time and ever afterwards; their exploits were followed in the Anglo-American newspapers of the day, and reached a wider audience when the tough partisan published his *Journals* in 1765. Because such ranger operations as the St Francis raid of 1759 became enshrined in frontier folklore, it is perhaps inevitable that modern historians should have begun to take a less eulogistic view of Rogers and his men.[92] Rogers's commands did indeed sustain bloody defeats on several occasions: for example, in March 1758, Rogers suffered casualties of nearly 75 per cent when his 180-strong force clashed with a superior column of French and Indians.[93] Yet, as far as contemporary commentators were concerned, Rogers and his men had at least demonstrated a laudable inclination to take the war to the enemy. Recounting this same costly encounter, one journal reported how the 'famous Capt. Rogers' and his men 'behaved themselves with the most signal calmness and bravery during the whole action': such detailed coverage was warranted by the motive of 'doing justice to the memories of those brave men who have signalized themselves in their country's service, at a period when national

89 In a breakdown of officer fatalities in the units under his command between 1758 and 1763, Amherst drew a distinction between Gorham's corps and the other 'Independent Companys of Rangers'. See 'List of Officers Killed, Dead, or Missing & ca, in the American Army . . .', in 'Amherst's Personal Journal', p. 155. Returns for Abercromby's army in June 1758 and Amherst's in August 1760 both included the rangers in the total of regulars. See Abercromby to Pitt, Camp at Lake George, 29 June 1758, in *Correspondence of Pitt*, I, 285; *Hervey's Journals*, p. 57. The question of ranger status is complicated by the fact that besides those companies in Crown pay, others were raised by individual provinces.

90 *Rogers' Journals*, p. 49; Pargellis, *Lord Loudoun*, p. 283.

91 John Gorham (d. 1751) was the brother of Joseph. See Krugler, 'Gorham, John', in *DCB*, III, 260–61.

92 W. J. Eccles considers that Rogers's rangers were 'highly overrated', while C. P. Stacey feels they were 'probably not quite so formidable as they have been made out to be'. See Eccles, review of Leach, *Arms for Empire*, in *WMQ*, XXXI (1974), 502; Stacey, 'The British Forces in North America during the Seven Years' War', in *DCB*, III, xxix.

93 This 'unfortunate scout' was the 'Battle on Snowshoes'. See *Rogers' Journals*, pp. 83–90, and for a French account, *Adventure in the Wilderness*, pp. 198–9.

virtue seems at a low ebb'.[94] In addition, those who seek to question the effectiveness of Rogers's rangers must themselves be wary of underrating the unusual risks inherent in wilderness warfare. Patrols often staggered home frost-bitten and delirious with fatigue, whilst battle casualties were frequently far heavier than in 'conventional' warfare. Such losses stemmed both from the merciless nature of the fighting and the fact that clashes often occurred deep within hostile territory. Captain James Abercrombie, a regular officer with ranging experience, had no illusions about the high stakes at play in the blood-stained no-man's-land around lakes George and Champlain. When Rogers was worsted after a fierce skirmish in January 1757, Abercrombie regarded the reverse as a natural consequence of that mode of warfare, observing that it was 'impossible to play at bowls without meeting with rubs'.[95]

It was in a bid to exploit this hard-earned expertise that Loudoun ordered Rogers to form a training cadre of 50 volunteers from the regulars at Fort Edward. During the summer and autumn of 1757, young gentlemen such as Francis Carruthers of the 44th Foot and Charles Humbles of the 22nd were instructed in the rangers' methods of 'marching, retreating, ambushing and fighting ... that they might be better qualified for any future service against the enemy we had to contend with'.[96] For the further enlightenment of these neophytes in wilderness warfare Rogers compiled a set of rules based upon his own experience. Rogers's biographer, John Cuneo, has described the result as 'the first written manual of warfare in the New World'.[97] These instructions represented a codification of techniques already tested in years of guerrilla warfare. For example, small patrols were recommended to march in single file, with one man forward twenty yards, and another at a similar distance on each flank to prevent surprise. If pursued by the enemy, Rogers advised making 'a circle till you come to your own tracks, and there form an ambush to receive them'. After ten pages of such hints, Rogers added a comment that underscores the sheer unpredictability of wilderness warfare: there remained 'a thousand occurences and circumstances' for which no established procedure existed; on these occasions 'every man's reason and judgement must be his guide'.[98]

Rogers's record as an aggressive leader of irregulars earned him the respect of such critical professionals as Amherst and Wolfe, but not all rangers shared his high reputation. The sloppy discipline of some ranging

94 *The American Magazine and Monthly Chronicle for the British Colonies, 1758* (March), pp. 299–300.
95 Abercrombie to Rogers, Albany, 6 February 1757, in *Rogers' Journals*, p. 47.
96 Ibid., pp. 56–9.
97 Cuneo, *Robert Rogers of the Rangers*, p. 55.
98 *Rogers' Journals*, pp. 60; 67; 70.

units had long worried officers schooled in the stringent standards of the regulars. With the steady expansion of the rangers the quality of personnel dropped: the pool of genuine woodsmen was not bottomless, and recruits taken from the long-settled coastal colonies knew no more about fighting Indians than the rawest redcoat. Wolfe was not merely voicing his customary dislike of all things American when he remarked that the rangers assembled for the campaign against Quebec were 'in general recruits without service or experience, and not to be depended upon'.[99]

The British Army's response (ii): Adapting the redcoats

Like the Indians, the rangers were tolerated despite lingering doubts over their worth. While retaining these native irregulars, the British Army also sought to adapt its own regular battalions to wilderness requirements. Such initiatives did not enjoy the universal support of the officer corps; in the eyes of Captain-Lieutenant Ralph Hill of the 45th Foot they went against the grain of sixteen years' service. Hill had become embroiled in a convoluted dispute with Captain George Scott of the 40th Foot – an officer who possessed extensive experience of local conditions and strong views on how they should best be mastered. Hostility between the pair centred on the issue of who should command the troops at Fort Cumberland, Nova Scotia; it first surfaced in November 1755, when Hill headed a detachment of regulars ordered to support Joseph Gorham's rangers in a raid on the settlement of Memramkook. According to Scott, the plan specified a surprise attack at 'peep of Day'. In order to intercept any fugitives, Scott placed ambushes in the woods 'with Orders to conceal themselves as much as possible, and not to Stir nor fire, untill the Enemy came just upon them'. Checking his dispositions before breaking open the houses, Scott was surprised to find the regulars standing up and fully exposed to view. Hill explained that he had marched his men to the place indicated by Scott,

> but it being broken Ground by some Trees being felled, and under Wood, on my coming to the Spot I found my Detachment in great Confusion and Disorder, being a mere Huddle & Group of Figures & more likely to do hurt to one another than fit for any Service.

99 Wolfe to Pitt, Halifax Harbour, 1 May 1759, in Willson, *Life and Letters of Wolfe*, p. 424.

In consequence, Hill instead ordered his men to form their platoons as fast as possible, assuring Scott that he would sit them down directly they had done so. Hill later expressed his creed in a letter to Scott: 'Order, Sir, is the Soul of Discipline, the more Compact all Bodys are kept, the more ready all general Orders will be executed.'[100]

Other soldiers were quicker to grasp the importance of concealment for survival in the woods. Amid the chaos of Braddock's defeat, Martin Lucorney of Captain Peter Wraxall's New York Independent Company was one of the few redcoats to keep his head and attempt to fight the Indians in their own way. Lucorney's courageous conduct came to light after he denied deserting from Wraxall's unit in 1756. During the frenzied flight from the Monongahela, Lucorney had the presence of mind to recover a pair of colours and deliver them to a sergeant of the South Carolina Independents; in addition, another soldier, Alexander McFall, testified how he and Lucorney 'had several turns for two days in carrying General Braddock after he was wounded'. In the action itself, John Jones of Wraxall's company 'saw the prisoner several times behind a Tree ... fireing and watching his opportunity to fire upon the enemy'. Another of the Independents, Andrew Holms, said that Lucorney – a Hungarian who spoke little English – 'Struck upon a Tree making the Deponent understand, that it was the proper method for the Troops to take for their defence'.[101]

The resourceful Lucorney had unknowingly anticipated the Army's initial response to the challenge of bush-fighting. At Loudoun's New York headquarters, Colonel John Forbes devoted considerable thought to 'the Genius of the Ennemy and their manner of fighting'. Grappling with this problem before the onset of the 1757 campaigning season, Forbes concluded that every subaltern and soldier must become acquainted with 'Wood fighting' and be ready to respond to a surprise attack: unlike the inexperienced soldier, who 'either falls a Sacrifice to a merciless ennemy or betakes to shamefull flight', his acclimatised counterpart would immediately secure himself 'behind some tree stumps or stone, where he becomes his own Commanding officer, acting to the best of his judgement for his own defence and General Good of the whole'. In addition, Forbes believed it would be beneficial for the regulars to imitate the 'ruzes' employed by the ranging companies.[102] It is likely that Forbes's

100 GCM, Halifax, 10 January 1757, in WO/71/44.

101 The court found Lucorney guilty as charged, but 'in Consideration of his former Gallant behaviour and particularly his turning out a Volunteer in carrying of General Braddock after he was Wounded', mitigated the punishment to a mere 500 lashes. See GCM, Fort Edward, 13 July 1757, in WO/71/65.

102 Undated memorandum in Forbes's hand (*c.* spring to early summer, 1757), in RH 4/86/2.

proposals lay behind the introduction of simple drills designed to cope with combat in wooded conditions: the official report of a General Court Martial held at Fort Edward that summer suggests not only the nature of such efforts, but also the limits of their effectiveness. The court heard how a detachment of twenty men drawn from the 60th and 35th Foot and the Massachusetts provincials had set off in pursuit of deserters. The patrol marched through the woods in Indian file, with its commander, Sergeant William Isaac, leading an advanced party of two men while a corporal brought up the rear.[103] On the morning of the second day, the patrol had barely begun its march when the tail of the column came under fire. Sergeant Isaac shouted the order 'tree all!', and in obedience to these instructions, Private Henry Garman of the 35th took shelter behind a tree. In his evidence to the court, Garman described the confused skirmish that followed:

> by a Flash from the pan of the Enemy he thinks he saw two Indians upon whom he fired; he then was retreating to another Tree in order to reload, and hit his foot against a stump which threw him down, cut his knee, dirtied his Breeches, and his Piece was knocked out of his hand by the Shock of the fall. That he got up again and searched for his firelock, but being so dark, together with the smoak of the fireing, he could not find his peice.

The command to 'tree all' had prompted a very different response from John Griffiths. A 'Staunch Old Soldier' with 23 years' service, Griffiths was having nothing of such new-fangled drills. Instead of taking to a tree as ordered, Griffiths 'kneeled down, with his firelock cocked, in the position as the front Rank of a Platoon preparing to fire, in which position he remained for some time intending to reserve his fire, till he should see an Enemy near enough to make sure of him'. One man had been killed, and another wounded in the brief skirmish: in the confusion, a further eight soldiers became lost in the woods.[104] The incident shows that while a recognised drill had been evolved for ambush situations, it was easier to implement in theory than reality.

Whenever Anglo-American armies gathered, attempts were made to familiarise the men with fighting in wooded conditions. Troops mustered in 1757 for Loudoun's aborted Louisbourg expedition were 'Disciplined for the nature of the Country'; in the following year, when Amherst was

103 Sergeant Isaac of the 35th Foot was described as 'Old and worn out' when examined at Chelsea on 12 April 1758. Aged 58, Isaac was a weaver from County Cavan and had served in the army for no less than 38 years. See WO/116/5, fol. 20.

104 GCM, Camp at Fort Edward, 11 July 1757, in WO/71/65. Provincial troops attacked in the woods near Fort Edward later that month were likewise ordered to 'Tree and to behave in the best Manner'. See GCM, Fort Edward, 26 July 1757, in WO/71/66.

preparing his strike against the same objective, the battalions were exercised 'in the Woods, bush fighting, after the Indian manner'.[105] That August, during Forbes's campaign, the innovative Lieutenant-Colonel Bouquet of the Royal Americans was busy exercising 'his men in the woods and bushes in a particular manner of his own invention'.[106] Although such efforts demonstrated an admirable determination to confront local conditions, their practical value was seemingly minimal. For example, shortly before his disastrous raid on Fort Duquesne, Major Grant had attempted to teach his men 'the art of bush fighting'.[107] A more celebrated, but equally fruitless, effort to equip and train troops for the American woods was orchestrated by the popular Brigadier-General Lord Howe within the army poised to attack Ticonderoga in 1758. One admirer wrote of Howe's care in 'forming his regular troops to the method of bush-fighting all this season, so that he has now, it is said, made them as dexterous at it almost as the rangers'.[108] Howe's reforms gained widespread publicity and approval, but did nothing to prevent his battalions from degenerating into a disorderly mob when firing erupted as they attempted to negotiate woods near the French stronghold on 6 July. Charles Lee of the 44th Foot said that the panic was 'occasion'd by the Indian war cry'. He added: 'The darkness and thickness of the woods must have made this a very dismal tragedy, had not the officers exerted themselves to the utmost to rectify the error.'[109] It is significant that these same troops displayed no such nervousness when required to operate outside the woods: just two days after this embarrassing incident, they assaulted the French lines with a furious courage that impressed friend and foe alike. As Captain Pouchot of the *troupes de terre* recalled, 'The enemy behaved with the greatest bravery in this attack, bearing the brunt of terrible musket fire without flinching.'[110]

It was only repeated exposure to wilderness fighting that eventually enabled British soldiers to maintain their nerve when attacked by Indians amidst difficult terrain. During the siege of Quebec the redcoats frequently engaged in bush-fights with the French irregulars: the British usually came off worse in such clashes, but as one officer remarked, this

105 'Journal of Richard Humphrys', p. 3; 'Memoirs of an Invalid', p. 18.

106 Letter of Major Joseph Shippen, cited by E. D. Branch, in 'Henry Bouquet: Professional Soldier', *PMHB*, LXII (1938), 41–51; 45. Bouquet's extensive skirmish line apparently consisted of just 'one Rank entire'. See 'Thomas Barton and the Forbes Expedition', ed. W. A. Hunter, in Ibid., XCV (1971), 431–83; 449–50.

107 'Thomas Gist's Indian Captivity', ed. H. H. Peckham, *PMHB*, LXXX (1956), 285–311; 289.

108 'Letter from New York, 31 May; 1758', in *Scots Magazine, 1758* (August), p. 442.

109 'Narrative', enclosed in letter to Miss Sidney Lee, Albany, 16 September 1758, in *NYHSC: Lee Papers*, I, 10.

110 *Pouchot's Memoirs*, p. 149.

continuous bickering had 'the good effect of using our men to the woods, and familiarizing them with the Canadians and Indians, whom they soon began to despise'.[111] In 1760 and 1761, the expeditions against the Cherokees again proved that British regulars were capable of keeping calm under Indian assault. Describing his skirmish of 27 June 1760, Colonel Archibald Montgomery reported the 'Spirit and Coolness' displayed by the troops throughout the engagement.[112]

Whilst it is clear that the redcoats had made considerable progress since Braddock's day in coming to grips with American conditions, the competence acquired in Indian-fighting, and the degree to which 'conventional' tactics had been tailored to wilderness requirements, should not be exaggerated: it is revealing that even after their encounter with Montgomery's column the Cherokees continued to believe that they enjoyed an 'Advantage in War' over the Europeans. According to Governor William Bull of South Carolina, Anglo-American prisoners released by the Cherokees reported how

> their Young men from their past Observations Express no very respectable Opinion of our manner of fighting them, as by our Close order, We present a large & open Object to their fire, & our Platoons do little Execution as the Indians are thinly Scattered, & Concealed behind Bushes or Trees; 'Tho they Acknowledged our Troops thereby show they are not afraid, and that our Numbers would be formidable in open Ground, where they will never give us an oportunity of Engaging them.[113]

In the following year, Grant's punitive expedition encountered surprisingly light opposition from the Cherokees. The 'Indian Corps' commanded by Captain Quintin Kennedy flanked the column and scouted ahead of its advance-guard; on 10 June 1761, it was this formation that detected a Cherokee ambush. Two captured squaws revealed that during the day's fighting the Cherokees 'had not got a Hair [of a scalp], & Expressed much surprise that we seemed to take so little notice of them during the action'.[114] As Grant related to Amherst, his expedition had 'not met with a Single Rub', even though the mountains would have proved impenetrable if the 'Inhabitants deserved the name of an

111 'Journal of Major Moncrief [actually written by Major Patrick Mackellar, Royal Engineers]', in *Siege of Quebec*, V, 33–58; 47.

112 Montgomery to Amherst, Camp at Fort Prince George, 2 July 1760, in WO/34/47, fol. 17.

113 Bull to Amherst, Charlestown, 15 April 1761, in CO/5/61, fol. 277.

114 'Journal of the March and Operations of the Troops under the Command of Lieut. Col. Grant', in WO/34/40, fol. 97.

Enemy'.[115] The feeble Indian resistance on this occasion led Amherst to adopt a sweeping generalisation – that the 'savages' were 'a Dastardly Sett, and dare not face real Danger'.[116]

The inaccuracy of Amherst's verdict was to be demonstrated two years later during 'Pontiac's War' – an episode that remains central to any discussion of the British Army's record of Indian-fighting. Operations mounted against the Indians in 1763 are particularly revealing because they involved soldiers with considerable experience of wilderness warfare. Such veterans included Colonel Henry Bouquet of the Royal Americans, an officer who had rapidly appreciated that the New World demanded new tactics and was active in evolving them. In the summer of 1763 the Colonel was charged with relieving Fort Pitt and pursuing operations against the hostile tribes. On the afternoon of 5 August, when Bouquet's tired column of about 500 effectives was a mile short of a stream called Bushy Run, his advance-guard was attacked by a substantial body of Ohio Indians.[117] A general charge dispersed these warriors, but they soon returned to harass the column. Fierce fighting ensued as the Indians menaced Bouquet's defensive perimeter.[118] Robert Kirk of Montgomery's Highlanders recalled that the British made a rough barricade of flour bags, from which they launched bayonet charges whenever the Indians ventured close enough.[119] True to their tactical creed, these warriors merely 'gave way when pressed, and appeared again immediately'. British casualties mounted steadily and by nightfall the outlook for Bouquet's parched and weary command appeared bleak.[120] On the morning of the second day the Indians redoubled their efforts to break the British line. Bouquet was aware that the climax of the fight was approaching. The increasing audacity of the Indians prompted an attempt to lure them to close quarters. To achieve this design, Bouquet deliberately weakened one section of his line. Sensing victory, the Indians advanced, only to be caught off guard by a counter-attack. This crucial moment is described by Kirk:

115 Letter from Camp near Fort Prince George, 10 July 1761 (WO/34/47, fol. 94).

116 Extract of letter from Amherst to Grant, Albany, 1 August 1761, in CO/5/61, fol. 389. According to the Indian trader James Adair, the Cherokees were only prevented from staging a tenacious defence of their 'stupendous mountains' by a 'great want of ammunition'. See Adair, *The History of the American Indians* (London, 1775), p. 252.

117 Whilst the British considered that they had been attacked by at least an equal number of Indians, the Delaware warrior Killbuck later told Johnson that only 110 warriors were actually engaged (*Johnson Papers*, XI, 618).

118 See Bouquet's reports to Amherst, written from the battlefield itself on 5 and 6 August 1763 (*Papers of Bouquet*, VI, 338–40; 342–4).

119 *Kirk's Memoirs*, p. 77.

120 Writing on the evening of 5 August, Bouquet emphasised the desperate and uncertain situation of his command. This pessimistic passage was omitted when the despatch was published in London newspapers.

> the Indians thought we were going to break and run away, and being sure of their prey came in upon us in the greatest disorder; but they soon found their mistake, for we met them with our fire first, and then made terrible havock amongst them with out fixt bayonets, and continuing to push them everywhere, they set to their heels and were never able to rally again.[121]

The combat cost Bouquet the 'heavy loss' of 110 killed and wounded.[122] Bouquet's agile mind, combined with the tenacity of his Highlanders, had secured the survival of his column, although the transport requirements of the injured made it necessary to jettison the provisions destined for Fort Pitt.[123] Indian losses at Bushy Run are not known.[124] The outcome of the action excited widespread relief on the frontier, encouraging one newspaper to exclaim 'that Indians are no more invulnerable than other Men, when attacked on equal Terms and especially by British Troops'.[125] Although Bouquet's initial reaction was dampened by the scale of his losses, he rapidly grasped the significance of the combat. Writing from Fort Pitt on 11 August, Bouquet told Pennsylvania's governor James Hamilton of 'that Bloody affair in which the most Warlike of the savage Tribes have lost their Boasted Claim of being Invincible in the Woods'.[126] Modern historians have contrasted the fate of Bouquet's command with that of Braddock eight years earlier. In the 1920s, Colonel J. F. C. Fuller wrote that Bushy Run marked 'a complete effacement' of Braddock's disaster. More recently, Douglas Leach has seen Bushy Run as a 'clear vindication of British military discipline and valor when properly sustained in the wilderness by modified tactics based on experience', while King Lawrence Parker remarked that the action demonstrated that 'British regulars need not suffer the fate of Braddock and his army when properly trained and led by officers experienced in this kind of warfare'.[127]

121 *Kirk's Memoirs*, p. 79.

122 Bouquet to Amherst, Fort Pitt, 11 August 1763, in *Papers of Bouquet*, VI, 361.

123 *Annual Register*, 1763, p. 30.

124 An early report said '20 of their Great Warriors were found dead, besides a great Number wounded, and dragged away by their fellows' ('Extract of a letter from Lancaster, August 23', in *Pennsylvania Gazette*, no. 1809, 25 August 1763). Like the Plains Indians in the nineteenth century, the woodland warriors went to great lengths to prevent their wounded or dead from falling into enemy hands. For example, when the Cherokees fought Montgomery's column on 27 June 1760, the Indians 'retired hastily, dragging their killed and wounded with them by the legs and arms'. See Mante, *History of the Late War*, p. 291.

125 *Pennsylvania Gazette*, no. 1810, 1 September 1763.

126 Add. MSS 21,649, fol. 295.

127 J. F. C. Fuller, *British Light Infantry in the Eighteenth Century* (London, 1925), pp. 100–101; Leach, *Arms for Empire*, p. 501; Parker, 'Anglo-American Wilderness Campaigning', p. 310. See also Houlding, *Fit for Service*, p. 376; D. Gates, *The British Light Infantry Arm, c. 1790–1815, its creation, training and operational role* (London, 1987), p. 13.

Such findings are certainly logical, and suggest a natural learning process: Braddock and his men were novices in wilderness warfare, whereas Bouquet had accumulated extensive experience of local conditions, and commanded veterans. However, it could be argued that the true significance of Bouquet's victory at Bushy Run stems from the fact that it was untypical of the British Army's encounters with hostile Indians: on that occasion the Indians were beaten because they abandoned their usual 'skulking' tactics; by fighting at close quarters like Europeans they won the respect of their foes, only to lose the battle.[128]

A more realistic indication of the redcoats' Indian-fighting abilities is provided by an examination of that summer's events at Detroit and Niagara. Like Bouquet, Captain James Dalyell possessed ample experience of soldiering in America. In August 1758, Dalyell had earned the praise of Robert Rogers for his coolness when in command of a detachment of Gage's Light Infantry during a fierce encounter with French and Indians near Old Fort Anne;[129] after that fight Abercromby had thanked the officers and men involved for their fine conduct, hoping they were now 'satisfied that Indians are a despicable enemy, against men who will do their duty'.[130] Five years later, when Dalyell was serving as Amherst's aide-de-camp, the General chose him to head a reinforcement for Detroit after that settlement was blockaded by some 900 Indians under Pontiac. Gathering together about 250 men, Dalyell arrived safely, to the relief of the besieged commander, Major Henry Gladwin of the 80th Regiment. Gladwin's delight soon turned to anxiety when it became clear that Dalyell was determined to launch a night attack upon Pontiac's camp. Like so many other officers, Gladwin had gained his first taste of Indian-fighting with Braddock.[131] In his opinion the proposed sortie was too risky. Although out-ranked by Gladwin, Dalyell was a favoured member of the military family of Amherst, a man who despised Indians and now held a low opinion of their fighting abilities. In consequence, Dalyell gained his point, and in the early hours of 31 July, left

128 British commentators were deeply impressed by the Indians' determination at Bushy Run. Bouquet wrote: 'Indeed, they fought with the greatest bravery and resolution for two days' (Bouquet to Lt James McDonald, Fort Pitt, 28 August 1763 in Add. MSS 21,649, fol. 316).

129 *Rogers' Journals*, p. 118. Dalyell joined Gage's from the Royal Americans; he subsequently transferred to the prestigious Royal Regiment in 1760. See *Army List*, 1757; 1758; 1762.

130 'Monypenny Orderly Book', *BFTM* (December 1970), p. 91.

131 Gladwin was wounded at the Monongahela whilst a lieutenant in the 48th Foot. See *London Gazette*, no. 9505 (23–6 August), 1755.

Detroit with 276 men.[132] His officers included the veteran ranger, Major Rogers. The British marched two abreast along the 'Great Road' bordering the Detroit River; they were accompanied by a pair of boats – each mounting a 'paterrara' or swivel gun – intended to protect any retreat and remove casualties. As Gladwin had feared, Pontiac's warriors were waiting for the redcoats. The British advance-guard was ambushed as it negotiated a bridge, while another group of warriors, who had remained hidden as the British tramped past in the dark, now emerged to threaten Dalyell's line of retreat. Despite initial confusion the British regained their composure and counter-attacked. It was soon clear that the Indians sought to sever the column's line of retreat to Fort Detroit: indeed, the chiefs 'talked loud in the Front, animating their young Warriors to Courage in order to bring our Detachment on, that they might have the more time to get in the Rere'.[133] For some time Dalyell remained undecided whether to push on or retire. With the rear-guard facing mounting pressure, its commander Captain James Grant of the 80th Regiment urged decisive action. Grant 'took liberty to say, we should not give the Enemy time to Recollect, and recover themselves, that if he [Dalyell] intended to go on, we should push them, and if to retire, we should do it before they got in our Rear'.[134] The British finally withdrew in good order with the various parties covering each other, although Dalyell was killed along with twenty others. Another 42 men were wounded. The Indians later claimed to have lost only six warriors.[135] This rebuff stemmed directly from Dalyell's overconfidence. The result was predictable. One journal noted: 'Instead of surprising the Indians, our troops were themselves surprised, surrounded, and in the most imminent danger of a total defeat.'[136] When told of the setback, Amherst sprang to Dalyell's defence and sought to minimise the reverse.[137] The survivors no doubt viewed things differently: their opinions were more accurately expressed by one Detroit trader, who wrote of the 'damn'd Drubbing the savage Bougres gave us the 31st'.[138]

132 See 'Detail of the Action of the 31st July commanded by Capt Dalyell against the Indian Nations near Fort Detroit', in WO/34/49, fols 239–40. This report, which was sent by Gladwin to Amherst on 8 August, bears the signatures of fourteen officers, suggesting an 'official' version of events compiled in anticipation of an inquiry. Many passages are identical with an account forwarded to Sir William Johnson by Major Alexander Duncan of the 55th Foot (no date, in *Johnson Papers*, X, 762–6).

133 'Journal of the Siege of Detroit, By Lieutenant James MacDonald of the 60th Regt' in WO/34/49, fol. 8.

134 Duncan to Johnson, *Johnson Papers*, X, 764.

135 *London Magazine, 1763* (October), p. 545; *Siege of Detroit*, p. 263.

136 *Annual Register, 1763*, p. 26.

137 *Journal of Amherst*, p. 320; Amherst to William Johnson, 9 September 1763 (*NYCD*, VII, 547).

138 Cited in Cuneo, *Robert Rogers of the Rangers*, pp. 166–7.

Within weeks of the 'battle of Bloody Run', as Dalyell's action soon became known, further proof of the efficacy of traditional tribal tactics was given when the Senecas unleashed a devastating ambush on the Niagara portage trail. Like Pontiac's dispositions to baffle Dalyell's sortie, the tactics employed by the Indians on 14 September revealed thorough planning and considerable control. The Senecas baited their trap by attacking a convoy of wagons as it trundled down from the head of the falls towards Fort Niagara.[139] The firing alerted Lieutenants George Campbell and William Fraser, both experienced officers, who were encamped nearby with two companies of the 80th Regiment. These troops immediately marched to assist the convoy; one mile short of the site of the first ambush, they were themselves surprised and overwhelmed by the Senecas. According to a handful of shocked and wounded survivors, these warriors were naked, painted and disinclined to take prisoners. Altogether, this simple snare claimed the lives of more than 80 soldiers.[140] A Seneca chief named Dekanandi informed Sir William Johnson that 309 warriors were involved, and their sole loss amounted to one brave 'wounded with shot'. Indian participants had told Dekanandi that when pressed the two British relief companies had given ground: upon this the Indians 'filed of to the right & made a Wing so as to cut them of from the Fort'.[141] After examining the ground, Lieutenant-Colonel William Browning of the 46th Foot reported that the Senecas had launched their attack upon the companies from 'an advantagious hill coverd with brush and Commanding the Pass', whilst Major John Wilkins of the Royal Americans agreed that the site had been 'well chose by the Savages'.[142] As with Dalyell's defeat, Amherst refused to accept the potency of the Indian tactics. He concluded that the commendable zeal shown by Campbell and Fraser in hurrying to the convoy's aid must have left their men 'more Huddled together, & less on their Guard than they would have been on any other Occasion'.[143] The reverses at Niagara and Detroit offer a corrective to the belief that Bouquet's victory over the Ohio tribes had demonstrated the British Army's mastery of wilder-

139 See reports to Amherst from Lt-Col. Browning and Major Wilkins, dated Niagara, 16 and 17 September 1763 in WO/34/22, fols 176; 181–2; also Captain George Etherington, 60th Foot, to Johnson, 17 September, in *Johnson Papers*, X, 818, and *London Magazine, 1763* (October), p. 604.

140 'Return of the Killed Wounded and Missing in the Action on the Carrying Place of Niagara, the 14 Sept 1763' (WO/34/22, fol. 178).

141 'Journal of Indian Affairs', *Johnson Papers*, X, 892.

142 See Browning and Wilkins to Amherst, Niagara, 16 and 17 September 1763, in WO/34/22, fols 176; 181.

143 *Journal of Amherst*, p. 322; Amherst to Bouquet, New York, 3 October 1763, in Add. MSS 21,634, fol. 410.

ness warfare; by contrast, Bushy Run was in fact the exception that proved a very different rule.

The British Army's employment of Indian artefacts and techniques in the wilderness has already been noted. Ironically, the redcoats even adopted the characteristic Indian war cry that had once caused them such consternation. Describing the fighting on Martinique in 1762, Lieutenant John Grant of the 2/42nd recalled:

> we saw a large body of French immediately opposite to us, driving in the 60th who were slowly retiring before them to our right down the hill. We instantly gave the Indian Halloo, part of our Backwoods aquirements, the brave fellows of the 60th instantly stood, as if rivetted to the spot and advanced with us.[144]

Similarly, during skirmishing on Cuba that summer, British troops greeted charging Spanish cavalry with 'a fire (& a whoop) which kill'd & wounded a good many & set them scampering like the Devil'.[145] This yelping represented highly unorthodox behaviour: unlike the excitable French, who had a habit of shouting as they went into action, British soldiers were traditionally expected to maintain a 'nobly awful' silence on the battlefield.[146]

Whilst contributing to the distinctive identity of the redcoats who formed the 'American Army', such traits did not transform them into skilled woodsmen. The expeditions against the Cherokees had demonstrated that when operating in conjunction with 'friendly' Indians and other irregulars, British troops could penetrate the most difficult wilderness terrain; however, when forced to march in forests without such expert scouts, the redcoats continued to face the problems that had dogged them since Braddock's day. On his march to Fort Pitt, Bouquet lamented a dire need of 'men used to the woods' as his regulars had proved ineffective flankers. He added: 'I cannot send a Highlander out of my sight without running the risk of losing the man; which exposes me to a surprise from the sculking villains I have to deal with.'[147] To remedy this deficiency, Bouquet was obliged to recruit 'about thirty Woodsmen' to scout for the

144 'Journal of John Grant', p. 77.

145 See the anonymous journal, 'English against the Havana in 1762', dated Havana, 17 August 1762, in WO/34/55, fols 181–4; 181.

146 *Knox's Journals*, II, 78–9. Orders issued by Wolfe to the 20th Foot in 1755 read: 'The battalion is not to hallo, or cry out, upon any account whatsoever . . . till they are ordered to charge with their bayonets . . . [when] the battalion may give a warlike shout and rush in' (Entick, *General History*, IV, 92).

147 Bouquet to Lt-Col. James Robertson, Fort Bedford, 26 July 1763, in Add. MSS 21,634, fol. 335.

column.[148] Just months after Bushy Run, Major-General Gage likewise agreed with Bouquet that it was 'next to Impossible, to March in Woods with Regulars alone without being every moment Subject to a Surprise from which a Body of good Woodsmen would Affectualy Secure you'.[149] Bouquet had been unable to follow up his victory with an attack against the 'upper Delaware Towns' owing to a dearth of skilled frontiersmen.[150] During the methodical Muskingum expedition of 1764, Bouquet's army of 1,500 regulars and provincials was screened by just such a 'corps of Virginia volunteers advanced before the whole'.[151]

Indeed, the knowledge of 'irregular' warfare and local conditions accumulated by the redcoats during the long years of conflict in North America had made remarkably little difference to the British Army's ability to wage war against Indians. Though no longer unnerved by the mere shout or shadow of a tribesman, even Bouquet's seasoned veterans had much to learn before they could confront the woodland warriors on truly equal terms.[152] Yet, as will be seen, the redcoats' struggle to meet America's bush-fighting challenge had none the less prompted responses that would influence the British Army's conduct of operations far into the future.

148 Bouquet to Amherst, 26 July 1763, in *Papers of Bouquet*, VI, 326. Redcoats of the 49th and 74th Foot sent to quell the Tacky slave revolt on Jamaica in 1760 were likewise obliged to rely upon local scouts. Marching to attack a rebel camp in June, the regulars and militia were flanked by black Maroon auxiliaries who scoured the woods to prevent ambushes. After regulars had stormed the slave breast-work the Maroons completed the victory by flushing the fugitives out of the bushes from which they were maintaining a harassing fire. See Craton, *Testing the Chains*, pp. 135–6.

149 Letter from New York, 18 November 1763, in *Papers of Bouquet*, VI, 461.

150 Bouquet to Colonel Adam Stephen, Fort Pitt, 23 October 1763, in Ibid., p. 435.

151 Smith, *Expedition Against the Ohio Indians*, p. 8.

152 Bouquet's dispositions in 1764 emphasised *defensive* firepower, suggesting a reluctance to tackle Indians in the woods. See A. Starkey, 'European–Native American Warfare in North America 1513–1815', in *War in the Early Modern World, 1450–1815*, ed. J. Black (London, 1999), pp. 237–62; 255.

7

The tactical evolution of the redcoats

Long after the 'American Army' had marched into history, other redcoats faced the veterans of Napoleon Bonaparte's famed 'Army of Italy' among the sand dunes and palm groves of Egypt. During a remarkable fortnight in March 1801, a British task-force made good its amphibious landing at Aboukir Bay in the face of fierce opposition, then marched inland to confront and out-fight an experienced enemy at Mandara and Alexandria. Following upon depressing years of defeat at the hands of Republican France, the victorious Egyptian campaign provided a tonic that revived the jaded morale of the British Army.[1]

The redcoats who triumphed in Egypt were commanded by Sir Ralph Abercromby, a Scottish soldier with service dating back to the Seven Years War. Abercromby had spent his youthful campaigns in Germany rather than America, but the regiments he commanded in 1801 included no less than seven that had once formed part of the 'American Army'.[2] The presence of these units at the 'regeneration' of the British Army was singularly apt. Although the redcoats of Ticonderoga, Quebec and Martinique were long since dead or discharged, they had none the less bequeathed a significant legacy to those men who followed in their footsteps. Abercromby's victory in Egypt had rested on his men's mastery of a trio of key tactical skills: the amphibious assault landing; light infantry skirmishing; and the disciplined delivery of firepower from linear formations. A marked proficiency in all three of these areas had already been displayed some forty years earlier by the men of the 'American Army': indeed, nothing demonstrates the remarkable tactical flexibility of that force better than its development of skills that would come to characterise the renowned British infantry of the following century. Referring to the seasoned troops he commanded in the Peninsula, Wellington famously observed that this was an army with which he could 'go anywhere and do anything'; by focusing upon the hallowed Trinity of tactical techniques that would distinguish the redcoats' resurgence in 1801, this chapter seeks

1 See P. Mackesy, *British Victory in Egypt, 1801: The End of Napoleon's Conquest* (London, 1995); also 'Abercromby in Egypt: The Regeneration of the Army', in *The Road to Waterloo: The British Army and the Struggle Against Revolutionary and Napoleonic France, 1793–1815*, ed. A. J. Guy (London, 1990), pp. 101–10.

2 These were the 2/1st (Royals), 27th, 28th, 40th, 42nd, 44th and 58th.

to suggest that the Peer's verdict could be applied with equal justice to the 'American Army' of half a century before.

The birth of Britain's light infantry

An important consequence of the British Army's efforts to respond to North American wilderness conditions was the evolution of regular light infantry. As the previous chapter has indicated, attempts were made to give all soldiers of the 'American Army' some experience of 'bush-fighting'; however, there was increasing recognition of the need to field numbers of more highly trained specialists. The impetus for this significant step stemmed from growing dissatisfaction with the performance of the rangers; rumbling discontent came to a head in November 1757 after the lax discipline of a ranger patrol was witnessed by Captain James Abercrombie.[3] A friend and admirer of Rogers, the Captain was also aide-de-camp to his namesake uncle, Major-General Abercromby. As the latter explained to Forbes, such misbehaviour had underlined 'the necessity of new modelling that Corps' into 'a respectable body of men under proper discipline'.[4] Loudoun had originally intended to achieve this object by the creation of two ranging companies within each of the larger redcoat battalions; he hoped that the knowledge acquired by the volunteers training under Rogers would be disseminated when these cadets returned to their parent units.[5] This solution was shelved when Lieutenant-Colonel Gage of the 44th Foot – the commander of Braddock's advance-guard – offered to raise and clothe a regiment of 500 light infantry at his own expense, with the cost to be reimbursed if the plan was approved. Gage's initiative scored on two grounds: the first was purely economic, as the new corps would be paid at the same paltry rate as the British regulars; second, it would provide Loudoun with 'a Corp of Rangers that would be disciplined, and have Officers at their head on whom I can depend, which, except a very few is not the Case at present'.[6] Gage therefore secured his regiment, although the scheme was not without its critics. Sceptics included Forbes, who viewed the initiative as a 'most flagrant jobb' by which Gage would gain both fame (through 'the puff of assisting the Government in distress') and fortune (by

[3] At the time Rogers was sick with scurvy, and Captain John Stark commanded in his stead (Cuneo, *Robert Rogers of the Rangers*, pp. 61–2).

[4] Letters from Abercromby to Forbes, dated Albany, 29 November and 14 December 1757, in RH 4/86/1. Despite their kinship, uncle and nephew spelled their surnames differently.

[5] Pargellis, *Lord Loudoun*, pp. 304–5.

[6] See Loudoun to Pitt, New York, 14 February 1758, in *Correspondence of Pitt*, I, 191; also J. R. Alden, *General Gage in America* (Baton Rouge, 1947), pp. 41–3.

advancing to colonel's rank). On a more practical level, Forbes doubted whether regular pay would prove sufficient to attract men expected to undertake the notoriously onerous duties of the rangers.[7] In fact, when Gage set about raising his regiment, some recruits enlisted in the belief that they would be paid the same generous wage as the rangers – an illusion which unscrupulous officers like Quintin Kennedy (whose bush-fighting background had gained him a captaincy in the corps) did nothing to dispel.[8] Raised on a five-company establishment, Gage's regiment received a starter fund of 96 men drafted from Loudoun's regular battalions: all were to be 'active, young, strong, and healthy, for which the Commanding Officers will be answerable'.[9] Gage's battalion emerged early in 1758 as the '80th Regiment of Light Armed Foot' and saw much hard service over the next six years. Ironically, like the very rangers it sought to supplant, 'Gage's Light Infantry' also included an unusually high quota of men who bridled at regular discipline.[10]

Gage's regiment was the first officially recognised formation of regular light infantry in the British Army. Within months, other moves to swell Britain's light troops were also under way. In the force destined to attack Ticonderoga under Abercromby, rifle-barrelled carbines were issued to the ten best marksmen in each battalion, while Forbes also took a number of these weapons on his expedition to Fort Duquesne.[11] Meanwhile, the army bound for Louisbourg under Amherst was evolving its own light infantry. Orders issued at Halifax on 12 May announced the formation of a 'body of light infantry, from the different corps to act as irregulars'. Each regular battalion was to furnish 30 or 40 men: units with American service would give 'such as have been most accustomed to the woods, and are good marksmen', while those recently arrived from Europe were to supply 'active marchers, and men that are expert at firing ball'. All must be 'alert,

7 Unsigned memorandum in Forbes's hand (undated, but *c.* December 1757), in RH 4/86/2.

8 See, for example, GCM, Lake George Camp, 21 August 1758 (WO/71/66). Deserters William Moore, John Andrew, John Harrison and Thomas Vincent all claimed that they had enlisted in Gage's on the promise that they would receive 'Rangers Pay' of half a crown per day. All four were sentenced to death.

9 Orders, New York, 28 December 1757, in RH 4/86/1 (General Order Books of Loudoun's Commands).

10 Men of the 80th make frequent appearances within the courts martial records of the 'American Army'. According to Lieutenant Grant of the 2/42nd, Gage's was 'formed of all the Jail birds of america' ('Journal of John Grant', p. 65).

11 'Monypenny Orderly Book', in *BFTM* (December 1969), p. 348; an undated rough list of 'Artillery' (for Forbes's 1758 expedition) includes 100 'Carbines with rifled Barrels & Bayonets & moulds' (in RH 4/86/1). Twelve rifled carbines had been included in the munitions sent to North America with Braddock. See *Military Affairs in North America*, p. 483. However, while many Virginian and Pennsylvanian provincials employed 'grooved rifles', such weapons were never widely adopted by British regulars. See H. L. Blackmore, *British Military Firearms, 1650–1850* (London, 1961), p. 68. For a detailed discussion of the evidence see Parker, 'Anglo-American Wilderness Campaigning', pp. 384–97.

Spirited soldiers, able to endure fatigue'. This body was joined with the five companies of rangers allocated to the expedition and placed under the command of Major of Brigade George Scott.[12] Scott, who retained his captaincy in the 40th Foot, had recently lobbied Loudoun with suggestions for modifying the Army's dress and equipment.[13] Scott's notions may have influenced the ranger-like appearance of the light infantry at Louisbourg. According to one observer, this 550-strong corps was clad in a makeshift mufti:

> some in blue, some in green jackets, and drawers, for the easier brushing thro' the woods, with ruffs of black bear's skin round their necks, the beard of their upper lips, some grown into whiskers, others not so, but all well smutted on that part, with little round hats like several of our seamen – Their arms were a fusil, cartouch box of balls and flints, and a powder-horn flung over their shoulders.[14]

These 'chosen men' proved 'inconceivably useful' during the subsequent operations;[15] indeed, when the Louisbourg regiments dispersed to winter quarters they were retained as light companies within their own battalions. Before the onset of the new campaigning season the light infantry experiment was taken a stage further with the formation of light companies in all the regular battalions on the North American continent. Writing to Robert Rogers from New York on 26 February 1759, Lieutenant-Colonel Roger Townshend reported:

> We have chose out one hundred men from each regiment, and pitched upon the officers to act this year as light infantry; they are cloathed and accoutred as light as possible, and in my opinion are a kind of troops that has been much wanted in this country.[16]

Uniforms were modified by cropping the tricorne hat into a cap, shortening the coat, and removing the regimental lace. Colonels enjoyed some discretion over minor details, but the basic message was clear: 'The less they are seen in the Woods the better.'[17] The utility of such soldiers was quickly appreciated: besides raising light companies of their own, each of Wolfe's battalions was to provide 'well-chosen men' for a further three-company unit under Major John Dalling: this remained distinct from the

12 Fraser's Highlanders were to contribute 100 men. See *Knox's Journal*, I, 207.
13 See Scott to Loudoun, Halifax, 14 October 1757 and 13 February 1758 (LO 4641; 6927).
14 'An Authentick Account of the Reduction of Louisbourg', in *London Magazine, 1758* (December), p. 615.
15 *Knox's Journal*, I, 253; 279.
16 *Rogers' Journals*, p. 135.
17 'Monypenny Orderly Book', *BFTM* (June, 1971), pp. 169–70.

light infantry companies 'of the line', which were brigaded under the command of Lieutenant-Colonel William Howe of the 58th Foot.[18] During the Seven Years War the light companies never constituted an official part of the regimental establishment, but were instead created on an *ad hoc* basis according to demand.[19] For example, following the British capture of Quebec, the light infantry under Howe were ordered to rejoin their regiments: just two months later, every regiment reformed its light company.[20] Such units were often mustered from among the total available manpower, suggesting that all the regulars of the 'American Army' might be expected to fulfil this role if necessary; hence two of the light companies sent against the French invaders of Newfoundland in 1762 were composed of invalids from regiments serving in the West Indies who had been recuperating in New York's hospitals.[21] Similarly, considering the sickly condition of the Highland battalions returned to the mainland from Havana, the light companies who were soon after sent to counter the Ohio Indians must have comprised the fittest men that the residue of these depleted units could furnish. British regiments operating outside the Americas did not employ light companies;[22] those arriving in the theatre from elsewhere, like the Belle Isle regiments who joined the veterans of the 'American Army' for Monckton's Martinique expedition, were obliged to raise them forthwith.[23] Such companies were often organised into temporary brigades: an officer who served at Havana in one of the four regiments to sail from England with Albemarle reported engaging

18 *Knox's Journal*, I, 333–4; also 'Journal of Richard Humphrys', p. 33.

19 Official light companies were only established in 1771, when looming war with Spain over the Falkland Islands prompted augmentations. See Shy, *Toward Lexington*, pp. 372–3. Some regiments retained an 'unofficial' light company before this date: when Maj.-Gen. Hamilton Lambert reviewed the 28th Foot at Limerick on 28 May 1768, he noted that everything was according to regulations save for 'a Company called a Light Infantry one, which appeared cloathed in short Coats and Caps, but have notwithstanding proper Cloathing like the other Companys when required to be worn'. The 28th Foot had arrived in Ireland in August 1767 after a decade of service in America (WO/27/14).

20 Orders of 22 September and 22 November 1759, in *Knox's Journal*, II, 137; 281.

21 WO/1/5, fol. 246.

22 During the German campaigns, the army of Ferdinand of Brunswick in which the British contingent served was already well supplied with light troops, including hussars and Jägers. See Savory, *His Britannic Majesty's Army in Germany*, p. 484. C. T. Atkinson argued that the 87th and 88th regiments of Highlanders sent to Germany constituted 'light infantry', but his article 'The Highlanders in Westphalia, 1760–62 and the Development of Light Infantry' (in *JSAHR*, XX (1941), 208–33) offers no real evidence that these units performed such a role, and it is significant that Savory omits them from the total of Ferdinand's light troops. However, Atkinson does note a development in the autumn of 1761 when selected volunteers from the British infantry were 'appointed Chasseurs' (ibid., p. 219). Known as 'Major Fraser's Chasseurs', this unit earned a high reputation in the campaigns of that year and 1762 (Savory, *His Britannic Majesty's Army in Germany*, pp. 354; 372).

23 Orders, 31 December 1761, in 'Hamilton Notebook', p. 218.

himself 'into a service called the Light Infantry, a company of 'em having been formed out of each regiment and the whole joined together'.[24]

The influential military historian Peter Paret has traced the roots of the British light companies to European rather than American traditions: Paret bases this conclusion on two misconceptions: first, that the Royal American Regiment raised in 1756 was itself a light infantry formation; second, that the 60th Foot was actually recruited – as originally intended – from German and Swiss immigrants.[25] Building on these assumptions, Paret concludes that the origins of Britain's light infantry tradition rest among the gamekeepers and hunters of Europe's forests. On Paret's initial point, it is certainly true that on the formation of the Royal Americans, Lord Loudoun ordered its recruits to be trained in marksmanship and more flexible manoeuvres 'in order to qualify them for the Service of the Woods'.[26] Loudoun was acting on the recommendations of Lieutenant-Colonel Frederick Haldimand, a Swiss mercenary who had served in the Prussian Army throughout the War of the Austrian Succession before joining the 60th.[27] It is not known to what extent Loudoun's instructions were actually followed, but in May 1757, another Royal American, Colonel Jacques Prevost, was busy promoting his own proposals for the regulars in America to be clothed, armed and trained on a different footing from those in Europe.[28] More important, the fact that Henry Bouquet was still calling for similar reforms after 1764 strongly suggests that these early initiatives fell by the wayside.[29] In addition, throughout the Seven Years War the four battalions of the Royal Americans were employed as standard 'line' infantry; all raised light companies in 1759, a measure that would have been unnecessary if these battalions already fulfilled this specialist function. To address the second strand of Paret's argument, whilst the Royal Americans did muster Germans recruited on both sides of the Atlantic, the regiment's eventual composition was far more mixed: it would therefore be misleading to suggest that this unit fielded large

24 'Letters of Nicholas Delacherois', *JSAHR* (1973), p. 9.

25 P. Paret, 'Colonial Experience and European Military Reform at the End of the Eighteenth Century' in *BIHR*, XXXVII (1964), 47–59; 52.

26 These instructions were issued on 28 December 1756. See Pargellis, *Lord Loudoun*, pp. 299–300.

27 See Stuart R. J. Sutherland, Pierre Tousignant and Madeleine Dionne-Tousignant, 'Haldimand, Sir Frederick', in *DCB*, V, 887–904.

28 Prevost's 'Memoire Sur La Guerre D'Amerique' was addressed to the Duke of Cumberland. See *Military Affairs in North America*, pp. 337–40.

29 The whole question of the training and role of the Royal Americans at this time has been confused by J. F. C. Fuller. In his *British Light Infantry* (pp. 102–4), Fuller quoted information given by Lewis Butler in *Annals of the King's Royal Rifle Corps*, I, 160–61. This material was derived from Smith, *Expedition Against the Ohio Indians* (pp. 48–9) and concerned the training techniques that Bouquet advocated for his proposed battalion of 'hunters', not those in use by the Royal Americans.

numbers of the hereditary foresters who staffed the Jäger companies of the German princelings.

Rather than drawing upon European antecedents, the British light infantry boasted a New World lineage.[30] As the evidence considered above makes clear, the British Army's first regular light infantry unit, Gage's 80th Foot, was raised with the avowed intention of providing a more disciplined version of the existing American rangers; five of the ensigns employed in that unit had actually learned ranging techniques under the supervision of Robert Rogers.[31] The light infantry employed at Louisbourg were commanded by George Scott, a native-born officer whose knowledge of irregular warfare once again reflected experience of American rather than European conditions. Just as America's wilderness environment had first highlighted the need for light infantry, so that continent's indigenous irregulars were to provide the natural inspiration for such troops.

Paret has also argued that the British light infantry evolved in America during the second half of the eighteenth century were essentially units of regular line infantry rather than authentic 'light' troops.[32] This verdict holds true for the Revolutionary War of 1775 to 1783, when the light infantry usually operated as 'élite' battalions within the main line of battle, relinquishing genuine skirmishing duties to the Hessian Jägers.[33] The light infantry of Wolfe and Amherst were likewise employed as 'crack' assault troops on occasion, often operating in conjunction with the brigaded regimental grenadier companies; however, these first light companies were also expected to adopt a skirmishing role when required. The flexibility demanded of these units emerges from surviving orders. Those issued in 1758 to the light troops intended 'to oppose the Indians, Canadians, and other painted Savages' of Cape Breton deserve quotation at length: they represent the British Army's earliest surviving statement of light infantry doctrine:

> The Commander of the light troops must teach his Corps to attack & to defend themselves judiciously always endeavouring to get upon the Enemy's Flank, and equally watchfull to prevent them surrounding them: They must be instructed to chuse good Posts, & to lay themselves in ambuscade to advantage ... They

30 The importance of North American irregular warfare for the genesis of the light infantry is emphasised in E. Robson, 'British Light Infantry in the Mid-Eighteenth Century: The Effect of American Conditions', *Army Quarterly* (1952), 209–22.

31 Cuneo, *Robert Rogers of the Rangers*, p. 61.

32 Paret, 'Colonial Experience and European Military Reform', *BIHR* (1964), p. 52.

33 See R. Atwood, *The Hessians: Mercenaries from Hessen-Kassel in the American Revolution* (Cambridge, 1980), pp. 96; 130–38.

> must always march in [single?] Files, & generally fight in a single rank; pushing at the Enemy when they see him in Confusion, and that the Ground favours their Efforts; never pursue with too much eagerness, nor to give way, except in a very great inequality of numbers. They must avoid huddling together, & running into a Lump; In such a situation they are a fair object for their adversaries, & not able to employ their Arms to purpose.[34]

This versatile role, which combined the skills of the skirmisher with the determination and discipline of the regular line soldier, was also specified in Wolfe's army during the following summer. At Quebec on 7 September 1759, orders stated that the 'Light Infantry have no fixed post in the order of battle, they will be thrown upon one or other of the wings, with a view to take the enemy's flank, or rear if occasion offers'. Exactly one year later, when Murray's Quebec army approached Montreal, the light infantry and rangers were instructed to concentrate on harrying the enemy's flanks and mounting an active pursuit. Should the army be attacked while forming up, the light infantry would provide cover 'by skirmishing to check the enemy'.[35] Orders for the landing at Newfoundland in 1762 tasked the light companies with securing the landing place to cover the disembarkation of the battalions. If the enemy fell back, the light infantry should

> strive to get upon their flanks [and] cut off their retreat if possible ... but ... must not pursue out of the reach of support from the Battalions. Upon the march, the light Infantry will cover the front and flanks of the Line, seizing every commanding ground till the line has passed; wherever they may chance to fall in with the enemy they will stand their ground, and never retire to the Battalions, which shall always march up and support them.[36]

From their début at Louisbourg, where they spearheaded the amphibious assault upon Gabarus Bay, the light infantry were distinguished by dash and aggression. Perhaps the most celebrated instance of light infantry work was provided at Quebec on 13 September 1759. Howe's light companies led the amphibious landing during the hours of darkness, then scrambled up the cliff to rout the French picket posted in defence of a more practicable path. During the subsequent action on the Plains of Abraham the light infantry covered the vulnerable rear of the army's left flank.[37]

34 'Orders before Landing at Louisbourg, 1758' (CKS, U1350/030/1).

35 'Orderly Books at Quebec', in *Northcliffe Collection*, p. 163; *Knox's Journal*, II, 518.

36 Fyers, 'Loss and Recapture of St John's, Newfoundland', in *JSAHR* (1932), p. 201.

37 See General Townshend to Pitt, camp before Quebec, 20 September 1759, in *Correspondence of Pitt*, II, 165–7.

The ubiquitous light infantry were much in evidence during the fighting on Martinique in 1762. Along with the massed grenadier companies these light troops dominated the fight for the island, making short work of the terrain and defenders that had baffled other redcoats three years before. Describing the attack upon Morne Tartenson on 24 January, an officer in Lieutenant-Colonel George Scott's light infantry corps told how the men negotiated a deep gully while under 'a very smart fire' from French posted within a sugar-cane plantation: 'several of the men tumbled to the bottom, others let themselves down by the help of the trees, and then flinging their muskets at their backs, clambered up again as fast as they could'. Under the covering fire of a battery, the light infantry re-formed and pushed forwards, at which 'the Monsieurs' rapidly withdrew.[38] Three days later the light infantry corps under Scott and Major John Leland played a key role in repulsing the determined French sortie. Ordered to turn out, the light infantry ran to their arms and without bothering to form into 'very regular order' attacked so furiously that the French were driven from 'hill to hill'. With night coming on, cautious senior officers attempted to halt the headlong advance. However,

> Leylands Light Infantry never stopped till they found themselves, about 8 o'clock, unexpectedly in possession of the French camp batteries and guns on Morne Grenier. The fugitives proved our guides through passes which we possibly might never have found without them.[39]

Summing up the campaign, Monckton lavished praise upon the grenadiers, light infantry and rangers – 'the Warmest part of the Service having fallen to their Lot';[40] he later observed that the light infantry constituted 'a chosen body of men, on whom I had the utmost dependence'.[41] Light infantry bore the brunt of the fighting at Newfoundland later that summer. Early on 15 September, Captain Charles McDonell's company of 'recovered' men and the provincial light infantry executed a particularly daring feat by scaling the crags of Signal Hill. Although the French fired upon the climbers, the light infantry did not respond until they reached the summit: in his journal of the campaign William Amherst recorded how these troops subsequently 'drove three Companies of the French Grenadiers and two pickets from the most advantageous ground I ever

38 'Letter from an Officer in Col. Scott's Light Infantry', Martinique, 10 February 1762, in *Gentleman's Magazine, 1762* (March), pp. 130–31.

39 Dr Richard Huck to Captain James Dalyell, Martinique, 6 February 1762, in NAM MSS 7905–48.

40 Monckton to the Earl of Egremont, Fort Royal, Martinique, 9 February 1762, in *Gentleman's Magazine, 1762* (March), p. 126.

41 *Proceedings of A General Court Martial . . . For the Trial of a Charge Preferred By Colin Campbell, Esq Against the Honourable Major General Monckton* (London, 1764), p. 90.

saw – really, almost inaccessible'.[42] As Amherst informed his brother, this performance had made such an impression upon the defeated French commander at St John's, Joseph Louis, Comte d'Haussonville, that he had 'formed a plan of turning his own Regiment of four Battalions into light Infantry as soon as ever he arrives in France'.[43] Indeed, although initially formed to counter the Indians and other irregulars fielded by New France, the light infantry evolved within the 'American Army' had proved equally useful against more conventional opponents.

By the close of the Seven Years War, the light companies employed during that conflict's American campaigns had acquired a formidable and enduring reputation. Commenting upon the heavy losses sustained by British troops during the confused retreat from Concord in April 1775, Lord George Germain drew a parallel with the fate of Braddock's men twenty years earlier. Braddock's redcoats had also been tormented by enemies they could not see; however, as Lord George pointed out with pardonable exaggeration,

> Another discipline was then establish'd and all our light troops in America were taught to separate and secure themselves by trees, walls or hedges, and became so formidable both to the Indians and Canadians that they were victorious upon all occasions, and ever protected the main body of the army from surprise or insult.

Given this encouraging precedent, Germain had no doubts that Wolfe's light infantry specialist William Howe – who was once again serving in America – would soon 'teach the present army to be as formidable as that he formerly acted with'.[44]

The amphibious assault landing

When Thomas Pingo designed a medal to commemorate the capture of Louisbourg he emphasised cooperation between Britain's land and sea services: the obverse depicted a globe crushing the prone figure of France, flanked by a British grenadier and sailor; the motto 'Pariter-in-Bella' ('equal in wars') reinforced the clear visual message.[45] As has been noted in Chapter 1, the ability of the redcoats to work effectively with the

42 Fyers, 'Loss and Recapture of St John's, Newfoundland', in *JSAHR* (1932), p. 198.
43 Letter from St John's, 22–3 September 1762, in ibid., p. 203.
44 Germain to Lord Suffolk, 16 or 17 June 1775, in *HMC: Stopford-Sackville Manuscripts*, II, 2.
45 When exhibited in 1760, the medal was dedicated to the 'Union of the Army and Navy at Louisburg'. See C. Eimer, *The Pingo Family and Medal Making in 18th-Century Britain* (London, 1998), p. 47.

Royal Navy was a crucial component of Britain's war effort in the Americas. The proficiency in amphibious warfare that Pingo's design celebrated had been apparent at Guadeloupe and Quebec in 1759, and was to prove equally decisive during the Caribbean operations of 1762: these reached their zenith on 7 June, when 11,800 redcoats were landed at Coximar, near Havana, without the loss of a single man. While the warships' guns shattered the Spanish shore defences, the assault craft were assembled in a fashion approximating the ultimate combat formation of the troops. The landing then proceeded under cover of the ships' broadsides, with the leading waves being disembarked swiftly and efficiently. The Havana landings went exactly to plan, and the whole episode has been hailed as a model of its kind.[46] Yet this expertise had not been acquired easily; it reflected the experience of combined operations accumulated by soldiers and sailors alike over the previous five years; indeed, many of the redcoats that Albemarle inherited from Monckton had already participated in the expeditions to Louisbourg, Quebec and Martinique.[47]

The 'American Army''s development of an amphibious capacity was all the more remarkable given the traditional hostility between soldiers and sailors. In keeping with the spirit of Pingo's medal, the official despatches of British generals and admirals habitually emphasised the amity of their relationship: the word most often employed to describe this apparently blissful state of affairs was 'harmony'. However, such surface tranquillity often concealed hidden tensions. Although Wolfe's official despatch to Pitt from Quebec contained no hint of displeasure at Saunders and his crews, the General's personal journal tells another story. Noting on 8 July that the frigates and bomb ketches were keeping their distance from the French defences, Wolfe remarked on the 'Amazing backwardness in these matters on the side of the fleet'. Three weeks later, following the failure of his attack at Montmorency, Wolfe reported that the 'Accident of our boats running aground upon a shoal lost us a great deal of time'.[48] Again, whilst both General Monckton and Admiral Rodney had stressed the 'harmony' of their operations at Martinique in 1762, Albemarle arrived to find a very different situation: as he reported in his informal letter to Amherst, everything was 'in the greatest confusion' because Monckton and Rodney were 'upon ill terms', with the consequence that the 'service suffers'.[49]

46 See D. Syrett, 'The British Landing at Havana: An Example of an Eighteenth-Century Combined Operation', in *Mariner's Mirror*, LV (1969), 325–31.

47 Five battalions – the 15th, 28th, 35th, 48th and 3/60th – were present on all three of these occasions.

48 Willson, 'Fresh Light on the Quebec Campaign', in *Nineteenth Century & After*, (March 1910), pp. 452, 456. Writing to Saunders on 30 August 1759, Wolfe agreed to amend his official despatch in line with the Admiral's opinion that he was too critical of the Navy's role on 31 July (Willson, *Life and Letters of Wolfe*, pp. 460–63).

49 Letter of 6 May, in WO/34/55, fol. 139.

Given the polarity of Georgian Englishmen's attitudes towards their land and sea services, it is unsurprising that friction should exist between the two. According to the prevailing stereotype, soldiers were downtrodden minions poised to oppress their fellow countrymen; by contrast, sailors were roistering 'Hearts of Oak' whose carefree daring held foreigners at defiance and secured the seas for Britain's commerce. While a standing army allegedly threatened English liberties, a powerful navy guaranteed their survival. Newspapers regaled their readers with anecdotes of such 'Jolly Tars' as the men of the *Active* who lavished their prize money from the *Hermione* on a succession of 'uncommon pranks': dissatisfied with the fare offered at a Plymouth inn, one group promptly demanded a pan and butter so that they could 'fry their watches' instead. There was also something admirably eccentric about the sailor who received 250 lashes at Portsmouth – and insisted upon dancing a brisk hornpipe after every 50 strokes of the 'cat'.[50] Despite the Army's well-publicised victories, few such tales were told about soldiers. Like many of their land-locked countrymen, sailors frequently viewed the redcoat with contempt. As the old adage put it: 'A messmate before a shipmate; a shipmate before a landsman; a landsman before a dog; but a dog before a soldier.' Such ingrained prejudices were hardly conducive to the 'harmony' essential for successful 'conjunct expeditions'. When soldiers and sailors mingled, traditional enmities could escalate into violence. In March 1757 there were serious disturbances at Plymouth Dock after men of Anstruther's 58th Foot clashed with seafarers: triggered by 'a meer triffle', the fracas none the less resulted in 'broken heads on both sides'.[51]

Soldiers embarked upon amphibious operations were creatures out of their natural element – the lumbering redcoated 'lobsters' of contemporary slang. Conditions encountered aboard the transport ships did little to increase the soldier's confidence. In the summer of 1757, as the 15th Foot prepared to join the expedition to the Bay of Biscay, James Murray revealed his forebodings: Murray, an 'old expeditioner' who had survived the Carthagena débâcle, feared that the cramped conditions on board the transports, compounded by a lack of ventilators to clear the fetid atmosphere below decks, would cost the lives of 'many brave fellows' through the 'corruption of the air'.[52] In the opinion of James Miller, who participated in this expedition, the accommodation provided for soldiers between decks was 'not very conducive to ease or health'. Berths measuring six feet square by three feet six inches high, and

50 *Felix Farley's Bristol Journal*, 29 January and 10 September 1763.

51 Colonel Robert Anstruther to Barrington, Plymouth Dock, 18 March 1757, in WO/1/973, p. 45.

52 Murray to Amherst, Newport Camp, 20 August 1757 (CKS, U1350/013/5).

arranged in tiers, each housed four or five men who were obliged to 'creep into these holes' as best they could. Miller was loath to go below, 'for there proceeds, such a disagreeable stench, of putrid breaths, when you are going down the hatchway, that no being, accustomed to fresh air, can bear'. In particular, when cheese or 'grog' was being served, the resulting 'compound of Villainous Smells' was 'enough to Suffocate a Hottentot'.[53]

Vessels often shipped more soldiers than their tonnage could comfortably accommodate. In May 1758, when 'Jonas' embarked at the Isle of Wight for France, his transport the *Constant Jean* – a ship of 'about three hundred tons burthen' – was so 'extremly thronged' by the 500 soldiers, women and crew on board, that half had to remain on deck at any one time.[54] At the embarkation all was bewildering bustle:

> If by chance a soldier was in the sailors way, presently it was 'D——e get out you land-lobster' or 'give us a pull at this fore tackle to get the yaul in, or by G—— some of you lobsters will run away with her in the night'.

As the breeze freshened, those who were strangers to the sea soon began to suffer. With few soldiers now able to remain upon deck, conditions below grew hellish. The atmosphere was not improved when water shipped through the hatch-ways 'set the women a screaming'. The aftermath of the gale disclosed a sorry sight. 'Jonas' recalled: 'Most of the poor soldiers looked very dejected by the sickness, and the ship was in a nasty condition'. The fruitless cross-channel expeditions of that summer exerted a heavy toll upon the redcoats employed: many sickened and died, 'chiefly occasioned by lying so thick on board'.[55]

The inauspicious landings upon the Breton and Norman coasts had employed purpose-built landing craft rather than the customary ship's boats. Evolved in response to the notorious setbacks encountered by the previous year's Rochefort expedition, specimens were tested and approved in April 1758.[56] These 'flat-bottomed boats' incorporated a shallow draft designed to ferry troops close inshore; carried on board the men-of-war and transports, they were hoisted out immediately before use.[57] One authority on amphibious operations, the army officer Thomas

53 'Memoirs of an Invalid', pp. 12–13.

54 At this period the official ratios were two tons per man for long voyages, and one and a half or one tons for shorter trips. See D. Syrett, 'Living Conditions on the Navy Board's Transports during the American War, 1775–1783', in *MM*, LV (1969), 87–94; 88.

55 *A Soldier's Journal*, pp. 13–15; 19–21; 37.

56 Middleton, *Bells of Victory*, p. 66.

57 See H. Boscawen, 'The Origins of the Flat-bottomed Landing Craft 1757–58', in *Army Museum '84* [*National Army Museum Report*, 1984], 23–30; also D. Syrett, 'The Methodology of British Amphibious Operations During the Seven Years and American Wars', *MM*, LVIII (1972), 269–80; 272–4.

Molyneux, remained critical of the new craft, noting the 'Crouding and Confusion' that resulted when they were employed during an unopposed landing that August.[58] Refinements followed, and four years later the German traveller Count Frederick Kielmansegge could report how these 'flat boats' had 'very much accelerated the embarkation and disembarkation of troops'. In February 1762, Kielmansegge accompanied senior officers as they watched one of the regiments bound for Cuba, Lord Frederick Cavendish's 34th Foot, board their boats at Portsmouth.[59] The drill that so impressed the Count was soon duplicated under active-service conditions at Havana.

Things had not always gone so smoothly; indeed, Britain's first significant success of the war – the morale-boosting capture of Louisbourg – had only followed on an extremely risky assault landing. Unlike those troops raiding the French coast, the Louisbourg army lacked the new landing craft: instead, Amherst's men employed a motley flotilla including men-of-war's boats, flat-bottomed New England bateaux, and whaleboats requisitioned from the Greenland fisheries.[60] The weeks before the onset of the campaign saw elaborate exercises at Halifax intended to give the men some experience of amphibious warfare.[61] Orders issued on 21 May specified procedures destined to become standard practice during subsequent operations: firing from the boats was strictly forbidden; bayonets were only to be fixed once the troops were ashore. As soon as the men quit their craft they were to 'form and march directly forwards to clear the beach and charge whatever is before them'; they were warned against pursuing too far, and instead instructed to secure the beach-head for the comrades who followed.[62] For the attack at Gabarus Bay on 8 June, the British had arrayed their boats in three divisions: the left under Brigadier Wolfe, consisting of the light infantry, rangers, grenadiers and Fraser's Highlanders, encountered heavy fire as it attempted to land in Freshwater Cove. Withdrawing towards the centre, it luckily secured a beach-head after a handful of light infantry gained a lodgement on an undefended spur of rocks. At this Wolfe had leapt ashore at the head of reinforcements, taking the French lines in the rear and forcing the defenders to abandon their positions in panic. The remainder of the army had thereafter landed with

[58] Thomas More Molyneux, *Conjunct Expeditions: Or Expeditions that have been carried on jointly by the Fleet and Army* ... (London, 1759), pp. 211–13; 234.

[59] See *Diary of a Journey to England in the Years 1761–1762, By Count Frederick Kielmansegge*, trans. Countess Kielmansegge (London, 1902), pp. 258–9.

[60] Boscawen, 'Origins of the Flat-Bottomed Landing Craft', *Army Museum '84*, pp. 24; 30 (note 7).

[61] Hitsman and Bond 'Assault Landing at Louisbourg', *CHR*, 1954, pp. 321–2; also, James Cuninghame to Lord George Sackville, 'on board the *Ludlow Castle* at sea', 30 May 1758, in *HMC: Stopford-Sackville Manuscripts*, II, 262.

[62] 'Lt. Gordon's Journal of the Siege of Louisburg', *Journal of the Royal United Service Institution*, LX (1915), 117–52; 121.

little opposition, although a 'boisterous surf' staved many boats and left several men badly hurt.[63] According to another eyewitness, the first troops ashore followed their orders to the letter: not a single musket was fired until they 'gained Footing', upon which 'they immediately fix'd their Bayonets' and stormed the French breastworks. The same correspondent reported the enemy's astonished verdict that 'none, but Englishmen, or Madmen would have attempted what we did'.[64] Wolfe himself considered the attempt to be 'rash and ill-advised', only succeeding 'by the greatest of good fortune imaginable'.[65] He later confessed: 'I wouldn't recommend the Bay of Gabarouse for a descent, especially as we manag'd it.'[66] The Brigadier's sentiments were echoed by other redcoats. James Miller reported how, despite a 'great Swell, the troops embarked, on board the flat boats, and pushed for the shore'. Behind their abatis, the French held their fire until the boats drew near, then poured in a torrent of shot. Several craft were sunk by gunfire, and others capsized in the surf; these included a boat carrying part of the 15th's grenadier company, 'by which, one Officer, two sergeants, and thirty fine fellows, were lost'; the only survivors were those few men who could swim, and the drummer, who was found 'bouyed'd up' by his instrument.[67]

When James Thompson joined the assault with the grenadier company of Fraser's Highlanders the men were packed so tightly into their craft that there was no room for rowers; they were instead taken in tow by a ship's boat. Nearing the shore, the grenadiers were caught in a murderous crossfire. Those slain included Thompson's friend and patron Captain Charles Baillie, while one 24lb roundshot killed Lieutenant John Cuthbert, a sergeant and the tillerman before lodging itself in the stern post. The boat was struck so frequently that the Highlanders were obliged to plug the holes with their bulky plaids. As the vessel began to founder, the grenadiers were transferred to another craft: according to Thompson, their own boat was later recovered and taken to England as a curiosity, 'for she was completely riddled with shot-holes, and nearly a bucket-full of musket balls and other small shot was taken out of her'. Under covering fire from the warships, Thompson and his comrades were finally landed, although nearly swamped by the surf.[68]

63 'An Authentick Account of the Reduction of Louisbourg', in *London Magazine*, 1758 (November), pp. 550–52. Invalids of Fraser's Highlanders included Alexander McTavish, described as 'Bruised at landing at Louisbourg' (WO/116/5, fol. 35).

64 'Letter from a Gentleman ... Camp at the Light-House Point, the East Side of Louisbourg Harbour, August 4, 1758', in *American Magazine, 1758* (August), p. 559.

65 Wolfe to Major Walter Wolfe, Camp before Louisbourg, 27 July 1758, in Willson, *Life and Letters of Wolfe*, pp. 384–5.

66 Wolfe to Lord George Sackville, [Louisbourg, 30] July, 1758, in *HMC: Stopford-Sackville Manuscripts*, II, 263.

67 'Memoirs of an Invalid', pp. 20–21.

68 Harper, *Fraser Highlanders*, pp. 48–9.

Like the redcoats bound for Louisbourg, Hopson's battalions received some basic training in amphibious warfare before reaching their objective; waiting for their scattered ships to gather at Barbados, the General and Commodore Moore put the time to good use 'and exercised the Troops frequently in Landing', which was 'of much Service to them'.[69] At Martinique and Guadeloupe, the redcoats were disembarked safely after Holmes's warships overawed the shore batteries. The troops sent to storm Fort Louis on Valentine's Day 1759 were not so lucky; they included Lieutenant Grant of the Black Watch, whose account of the attack provides some valuable insights into the particular hazards of amphibious warfare. Initially, all had gone to plan, with the Highlanders and marines of the landing party remaining as 'mere spectators' while two ships of the line unleashed their broadsides upon the fort; however, once the landing party clambered into the flat-bottomed boats the barrage was lifted for fear of hitting them. At this, hundreds of French had reoccupied the battered bastion and opened such a heavy fire that the colonel of marines ordered the boats to retire. There now followed a bizarre incident which serves as a reminder of the importance of reputation among army officers, and warns against taking an overly rosy view of Georgian combined operations. As the boats returned alongside the *Berwick*, the disappointed commodore, Captain William Harman, shouted 'dont give the d——d cowardly fellows a rope'. Aggrieved at this slur upon his honour, Captain William Murray of the Highlanders stood and uttered a menacing response: 'Capt Harman, we are under command and were forced to obey but rest assured you shall answer to me for the expression you have used.' A chastened Harman hastily explained that his rebuke had not encompassed the Highlanders, but rather the marines. Murray remained so indignant that he ordered his boat to shove off for the shore, at which the others were shamed into following. On this occasion the attack was pressed home, although in some confusion. Grant recalled:

> Getting out of the Boat, I stumbled over a stone and fell forward into the water. My servant thinking me mortally wounded, seized me and was dragging me on shore, in doing so he scraped my shins against the Grapnall. We all rushed on pell mell, and the French ran like hares up the hill at the back of the battery.

During the first attack, the band of the *Roebuck* had played 'Britons Strike Home', only to cease upon the landing party's ignominious return. Once the fort was stormed, the sailors cheered and manned the yards to the

[69] Hopson to Pitt, Basseterre, Guadeloupe, 30 January 1759, in *Correspondence of Pitt*, II, 20; Moore to John Clevland, *Cambridge*, Basseterre, Guadeloupe, 30 January 1759 (ADM/1/307), fol. 109.

strains of 'God Save the King'. Grant was relieved to survive this watery baptism of fire with both his person and honour intact, although the experience left a deep impression on the young Scot. In a comment that encapsulates the inevitable disorientation of the soldier embarked upon an amphibious assault, Grant observed: 'of all the species of warfare that of landing is the most unpleasant [as] you present a mark for your en[e]my and you are not in your element'.[70]

The river-borne raids that prefaced Wolfe's victory on the Plains of Abraham offer another facet of the redcoats' experience of American amphibious warfare. A detailed account of these operations from the perspective of the private soldier survives in the journal of Richard Humphrys of the 28th Foot, who served the Quebec campaign in the ranks of Dalling's Light Infantry. In early August 1759, this corps was joined with Gorham's rangers, the 15th Foot and the 3rd Battalion of the Royal Americans; placed under the command of Brigadier Murray, these units sailed upriver to disrupt the French communications above Quebec. On 8 August, the small flotilla reached Pointe-aux-Trembles, where preparations were made to land; Dalling's corps would lead the assault, covered by the battalions. At 3.00 am the troops occupied the 'flat bottom'd boats'. An hour later the boats set off, but the crews lay on their oars within musket shot of the shore while the *Squirrel* frigate, two sloops of war and a pair of floating batteries silenced a trio of French floating batteries. At six the signal to land was given and the light infantry headed for the shore. Two companies reached the shallows and maintained a brisk fire from behind sheltering rocks. Offshore in his barge, Murray spotted French troops arriving to reinforce the Indians who were 'lying in the Bush', and ordered a withdrawal. As Humphrys and his comrades retreated, the boats pulled away, leaving them waist deep in water. The stranded light infantrymen threatened to fire upon the sailors 'if they did not Instantly Return and take us in'. At this the boats turned back, although 'at last some was Obliged to Swim for it the Enemy firing so hot at them'. Once out of range the soaked survivors cleaned their muskets and were issued dry ammunition. The British had suffered heavily, although it was impossible to gauge the enemy's losses, 'they being in the Bush, and we never having the Satisfaction to get on the Sod'. That afternoon a second attack was made. On this occasion one of the light infantry's boats 'unfortunately Struck upon a Rock', with the result that all save eleven of the men on board became casualties. As Humphrys observed,

70 'Journal of John Grant', pp. 30–35. See also the account in Moore to Clevland, aboard *Cambridge*, Basseterre, Guadeloupe, 6 March 1759 (ADM/1/307, fol. 139). Sadly, Harman's letters for 1759 are missing from the Admiralty Papers in the Public Record Office.

> everything went against us for this day, the Light Infantry being in the morning at the First attempt, three hundred and Seventy strong, and after the Second we had but One hundred and Twenty eight, but what was either kill'd wounded or taken prisoner.

That night they had returned aboard the warships in a 'forlorn Condition'.[71] Despite these discouraging setbacks, two days later a successful landing was made on the south shore at Sainte-Croix, followed soon after by a destructive raid upon a French military depot at Deschambault.[72]

Experience gained during these arduous amphibious probes was to prove invaluable in the coming weeks as the Quebec campaign moved towards its spectacular finale: survivors from the light companies involved in the up-river operations led the audacious landing above the city on the morning of 13 September 1759. The veterans of the 'American Army' emerged with credit from the events of that remarkable night. Orders issued on the eve of the assault once again emphasised the need for the 'Men to be quite silent' in the boats, while the first body to get ashore was to 'march directly to the Enemy & drive them from any Little Post they may occupy'.[73] The discipline maintained throughout the nail-biting approach to the landing zone proved beyond reproach. According to a volunteer among the light infantry in the leading boat, a French sentry who challenged the vulnerable flotilla was pacified by 'Capt. Fraser in the French tongue, saying we are the provision boats from Montreal, [and] cautioning the sentry to be silent'.[74] In the wake of the light infantry, the succeeding waves of redcoats disembarked with 'great good order and discretion', and formed up with 'much regularity'.[75] Admiral Saunders observed that 'considering the Darkness of the Night & the Rapidity of

71 'Journal of Richard Humphrys', pp. 48–54. Although Humphrys dates these attacks to 8 August, they actually occurred four days later. See the fragment of 'Murray's Journal' in *Knox's Journal*, III, 161–3. For another detailed description of this day's events, written by an anonymous volunteer in Dalling's Light Infantry, see 'Journal of the Particular Transactions' in *Siege of Quebec*, V, 177–9. This gives total casualties of 72 soldiers and ten sailors killed and wounded.

72 Stacey, *Quebec, 1759*, p. 82.

73 See orders issued on board the *Sutherland*, 11–12 September 1759, in 'Orderly Books at Quebec', in *Northcliffe Collection*, pp. 166–7.

74 'Journal of the Particular Transactions', in *Siege of Quebec*, V, 187. Captain Fraser had acquired his fluency in French whilst in 'the Dutch service' ('Townshend's Rough Notes', in *Northcliffe Collection*, pp. 422–5; 424). It is likely that this quick-thinking Highlander was Simon Fraser, who, as a brigadier-general, was killed at Saratoga in 1777. Fraser had been wounded in the service of Holland at the siege of Bergen-op-Zoom in 1747. See 'Fraser, Simon (d. 1777)', in *Dictionary of National Biography*, eds L. Stephen and S. Lee (63 vols, London, 1885–1900), XX, 222–3.

75 *Knox's Journal*, II, 96.

the Current, this was a very critical Operation, and very properly & successfully conducted'.[76] In the opinion of C. P. Stacey, the cooperation exhibited by the Army and Navy that night represented a 'professional triumph' which fully justified 'the reputation of the enterprise as a classic of combined operations'.[77]

The proficiency in amphibious warfare acquired by the redcoats in America during the Seven Years War would be reflected in succeeding conflicts. Successful 'Conjunct Expeditions' involving the Army and Navy were conspicuous during the American Revolutionary War; indeed, between 8.00 am and noon on 22 August 1776 some 15,000 crown troops were landed on Long Island in the most ambitious combined operation then recorded.[78] On the eve of his Egyptian expedition Sir Ralph Abercromby could characterise the amphibious attack as a distinctly 'British' mode of warfare, and one that embodied unique hazards.[79] That same fact had been all too apparent to the men of the 'American Army'; but as the boldy executed assault landing at Aboukir Bay in 1801 would demonstrate, their hard-earned lessons had not been forgotten.

The 'thin red line'

Alongside its efforts to meet the challenges of irregular and amphibious warfare, the 'American Army' continued to school itself in the very different skills of 'conventional' combat. Orderly books and journals from the American campaigns show that the Army as a whole was subjected to a rigorous training regime calculated to perfect key tactical techniques. It is clear from such evidence that regiments in the field did not aspire to the kind of meticulous parade-ground precision usually associated with eighteenth-century armies. In May 1759, when commanding officers of battalions bound for Quebec apologised that their men had been too scattered to practise a 'new system of discipline', Wolfe had replied: 'Poh! poh! – new exercise – new fiddle-stick; if they are otherwise well disciplined and will fight, that's all I shall require of them'.[80] Mastery of basic drills was likewise emphasised within Amherst's army at Albany in spring 1759. With little time to spare before the onset of the campaign, colonels were urged to concentrate upon perfecting such crucial techniques as target practice and manoeuvring in

76 Saunders to Clevland, *Stirling Castle* off Quebec, 21 September 1759 (ADM/1/482, fol. 58A).
77 Stacey, *Quebec, 1759*, p. 133.
78 See *1776. The British Story of the American Revolution* (London, 1976), p. 102.
79 Mackesy, *British Victory in Egypt*, p. 24.
80 *Knox's Journal*, I, 348–9.

the woods.[81] Similarly, at Montreal in July 1761, officers were told 'not to take pains about trifles, but to make their men expert in everything useful, particularly firing at marks and firing ball in battalions'.[82] Orders issued before the siege of Louisbourg were also terse in the extreme: when confronted by French regulars, the British battalions were to 'march up close to them, discharge their pieces loaded with two Bullets, and then rush upon them with their Bayonets'.[83]

Whilst the fire-fight might well be followed by a menacing advance with the bayonet, little formal attention was devoted to training the redcoats in the use of cold steel.[84] Such half-hearted instruction as was provided left much to be desired: when the 43rd Foot were shown 'a new method of pushing bayonets' in July 1759, the 'ludicrous' display provoked guffaws from the spectators.[85] On the open battlefield, actual hand-to-hand combat was rare, with 'bayonet charges' instead employed primarily as a means of intimidating a wavering foe into flight. For example, the 'Louisbourg Grenadiers' 'ran in with their bayonets' to complete the rout of Montcalm's troops on the Plains of Abraham. On this occasion at least, the blades were actually used: the grenadiers' commander, Major Alexander Murray of the 45th Foot, reported that several of their 'bayonets were bent, and their muzzles dipped in gore'.[86] According to the Jacobite exile James Johnstone, who served as aide-de-camp to the Chevalier de Lévis in 1760, the shaken British line at Sainte-Foy was finally broken by a vigorous application of the bayonet.[87] One British participant in the battle, the fiercely patriotic John Knox, scoffed at such reports. Knox observed: 'I have frequently had the honour of meeting them [the French] in the course of my service, and I never saw them disposed to come to the distance of pistol-shot, much less to bayonet-pushing.'[88] Genuine bayonet-fighting was usually restricted to combats for possession of field-works or other strong-points. For example, after the French sallied from Louisbourg in June 1758 they captured a small redoubt whose outnumbered and constricted defenders were obliged to

81 'Monypenny Orderly Book', *BFTM* (June 1971), p. 178.

82 'Brigade Order Books', in *Hervey's Journals*, p. 150.

83 'Orders before landing at Louisbourg, 1758' (CKS, U1350/030/1).

84 Bennett Cuthbertson called for British soldiers to be made 'more familiar with the bayonets than is the custom' (*Interior Management*, pp. 170–71).

85 *Knox's Journal*, I, 422.

86 See Murray to his wife, Quebec, 20 September 1759, in 'The Letters of Colonel Alexander Murray, 1742–59', in *1926 Regimental Annual. The Sherwood Foresters, Nottinghamshire and Derbyshire Regiment*, ed. Col. H. C. Wylly (London, 1927), pp. 181–220; 216.

87 *The Campaign of 1760 in Canada. A Narrative Attributed to Chevalier Johnstone: Literary & Historical Society of Quebec, Historical Documents* (Second Series, Quebec, 1887), p. 12.

88 *Knox's Journal*, II, 443–4.

surrender 'after being forced on by fixed Bayonets'.[89] The same fortification was recaptured soon after by the grenadiers of the 22nd Foot, 'who, with their Bayonets, drove them out of the work without firing a shot till they began to run'.[90] Cramped conditions left little choice when John Grant of the 2/42nd resorted to his bayonet during the fighting on Cuba in 1762. Alarmed while scavenging in a hamlet outside Havana, Grant took cover in a nearby house, only to be confronted by a 'fine looking Spanish creole' who promptly levelled his musket and fired. As the room filled with smoke Grant instinctively lunged forward with his own bayoneted musket. Grant recalled:

> an agonized groan soon informed me that my aim had been too fatal, I found my fuzee grasped, when attempting to withdraw it, and the smoke clearing, I found I had run my opponent through the body and fairly pinned him to the wall, whilst his face glaring with rage and pain, was close to me.

It was only with a violent effort that the shocked Grant was able to wrench his musket free and quit the room.[91]

As orders quoted above indicate, the British Army in North America spared no pains to maximise its firepower – a stance possibly encouraged by a desire to compensate for the relative dearth of field artillery on that continent.[92] This approach built upon ground-work already laid in Britain. A year before arriving in America, Amherst's 15th Foot was devoting considerable attention to musketry. As Lieutenant-Colonel James Murray reported:

> We have three field days every week, seven rounds of powder and Ball each, every man has fired about eighty four rounds, and now load and fire Ball with as much coolness and allacrity in all the different fireings as ever you saw them fire blank powder ... We have not neglected fireing singly at a mark, and ... have a great many very good marks men who may do notable service upon occasion.[93]

89 'Journal of Richard Humphrys', p. 17.

90 Major Alexander Murray to his wife, 'Camp before Louisburg', 21 July 1758, in 'Letters of Alexander Murray' (*1926 Regimental Annual. Sherwood Foresters*), p. 203.

91 'Journal of John Grant', pp. 90–91.

92 Unlike their comrades in Germany, the redcoats of the 'American Army' did not enjoy the tactical support of 'battalion guns'. During the eighteenth century, it was customary for a pair of these light and manoeuvrable brass field-pieces to be issued to each battalion in wartime. For use of battalion guns in Germany, see, for example, 'Military Order Books, 1758–1759' (orders issued at 'Camp at Geosfeldt', 20 and 22 August 1758), in *HMC: Reports of Manuscripts in Various Collections*, VIII (London, 1913), 434; 436.

93 Murray to Amherst, Maidstone, 7 June 1757, in CKS, U1350/013/4.

In America, great pains were taken to ensure that regulars and provincials alike possessed ample experience of live firing: at Fort Edward on 29 May 1757, those men of the 35th Foot 'That Have not as Yet Fired', were to be ready that afternoon to 'Fire at a Mark'; soldiers on duty would be relieved until they had taken their turn at the butts.[94] In April 1759 the 43rd Foot in Nova Scotia were out every afternoon, 'firing at targets, in which they are encouraged by presents from their Officers'.[95] That same month, the Royal Highland Regiment at New York was also engaged in an intensive programme of musketry with the emphasis once again on accuracy.[96] By the spring of 1761, when the battalions of the 'American Army' were preparing for service in the Caribbean, Amherst could observe that 'in general all the men are so good marksmen that it requires only a little practice to keep their hands in'.[97]

Such repeated references to target practice sit uneasily alongside contemporary and modern comments regarding the limitations of the smooth-bore musket.[98] However, when discussing the question of 'aimed fire' it is necessary to draw a distinction between what occurred on the European battlefield and the very different conditions prevailing in America. In Europe, dense masses of troops and the thick powder smoke that their volleys soon generated rendered unaimed fire not only viable but virtually inevitable. Amidst such congestion it was enough for the soldier to point his firearm in the general direction of the enemy; the musketeers of Frederick the Great were actively discouraged from aiming and priority was instead given to rapidity of fire.[99] Across the Atlantic such confrontations between close-order troops were rare, with potential targets more likely to be scattered and employing cover. In addition, it would be wrong to suggest that Prussian methods prompted slavish imitation; for all its admiration of Frederician drill, the British Army had long prided itself on its own traditions of fire discipline. As Wolfe informed the 20th Foot in 1755, 'There is no necessity for firing very fast; a cool well-levelled fire, with the pieces carefully loaded, is much more destructive and formidable than the quickest fire in confusion.'[100] A year later, when Lord George

94 *General Orders of 1757, issued by the Earl of Loudoun and Phineas Lyman in the Campaign Against the French*, ed. W. C. Ford (New York, 1899; repr. 1970), p. 13.

95 *Knox's Journal*, I, 301. See also ibid, 306.

96 On 3–4 April the Highlanders shot at targets marked with a 'black spot in the middle'. See R. F. H. Wallace, 'Regimental Routine and Army Administration in North America in 1759', *JSAHR*, XXX (1952), 8–19; 11.

97 Amherst to Brigadier-General Gage, New York, 16 April 1761, in WO/34/7, fol. 30.

98 For examples of both see Gates, *British Light Infantry Arm*, p. 139.

99 This trend was encapsulated by the redesigned musket issued to the Prussian infantry in 1782, which was 'so constructed as to make aiming nearly impossible' and 'designed not to minimize its limitations of accuracy but to maximize its advantages as a quick-firing weapon'. See Showalter, *Wars of Frederick the Great*, 332–3.

100 'Instructions drawn up by the late Major General Wolfe', in Entick, *General History*, IV, 94.

Beauclerk reviewed Lord Charles Manners's regiment at Newcastle, he noted how the men 'fired very well, and took very good aim'.[101]

It is scarcely credible that so much time and energy should have been devoted to marksmanship in the 'American Army' if its officers did not believe that this training made a difference to the combat performance of their men. Although muskets of the period lacked sights and were prone to numerous technical faults, it is none the less apparent that troops who frequently undertook 'aimed fire' exercises were more likely to hit a given target than those who did not. Describing the formation of the regimental light companies in February 1759, Lieutenant-Colonel Roger Townshend suggested that when it came to marksmanship, practice made perfect: 'They ... have what ammunition they want, so I don't doubt but they will be excellent marksmen.'[102] Such comments appear more realistic when it is remembered that combat often commenced at ranges far closer than the 80 to 100 yards at which fire with the 'common' musket was theoretically practicable against individual targets. For example, eyewitnesses agree that the volleys which staggered Montcalm's advance at Quebec were administered at 40 yards.[103] Four years earlier, Wolfe had himself recommended that troops attacked by column should reserve their fire until the enemy was 'within about twenty yards': at that range fire delivered 'with a good aim' would – he added with some understatement – 'necessarily stop them a little'.[104] During the fighting on Guadeloupe in February 1759, George Durant remarked that the British defending the entrenchments around Basseterre 'reserved their Fire 'till they [the French] came within *ten* yards of them'.[105]

Besides a desire to increase accuracy, there was another important justification for 'reserving' fire. Given the low muzzle-velocity of the musket, the energy of its spherical projectile decreased rapidly with distance. Hence the carefully husbanded volley possessed a lethal 'weight' that was lacking in long-range fire. At Quebec on 13 September 1759, one observer noted that whereas the British suffered some 600 wounded, only 40 men were killed because the French opened fire at too great a distance: in consequence, 'their balls were almost spent before they reached our men; several of our people having received contusions on

101 Review of the 58th Foot (56th from 1757), Newcastle-upon-Tyne, 28 October 1756, in WO/27/4.

102 Townshend to Robert Rogers, New York, 26 February 1759, in *Rogers' Journals*, p. 135.

103 One authority has remarked that both the French 'Charleville' musket and the British 'Brown Bess' were 'capable of hitting a target the size of a man quite consistently at 50 or even 60 yards'. See E. P. Hamilton, *The French Army in America* (Ottawa, 1967), p. 7. On British flintlock weapons see D. F. Harding, *Smallarms of the East India Company 1600–1856* (4 vols, London, 1997–9).

104 'Wolfe's Instructions', in Entick, *General History*, IV, p. 97.

105 'George Durant's Journal' (*Army Records Society: Military Miscellany I*), p. 41 (my italics).

parts where the blow must have been mortal, had they reserved their fire a little longer'.[106] The British wounded included Malcolm Fraser, who sustained a contusion to his right shoulder during the initial skirmishing. As he recalled, this blow 'pained me a good deal, but it did not disable me from my duty then, or afterwards'.[107] Fraser's colonel survived two close shaves at the battle of Sainte-Foy: Simon Fraser was struck first in the right breast, but the ball was deflected by the belt-plate of his slung cartridge box; as Murray's troops retreated the colonel was hit again; this time the queue of his plaited hair absorbed the impact and he escaped with no more than a stiff neck.[108] Such phenomena explain the bullet-dented snuff-boxes, watches and coins still preserved in regimental museums, and give credence to the curious anecdote that Charles Lee of the 44th Foot told about his friend Dick Mather following the defeat at Ticonderoga. In a teasing letter to his sister, Lee claimed that a musket-ball was 'absolute'ly flatten'd' against Mather's forehead, like 'a bullet of clay when it has been thrown against a stone wall'. Lee had advised Mather to bequeath head and ball alike to the Royal Society, 'as a much greater curiosity than they were ever before presented with'.[109] Despite such badinage, at close quarters the heavy lead musket balls were capable of inflicting terrible wounds. A more harrowing account of the injuries sustained during the Ticonderoga assault was provided by chaplain John Cleaveland of the Massachusetts provincials. On July 11, as Abercromby's army licked its wounds at Lake George, Cleaveland wrote to his wife: 'It was a fearful sight to see numbers of men, some with their eyes shot out, their noses cut off by a ball, others shot in their head, neck, shoulders, arms, belly, thighs, legs & c.'[110] John Peebles, who accompanied the Newfoundland task-force as a surgeon's mate, was kept busy in the aftermath of the Signal Hill escalade; as Peebles explained, most of the men wounded on that occasion were 'very bad they being Extremely near to the Enemy' when hit.[111] Much the same point was made by Archibald Montgomery when describing his confrontation with the Cherokees in June 1760: he assured Amherst that 'as our men never fired but when they were near them, most of the shot which took place I fancy did the Bussiness'.[112]

106 *An Accurate and Authentic Journal of the Siege of Quebec*, p. 41. In fact, the casualty list of 664 killed, wounded and missing included 61 combat fatalities (*Knox's Journal*, II, 118).
107 'Journal of Malcolm Fraser', *JSAHR* (1939), p. 159.
108 Ibid., p. 165.
109 Lee to Miss Sidney Lee, Albany, 16 September 1758, in *NYHSC: Lee Papers*, I, 8.
110 See 'Cleaveland's Letters and Diary: A Chaplain at Ticonderoga 1758', in *Narratives of Colonial America 1704–1765*, ed. Howard H. Peckham (Chicago, 1971), pp. 125–54; 153.
111 Peebles to —— (Mr Fleming?), St John's, Newfoundland, 20 September 1762 (GD 21/487).
112 Letter dated Camp at Fort Prince George, 2 July 1760, in WO/34/47, fol. 17.

In the 'American Army' such musketry was increasingly dispensed by methods differing from the regulation platoon fire that Wolfe denigrated as 'the impracticable chequer'.[113] For the purpose of administering the simplified tactical system, known as 'alternate fire', each company was dubbed a 'subdivision' (two of which constituted a 'grand-division'). Unlike the official drill, which required the battalion to form eighteen separate platoons, alternate fire involved just ten subdivisions. Like the platoons, these larger units were numbered so that they could discharge their muskets in a specified sequence. Subdivisions gave their fire in three different ways: consecutively from right to left along the line; from the centre outwards to each flank; or from the flanks inwards. Alternate fire could also be given by platoons, which were created by simply dividing each company in two.[114] For all its efficacy, alternate fire none the less flew in the face of the official regulations promoted by Cumberland during his tenure as captain-general. The Duke was irate that his orders were 'changed according to the Whim & Supposed Improvements of every fertile Genius'.[115] Cumberland's broadside was triggered by developments in the force poised to invade the French coast under Lieutenant-General Sir John Mordaunt; in the south coast camps the tedious 'one two' of the manual arms drill was ignored and training concentrated upon alternate fire rather than the regulation platoon system.[116] As John Houlding has demonstrated, Cumberland's resignation that same year allowed the unofficial drill to spread to the British battalions serving in both America and Germany, a process culminating in acceptance in the 1764 *Regulations*.[117] The necessity for such practical formations had long been appreciated by the 'American Army'. The organisation of Braddock's regulars into company-sized fire-units has already been noted, and this expedient continued to find favour. When Amherst allocated two battalions composed of raw independent companies to James Grant's expedition against the Cherokees, he instructed their commanding officers to 'form their respective Corps into four grand Divisions & eight Sub

113 Wolfe to Lord George Sackville, Halifax, 24 May 1758, in *HMC: Stopford-Sackville Manuscripts*, II, 261.

114 Houlding, *Fit for Service*, pp. 318–21. The difference between the alternate fire and the regulation platoon fire has been characterised as a 'rolling' rather than 'flickering' effect. See Piers Mackesy, *The Coward of Minden. The Affair of Lord George Sackville* (London, 1979), p. 46.

115 Cumberland to Barrington, Headquarters at Rothenburg, 28 August 1757, in *Military Affairs in North America*, p. 398.

116 On Mordaunt's innovations see the Duke of Richmond to Lord George Lennox, Barham Downs Camp, 9 September 1757, in *HMC: Bathurst Manuscripts* (London, 1923), p. 681.

117 Houlding, *Fit for Service*, pp. 370–73. In 1768 Cuthbertson observed that as alternate fire was 'the most simple, plain and easy, and least liable to confusion in all situations, [it] should be principally attended to'. See *Interior Management*, p. 169.

Divisions, which I think is better than subdividing them into Platoons which might be subject to create confusion among them in Service'.[118]

By the crucial campaigning season of 1759 the redcoat battalions in America possessed considerable experience of active service and had undergone intensive training. The tactical proficiency destined to be demonstrated so famously on the Plains of Abraham had been anticipated in miniature earlier that summer when British regulars rebuffed a bid to break the siege of Niagara. The combat fought at La Belle Famille on the morning of 24 July involved a confrontation between 464 redcoats under the command of Lieutenant-Colonel Eyre Massy of the 46th Foot, and about 800 French regulars and militia led by Captain Francois Le Marchand de Lignery of the *compagnies franches de la marine*.[119] The tactics employed by the British on this occasion can be reconstructed with unusual precision owing to the survival of a trio of letters written by Massy after the skirmish; taken together, these provide a wealth of technical detail that is all too rare in contemporary accounts of combat. On learning of the approach of the French relief force, Massy had deployed elements of the 46th Foot in support of three companies of light infantry to contest the road to Fort Niagara. The regiment was positioned on the right of the light companies; the 46th's right flank was covered by its own grenadier company backed by a detachment, or 'picket', of the 44th Foot.[120] Observing that the approaching French column included 'a good number of Regulars', Massy ordered his front rank to fix bayonets: the whole command were to lie down and withhold their fire until he gave the word. The French emerged from the wood-fringed track into the clearing of La Belle Famille. Firing as they came, Lignery's men began to deploy from column into line. Although wounded by this scattered shooting, Massy finally ordered his patient redcoats to rise and respond. The men of the 46th did so with devastating effect. 'To do justice', Massy reported,

> I never saw a Grand Division (for so I must call my number) give so plump a fire, after firing standing seven Rounds I gave the

118 'Instructions to Lt Col Grant, 15 December, 1760, Extracts', in 'Amherst's Personal Journal', p. 103.

119 On the eve of the combat both sides had enjoyed the theoretical support of several hundred Indians. However, on the morning of 24 July the Iroquois allies of the British had informed the 'French' Indians that they intended to take no part in the impending clash, and requested them likewise to remain neutral: at this, the bulk of the latter abandoned Lignery. For events at Niagara that summer, see Dunnigan, *Siege, 1759*.

120 Massy to Pitt, Oswego, 30 July 1759, in PRO 30 (Gifts and Deposits)/8 (Chatham Papers)/49, fol. 93. The extreme left of the line was held by 'pickets' of the 46th Foot and the New York provincials. See the sketch map of the action (PRO, MP. I/277) originally enclosed in Massy to Pitt, Fort Stanwix, 11 July 1760 (PRO 30/8/49, fol. 91).

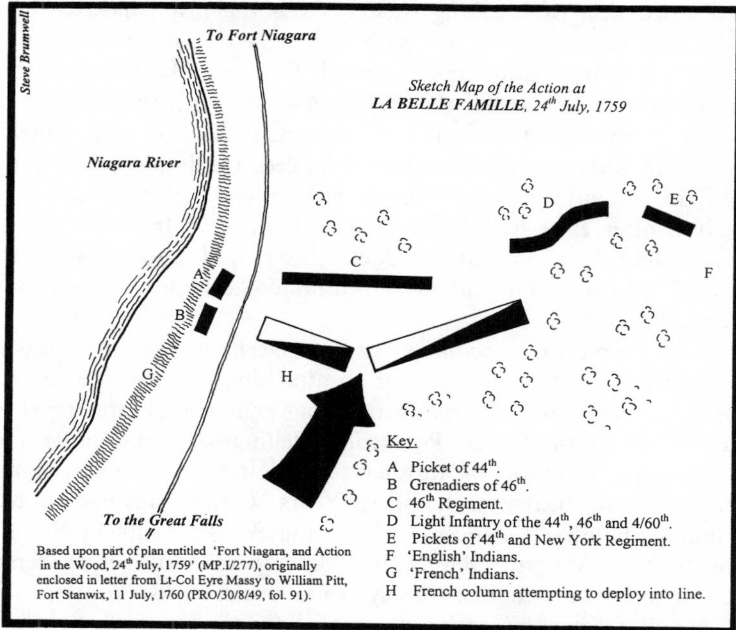

Map 2 The action at La Belle Famille, 24 July 1759.

> word for the whole to advance by constant firing, which was done in great order and ye most of ye 46 fir'd sixteen rounds.[121]

The 130-odd men of the 46th under Massy's personal command – corresponding to a 'grand-division' composed of two companies or 'subdivisions' – apparently delivered their fire simultaneously as massed volleys.[122] Although Massy failed to specify the distances involved, this concentrated musketry was clearly unleashed at very close range. As Massy later informed Pitt: 'The Men receiv'd the Enemy with vast Resolution, and never fir'd one shot, untill we cou'd almost reach them with our Bayonets.' There was special praise for the 46th's grenadier company, who 'behav'd most gloriously, and by their pouring in all their fire, in the Enemy's Flanks, kill'd great numbers, and in my oppinion

121 Massy to Amherst, Oswego, 30 July 1759, in WO/34/53, fol. 6.

122 Exclusive of men manning the siege trenches or on detailed duties, the 46th numbered 256 (Massy to Pitt, Oswego, 30 July 1759). From this number must be deducted the light infantry and 'picket', consisting of 50 men each, and a very weak grenadier company of about half that strength.

was the occasion of breaking them'.[123] As the firing halted, the redcoats 'immediately rush'd in with their Bayonets' to complete the rout.[124] It was only now, as the French fled, that the large contingent of Iroquois warriors joined the fray. Massy was mortified that printed accounts of the action reflected 'great credit' on 'Savages' whose behaviour had proved 'most dastardly'. Indeed, the Indians had done no more than to 'pull out the Prisoners, hid under Logs, and Scalp'd poor Wretches, after they had fallen by our hands'.[125] Irate that his own battalion had been denied its due, Massy had good reason to be proud of soldiers who had clearly attained a high pitch of combat efficiency.[126]

With its triumph of disciplined close-range firepower, delivered from lines against the front and flank of an attacking column, the combat at La Belle Famille prefigured the dispositions that would later repel other French armies on the Iberian Peninsula. Wellington's veterans also benefited from the adoption of another tactical innovation evolved in the North American theatre of the Seven Years War. As has been noted, in common with other European powers the British Army of the 1750s customarily arrayed its infantry in a line formation with a depth of three ranks. In the 'American Army' – unlike the British contingent sent to Germany – it was increasingly common for the troops to fight in two ranks. The rationale behind this development emerges from standing orders issued in Amherst's army on 9 July 1759. During the coming campaign the regulars were to be 'drawn up on all services two deep' because 'the enemy have very few regular troops to oppose us, and no yelling of Indians, or fire of Canadians, can possibly withstand two ranks, if the men are silent, attentive, and obedient to their Officers'. As this order indicates, the new formation marked a response to local conditions; it was not primarily intended for use against regular troops in 'conventional' combat. Indeed, steps were taken to ensure that 'in case the service should

123 Massy to Pitt, Fort Stanwix, 11 July 1760, in PRO 30/8/49, fol. 91.

124 Captain Charles Lee, 44th Foot, to Sir William Bunbury, Niagara, 9 August 1759, in *NYHSC: Lee Papers*, I, 21.

125 Massy to Pitt, Fort Stanwix, 11 July. Although not present during the action at La Belle Famille, it was Sir William Johnson, as overall commander of the force besieging Niagara, who provided Amherst with the 'official' version of events: he wrote that the French were 'so well received by the troops in front, and the Indians on their flank, that in an hour's time, the whole was completely ruined'. See Johnson to Amherst, Niagara, 25 July 1759, in *Johnson Papers*, III, 108–10. Johnson's account was reproduced by newspapers on both sides of the Atlantic and Massy's attempt to set the record straight proved futile.

126 Brig.-Gen. Prideaux considered the 46th Foot to be 'a very fine Body of Men' and only wished they were more numerous. See extract of letter from Prideaux to Amherst, Fort Stanwix, 15 June 1759, in CO/5/55, fol. 188.

require it, the whole battalion can be formed three deep, in an instant'.[127] It is probable that British troops had previously employed this formation when there was little likelihood of encountering regular opposition: for example, in June 1755, the men of Braddock's expedition were told that upon the signal to assemble, 'all the troops are to turn out, accoutre and form two deep at the head of their encampments'.[128] During the summer of 1758 Abercromby's redcoats at Lake George received orders to adopt a two-deep 'order of Battle' that could be swiftly doubled in depth to four ranks as required. The shallow two-deep line was certainly being used in Wolfe's army before Quebec in August 1759:[129] it is likely that this famous formation made its major battlefield début soon after on the Plains of Abraham.[130] On this occasion the redcoats faced significant numbers of French regulars, and the thinner line was seemingly adopted from necessity rather than choice. John Johnson of the 58th Foot explained: 'Our line of Battle would admit of us to be drawn up two deep only, from the smallness of our number, as well as the quantity of ground we had to cover to secure our flanks.' Owing to this the files were 'at least three feet asunder' instead of being closed up elbow to elbow as was usual, whilst 40-yard intervals divided the battalions.[131]

When Brigadier-General James Murray's sickly garrison marched out to confront the French at Sainte-Foy on 28 April 1760, the two-deep line was again employed; as with Wolfe's fight, a dearth of British manpower left little choice in the matter. Malcolm Fraser observed that Murray 'ordered the whole to draw up in line of Battle, two deep, and take up as much room as possible'. Once again, there were 'large intervalls' between the regiments in the line.[132] The battle that followed proved more prolonged and hard fought than Wolfe's victory on the same ground. Although ending in defeat for the redcoats, it was conceded that the action had been exceptionally well contested: the experience left a strong impression upon many participants and the resulting wealth of eyewitness accounts permits the British viewpoint to be reconstructed in some detail.

127 *Knox's Journal*, I, 487–8. The order of 9 July 1759, requiring that the troops be proficient in forming both the two- and three-deep lines, was repeated in the following summer. See Amherst to Colonel Haldimand, Oswego, 3 August 1760, in Add. MSS., 21,661, fol. 80.

128 'Orme's Journal', in *History of an Expedition Against Fort Duquesne*, p. 333.

129 'General Orders, 3 July, 1758' (AB 407); *General Orders in Wolfe's Army*, pp. 35–6.

130 This is the verdict of C. P. Stacey in his careful study of the battle. See *Quebec, 1759*, p. 138.

131 'Memoirs of John Johnson' in *Siege of Quebec*, V, 107.

132 'Journal of Malcolm Fraser', *JSAHR* (1939), p. 164; 'Account of Life in Quebec During Winter of 1759–60', in *Northcliffe Collection*, pp. 426–9; 427.

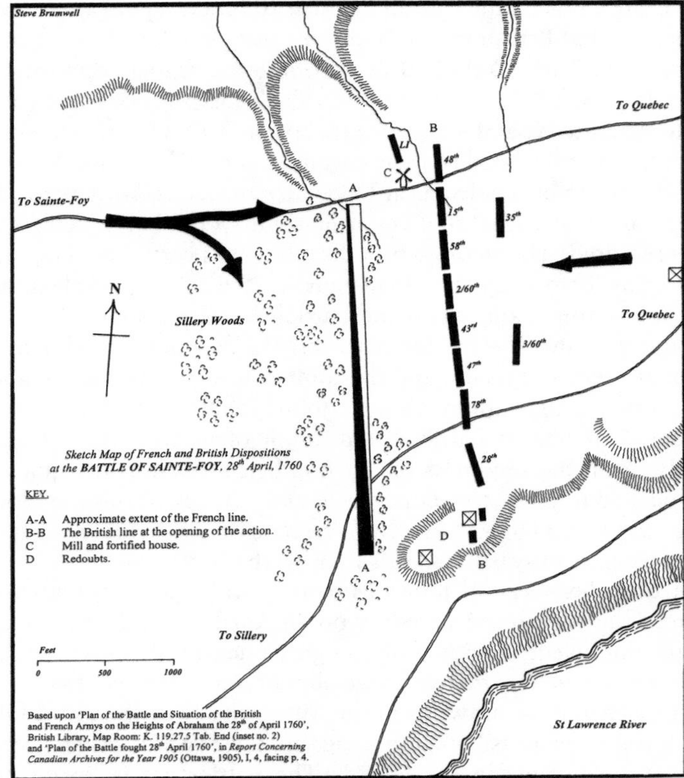

Map 3 French and British dispositions at the Battle of Sainte-Foy, 28 April 1760.

The bare outlines of the battle are best followed in the reports of the rival generals.[133] Early on 27 April 1760, Murray received intelligence

[133] See *Murray's Journal of the Siege of Quebec*, pp. 26–7; Murray to Amherst, Quebec, 30 April 1760 (CO/5/58, fols 191–3), and to Pitt, Quebec, 25 May 1760 (*Correspondence of Pitt*, II, 291–7). For Lévis's perspective see 'Bataille Gagnée Par L'Armee Française Commandée Par M. De Lévis Sur Les Troupes Angloises, Le 28 Avril, Près De Quebec', in *Collection des Manuscripts du Maréchal de Lévis: Volume I, Journal des Campagnes du Chevalier de Lévis en Canada De 1756 a 1760*, ed. H. R. Casgrain (Montreal, 1889), pp. 263–8; also Vaudreuil to M. Berryer, Montreal, 3 May 1760, in *NYCD*, X, 1,075–7; and 'Journal of the Battle of Sillery and Siege of Quebec', in ibid., 1,077–86. Two contemporary British maps of the battle were also examined: 'Plan of the Battle fought the 28th of April 1760 . . .', in *Report Concerning Canadian Archives for the Year 1905* (Ottawa, 1905), I, 4, facing p. 4; and 'Plan of the Battle and Situation of the British and French Armys on the Heights of Abraham the 28th of April 1760'. See British Library, Map Room: K. 119.27.5 Tab. End (inset no. 2).

that a substantial French army had landed at Pointe-aux-Trembles;[134] he responded by heading a strong detachment to cover the withdrawal of his vulnerable outposts. Aware that Quebec's feeble fortifications were dominated by the Heights of Abraham, Murray decided to march forth and deny the enemy this commanding position. At 7.00 am on Monday 28 April, Murray led out all the men he could muster, amounting to less than 4,000, and formed his 'Little Army' on the Heights.[135] The British line consisted of eight battalions organised into two brigades, with two battalions in reserve. The right flank was covered by a corps of light infantry; the left rested on two companies of rangers and volunteers. The battalions were accompanied by twenty field-pieces and a pair of howitzers taken from the walls of Quebec; by contrast, the French deployed just three cannon. As his own line was forming, Murray reconnoitred the enemy. Lévis's vanguard only was in position, holding the line that the main army was intended to occupy: this stretched from two redoubts above the St Lawrence on the right, via 'rising grounds' in the centre, to a fortified house and a windmill on the left. From Murray's position, the French main body appeared to be 'upon the March, in one Column'. Considering this to be 'the lucky Moment', Murray decided to attack before the enemy were ready to receive him. Although the three brigades of the French right had actually deployed, the left remained unformed. In consequence, Lévis resolved to withdraw those troops already in position within the shelter of Sillery Woods. On the British right, the light infantry dislodged five companies of grenadiers from the house and windmill. Pursuing too far, these troops were themselves rebuffed as the French left advanced on its own initiative. With the light infantry dispersed along the front of Murray's right wing, the British were prevented from exploiting the initial success gained against the French left. In attempting to regain their original post the light infantry were charged and scattered: they took no further part in the action. At this crisis, the 35th Foot shored up the threatened British right, which 'soon recovered Everything there'. Lévis decided to capitalise on the enthusiasm of his left-hand battalions by ordering those on the right likewise to attack with the bayonet. On this wing the British had at first captured the two redoubts, but came under increasing pressure 'till at last fairly fought down, and reduced to a handfull'. In an effort to stabilise this situation, the 3/60th

[134] Troops allocated for the expedition against Quebec numbered 6,910. Of these, 3,889 were regulars, including all eight battalions of the *troupes de terre*, and two others formed from the *compagnies franches de la marine*. The remainder consisted of militia and a small number of Indians (See *Collection de Lévis*, I, 257). Some 5,000 of Lévis's army were actually present at Sainte-Foy (ibid., 268).

[135] Of Quebec's garrison, 3,866 officers and men 'March'd into the Field' with Murray (CO/5/64, fol. 65).

was sent from the reserve and the 43rd quit the centre, an area where the British had so far held their own. Despite this reinforcement, Murray's left buckled under the French onslaught: according to Lévis, it was only a garbled order – which resulted in one of his right-hand brigades moving to support the left rather than advancing to its front – that prevented the British from being cut off from Quebec.[136] With disorder spreading from left to right, the redcoats retreated under the cover of several blockhouses, spiking their guns before abandoning them to the enemy. Three hours of fighting had cost both sides a heavy toll in killed and wounded. One third of Murray's men were casualties; the French army also suffered severely.[137]

The battle of Sainte-Foy went far to redeem the performance of Montcalm's regulars seven months earlier. Lévis had fought a skilful action by first halting Murray's advance and then concentrating his forces upon the exposed extremities of the British line. At these points, the attack was pressed home by columns.[138] As Murray's chief engineer Major Patrick Mackellar observed, the action was 'chiefly upon the Flanks', even though the French were numerous enough to 'make a push' elsewhere.[139] John Knox of the 43rd also noted that the French 'seemed regardless of our centre' instead reinforcing their own right and left wings in an effort to outflank the British and sever the route back to Quebec.[140] The coolness of Lévis was in marked contrast to the impetuosity displayed by his opponent. Like Montcalm before him, Murray abandoned an advantageous position for an impulsive advance: his officers and men were not slow to record their disapproval. As Lieutenant Malcolm Fraser noted, upon quitting Quebec the army did not believe that Murray sought battle: the men carried picks and shovels, and assumed they would entrench themselves on the Heights. In this dominating

136 Several historians have concluded that as the two regular battalions of this brigade did not attack as ordered, they should not be counted in the total of the French troops who actually participated in the battle. See G. F. G. Stanley, *New France. The Last Phase 1744–1760* (Toronto, 1968), p. 248; also W. J. Eccles and Susan L. Laskin, 'The Battles for Quebec, 1759 and 1760', in *Historical Atlas of Canada, Volume I, From the Beginning to 1800*, ed. R. Cole Harris (Toronto, 1987), plate 43. Such efforts to recast the battle as a confrontation between armies of equal size remain unconvincing: the brigade concerned was deployed on the battlefield and formed part of the force at Lévis's immediate disposal. The fact that it moved to the wrong part of the line is irrelevant to any assessment of the available French strength.

137 In casualty returns for 27 April to 21 May 1760, Murray recorded 292 killed, 837 wounded and 53 prisoners (CO/5/64, fol. 65). Lévis lost 193 killed and 640 wounded. See *Collection de Lévis*, I, 269.

138 'Letter from an Officer of the Royal American Regiment', Quebec, 24 May 1760, in *Gentleman's Magazine, 1760* (July), p. 314.

139 See Mackellar's comments included with a 'Plan of the Battle Fought the 28th of April, 1760', in *Report Concerning Canadian Archives for the Year 1905*, I, 4, facing p. 4.

140 *Knox's Journal*, II, 394.

position, Fraser continued, the British artillery enjoyed a clear field of fire of some 500 yards. This advantage was thrown away on Murray's 'passion for glory getting the better of his reason'.[141] John Johnson of the 58th Foot likewise accused Murray of wasting the lives of brave men in a bid to gain himself 'great honour'. Given the paucity of the garrison, and the weakness of many through illness, it would have been more prudent to remain within the city and defend it 'to the last extremity'. During the course of the battle the British had been lured forward 'into low swampy ground' where they were obliged to fight 'almost knee-deep' in the slush; it was these same conditions that made it impracticable to retrieve the field-pieces.[142]

A convincing description of the fighting, emphasising the importance of the terrain, is provided by private James Miller of the 15th Foot. Miller's battalion advanced and drove the enemy back, only to fall victim to its own success:

> at first we were drawn up in a hollow, with a height, in front, on which the enemys balls struck, and flew over our heads. The fireing continued, in the center and left, where we repuls'd the enemy; in our front, we unfortunately advanced, which gave them, an opportunity of cutting us up, they being drawn up under cover, and taking aim at leisure, while we could only see them, through the intervals, of the trees. In short, in half an hour, Ten Officers, from Twenty, were dropped, twelve serjeants, from twenty four, and near two hundred Rank and file, from less than four hundred in the field! The corps, was broken, and Retreated, to their former ground; happy would it have been had they never left it.[143]

Further to the left, the same 'heights' that had created crucial 'dead ground' for Miller and his comrades afforded equal protection to the 47th Foot. Malcolm Fraser, who served in the same brigade, noted that before being ordered to retire, the 47th 'were drawn up with a small rising ground in their front, which till then covered them pretty much from the enemy's fire'.[144]

A glimpse of the bitter fighting for the windmill emerges from the records of a General Court Martial called to investigate the alleged

141 'Journal of Malcolm Fraser', *JSAHR* (1939), p. 166.

142 'Memoirs of John Johnson', in *Siege of Quebec*, V, 120–23; *Knox's Journal*, II, 394.

143 'Memoirs of an Invalid', pp. 36–7. According to Murray's casualty returns (CO/5/64, fol. 65) the 15th Foot suffered 138 killed, wounded and taken prisoner, or 34 per cent of the 386 of all ranks on the field. It is unlikely that these figures include those who escaped with superficial contusions.

144 'Journal of Malcolm Fraser', *JSAHR* (1939), p. 164.

'misbehaviour' of one of the officers present, Lieutenant Eubule Ormsby of the 35th Foot.[145] When Ormsby's battalion was ordered to cover the right wing of the army, its grenadier company had the task of capturing the mill to their front. A fellow subaltern in Otway's, Cornelius Lysaught, claimed that instead of leading his grenadiers in the fashion expected of a British officer, Ormsby spent the crisis of the action cowering behind an ammunition tumbril. Sworn testimonies from those men of Ormsby's company called to give evidence regarding his conduct provide a useful reminder that the combatant's perspective of the battlefield is invariably more limited than that of the historian: in the case of the private soldier, this view may be restricted to the few square yards that form his immediate surroundings.

Ormsby hoped the hearing would prove that he did his duty 'where the heat of the action was'. In court Orsmby recalled that the grenadier company had given its 'first Fire . . . in a regular manner, the front Rank kneeling', with a ravine to their front and at a range of about 50–60 yards from the windmill. When this musketry forced the French to withdraw, Captain Charles Ince called out loudly for the company to follow him, and led them across the snow-clogged gully by a path that could accommodate only one or two men abreast. As his own post was on the left of the company, Orsmby crossed last of all. Ince was wounded soon after the company reached the mill: summoned to his side, Ormsby was urged to 'keep what we have got'. One man with good reason to recall that Ormsby was present 'nigh the mill' was John Maxwell. With the company in confusion, Maxwell 'set up a kind of Indian Hollow': upon hearing this unsoldierly whooping, Ormsby ordered him to 'hold his tongue'. Another soldier, Joseph Scott, fell slightly behind the company as he paused to 'put in a Flint'; despite this distraction, he remembered that Ormsby had ordered the men to fire. John Stone was also well aware that Ormsby did his duty. The lieutenant 'advanced with the company to the Mill, pointed out to me, and Ordered me to Fire, where he saw them stand very thick, and that he retreated with the company'. By this time Ince was already wounded, and Stone recalled that Ormsby ordered him and some others to help draw off an artillery piece. Lieutenant John Fraser of the 48th Foot testified that it was only owing to the 'singular good behaviour' of Otway's grenadiers that the howitzer and ammunition cart that he commanded were not captured before the line retreated; indeed, Fraser had told Ormsby that he would 'ever esteem them for it'.[146] Lieutenant William Johnston of the Royal Artillery had not seen Ormsby behind a

[145] GCM, Quebec, 1 June 1761, in WO/71/68.

[146] In his despatch to Pitt of 25 May 1760, Murray praised the distinguished conduct of Captain Ince's company of grenadiers (*Correspondence of Pitt*, II, 294).

cart during the battle. However, Johnston had received messages from Captain Ince, requesting permission to be carried back in the ammunition cart. Ormsby therefore submitted that if any officer of the 35th's grenadiers had been seen behind a carriage, it was likely to have been the stricken Ince. After considering the evidence, the court entered a unanimous verdict of 'not guilty', commenting that 'there is not the least Foundation for the accusation, and the Aspersion upon said Lieutenant Ormsby is Scandalous, and Infamous'.[147]

The battle of Sainte-Foy demonstrated that the kind of thin, open-order firing line that was perfectly adequate for defying Indians or militia on clear ground was inadequate to cope with attack by superior numbers of determined regulars. Formed two deep and with large gaps between the files, there were simply not enough redcoats in the line to halt the French assault columns. In the opening phase of the action this weakness had been disguised as the powerful British artillery plied the opposition with grape. John Johnson maintained that while these guns kept up their fire the French were obliged to seek protection in the woods behind them. Once the cannonade slackened, owing to the ammunition carts becoming 'bogged in deep pits of Snow', the French grew bolder; they became more so upon realising that the musketry emanating from the scanty British line 'was so very light'.[148]

At Sainte-Foy, the 'thin red line' had been stretched to breaking point. In the remaining American campaigns of the war, the redcoats would never again face such a test at the hands of regular opponents. The fluid and headlong assaults by light infantry and grenadiers that carried the formidable strong-points on Martinique were far removed from the 'conventional' battlefield confrontation. There were those who felt that the conquest of Martinique had proved too easy, thereby giving the victors an inflated opinion of their own prowess and tactics. Such sceptics included Lieutenant-General George Earl of Albemarle, the commander of the land forces in the expedition to Havana. Albemarle expressed his doubts in a personal letter to his friend 'Jeff' Amherst:

> Your army is a fine one, brave to the last degree, almost spoilt by the expedition *up the River St. Lawrence*. Your officers are all

147 This finding failed to end the bickering between Ormsby and Lysaught. In 1764, at the instigation of his old antagonist, Ormsby was charged with behaviour unbecoming an officer and gentleman after it was alleged that he failed to appear for a duel with Lysaught. In issuing his challenge, Lysaught assumed that Orsmby would have embraced the opportunity to wipe away any 'former suspicions' – a thinly veiled reference to his alleged misconduct at Sainte-Foy. Once again, the court returned a 'not guilty' verdict, ruling that the exasperated Ormsby be 'most honourably acquitted'. See GCM, Mobile, West Florida, 13 August 1764, in WO/71/74.

148 'Memoirs of John Johnson', in *Siege of Quebec*, V, 121.

> generals, with a thoro' contempt for everybody that has not served under *Mr. Wolfe* ... They have conquered in a few days the strongest country you ever saw, in the american way, running or with the Indian [w]hoop. That manner of fighting will not always succeed, and I dread their meeting of troops that will stand their ground. They are certainly brave and will be cut to pieces.[149]

Albemarle boasted precious little combat experience to justify the responsibility placed upon him, and his sentiments may reflect the inferiority he felt when among the seasoned veterans of the 'American Army'.[150] However, other more experienced soldiers were also disturbed at the 'running and whooping' tactics of the conquerors of Montreal and Martinique. One such officer was clearly concerned at what he saw after the army landed on Cuba; recalling the skirmish with Spanish cavalry on 8 June, he described how the bold front maintained by 500 light infantry caused the troopers to recoil when within 60 yards. Had the cavalry charged home, the consequences could have proved serious, as the light infantry had left their bayonets on the transport ships: being 'accustomed only to act in the woods, they never dreamt of such an adventure in open ground'.[151] The young officer was David Dundas, who served the campaign as an aide-de-camp to Major-General George Augustus Eliott. Dundas did not write his memoir until 1800, when he was quartermaster-general of the British Army and regarded as the leading authority on infantry drill, an obsession which had earned him the nickname of 'Old Pivot'.[152] Before serving at Havana, Dundas had campaigned in Germany: what Dundas witnessed on the open battlefields of Europe convinced him that only disciplined close-order infantry, formed up in three ranks and moving at an unhurried pace, could be counted upon to defy regular horse and foot alike.

Dundas had to await the termination of another, less glorious, American war for the opportunity to preach his tactical gospel to a wider congregation. From Bunker Hill to Guilford Court House the redcoats had fought in the thin line first employed by the 'American Army' of

149 Albemarle to Amherst, 6 May 1762, in WO/34/55, fols 139–40.

150 As Lord Bury, Albemarle served as aide-de-camp to Cumberland at Fontenoy and Culloden. Despite steady promotion, he had seen no active service since. There was no love lost between Albemarle and Wolfe. When the former gained the colonelcy of the 20th Foot in 1749, Wolfe (the regiment's lieutenant-colonel) dismissed him as a 'showy' place-seeker. See 'Keppel, George, third Earl of Albemarle, (1724–1772)', in *DNB*, XXXI, 42–3.

151 'Lieutenant-General David Dundas's Memorandum on the Capture of Havana', in *Siege and Capture of Havana*, pp. 314–26; 316–17.

152 Dundas compiled his account with the aid of memoranda and plans made at the time (ibid., p. 326).

the previous conflict. This formation had been adopted at the urging of Wolfe's disciple William Howe, who gained command of Britain's North American army in 1776. Howe's successor, Sir Henry Clinton, was a product of the rival 'German' school of tactics. While disapproving of 'the open, flimsy order of two deep in line', Clinton none the less retained it because the American rebels employed it themselves and fielded few cavalry to menace such a formation.[153] The redcoats performed well during the Revolutionary War, and Britain's ultimate defeat stemmed from strategic rather than tactical shortcomings. However, Dundas maintained that one legacy of the war was a regrettable lack of solidity amongst the redcoats, who instead favoured a 'loose and irregular system' more calculated for Virginia than Flanders.[154] Dundas published his notions in 1788, and was to see them enshrined in the *Regulations* of 1792. Although it was left to other soldiers to revive the light infantry skills that Dundas marginalised, the work of 'Old Pivot' did much to underpin the re-emergence of the British infantry from 1801 onwards.[155] When the British Army countered Napoleonic France its infantry fought elbow to elbow in Dundas fashion; they none the less employed a unique tactical device that can be traced back through the American War of Independence to the redcoats of Quebec – the 'thin red line' of two ranks. In addition, the battalions composing the line were now screened by skilled light infantry who likewise drew upon techniques pioneered in America half a century before: this belated alliance between the best traditions of James Wolfe and Frederick the Great was destined to prove the nemesis of Napoleon's infantry from Alexandria to Waterloo.[156]

153 *The American Rebellion. Sir Henry Clinton's Narrative of His Campaigns, 1775–1782* . . ., ed. W. B. Willcox (New Haven, 1954), p. 95, note 16.

154 Colonel David Dundas, *Principles of Military Movement, Chiefly Applied to Infantry* . . . (London, 1788), p. 11.

155 In the opinion of Piers Mackesy, Dundas's reforms were vindicated during Abercromby's Egyptian campaign of that year. See *British Victory in Egypt*, p. 30.

156 P. Mackesy, 'What the British Army Learned', in *Arms and Independence. The Military Character of the American Revolution*, eds R. Hoffman and P. J. Albert (Charlottesville, Virginia, 1984), pp. 191–215. Whilst the three-deep formation remained official doctrine as late as 1824, Sir Arthur Wellesley ordered his troops to fight in two lines from their first landfall in Portugal in 1808 (ibid., p. 215).

8

The Highland battalions in the Americas

During the summer of 1775, as Britain faced the task of bringing her rebellious North American colonies to heel, army recruiting parties were busy in the Highlands of Scotland. Squads from the Black Watch sought men capable of upholding what was already a proud tradition of service to 'their king and country'. The regiment's recruiting proclamations – made in the Gaelic language of the Highlands – listed the battle honours gained 'during two long bloody wars' in Europe and America: at Fontenoy, Bergen-op-Zoom, Ticonderoga, Guadeloupe, Martinique and Havana, and 'in the hard battle of Bushi-run which broke the courage of the Indians', the men of the Royal Highland Regiment had acquired 'honour and fame', both 'for Scotland and for themselves'. Now, as the redcoats prepared to campaign in America once more, what was needed were 'men in whom there is spirit and bravery, who are willing and able to stand in the place of those who went before them'.[1]

Such recruits had much to live up to: of all the British battalions that formed the 'American Army', none saw harder service, or gained a higher reputation, than those composed of Scottish Highlanders. Although the Black Watch had served with distinction during the War of the Austrian Succession, it was in the following decade, in the course of the Seven Years War, that the Highland contribution to the British Army underwent a major expansion. As that war escalated into a truly global conflict, regimented Highland troops were employed as far afield as India and Germany. However, service in both these theatres only followed upon the successful deployment of Highland battalions in North America and the Caribbean. It was through these costly campaigns that the Highlanders established the reputation that was to gain them a permanent place within the structure of the British Army. The first regimented Highland corps to serve in North America was Lord John Murray's

1 See L. Leneman, *Living in Atholl. A Social History of the Estates 1685–1785* (Edinburgh, 1986), pp. 130–31.

42nd Foot, which arrived at New York in June 1756.[2] Within a year these Highlanders had been joined by two more battalions of kilted troops which were named after their lieutenant-colonel commandants, Archibald Montgomery and Simon Fraser.[3] Although the Highland regiments were absorbed into the British Army as 'regular' troops, they none the less formed a distinctive component within it and accordingly require examination in their own right.

Dress, language and cultural background all set the Highlanders apart from the 'English' battalions. From their first deployment these picturesque soldiers attracted considerable attention: their exploits figured prominently in letters sent home from America and the West Indies, many of which subsequently appeared in London and provincial newspapers. Such reports frequently credited the Highlanders with spectacular feats of courage and tenacity. For example, an officer in the 55th Foot who witnessed the costly attack of the Black Watch upon the French lines at Ticonderoga in 1758 likened the Highlanders to 'roaring lions breaking from their chains'.[4] Similarly, the performance of Fraser's Highlanders at Quebec in 1759 prompted widespread admiration and generated much colourful prose. According to one account, Fraser's casualties that day included Ewan Cameron, 'a common highlander' who reputedly slew nine Frenchmen before his sword arm was smashed by a cannon-ball. Nothing daunted, Cameron fought on with a bayonet until felled by an 'unlucky bullet'.[5] In 1762, Daniel Gun of Montgomery's Highlanders gained celebrity after he single-handedly captured four French grenadiers on Martinique. On being presented with a guinea per captive, Gun, who was 'scarce five foot high, but a broad well set Man', gave a bow and told his comrade 'Donald': 'gin I had kenned, these Childs wad ha' come to sa gud a Market, by the Lard, I wad ha' brought twa more of them'.[6]

2 Formed from the Highland Independent Companies of the 'Black Watch' in 1739 as the 43rd Foot, the regiment was renumbered after the existing 42nd Foot was disbanded in 1749. Although the Black Watch was the first regiment of Highlanders to serve in North America, a company of Highland troops had been raised in Georgia in 1739–40 by the colony's governor, James Oglethorpe, who was himself the colonel of the original 42nd Foot. See A. J. Guy, 'King George's Army', in *1745: Charles Edward Stuart and the Jacobites*, pp. 55–6, note 28; J. M. Johnson, *Militiamen, Rangers, and Redcoats: The Military in Georgia, 1754–1776* (Macon, Georgia, 1992), pp. 10–13.

3 Originally termed the 1st and 2nd Highland Battalions, and ranked as the 62nd and 63rd Foot, Montgomery's and Fraser's were subsequently renumbered the 77th and 78th.

4 'Extract of a letter from a lieutenant in Howe's regiment, dated at Lake George, July 10 [1758]', in *Scots Magazine, 1758* (August), p. 439.

5 'Letter of Captain James Calcraft, Quebec, 20 September, 1759', in *Siege of Quebec*, VI, 146.

6 *Felix Farley's Bristol Journal*, 17 April 1762 (citing a 'private Letter from Fort Royal in Martinico'). Orders given in Monckton's army at Martinique on 19 January 1762, announced the General's award of the cash to Gun in recognition of his 'gallant behaviour'. See 'Hamilton Notebook', p. 253.

Such anecdotes credited the Highlanders with almost superhuman qualities, yet the service record of the Highland battalions in the Americas required no exaggeration: indeed, sober professional soldiers were unanimous in praising their endurance and bravery. At Nova Scotia in May 1758, the notoriously picky James Wolfe described Fraser's battalion as 'very useful Serviceable soldiers, and commanded by the most manly corps of officers I ever Saw'.[7] Recording the services of Montgomery's Highlanders during the Cherokee War of 1760, the soldier and historian Thomas Mante extolled the 'unrepining chearfulness and implicit obedience to their officers which justly characterises the soldiers of North Britain'.[8] In 1763, Colonel Henry Bouquet attributed his hard-won victory over the Ohio Indians at Bushy Run to the fighting qualities of the 42nd and 77th Regiments. He wrote: 'The Highlanders are the bravest men I ever saw, and their behaviour in that obstinat affair does them the highest honor.'[9]

The contribution of the Highlanders was significant in terms of numbers as well as deeds. In September of 1757 the trio of Highland units together mustered 3,306 men of all ranks.[10] By the following spring, the addition of three more companies to each of the battalions had raised the number of Highlanders to 4,200 out of a total of 24,000 British regulars in North America.[11] Subsequent returns are incomplete, but this figure probably shows these Highland regiments at their numerical peak: although a second battalion of the Black Watch was raised in 1758, and both Montgomery's and Fraser's gained a fourteenth company, these and other reinforcements scarcely balanced the heavy casualties sustained during the campaigns waged from that summer onwards. The high overall percentage of Scots in the 'American Army' has already been noted; it offers a reminder that many other Highlanders spent all, or part, of their service in non-Highland battalions. Units possessing traditional territorial links with Scotland, such as the 1st Foot, or 'Royal Scots', or which had recruited heavily in that country, like the 55th Foot, included many Highlanders in their ranks. Even units with no particular Scottish connection might include a significant number of men born in the 'Highland' zone north of the Tay. For example, of the 569 men serving in Anstruther's 58th Foot in December 1759, no less than 51 (9 per cent) were Highlanders.

7 Wolfe to Lord George Sackville, 12 May 1758, in Willson, *Life and Letters of Wolfe*, p. 363.
8 Mante, *History of the Late War*, p. 293.
9 Bouquet to Lieutenant James McDonald, 28 August 1763, in Add. MSS 21,649, fol. 316.
10 Monthly Returns, 24 September 1757 (GD 45/2/13/2).
11 CO/5/50, fols 55–6: 'Distribution of His Majesty's Forces in North America for the Campaigns of 1758 according to the Returns of 24th February, 1758'.

The Highland battalions participated in some of the fiercest fighting of the war – a commitment reflected in their casualty rates. The Black Watch sustained massive losses at Ticonderoga in July 1758: of the ten companies present at the action – a total of 1,100 officers and men – more than 500 of all ranks were subsequently listed as killed, wounded or missing.[12] Two months later Montgomery's new battalion also suffered heavily on the Ohio front: out of 389 Highlanders who accompanied Major Grant in his attempt to surprise Fort Duquesne in September, no less than 223 were lost.[13] That summer saw Fraser's Highlanders serving at Louisbourg, where they escaped lightly compared with the Highland battalions employed elsewhere. This respite was merely temporary: on 13 September 1759, during the action on the Plains of Abraham, Fraser's sustained 18 killed and 148 wounded – by far the heaviest loss of any British battalion present that day. At Sainte-Foy in the following April, Fraser's Highlanders suffered even more heavily, losing another 213 casualties.[14]

Such battlefield losses were heavy enough, but remained insignificant when set beside the attrition stemming from sickness during the Caribbean campaigns of 1762. Both battalions of the 42nd Regiment and nine companies of Montgomery's Highlanders were employed in these operations. When these units sailed from New York for the West Indies in May and November 1761 they mustered 2,075, officers included.[15] A year later, following the conquest of Martinique and Havana, these same units returned in a very different condition. In November 1762, of the three battalions, just 795 remained alive. The two battalions of the Black Watch fielded only 480 men, requiring another 231 merely to complete a single battalion on the reduced establishment.[16] Such stark statistics are shocking enough, but the real condition of these troops is better conveyed in the words of surgeon John Adair, who reported to Amherst that even these men were in a 'deplorable Situation', being 'reduced to the lowest state with dangerous Fevers & Fluxes'. It was Adair's opinion that the entire brigade, which also included the remnants of the 17th Foot, did not contain 30 men who were fit for service.[17] Even now, the ordeal of these sickly

12 Returns, Lake George, 29 June 1758 (CO/5/50, fol. 174); Casualty returns in WO/1/1, fol. 199. See also '"Like Roaring Lions Breaking From Their Chains": The Highland Regiment at Ticonderoga', documents compiled and edited by N. Westbrook, *BFTM*, XVI, 2 (1999), 16–91.

13 See casualty returns in *Papers of Bouquet*, II, 508–9.

14 *Knox's Journal*, II, 118; CO/5/58, fol. 194. Fraser's losses at Sainte-Foy totalled nearly half of those present that day ('Journal of Malcolm Fraser', *JSAHR* (1939), p. 166).

15 'Amherst's Personal Journal', pp. 110; 115.

16 See 'State of the Brigade Arrived from the Havana ... Taken from the Returns 24 Novr 1762' (CKS, U1350/042/11A).

17 'Report of the State of the 17th, two Battalions of the 42d, and 77th Regiments', 18 September 1762, in CKS, U1350/042/8A.

troops was not over. In the early summer of 1763, when 'Pontiac's War' erupted on the western frontier, the remains of the three Highland battalions, amounting to about 600 of all ranks, were despatched to counter the threat.[18] Some 60 of these men were still so weak that they had to be left behind to garrison the posts of Bedford and Ligonier.[19] The remainder were heavily engaged with the Indians at Bushy Run, where they lost a further 80 killed and wounded. By late August 1763, of more than 2,000 Highlanders who had sailed for the West Indies two years before, just 245 remained fit for duty.[20]

From rebels to redcoats

The large-scale employment of Highland manpower across the Atlantic was all the more remarkable because it began merely a decade after a rebel Highland army under Bonnie Prince Charlie had marched as far south as Derby before turning back to meet final defeat at Culloden Moor. In the wake of Culloden, and in a bid to stamp out the potential for rebellion in the Highlands, the victorious Hanoverian regime had made determined efforts to destroy the tribal and militaristic clan society of the region. The system of land-holding whereby tenants owed military service to clan chiefs was abolished, and the carrying of traditional weapons, and even the wearing of tartan, was banned. Although keen to eradicate the traditional roots of Highland warrior society, English commentators were not slow to grasp the potential for harnessing such martial spirit to the service of the state. In the year after Culloden a report on the Highland 'problem' noted that, for all their faults, the 'Common Highlanders' did not lack courage. With proper care, this 'natural Genius' of the Highlanders could be used to transform 'the worst of Rebels into Loyal Subjects'.[21] Four years later James Wolfe wrote to a friend in Nova Scotia that Highlanders could prove useful in that theatre:

> I should imagine that two or three independent Highland companies might be of use; they are hardy, intrepid, accustomed to a rough country, and no great mischief if they fall. How can you

18 *Journal of Amherst*, p. 309.

19 Bouquet to Major Henry Gladwin, 28 August 1763, in Add. MSS. 21,649, fol. 314.

20 See Bushy Run casualty returns in WO/34/40, fol. 326; Bouquet to Amherst, Fort Pitt, 26 August 1763 (Add. MSS 21,634, fol. 365).

21 'Proposals for Civilizing the Highlands', enclosed in Lord Justice-Clerk Andrew Fletcher and Commander-in-Chief Scotland, Lt-Gen. Humphrey Bland to the Duke of Newcastle, Edinburgh, 4 December 1747, in *The Albemarle Papers: Being the Correspondence of William Anne, Second Earl of Albemarle, Commander-in-Chief in Scotland, 1746–1747*, ed. C. Sanford Terry (2 vols, Aberdeen, 1902), II, 490.

outlaws as his 'Privy Council'.[30] The Reverend Forbes added that in the summer of 1759, Patrick Grant was forced into the Army for service in North America. There, Grant made a notable figure in the fighting against the French, and returned to Glen Moriston in 1761 or 1762, in possession of a Chelsea pension.[31]

Given the bitter fighting during the '45, and the brutality of the British Army's subsequent punitive expeditions in the Highlands, the apparent lack of ill-feeling between old enemies is perhaps surprising. Of course, many humble Highlanders were unconcerned with political niceties and simply did what their chiefs told them to do. In the case of those Highlanders who had backed the Stuarts through personal choice, any lingering grudge against the Hanoverian regime appears to have taken second place to other motives. For example, Malcolm Macpherson of Phoiness, who distinguished himself at Quebec in 1759 with Fraser's Highlanders, justified his service in the British Army on the grounds of a costly law-suit, and 'a desire of being revenged on the French for their treacherous promises in 1745'.[32] As far as the Jacobites' late opponents were concerned, dislike for the Highlanders was quickly replaced by an appreciation of their qualities as fighting men. This stance was encountered by Lieutenant John Grant of the Black Watch, who was en route to join the army destined for Guadeloupe when the two companies of Highlanders to which he was attached fell in with a convoy carrying marines for a projected assault upon Dominica. Grant recalled that one of the officers was keen for the Highlanders to join this force:

> He called our two captains onboard, and said Gentleman, I could not bear a Scotch talk [until] lately – for I got so many wounds from the Highlanders at Preston Pans that I could not bear them. But now I have changed my mind and would command them sooner than any other people.[33]

Because of their rugged homeland, Highlanders were viewed as particularly suited to the rigours of campaigning in North America. For example, the Indian trader James Adair stressed the ability of Montgomery's 'brave,

30 Robert Forbes, *The Lyon in Mourning*, ed. H. Paton (3 vols, Edinburgh, 1896), III, 97–8. See also R. K. Marshall, *Bonnie Prince Charlie* (Edinburgh, 1988), p. 164.

31 *Lyon in Mourning*, III, 117; 203–4. Grant may be the same man as the Sergeant Peter Grant, described as a 58-year-old labourer from 'Glenmorrison', who was among a batch of 20 disabled veterans of Fraser's Highlanders examined at Chelsea on 28 October 1760. Sergeant Grant received a pension on account of 'Scurvy & age' and having served for 30 years. Although only re-enlisted in 1759, in common with all the other 'Glenmoriston men' Patrick Grant had soldiered in the Black Watch before the '45 rebellion (see WO/116/5, fol. 53; *Lyon in Mourning*, III, 103).

32 Stewart, *Sketches of the Highlanders*, I, 333, note.

33 'Journal of John Grant', pp. 29–30.

hardy highlanders' to penetrate the mountainous territory of the Cherokees in 1760.[34] It was also widely believed that the Highlanders enjoyed some form of mysterious kinship with the woodland Indians of north-eastern America. However bizarre this notion might appear today, it was far from strange to the thinking man of the 1750s. In the summer of 1758, as he prepared to march on Fort Duquesne, Brigadier-General Forbes hoped that the arrival of Montgomery's Highlanders would help him to retain the services of his restless Cherokee allies, their 'cousins'.[35] Twenty years before, when James Oglethorpe planted a colony of Highlanders in Georgia, their adherence to the 'true Highland habit, which is without any breeches' convinced the local Indians that they were 'just such a people as themselves'.[36] On occasion, this alleged affinity with the Indians could have tragic results. In September 1757, a Highlander in Nova Scotia was shot dead by a nervous redcoat: wrapped up in his plaid, and with his long hair worn loose, this Gaelic-speaking recruit proved unable to comprehend the sentry's challenge and was mistaken for a lurking Micmac warrior.[37]

In some respects the ties between Highlanders and American Indians were indeed stronger than a shared distaste for constricting breeches. Both belonged to martial and tribal societies that appeared exotic and barbaric to eighteenth-century Englishmen, and indeed Lowland Scots. For example, the author of a pamphlet written in the immediate wake of the Black Watch mutiny of 1743 said that when the Highlanders walked the streets of London, they had proved to be a greater object of curiosity than either the Moroccan ambassador or even a group of visiting Indian chiefs.[38] Even after their celebrated services in the Seven Years War, Highlanders could still appear both alarming and outlandish to the average Englishman. For example, when Allan Macpherson of Cluny returned from the West Indies in 1762, wearing the uniform of the Black Watch, he prompted considerable interest upon landing at Bristol. He recalled: 'a great crowd of people came round me and a respectable looking man asked me "Pray sir, forgive me for asking whether you be with us or against – for I never saw such a dress before"'.[39] In the 1740s writers south of the Highland Line had often referred to the clansmen as 'savages' and 'barbarians', and it was ironic that identical terminology should be applied to the Indians the

34 Adair, *History of the American Indians*, pp. 251–2.
35 Forbes to Pitt, Philadelphia, 17 June 1758, in *Writings of Forbes*, p. 117.
36 *London Magazine, 1757* (November), p. 544.
37 *Knox's Journal*, I, 73–4.
38 Anon, *A Short History of the Highland Regiment* ... (London, 1743), p. 1.
39 From *The Red Hackle*, no. 213 (August, 1985), p. 2, cited in D. M. Henderson, *Highland Soldier: A Social Study of the Highland Regiments, 1820–1920* (Edinburgh, 1989), p. 14.

Highlanders were sent to fight a decade later. Charged with destroying Cherokee towns in 1760, Lieutenant-Colonel James Grant found himself pitying the victims of this harsh policy.[40] Even for a Whig Highlander like Grant, such work may have stirred uncomfortable memories of what another British punitive expedition had done in the glens after Culloden.

Harnessing Highland manpower

In common with the orthodox redcoat battalions, the ranks of the Highland regiments included men enlisted against their will. In one sense, this was itself an extension of traditional Highland military organisation. The clan regiments that fought for Prince Charles Edward Stuart had been raised by a combination of factors: these might include the traditional hold of the landowner over his tenant, appeals to a shared pride in clan and culture, and simple unvarnished threats. Indeed, a common defence of Jacobite prisoners after the '45 was that they had been obliged to join the rebellion under duress.[41] The Highlanders who served in the Americas were recruited by a variety of methods, some of which mirrored those employed in raising the old clan regiments. Despite the government's attempts to destroy the clan system, ancient loyalties and obligations endured. For example, even though the Fraser estates in the Highlands had been forfeited after the '45, Simon Fraser none the less enjoyed spectacular success in raising men on his family's former domains. Announcing the completion of his battalion at over 1,000 rank and file, Fraser reported that he had recruited 306 of these in just three days in the 'Fraser Country'.[42]

Coercion, whether applied by landowners or the commissioners responsible for pressing the 'idle able-bodied' under the Recruiting Acts (often one and the same), played a key role in filling the ranks of Fraser's and Montgomery's battalions. Robert Kirk, who served in Montgomery's Highlanders throughout the Seven Years War, recalled that the unit was 'mostly composed of impress'd men from the Highlands'.[43] Kirk's statement is supported by other evidence. Commenting on the successful recruitment of men for Montgomery's, Lady Ballandalloch doubted that so many could have been raised 'without takeing some men from their

40 *Gentleman's Magazine, 1760* (July), p. 306 (extract of undated letter from Grant to Lt-Gov. Bull of South Carolina).

41 Sir Bruce Gordon Seton and Jean Gordon Arnot, *The Prisoners of the '45* (3 vols, Edinburgh, 1928), I, 269.

42 Copy of a letter from Lt-Col. Simon Fraser to Captain Stewart, Secretary to Lord George Beauclerk, Inverness, 1 March 1757, in WO/1/974, p. 365.

43 *Kirk's Memoirs*, p. 2.

poor wives and childeren'.[44] Such arbitrary methods of recruitment did not go unresented: men who deserted from Fraser's before the battalion sailed for America justified this action on the grounds of 'their having been forced into the service without any shew of legal authority'.[45] Force could be brought to bear in more subtle ways. The MP and Highland landowner Ludovick Grant employed a mailed fist within a velvet glove to ensure that sufficient recruits volunteered for the company of his cousin, Major James Grant of Montgomery's Highlanders. Grant told his tenants that as it was necessary for his own honour and the credit of his family that Major Grant's company should be amongst the first to be completed, he trusted that they would 'mannage matters so as that all the young fellows upon Esteat who incline the armie goe into his Companie preferable to any other'. In a thinly veiled threat, Grant added: 'if you have the least reguard all of you upon this occasion will have ane opportunitie of giving Proofs of your friendship to me and my familie ... I hope by your Conduct at this time you'll give me reason to continue your affectionate friend and humble servt.'.[46] Grant's approach had the desired effect: within a month Major Grant already possessed a company some 160 strong, of whom 40 had been recruited by 'the Gentlemen in Strathspey'.[47]

Other men enlisted willingly: at a time when redcoat patrols were still enforcing the ban on tartan and Highland weaponry, service in the British Army was the only means by which a Highlander could bear arms and wear the garb of his ancestors.[48] In addition, in the 1750s, before large-scale emigration to the Scottish Lowlands and North America had begun, the Highlands held a population that was too numerous for its scanty natural resources to support.[49] During the bleak winter of 1756–57, hunger therefore provided a further incentive to serve King George in America. In such harsh times, recruiters who dangled the prospect of cash bounties had no problem in attracting men. This financial factor

44 Penvel Grant (Lady Ballandalloch), to Robert Grant of Tammore, Edinburgh, 17 February 1757, in Add. MSS. 25,411 (Grant Family Correspondence, Volume VII, 1754–57), fols 230–31.

45 Beauclerk to Barrington, Edinburgh, 15 June 1757, in WO/1/613, p. 138.

46 Grant to 'the Gentlemen Woodfellers & tenants of Strathspey, Delnabo & Dunphaill', Panton Square, London, January (?) 20, 1757, in GD 248/507/3/7.

47 James Grant to Robert Grant of Tammore, Lethen, 18 February 1757 (Add. MSS 25,411, fol. 232). The coercive aspects of Highland recruitment are emphasised in A. Mackillop, *'More Fruitful than the Soil': Army, Empire and the Scottish Highlands 1715–1815* (East Linton, 1999).

48 Recruits rejected by Montgomery's and Fraser's battalions had a clause inserted in their discharge papers 'that they were to wear no part of the Highland Dress, longer than fifteen Days from the date thereof'. See Beauclerk to Barrington, Edinburgh, 6 May 1757, in WO/1/613, p. 115.

49 B. Lenman, *Integration, Enlightenment, and Industrialization: Scotland 1746–1832* (London, 1981), p. 10.

emerges in a series of letters regarding the recruitment of Major James Clephane's company of Fraser's Highlanders. In the Major's absence this duty was conducted with great enthusiasm by his sister Mrs Elizabeth Rose, and her husband Hugh. On 2 February 1757, Mrs Rose was already able to report the presence of a 'very numbrous band' of recruits around her home at Kilravock. Displaying a distinctly maternal interest in 'our Troops', 'Betty Clephane' explained that rather than send her recruits to Inverness, she preferred to keep them nearby so that 'their Bellys may be well filled, and if thay be, thay will cast a dash, for thay are realy hansome Boys . . . tip top fellows'. Mrs Rose was prepared to pay generous bounties for her brother's men, a procedure that exasperated her thrifty husband: 'Mr Rose goes Mad, at not haveing them Cheap', she confessed. In consequence, however, the Major's recruits were all 'Sterling volenteers', in contrast to those raised by local 'Grandees' who 'takes out their people as if they had their press act in force for it'. To illustrate her point, Mrs Rose told how two tradesmen had approached her to enlist. Neither actually wanted to become a soldier, but as their landlord intended that they should enlist regardless, they instead offered themselves to Mrs Rose 'on such and such terms and on those terms thay were accepted of'.[50] Two days later, Hugh Rose reported that his wife had indeed been 'as busy as a Bee', to the extent that he could now march the Major's full complement of men to headquarters whenever he pleased.[51] Other time-honoured methods of recruitment also helped to swell the ranks of the Highland battalions. In 1758 John Grant was offered a lieutenancy in the 2nd Battalion of the Black Watch on condition of raising 25 men. After finding a good piper and four expert dancers, Grant established himself at an alehouse. Grant's own 'Serjeant Kite' then delivered his flowery harangue and the reels commenced. Grant recalled that 'this collected a crowd & drink was not scarce . . . I soon enlisted my number'.[52]

By the spring of 1757, both Montgomery's and Fraser's had not only been raised to their full establishment of 1,000 men each, but also boasted 500 surplus, or 'supernumerary' men, of whom 260 were to accompany the battalions to America.[53] These figures are particularly impressive when it is appreciated that many other men had already been rejected: for example, of 1,029 recruits for Montgomery's Highlanders examined in March, no less than 472 were turned away.[54] If the orders issued to officers recruiting for Fraser's battalion are any indication, this wholesale

50 Mrs Rose to Dr John Clephane (GD 125/22/2/5).

51 Hugh Rose to Dr Clephane, 'Killraick', 4 February 1757, in GD 125/22/2/8.

52 'Journal of John Grant', p. 25.

53 Beauclerk to Barrington, Edinburgh, 6 May 1757, in WO/1/613, p. 115.

54 'State of the first Highland Battalion . . . Nairn, March 9th, 1757', in WO/1/974, p. 139. Four of the company commanders had their entire complement of recruits refused. By contrast, all 230 men produced by Major Grant were approved.

rejection probably stemmed from the recruitment of men who fell far below the physical standards usually applied by the Army. Fraser's officers were permitted to take 'Men of any Size who are fit for Service and of any Age from Eighteen to Forty'. By contrast, whilst British officers recruiting in North America that year applied the same age limits, they were supposed to enlist no recruits under five feet four inches tall, except for 'growing lads', who could be taken at that height.[55] Indeed, the commander-in-chief in Scotland, Lord George Beauclerk, had issued orders that every supernumerary man who was under five feet four inches tall and over 30 years old should be discharged immediately.[56] Whatever the deficiencies of the rejected men, the surplus of alternatives meant that on 12 May 1757, Beauclerk was able to inform Lord Barrington that the officers who had reviewed Fraser's and Montgomery's considered both battalions to consist of 'very Serviceable good men, and the same has been Confirmed to me by all the other accounts I have heard of them'.[57] Indeed, when Colonel Webb and Lieutenant-Colonel Worge inspected Fraser's battalion at Glasgow they could not find one 'Indifferent man', reporting 'That they were in General remarkably well limbed & shouldered, and a very fine Battalion'.[58] The abundance of manpower early in 1757 is all the more striking as recruiting parties from the Black Watch had already been at work in the Highlands during the previous spring, seeking to raise more than 500 men to augment the regiment before its departure from Ireland to America.[59]

It was probably to take advantage of this apparent glut of clansmen that the Black Watch, Fraser's and Montgomery's set about raising a further three companies each for American service. However, by this stage there were already signs that men were becoming scarcer. By October 1757, all three regiments were facing problems in completing these additional companies. Quality, as well as quantity, was also dropping: when two of the new companies of Fraser's were reviewed at Glasgow, 52 of the men had to be discharged as unfit for service. Four days later, Beauclerk observed that all the officers were facing severe problems in raising their complements.[60]

Further demands on the reserves of Highland manpower came as the campaigning season of 1758 began in earnest. In early July 1758, at the

55 Recruiting Instructions for Fraser's Highlanders, London, 13 January 1757, in GD 125/22/16/4; Recruiting Instructions, Albany, 16 November 1757, in GD 45/2/18/1A.

56 Beauclerk to Barrington, Edinburgh, 6 May 1757, in WO/1/613, p. 115.

57 WO/1/973, p. 25.

58 Beauclerk to Barrington, Edinburgh, 6 May 1757 (WO/1/613, p. 116).

59 Barrington to Robert Ince, 27 January 1756, in WO/4/51, p. 158. Stewart of Garth maintained that by June 1756, these recruiting parties had raised 700 men (*Sketches of the Highlanders*, I, 296).

60 Beauclerk to Barrington, Edinurgh, 11 and 15 October 1757, in WO/1/613, pp. 197; 201.

same time that the Black Watch was throwing itself against the French fortifications at Ticonderoga, but before news of that disaster had crossed the Atlantic, it was decided to honour the corps with the title 'Royal Highland Regiment', and to order the raising of seven new companies to provide it with a second battalion.[61] Within weeks, on the arrival of the lengthy Ticonderoga casualty lists, orders were issued for a further 350 men to be raised as replacements.[62] The seven companies were completed in three months and embodied at Perth in October at a strength of 840.[63] However, the officers left behind in Scotland to recruit the extra replacements were less fortunate. By January 1759 they were struggling to raise even a handful of men and were doubtful of enlisting any more unless they were allowed above the customary levy money of £3 per man. When these officers were recruiting men to secure their own commissions they had personally provided extra bounty money to attract volunteers, and also received the generous assistance of their friends. With both these lures now withdrawn Beauclerk feared recruits would be hard to find. Officers recruiting an extra company apiece for Fraser's and Montgomery's were more successful, raising some 300 men, but this total included 'most of the Deserters of the Thievish Tribes in the Highlands', who were persuaded to enlist in exchange for the Royal pardon.[64] The growing problem of finding recruits for the three Highland regiments fighting in America was exacerbated by initiatives to form new Highland units for service in Germany and elsewhere. The formation of Keith's 87th and Campbell's 88th Regiments only increased the competition for recruits. Indeed, if the recollection of Sir Robert Murray Keith is to be believed, Highlanders raised specifically for America were diverted to recruit his own unit. On 21 August 1759, on the day following his appointment as major-commandant of a corps of Highlanders, Keith attended a meeting with Pitt at which it was decided to form such a unit for service in Germany. As 300 recruits for the Royal Highlanders were already waiting at Newcastle – presumably the replacements that the Regiment's officers had been raising with such difficulty over the past year – these were promptly handed over to the Major. Keith recalled: 'Mr Pitt *removed all obstacles* and gave me the sole command of them.'[65] More than 960 men of Keith's and Campbell's corps sailed from Leith and Burntisland for

61 Barrington to Lord John Murray, 13 July 1758, in WO/4/56, p. 58. News of the royal decision was given out in orders by Maj.-Gen. Abercromby at New York on 24 November 1758. See 'Monypenny Order Book', in *BFTM* (June 1971), pp. 155–6.

62 Barrington to Lord John Murray, 1 September 1758, in WO/4/56, p. 184.

63 Stewart, *Sketches of the Highlanders*, I, 308.

64 Beauclerk to Barrington, Edinburgh, 9 January 1759, in WO/1/614, pp. 5–6.

65 'Mrs Gillespie Smith's "Memoirs of Sir Robert Murray Keith"', cited by J. M. Bulloch in *Territorial Soldiering in the North-East of Scotland During 1759–1814* (Aberdeen, 1914), p. 24.

Germany in the spring of 1760.[66] The officers who reviewed these units before their embarkation noted the presence of a few old men and boys in both, but added the significant observation that they were 'not to be Objected at this time when Men are so very difficult to get'.[67] Such men were badly needed to strengthen Amherst's dwindling Highland battalions in America: on 6 December 1759 he wrote to Barrington from New York that the 'Royal Highland Regt and Montgomerys want a great many men'.[68] In the following autumn, Amherst complained that 1,500 men were now needed to complete his Highland regiments.[69] This situation stemmed partly from the fact that only 'Highlanders' were theoretically acceptable to these corps: as a result, unlike the other British regular battalions, such units could not beat up for recruits in the colonies themselves, or receive drafts from non-Highland regiments. The scarcity of Highlanders at this time, and the value placed upon them, is illustrated by the minutes of a General Court Martial held at Montreal in December 1760. Two men of the Royal Highland Regiment's 1st Battalion – James Hardy and Neill Nicholson – had deserted after meeting with a women who plied them with rum, with the result that they became 'flustered'. Called upon as a character witness, Captain Allan Campbell testified that Hardy and Nicholson were members of his grenadier company, and had served in the regiment since before its first arrival in America. Both men were found guilty as charged and sentenced to death; however, as the result of a very strong application in the name of all the court members, recommending them as proper objects for mercy, Brigadier-General Thomas Gage pardoned the pair. Clearly, at a time when good Highland recruits were so scarce the Army could ill afford to execute two hardened veterans, particularly as both belonged to the élite grenadier company.[70]

Much information regarding the Highland battalions during the Seven Years War can be gleaned from the records of those men who applied for pensions from Chelsea Hospital. The first 'sample' considered here, taken from the Black Watch, involves 27 wounded men who were granted out-

[66] Beauclerk to Barrington, Edinburgh, 19 May 1760, in WO/1/614, p. 437.

[67] See WO/1/614, pp. 450–51; 458. Among the 'old men' in Keith's Highlanders was John McDonald, whose age was given as 80 when he was examined at Chelsea on 9 September 1760. On that occasion McDonald's application was queried because he had only served for one and a half years. Happily, McDonald was 'admitted' to his pension by order of the King himself on 23 December 1760 (WO/116/5, fol. 52). Colin Campbell's short-lived regiment of Highlanders, raised in 1760 as the 100th Foot, fielded equally unpromising material, being 'composed of very young Boys, or of old Men, without the Benefit of the intermediate Years'. See William Rufane to Charles Townshend, Martinique, 16 July 1762 (WO/1/19, fol. 194).

[68] WO/1/5, fol. 84.

[69] Amherst to Barrington, Crown Point, 18 October 1760 (WO/1/5, fol. 132).

[70] GCM, Montreal, 8 December 1760, in WO/71/46.

pensions in late March 1759. This wave of claims reflects the heavy casualties suffered by the regiment in the attack upon Ticonderoga during the previous summer.[71] All of the men included in this sample were 'true' Highlanders. Unlike applicants from typical 'English' regiments at this time, few of these Highlanders could boast of a trade. The only two men who gave a previous occupation were Donald Cameron, a 'doctor' from Argyleshire, and James Robertson, a weaver from Tay Bridge in Perthshire. The average age of this group was 32 – comparable to that of a standard redcoat battalion – although the age range itself was far more extensive. At one extreme was Duncan McDonald, 21, who, the register recorded, 'lost his left leg in America'. Wounded alongside him was a man old enough to be his grandfather, the 65-year-old Donald Munro. The average length of service of these men was 6.4 years: however, of the 27 sampled, eighteen had spent either three or four years in the Army, suggesting that they were recruited during the drive to bring the regiment up to full strength for American service.

As already noted, the scale of casualties sustained by the Black Watch at Ticonderoga triggered a fresh wave of recruiting in 1758. These new recruits, who eventually formed the regiment's 2nd Battalion, were soon in action in the West Indies. Some of the men wounded at Guadeloupe were examined at Chelsea on 7 September 1759.[72] Of the fifteen men involved in this sample, all but one had served for just one year. The exception was 60-year-old Alexander McKenzie, who had accumulated a total of seventeen years in the Black Watch and other regiments. If the aged McKenzie is removed from the sample, on the grounds of unreasonably distorting the results, the average age of the remaining fourteen Guadeloupe wounded emerges as 24 – or eight years younger than the Ticonderoga casualties. The most junior was Corporal John Fonlis, aged nineteen, who lost his left arm; the oldest was 35-year-old John Beatton, who was 'Shott thro' the body'. Unlike the Ticonderoga casualties, previous occupations were recorded for all but one of these men. Of the fifteen, there were ten labourers, three weavers, and a tailor. The former tailor, Corporal Fonlis, was the sole Lowlander. The registers therefore reveal that the men recruited for the Regiment's 2nd Battalion were generally considerably younger than those 'mature' clansmen who had

71 All but one of these cases can be found in WO/120/4, p. 502, under the admission date of 27 March 1759. In its 'Chronicle' section for 13 March 1759, the *Annual Register* noted that 'About eighty Highlanders, wounded at the battle of Ticonderoga in America, set out from Portsmouth in waggons, in order to be sent, some to hospital for cure, others to Chelsea Hospital, and the rest to return to their own country. Some of them were so lacerated by the slugs and broken nails which the enemy fired, that they are deemed incurable' (*Annual Register, 1759*, p. 77).

72 See WO/120/4, pp. 503–4.

formed the original core of the regiment. The presence of the elderly Donald Munro and Alexander McKenzie among these wounded veterans serves as a reminder of the wide age span encountered among the Highlanders; this is highlighted by a series of six pension applications in February of 1761, all of which involved men of the Black Watch aged 60 or over. One of them, John Fraser, was 67. Fraser, from 'County Inverness', was discharged on the understandable grounds of being 'old and paralytic'. It is interesting to note that four of these men, James Eglington, Hector Peacock, Hugh Anderson and John Catanack, had only been recruited two and a half years before. At that time, all were well past what could be considered a reasonable age for active service: John Catanack was already 63. Despite their advanced years, these men were on active service during the previous year.[73] The fact that men were enrolled for foreign duty at such an advanced age strongly suggests that the supply of 'prime' Highlanders was failing to keep pace with the rate of attrition resulting from the tough American campaigning. This hint that the once-fertile recruiting ground of the Highlands no longer offered a limitless pool of manpower is supported by the fact that both Eglington and Peacock were not even Highlanders, having been born in Glasgow. Standards were clearly slipping, with recruiters not only enlisting old men, but also scouring far beyond the geographical boundaries that traditionally gave the Highland regiments their distinct identity.[74]

Honour, clanship and community

In his *Sketches*, Stewart of Garth maintained that the high moral code of the early Highlanders meant that misconduct was virtually unknown within their regiments.[75] Although it is true that Highlanders feature far

[73] These five and another aged Highlander, William Thompson, were among invalids embarked at New York, on 8 December 1760 (WO/1/5, fols 143–4). All were admitted to the Chelsea 'out' pension on the grounds of being 'old and infirm', and in the case of Eglington, having been 'Bruised at Albany by a Battoe'. See WO/120/4, p. 505.

[74] The presence of Lowland Scots in the 2/42nd during the Seven Years War is interesting in the light of comments by Stewart of Garth that the only non-Highlanders in the regiment at this time were '18 Irishmen enlisted at Glasgow by two officers anxious to gain commissions' (*Sketches of the Highlanders*, I, 308, note). Although it was announced that Montgomery's and Fraser's were to be formed solely from Highlanders, the former unit included a significant number of men born outside the Highlands. Indeed, Lord Loudoun observed that Montgomery's contained 'a good many low Countrymen' alongside the 'Real Highlanders' (See *London Magazine, 1757* (January), p. 42; Loudoun to Henry Bouquet, New York, 8 September 1757, in WO/34/41, fol. 17). Fraser's battalion also included the occasional non-Highlander. For example, George Crookshank was a former weaver from Edinburgh; Thomas Carter was a native of Dublin. See WO/116/5, fols 43; 57.

[75] Stewart, *Sketches of the Highlanders*, I, 292.

less frequently in the General Courts Martial records than miscreants from such battalions as the 44th Foot, or Gage's Light Infantry, it would be wrong to go to the other extreme and suggest that their ranks were filled with plaster saints. To make such a claim would be extremely naive – particularly given the often lawless nature of traditional Highland society, where cattle-raiding and blackmail were a way of life. A worthy champion of this violent heritage was Corporal Angus MacDonald of Fraser's Highlanders, who was brought before a General Court Martial at Quebec in September 1761. MacDonald, described as 'above the middle size' and with 'Caroty hair', had been engaged in a freelance extortion racket amongst the French-Canadian inhabitants of three neighbouring parishes. Found guilty as charged, MacDonald was ordered to repay the money he had stolen, and to receive 2,000 lashes with a cat-o'-nine-tails.[76] Neither were Highland officers always the paragons of virtue that Stewart imagined. For example, six officers wearing 'Hyland dress' employed swords, canes and horsewhips to inflict a severe beating upon two respected colonial civilians simply because the unfortunate pair were unable to ferry them from Perth Amboy to New York as promptly as they demanded.[77]

Dress and language distinguished the Highlanders from the rest of the redcoats, and this strong sense of identity was reinforced by a strict code of honour. According to Stewart of Garth, the Highlander 'was taught to consider courage as the most honourable virtue, cowardice the most disgraceful failing'. In consequence, the Highland soldier went into the field 'resolved not to disgrace his name'.[78] The importance of *esprit de corps* for the redcoats of the 'American Army' has already been noted: nowhere was this sense of community and group loyalty stronger than among the Highlanders. For example, Lauchlin McPherson held the rank of sergeant in Hopson's 40th Foot in Nova Scotia: although he had no complaints about his treatment in that regiment, McPherson had grown restless after hearing that the 'Highland Watch' (42nd) was now serving in America. Being 'very well satisfied that some of his Friends and Neighbours must be among them', McPherson petitioned Loudoun for a transfer. Indeed, McPherson was prepared to accept demotion to 'Private in the Ranks' if he could 'Share the Fate of War with his Country Men'.[79]

The bond between a Highlander and his officer was also closer than the relationship between the English soldier and his superiors; for all their differences in rank, such men shared a common culture and heritage,

76 GCM, Quebec, 25 September 1761, in WO/71/71.
77 Petition of Aaron Edwards and Peter Lot to Jeffery Amherst, New York, 3 March 1759, in RH 4/98/2.
78 Stewart, *Sketches of the Highlanders*, I, 235–6.
79 Undated [1757] petition from McPherson to Loudoun (LO 5256).

and very often the same name. Highland officers were expected to provide an unswerving example of honourable conduct to their men: those who did so inspired extreme devotion. As Lord George Beauclerk told Lord Barrington in 1760, it was well known that men raised in the Highlands enlisted from 'principles of personal regard and attachment to their officers'.[80] An example of this almost filial devotion stems from the Black Watch's frenzied assault on Ticonderoga in 1758. The story concerns Gilbert MacBean, who was examined at Chelsea Hospital in June 1787. MacBean, who was then aged 59, had five years previously been discharged from the West Fencible Regiment of Foot at Glasgow. The discharge paper issued on that occasion testified that MacBean had served honestly and faithfully in the Fencibles for four and a half years, and in the 42nd Regiment for eleven years. MacBean was discharged because of a rupture, but he had previously been severely wounded in the attack upon Ticonderoga. When MacBean finally managed to appear before the Chelsea commissioners, one of his former officers, John Small, took the trouble to write a message of support on the back of his original discharge certificate. It read:

> I beg leave to mention as a favourable and Recommendatory circumstance in behalf of Gilbert MacBean, that having had the Honor to Command a Division of the 42d Regt at the attack of the Lines of Ticonderoga on the 8th July 1758 (where the said Regiment had 27 Officers and upwards of 500 non Commissioned officers & Privates Kill'd and wounded) I witness'd the remarkable good behaviour of McBean (who was then a servant to Major Duncan Campbell) and with a fidelity, and singularly meritorious attachment, carried his Master (who was then mortally Wounded) off the Field, and continued inseperably with him and his son, Lieut Alexr Campbell (who also Died of the Wounds he then and there received) Until they both Expired in his arms.

Small, who had since risen to become lieutenant-colonel of the 84th Regiment's 2nd Battalion, hoped that this testimony would help to secure MacBean the 'Royal Bounty' of a pension.[81] This incident neatly demonstrates the reciprocal bond between Highland officers and their men: it reveals not only MacBean's devotion to his officers on the battlefield, but also the fact that Colonel Small remembered a private soldier he

[80] Letter dated Edinburgh, 5 February 1760, in WO/1/614, p. 295.
[81] Chelsea Board of 18 June 1787, in WO/121/1.

had fought alongside nearly three decades before, and felt moved to help him.[82]

Further evidence of the close bond between Highland officers and their men – particularly where a clan tie also existed – is illustrated by an incident that occurred while Fraser's Highlanders were quartered in Connecticut during the winter of 1757–58. On this occasion Colonel Simon Fraser spared no effort to aid Sergeant Alexander Fraser, who was charged with murdering Corporal James Macky of the battalion. According to a court of inquiry, Macky had struck Fraser an unprovoked blow to the head with his broadsword; blinded by blood, Sergeant Fraser retaliated, administering a fatal dirk thrust to the Corporal's throat.[83] Rather than see the Sergeant tried by the local civilian authorities, Colonel Fraser was anxious that the accused should go before a court martial and made a strong appeal to Forbes to intercede with Lord Loudoun on the Sergeant's behalf: 'for God's sake My dear Sir, put my Lord in mind to do something about this poor unhappy man, whose life 'twere pity should be in the hands of uncultivated creatures, for the King has not a better soldier'.[84] According to Sergeant James Thompson of Fraser's, who had loaned Fraser the lethal dirk, Colonel Fraser subsequently took an even more personal role in the Sergeant's defence. When the Sergeant came to trial at the Superior Court, as he spoke little English, it was necessary to provide a Gaelic-speaking interpreter. This key office was fulfilled by Colonel Fraser himself. During the proceedings the Attorney-General observed that the evidence was 'too much to the same effect that he could not refrain from taxing Colonel Fraser with wishing to screen the prisoner'.[85] To the Colonel's surprise and delight, the jury returned a 'not guilty' verdict, causing him to remark that in consequence 'The Colony of Connecticut and the 2d highland Battalion are hand & glove.'[86]

'Celtic Warfare'?

The Highland regiments also stemmed from a culture with its own distinctive tactical doctrine: this combined firepower with the cold steel of the traditional broadsword charge. One modern scholar, Michael Hill, has emphasised these traits in his examination of the Highlanders' role

82 For Small's career see K. R. Stacy, 'Major General John Small, 1726–1796', *JSAHR*, LXXIV (1996), 102–4.

83 See GD 45/2/29/2B (enclosure with Fraser to Forbes, Stratford, 10 January 1758).

84 Same to same, Stratford, 10 February 1758 (GD 45/2/29/4).

85 Harper, *Fraser Highlanders*, pp. 61–2.

86 Fraser to Forbes, Stratford, 25 February 1758, in GD 45/2/29/5.

in America. Hill praises officers such as Wolfe for 'allowing the Highlanders to practice their primitive mode of warfare', giving them 'just enough discipline and stability to temper their customary blind rage'. Hill's picture of a barely restrained mass of clansmen brandishing swords and shields in the manner of their ancestors forms part of a more general thesis of 'Celtic Warfare': this itself fits into a wider argument that seeks to establish a continuity in the aggressive mode of warfare used by the Scottish and Irish Celts and their descendants.[87] Indeed, some American historians have suggested that the 'Highland charge' only reached its high-water mark when Pickett's attack foundered before the Union lines at Gettysburg.[88] Hill's thesis requires some discussion here, as it offers a distorted image of the Highland battalions in America.

On the question of control, it is certainly true that the Highlanders – like the British grenadiers – could occasionally allow their fighting spirit to override the strict conventions of discipline. For example, at Ticonderoga, the Black Watch was disgruntled at being placed in reserve, and instead attacked with such determination that a handful of its men apparently earned the grim distinction of dying within the enemy breastwork.[89] The French commander, the Marquis de Montcalm, was certainly impressed with the ferocity of the onslaught: he reported that a column 'consisting of English grenadiers and Scotch highlanders, continued charging for 3 hours without retreating or breaking'.[90] A similar independence surfaced a year later at Quebec, when Wolfe was repulsed beneath the slopes of Montmorency. Brigadier-General George Townshend, who had crossed the ford at Montmorency to support the main attack, recorded that two companies of Fraser's Highlanders under his command 'would not retire with him' until certain that the rest of their regiment, which was on the beach with Wolfe, had been safely re-embarked. A tense Townshend was obliged to linger until the tide was so high that his command 'could scarcely wade over ye ford'. Townshend's grumble led the Canadian military historian C. P. Stacey to observe that the '78th was really less a British regiment than a war party of Clan Fraser'. This exaggerates the situation, as Fraser's Highlanders were clearly a well-disciplined regular corps: indeed, when Wolfe rebuked his grenadiers for their headlong

87 J. M. Hill, *Celtic Warfare, 1595–1763* (Edinburgh, 1986), pp. 168; 178; 180.

88 See G. McWhiney and P. D. Jamieson, *Attack and Die: Civil War Military Tactics and the Southern Heritage* (Alabama, 1982).

89 Cadwallader Colden heard that the 42nd Foot 'renewed the attack three times & every time some of them got on top of the ennemies work but not being properly supported they were forced to retire with great loss' (Colden to Peter Collinson, Long Island, 23 August 1758, in *Collections of New-York Historical Society, 1921: Letters and Papers of Cadwallader Colden, Volume V, 1755–1760* (New York, 1922), p. 251.

90 'M. de Montcalm's Report of the Battle of Ticonderoga', in *NYCD*, X, 740.

attack at Montmorency, he deliberately contrasted their 'impetuous, irregular, and unsoldierlike behaviour', with the 'soldier-like and cool' conduct of Amherst's and Fraser's regiments.[91]

Modern scholars who seek to portray the Highland regiments in America as bodies of semi-trained tribal irregulars can draw some encouragement from the colourful memoirs of James Thompson. In 1818, when the Duke of Richmond visited Quebec, he took the opportunity to quiz the venerable Thompson – who was by now something of a celebrity himself – about the nature of Fraser's Highlanders. Thompson had explained:

> To be sure, they knew nothing about Parade-exercise, and figuring away with their Fuzees, and they could not bear to be taught to 'Prime & load', for every mothers' son of them knew that from his infancy – The only difficult matter to teach them was to 'Form the line', and then, it was just as difficult to make them keep it, that is to say, when they had an enemy in sight: – but, as for the rest of the business, they could do just as well as other soldiers.[92]

Accepting that Thompson was seeking to provide his royal visitor with an accurate description of the discipline of Fraser's Highlanders, his comments must surely embrace his old battalion's early days, rather than its subsequent service. It is certainly true that on disembarking in America, many of the Highland recruits that had been despatched across the Atlantic in such haste were still virtually untrained. For example, when Sir Allan MacLean arrived in the spring of 1758 with the three additional companies for Montgomery's Highlanders he emphasised that these raw recruits were ill prepared to take the field, even though he kept them 'constantly at the Exercise'. When it came to marksmanship, the performance of the recruits was particularly poor because 'the major part of them have been even thoroughly ignorant of the method of charging a piece'.[93] Brigadier-General Forbes hoped that these three companies might eventually prove useful, although they were currently inferior to 'the same number of the Militia, as none of them has ever as yet burnt powder or [is] any ways used to arms'.[94]

Such deficiences could be expected of any raw recruits, but whatever their initial level of efficiency, it is clear that the Highlanders were sub-

91 'Townshend's Rough Notes', in *Northcliffe Collection*, p. 423; C. P. Stacey, *Quebec, 1759*, p. 78; *Knox's Journal*, II, 3–4.
92 Anecdote related by Thompson to his son, also James, on 31 August 1828, in GD 45/3/422, fol. 500.
93 MacLean to John Forbes, Lancaster, 10 May 1758 (GD 45/2/51/1).
94 Note on preparations for the 1758 campaign against Fort Duquesne, undated and unsigned, but in the handwriting of Forbes, in RH 4/86/1.

sequently subjected to the same intensive training regime as the other regular battalions in America. For example, the four companies of Fraser's Highlanders at Fort Stanwix were carefully drilled in the 'New Manual Exercise'.[95] By the final campaign against Canada, the Highlanders were as well trained as any troops in an army which had been brought to an exceptionally high pitch of discipline. On 10 May 1760, Amherst reviewed the 2nd Battalion of the 42nd and noted that they 'went through their Exercise very well'.[96] Such evidence makes it clear that the Highlanders must be considered as a fully integrated component of the British Army, rather than outlandish auxiliaries.

Accordingly, while traditional 'Highland' tactics called for the broadsword charge to be prefaced by a single close-range volley from muskets and pistols, the Highland battalions were trained in the rolling fire by platoons that was the trademark of the British infantry. Eyewitness accounts of Major James Grant's defeat at Fort Duquesne in 1758 specifically mention the orderly platoon firing of the 77th regiment.[97] Similarly, in the Caribbean campaign of 1759, the 2nd Battalion of the 42nd was described as maintaining a 'regular platoon firing' as it advanced upon the French entrenchments at Guadeloupe.[98] During Wolfe's victory at Quebec, Fraser's Highlanders took their place in the British line, and 'continued firing very hot for about six or ... eight minutes' before Brigadier-General James Murray ordered them to 'draw their swords' and pursue Montcalm's shattered whitecoats.[99]

The experience of Fraser's Highlanders at Quebec reveals the strengths and weaknesses of the basket-hilted broadsword. While these formidable close-quarter weapons proved as intimidating to the French regulars on that September morning as they had to the redcoats themselves in 1745, the finest swordsmanship was useless against Indians and Canadian bush-runners, who refused to come within range of the swinging blades. Eyewitness accounts tell how Fraser's broadswords harried the French

95 Orderly Book, Fort Stanwix, 1 February to 9 April 1759, in GD 125/34/4, fols 15; 23.

96 *Journal of Amherst*, p. 199. For examples of the frequent and detailed orders issued to the Royal Highland Regiment during the previous year, see Wallace, 'Regimental Routine', in *JSAHR* (1952), pp. 8–19. One observer writing in 1743 noted that upon the outbreak of the War of the Austrian Succession the 'Black Watch' were already 'as well disciplined as any troops in the service' (See *Short History of the Highland Regiment*, p. 26).

97 *Kirk's Memoirs*, p. 6; 'Thomas Gist's Indian Captivity', *PMHB* (1956), p. 292.

98 Barrington to Pitt, Gaudeloupe, 9 May 1759, in *London Magazine, 1759* (June), pp. 317–18.

99 'Journal of Malcolm Fraser', *JSAHR* (1939), p. 156. Hill argues that the regiment contributed 'the Highlanders' traditional discharge' on this occasion (*Celtic Warfare*, p. 165). However, Malcolm Fraser is clearly describing a far more sustained period of firing than a single volley.

to the gates of Quebec with considerable carnage.[100] However, when the Highlanders were directed to dislodge skirmishers from some rough ground near the General Hospital, the tables were turned with a vengeance. Having left their own firearms behind, Fraser's Highlanders suffered heavy losses from the musketry of these evasive foes. The Highlanders were forced to give ground and re-form, while the 58th Regiment and the Royal Americans came to their aid. As Malcolm Fraser recorded: 'It was at this time and while in the bushes that our Regiment suffered most.'[101]

Broadswords were swiftly discarded in 1776, when the Black Watch found itself in America once more, but this time opposed to rebellious colonists. It comes as no surprise to learn that the rejection of the broadsword by his own regiment was viewed as a black day by our old friend, David Stewart of Garth. He roundly condemned this break with the past, and bitterly regretted that a weapon Highlanders could employ so well, should be sent to 'rust and spoil in the stores'.[102] However, by the end of the Seven Years War, it seems that the broadsword had already fallen out of favour with the Highland regiments themselves. After that war, the lieutenant-colonel of the Royal Highland Regiment told reviewing officers how on several occasions in America his men had declined using broadswords, and regarded these weapons as incumbrances. When it came to close fighting, he said, they all preferred their bayonets.[103]

As noted at the beginning of this chapter, the daring deeds of Highland soldiers in America provided much colourful copy for English and Scottish newspapers: such coverage grew ever more enthusiastic as the roll of Britain's victories in the 'Great War for the Empire' lengthened. Malcolm Macpherson, who fought in the ranks of Fraser's Highlanders after volunteering at the age of 70, was feted when he subsequently visited London to swear allegiance to the King. As Macpherson strolled the

100 See, for example, 'Genuine Letters from a Volunteer in the British Service at Quebec', in *Siege of Quebec*, V, 13–25; 23–4.

101 'Journal of Malcolm Fraser', *JSAHR* (1939), p. 156.

102 Stewart, *Sketches of the Highlanders*, I, 399–400.

103 Houlding, *Fit for Service*, p. 151, note. As early as 1757, Archibald Montgomery had requested that his battalion be allowed to leave their broadswords at Philadelphia before campaigning in the backwoods. He argued: 'Our men are young and the less they are loaded the better, if you can give us a little help in carrying their baggage, they'l March like so many Grey-Hounds' (See Montgomery to Forbes, Charlestown, South Carolina, 27 April 1757, in GD 45/2/87/3). At Albany on 5 May 1759, all the 'English' regiments (the grenadier companies excepted) were ordered to leave their swords behind during the coming campaign. The 42nd and 77th were not included in the ban: their commanding officers were to act as they thought best (*Knox's Journal*, I, 459–60).

capital's streets the mob had cried, 'There goes the brave old highlander; Long live the gallant old Boy.'[104] Indeed, the well-publicised services of men like Macpherson looked set to secure a victory as remarkable as any won over King George's enemies on the battlefield: their efforts bade fair to surmount centuries of prejudice and gain the Englishman's acceptance of the Scot as fellow British subject. For example, on 19 June 1762, the *Briton* observed that for all their rebellious past, the Highlanders had quite literally 'washed away' the stain of Jacobitism by the blood shed so liberally at Ticonderoga, Guadeloupe, Quebec and elsewhere across the globe.[105]

The *Briton* was a pro-government journal: its comment suggests an attempt to counter a growing wave of anti-Scottish sentiment that even the exploits of popular heroes like Macpherson would prove incapable of stemming. This 'runaway Scottophobia' owed less to old rivalries than to the emergence of a Scotsman, John Stuart, 3rd Earl of Bute, as Prime Minister during the final phase of the Seven Years War. Bute, who became First Lord of the Treasury in May 1762, was widely attacked for his influence over the young George III, the affair he was allegedly conducting with the King's mother, and his role in peace negotiations that appeared to squander the gains acquired at such cost.[106] The animosity aroused by Bute was encountered by two officers of the Black Watch who attended an opera at Covent Garden in December 1762 clad in their plaids. As James Boswell recorded, on entering the theatre the pair drew forth chants of 'No Scots! No Scots! Out with them!' and were pelted with apples. With his own Scottish blood boiling, Boswell spoke to the officers and discovered that they had recently arrived from Havana: 'And this', they said, 'is the thanks that we get – to be hissed when we come home. If it was [the] French, what could they do worse?' Boswell noted that the mob 'soon gave over',[107] but the incident none the less provides a further reminder of the fickleness of civilian attitudes towards the soldier during the Georgian era. It likewise warns against exaggerating the degree to which the impressive performance of Highland soldiers during the Seven Years War contributed to the integration of Scots as bona fide Britons. Whilst the sterling services of the Highland battalions from Ticonderoga to Bushy Run ensured that such formations would become a fixture within the British Army, the general acceptance of both Highland and Lowland

104 See *Derby Mercury*, 11–18 January and 1–8 February 1760.

105 Cited in J. Black, *Britain as a Military Power, 1688–1815* (London, 1999), p. 277.

106 On Bute see Colley, *Britons*, p. 117; Langford, *Polite and Commercial People*, pp. 351–5.

107 *Boswell's London Journal*, pp. 71–2; see also the report of the same incident in *Felix Farley's Bristol Journal*, Saturday, 11 December 1762.

Scots by English and Irish soldiers in America remained at striking variance with the attitudes expressed by their civilian countrymen across the Atlantic. In this sense, the 'American Army' prefigured notions of 'Britishness' that would only reach fruition within society at large during the more protracted struggle against Revolutionary and Napoleonic France.[108]

[108] In *Britons*, Colley argues that the British nation was 'forged' during successive eighteenth-century wars with France – particularly the final conflict waged between 1793 and 1815. M. G. H. Pittock agrees on the importance of the latter era for the formation of British identity. See *Inventing and Resisting Britain. Cultural Identities in Britain and Ireland, 1685–1789* (London, 1997), p. 173. J. E. Cookson argues that it was not until these same campaigns that the Highland regiments acquired the wider reputation that transformed them into symbols of Scottish 'national valour'. See 'The Napoleonic Wars, Military Scotland and Tory Highlandism in the Early Nineteenth Century', *SHR*, LXXVIII, I (April 1999), 60–75; 63.

9
The legacies of the 'American Army'

In 1762, during the closing phase of the 'Great War for Empire', the prolific Lancashire caricaturist 'Tim Bobbin' produced a print that hinted at the human price of Britain's victories. Entitled 'The Pluralist and Old Soldier', the broadside contrasted the desperate plight of a gaunt, peg-legged veteran of 'Gardeloupe' with the wealth and ease of a plump and uncaring clergyman.[1] As a soldier's son who was 'born in the Army', Bobbin's crippled soldier had no home parish from which to seek poor relief, and was therefore reduced to 'the Beggar's list'. Such mutilated ex-servicemen must have proved a familiar sight in the years after the Peace of Paris. The presence of crippled veterans of Quebec, Martinique and countless less-celebrated encounters offered one conspicuous legacy of the British Army's recent campaigns in America; other wider ramifications were less obvious in the short term, but would none the less become apparent within the lifetimes of such survivors of the Seven Years War. This final chapter seeks to address these different 'legacies' of the 'American Army', and to consider the wider significance of that organisation. First, it examines the demobilisation process and traces the fate of those 'Old Soldiers' who provided the inspiration for social commentators like Tim Bobbin; it concludes by considering the implications of their wartime service for the British Army, nation and empire – not least, for Britain's North American colonies themselves.

Demobilisation and resettlement

Brother Soldier do you hear of the news,
There's Peace both by Land and Sea,
No more the old Blades must be us'd,
Some of Us disbanded must be.

So runs the opening verse of 'The Soldier's Complaint' – a ballad believed to date from the Seven Years War. Subsequent stanzas capture something

1 'Tim Bobbin' was the pseudonym of John Collier. For this print, see Figure 4.

Figure 4 A crippled veteran in tattered regimental coat and uncocked hat approaches a well-fed clergyman for alms in Tim Bobbin's 1762 broadside, *The Pluralist and Old Soldier*. © Copyright The British Museum.

of the ambivalence with which military men viewed the close of hostilities: whilst the private soldier of 'Rear, File and Rank' gives thanks for a long-awaited discharge, his comrades are split between those returning to civilian trades and others obliged to take 'to the Highway'.[2] On the return of peace in 1763, it was fear of the latter group that dominated the thoughts of men of property. Like other societies before and since, mid-Georgian Britain was haunted by a morbid dread of crime; at no time was

[2] R. Palmer, *The Sound of History. Songs and Social Comment* (Oxford, 1988), p. 297.

this paranoia more acute than in the wake of war. Modern historians suggest that such fears were justified; their researches reveal a close relationship between war and levels of criminal activity, with serious property offences declining during the duration of the conflict, only to rise again with the coming of peace.[3] The natural conclusion drawn from this correlation is that war temporarily removed the kind of young, labouring men who provided the bulk of the criminal orders, merely to return them to a civilian life where the inevitable post-war economic slump had narrowed the prospects of honest toil.[4]

At the victorious close of the Seven Years War, the customary dread of a demobilised soldiery was accompanied by something else – the first stirrings of sympathy for those men whose valour had conquered new territories around the globe, and who now faced the bleak prospect of disbandment and poverty. In particular, the Army's losses at Havana – and the unequal division of the prize money extorted from that city – had excited considerable indignation. As one journalist observed, for a commander to gain £70,000, while a subaltern received only £80, and a private soldier a mere £2.10 shillings was 'certainly a wide Disparity'. He asked: 'Is not this making one Man as valuable as near 30,000; and making the Lives of so many as equivalent only to one?'[5] The prevailing mood in support of the humble redcoat was reflected by a contributor to the popular *Gentleman's Magazine*, who observed that the veteran home from the wars to find his job taken by another man was obliged to 'sue for hard labour, or starve'. In the writer's opinion, it was scarcely to be wondered at that men who had risked life and limb for their country's good should now turn to crime; indeed, 'They who scaled rocks at *Quebec*, will treat *a man of business* with little ceremony if they meet him near Paddington in an evening.' It was the responsibility of the wealthy to do all in their power to preserve such deserving veterans from an ignominious death on the gallows.[6] A similar theme surfaced during the widespread attacks on the Bute ministry: one print, sardonically entitled 'Places of Honour', depicted a knot of crippled soldiers and sailors observing their former comrades heading for Tyburn in a long

[3] See J. M. Beattie, 'The Pattern of Crime in England 1660–1800' in *Past and Present*, LXII (1974), 47–95; 93–5; also *Crime and the Courts in England, 1660–1800* (Oxford, 1986), pp. 213–35; D. Hay, 'War, Dearth and Theft in the Eighteenth Century: The Record of the English Courts', in *Past and Present*, XCV (1982), 117–60; 125–6. See also McLynn, *Crime and Punishment in Eighteenth-Century England*, Chapter 17, 'The Impact of War' (pp. 320–40).

[4] John Styles believes that the low level of indictments during wartime may simply reflect a decline in prosecutions rather than a fall in crime. See 'Crime in 18th-Century England', in *History Today*, XXXVIII (March 1988), 36–42; 38–9.

[5] *Felix Farley's Bristol Journal*, Saturday, 12 February 1763.

[6] 'An Address to the Public in favour of disbanded Soldiers', in *Gentleman's Magazine, 1763* (March), pp. 119–20.

cavalcade of tumbrils carrying banners emblazoned with the names of recent conquests: a commentary lamented the dismal reward of 'Honour and Victory' and suggested that 'the Authors of an infamous P[eac]e' should change places with the veterans destined for the 'triple tree'.[7]

Appeals to save returning servicemen from a life of crime struck a chord with some patriotic landowners. In the spring of 1763, Charles Watson-Wentworth, Marquis of Rockingham, and Sir George Saville subscribed a donation of £5 to each man of the 51st Foot who had enlisted to serve for three years or the duration of the war, and was now entitled to his discharge. The battalion had been raised in Yorkshire's West Riding in 1755; the 'bounty' was given in recognition of the men's valour at Minden and elsewhere, which had been to their own honour and that of the county where they were recruited. More significantly, it was hoped that the cash would help these veterans readjust to the 'honest industry' of civilian life.[8] Sir Ludovick Grant, who had been instrumental in 'encouraging' his own tenants to enlist in the ranks of Montgomery's Highlanders, was among those Scottish landowners who subsequently invited 'reduced soldiers' to settle upon new estates on favourable terms.[9]

The peace of 1763 saw Britain's regular army axed from a theoretical establishment of about 120,000 to less than 45,000 men.[10] It is tempting to imagine that the spring of 1763 therefore witnessed the country's lanes and turnpikes clogged with some 75,000 sullen veterans, clad in their faded regimentals and with nothing but a fortnight's 'subsistence' money to carry them back to their former homes. This dramatic picture meshes neatly with the pattern of crime identified by historians, but requires modification on several counts. First, while there is no doubting the basic link between the onset of peace and rising crime levels, what is less clear is the extent to which this increased criminal activity was actually the work of such disbanded servicemen. Although newspapers in 1763 certainly report an upsurge of robberies, the perpetrators are usually identified only as generic 'footpads' or 'highwaymen' rather than former soldiers and seamen. It is also necessary to question the implication that

7 *The Butiad, or political register; being a supplement to the British antidote to Caledonian poison ...* (London, 1763), p. 70.

8 *Boddely's Bath Journal, 1763* (Monday, 30 May), p. 86.

9 *Felix Farley's Bristol Journal*, Saturday, 23 April 1763. Other former servicemen were invited by the Commissioners of the Forfeited Estates to relocate upon the confiscated lands of Jacobites. See J. Innes, 'The Domestic Face of the Military–Fiscal State. Government and Society in eighteenth-century Britain', in *An Imperial State at War. Britain from 1689 to 1815*, ed. L. Stone (London, 1994), pp. 96–127; 116.

10 As far as the infantry was concerned, all regiments 'junior' to the 70th Foot were to be disbanded. See Whitworth, *Field Marshal Lord Ligonier*, pp. 373–6; Fortescue, *History of the British Army*, III, 10–11.

soldiers were any more predisposed towards crime than the population in general: as has been seen, the redcoat battalions that fought in America reflected a genuine cross-section of the 'labouring' classes rather than a concentration of reprieved gaol-birds; hence the small minority of hardened criminals were viewed as 'notorious offenders' and ostracised by the majority of 'steady' soldiers.

In addition, the sheer scale of demobilisation can never have approached that feared by contemporary commentators and assumed by modern historians. Nothing emerges more clearly from a study of the 'American Army' than the ongoing battle to maintain manpower; it followed that the 'paper' strengths carried on the official establishment bore little relation to the actual number of men in service and destined for discharge at the peace. As this book has emphasised, many redcoat battalions that were already badly undermanned at the onset of 1762 subsequently suffered far more heavily during the Caribbean operations of that year. Some indication of the wastage involved can be gained from an examination of the 'Succession Book' of the 58th Foot. On Christmas Eve 1759, the battalion mustered 614 NCOs and men – requiring one drummer and 159 private soldiers to complete the establishment.[11] Of the 569 men identified as serving with the regiment at that time, more than one in five (124 men; 22 per cent) were dead before the battalion returned to Britain in 1763. Of these fatalities, just 12 (9.6 per cent) were killed in action or died of wounds. No less than 71 men (57 per cent) lost their lives at Havana in the summer and autumn of 1762, or while on passage from Cuba to Britain. These losses are all the more telling when it is appreciated that they fell among the 178 men of the regiment who evaded capture by French privateers while sailing from New York to Havana.[12] The 58th's casualties on Cuba therefore amounted to 40 per cent of the men landed, so mirroring the mortality rate within Albemarle's army as a whole.

Other units suffered even more heavily, soaking up successive drafts sent to replenish their ranks. On the return of the King's Own to England in August 1764, following a six-year stint in the West Indies, it was reckoned that the regiment had 'lost by war, sickness, & c. one lieutenant-colonel, one major, three captains, two adjutants, several lieutenants and ensigns, one surgeon, and upwards of twelve hundred private men'.[13] Again, when Webb's 48th Foot sailed to Ireland from Havana in the autumn of 1763 after eight years in America, it was reported with some dismay that the regiment now numbered just 36

11 WO/25/435, fol. 43.

12 See 'State of the 58th Foot when Captured by the French' (WO/1/5, fols 309–10). Another ten men died in August and September 1762 on St Domingue while prisoners-of-war.

13 *A Soldier's Journal*, p. 169.

rank and file.[14] Such examples could be multiplied; they clearly warn against the danger of exaggerating the number of men demobilised after the Treaty of Paris.

As far as the 'American Army' was concerned, it is also necessary to remember that the official end of strife between Britain and the Bourbons did not signal an automatic return of manpower to the mother country. While 'young' corps such as Montgomery's and Fraser's Highlanders were disbanded, older-established formations remained in being, albeit on the reduced peacetime establishment.[15] The majority of units that had been serving in the Americas in 1762 stayed where they were at the peace; as is notorious, it was the decision to retain fifteen battalions on the North American continent, and oblige the provinces to help pay for them, that paved the way for colonial revolt. Redcoats hoping to return home after long years of foreign service were distraught to discover orders posting them elsewhere; they included James Miller of the 15th Foot, who had arrived in America with his regiment in 1758 to join Amherst's siege of Louisbourg. Five years later, after witnessing the return of Havana to the Spaniards, Miller and his comrades had anticipated 'the happiness of being blessed once more, with a sight of all that is dear to man, his country, parents & ca'. However, before the transports had even cleared the Gulf of Florida a packet boat from England brought orders for a new distribution of the troops, and the 15th Foot was returned to Canada. Miller recalled:

> It is astonishing what effect this disappointment had on some of the men, several of whom, absolutely fell sick and Died! Others never held up their heads, untill we arrived at N. York, which was near three weeks after.[16]

Miller's battalion finally sailed for England in 1768, by which time a decade of American service had clearly taken its toll. When reviewed by Major-General John Clavering at Stroud on 3 October, many of the men were old and 'very low'; although they performed the exercise 'Tolerably well', the timing was sluggish, while their manoeuvres 'wanted both Steadiness and Precision'. Clavering, himself a veteran of Caribbean service, was prepared to make allowances. He concluded:

> Considering this Regiment's long Services in America, and having been Situated in a Country where only a small part of the year could be appropriated to the Discipline of the men, they made a better appearance than cou'd be Expected.[17]

14 *Felix Farley's Bristol Journal*, Saturday, 3 September 1763.
15 This consisted of nine companies totalling 500 of all ranks.
16 'Memoirs of an Invalid', pp. 75–6.
17 WO/27/12.

Casualties sustained in the West Indian campaigns of 1762 meant that those battalions of the 'American Army' which were spared disbandment at the peace struggled to field even the reduced establishment. The crisis posed by the outbreak of 'Pontiac's War' in the summer of 1763 therefore obliged Amherst to transfer all available manpower to formations most in need of such transfusions. Men who were not entitled to their discharge were simply drafted into other battalions. For example, the 46th Foot – a regiment devastated on Cuba – received a hefty draft of 155 men; these were drawn from the 44th Foot – which had escaped the Havana expedition – and the disbanding 4th Battalion of the Royal Americans.[18] Similarly, the 42nd Regiment, which had shrunk to a single battalion, received the fittest men of Montgomery's Highlanders.[19] When Amherst's own 15th Foot arrived at Quebec from Cuba in 1763, 'they were reduced to few in numbers, notwithstanding they had been filled up twice, since their leaving Quebec, in less than three years'; the battalion was only completed to the peacetime establishment by drafts from the disbanding Fraser's Highlanders.[20]

As far as those units which escaped disbandment at the peace were concerned, the only men to be returned to civilian life were the volunteers or pressed men who had completed their specified period of service, and those invalids – including the 'worn out', wounded and otherwise disabled – who were 'recommended' to Chelsea. The demobilisation process can be traced by examination of the 58th Foot, which began arriving back in England in January 1763. According to the regimental returns for April, the battalion consisted of 454 sergeants, drummers and 'effective' rank and file. During the following month a total of 117 men (26 per cent) were released; of these, 31 had been recommended to Chelsea Hospital.[21] This modest reduction by a unit which had escaped relatively lightly in the course of the American campaigns can have done little to swell the tidal wave of brutalised veterans feared by civilian pundits, particularly when it is remembered that around one quarter of those discharged were deemed sufficiently aged or disabled to qualify for a pension.

18 Return of drafts received by the 46th Foot, Niagara, 5 October 1763 (WO/34/22, fols 203–4).

19 Amherst to Bouquet, New York, 7 August 1763, in *Papers of Bouquet*, VI, 346.

20 'Memoirs of an Invalid', pp. 77–8. This explains why, when the regiment returned to England, Scots formed the largest ethnic group, representing exactly half of the battalion (Review of the 15th Foot, Stroud, 3 October 1768, in WO/27/12). In October 1756, Scots had accounted for just 13 per cent of the manpower. See Review, Shroton Camp (WO/27/4).

21 See WO/25/435, fols 50–51. The 'Succession Book' contains the personal details of 111 men discharged on 24–5 April 1763, mostly at Bideford in North Devon. According to this source, 43 men were recommended to Chelsea; of these, all save five appear on the Hospital's registers for the period from 19 May to 16 June 1763.

When considering the demobilisation of 1763, and the likely impact upon British society, it is likewise necessary to remember that many survivors of the 'American Army' opted to take their discharge in the colonies. Such redcoats naturally included the bulk of those men actually enlisted in America. Of those British-born redcoats discharged before the peace of 1763, most had little option but to remain in America: only those actually deemed to qualify for a Chelsea pension were guaranteed transportation back across the Atlantic. For example, when invalids of the 35th Foot were despatched from Albany to New York late in 1757, the unrecommended were 'sent about their business, and Were told, that none were to have a Passage to England but those Who were Recommended': according to Major Henry Fletcher, these men had opted to remain in America, 'as they think they have a better prospect of a Livelyhood'.[22] Other redcoats remained bewildered and helpless when cast adrift in the colonies: discharged from the Royal Americans in 1757, the aged and infirm Thomas Spence begged Loudoun to secure him a passage to England; Spence was 'in a Strange County, Destitute of friends' and unable to help himself.[23] By the close of the conflict, resettlement of veterans in the colonies was being actively encouraged. Ordering the 42nd Foot to be completed to the peacetime establishment, Amherst specified that 'genuine invalids' or those who had completed their service were to be discharged with passes to New York and recommended to Chelsea if so entitled. However, the General preferred that these veterans should take their discharges 'in this country as I think they may get their Livelihood by Working much easier here than at Home'.[24] Thomas Busby of the Inniskilling Regiment, who received 'seven Bullets through his Hat and seven thro' his Clothes' during the assault upon Ticonderoga, was among those men who stayed put after his unit left Quebec for Ireland in 1767; like several other Irish ex-soldiers, Busby established himself as an innkeeper.[25]

A major inducement for disbanding soldiers to remain in America was provided by a Royal Proclamation inviting them to apply for grants of land rent-free for a specified period of years; these ranged from 5,000 acres for field officers down to 50 acres for private soldiers.[26] This deal proved a tempting incentive to build a new life in the New World: on the disbandment of Fraser's Highlanders at Quebec in 1763, no less than 158 NCOs

22 Fletcher to Forbes, Philadelphia, 22 January, 1758 (GD 45/2/32/46).
23 See LO 2598.
24 Amherst to Bouquet, New York, 7 August 1763, in *Papers of Bouquet*, VI, 346.
25 Busby also served at Martinique and Havana. See A. J. H. Richardson, 'Busby, Thomas', in *DCB*, IV, 115–16; Lt-Col. I. MacCulloch, 'Men of the 27th Foot: Two Portraits (i) Thomas Busby, Grenadier, 1735–1798', in *BFTM*, XVI, 2 (1999), 119–27.
26 See *Scots Magazine, 1763* (October), p. 577.

and men chose to remain in North America, many settling along the banks of the St Lawrence River.[27] One old campaigner who took advantage of the Royal Proclamation to seek his fortune in America was John Curtin, who was discharged from the 48th Foot at Crown Point on 20 October 1763. According to his original hand-written discharge certificate, Curtin had served for twelve years 'faithfully & honestly as a good soldier'. At that time Curtin was already aged 68, and recommended to Chelsea on the grounds of being 'old unfirm & unfitt for Service'; instead, he accepted the offer of 200 acres of woodland near Lake Champlain. Curtin lived there with his family for several years and 'at Great Expense [did] Grub up Reclaim and Improve upwards of 100 acres of the said Land, Built a House, Barn and other offices thereon ... and planted Indian Corn, Wheat, Buck Wheat, Potatoes and other things'. When rebellion split New York province into rival factions, Curtin favoured King George: he paid the price for his loyalty in 1780 when he was dispossessed for refusing to swear the oath of allegiance to Congress. The old redcoat spent a miserable three years in jail before being released through the interest of General Clinton and Lord Rawdon. It was only in 1787, when Curtin was a venerable 92 years old, that he made a belated application for a Chelsea pension to keep him from want.[28] On that occasion Curtin was granted his pension by order of King George III himself.[29]

Pensions and poverty

Army pensions had originally taken the form of accommodation at Chelsea's Royal Hospital; completed in 1692, this establishment was funded by a 'poundage' of one shilling from every pound passing through the hands of the Paymaster-General, and an annual stoppage of one day's pay from every man in the Army.[30] For all its elegance, Sir Christopher Wren's structure was not calculated to cope with the human wreckage generated by King William's wars; indeed, the hospital was no sooner finished than all 472 of its beds were occupied;[31] as a result, it was only

[27] Harper, *Fraser Highlanders*, pp. 123–5.

[28] Board of 26 October 1787, in WO/121/2. Curtin's original discharge certificate, signed by Lt-Col. Ralph Burton, is accompanied in the file by petitions addressed to Sir George Howard, Bart, and Lord George Townshend, under whom Curtin had served at Quebec following the death of Wolfe.

[29] See Chelsea Board of 26 October 1787, in WO/116/9 (unfoliated). The 'worn out' Curtin was described as a former 'horse rider' from County Cork.

[30] Pensioners from the Irish establishment were accommodated at the Royal Hospital Kilmainham, Dublin; this foundation pre-dated Chelsea, being completed in 1684.

[31] See J. Childs, *The British Army of William III* (Manchester, 1987), pp. 153–4.

ever a small percentage of severely disabled or especially deserving veterans who secured the coveted status of 'in pensioners'.[32] Although obliged to perform guard duties, such invalids led a life of relative security that mirrored the order and comradeship of the Army: John Johnson of the 58th Foot wrote his memoir of the Quebec campaign while 'basking under the bright beams of His Most Gracious Majesty, in Chelsea Hospital', where he was 'plentifully provided with every comfortable necessary of life, by the Benevolence of his Country'.[33] This apparently cheery twilight was denied the vast majority of old soldiers; these so-called 'out-pensioners' remained at large in the community, collecting their pensions from designated centres at six-month intervals. Succeeding wars swelled their ranks: in 1757 there were 6,514 out-pensioners on the books of Chelsea Hospital; by 1764, the number had risen to 14,700.[34] At 5*d*. per day, the private soldier's pension fell far below the wage of even the casual agricultural worker. The limbless, ruptured or 'worn out' had little prospect of returning to the unskilled manual work of the 'labourer' or 'husbandman' and were reduced to begging to supplement their pension. It is significant that when a call went up for out-pensioners to form independent companies of invalids in 1755 it proved impossible to trace many of the men concerned. As Secretary-at-War Barrington observed, considerable numbers of out-pensioners were 'Itenerants without any Settled aboad'.[35]

The first Chelsea pensions were available to such soldiers as were 'disabled by wounds in fight or other accident, or who, having served the Crown twenty years, had been judged unfit for service'.[36] The same basic criteria applied during the Seven Years War, but as claimants reached unprecedented numbers applications became subject to increasing regularisation. Acceptance for pension was never a mere formality: just because a man was deemed 'intirely unfit for service' did not mean that he had qualified for the 'Royal Bounty of Chelsea Hospital'. For example, of thirteen unfit men of the 35th Foot discharged at Philadelphia in January 1758, only one was recommended: John Holmes, who had accumulated 35 years of service, was described as 'Old & worn out'. The remaining dozen were all either old, infirm, or both, but boasted insufficient service to qualify for the pension.[37] Even a 'recommendation' was insufficient

32 When Count Kielmansegge visited Chelsea Royal Hospital in 1762, the in-pensioners numbered 448 NCOs and privates. See *Diary of a Journey to England*, p. 276.

33 'Memoirs of John Johnson', in *Siege of Quebec*, V, 72–3.

34 *Journals of the House of Commons*, XXVII, 657; XXIX, 875.

35 Barrington to Lt-Col. Armstrong at Carlisle, 18 November 1755, in WO/4/51, p. 44.

36 Clifford Walton, *History of the British Standing Army, AD 1660 to 1700* (London, 1894), p. 602.

37 GD 45/2/35/6.

to guarantee a pension. When 41 recommended men of Fraser's were examined at Chelsea on 6 January 1764, nine were rejected outright, five 'referred' for further comment, and another seven considered fit enough to perform garrison duty: indeed, less than half of those recommended were actually 'approved' on the day of their examination.[38]

Recommended men were required to attend at Chelsea in person for examination; this onerous obligation even extended to those invalids of the 'American Army' who had been born in the colonies. At the beginning of the war, the Army had dabbled with schemes whereby soldiers discharged in America who were considered 'proper objects' for assistance could be placed on the Chelsea out-pension 'without their personal appearance at the Board'.[39] Such initiatives ultimately proved unworkable. The Chelsea registers consequently record a smattering of maimed Americans who journeyed to the mother country in quest of charity. For example, Joseph Hughs of Gage's Light Infantry had lost his right arm, a disability that precluded any thought of returning to his old trade of cobbler in Philadelphia. Hughs was lucky enough to gain accommodation within Chelsea Hospital itself.[40] Such favour was denied to most American applicants – men like 20-year-old John Thompson of the 44th Foot, who lost his right leg during the bloody assault on Ticonderoga.[41] This pathetic traffic in crippled colonial veterans is suggestive of the desperate plight of such invalids; it also lends weight to the contention that at the conclusion of the Seven Years War, the Anglo-American community remained bound by closer ties than the discord of the next decade would indicate.

Crippled veterans like Thompson highlight the realities behind Tim Bobbin's 1762 broadside. For other former soldiers the scars of service were less obvious but equally debilitating: Thomas Fitzgerald, who had soldiered in the 46th Foot for three years when he came before the Chelsea Board on 27 March 1759, had 'lost his senses in the Service', while Sergeant George Bidgood of the 28th Foot, who secured a pension in the following year, was both 'Wounded & Lunatic'.[42] Some of these sufferers, like Sergeant Edward Eades of the 43rd Foot, were admitted to the asylum at Bethlem Hospital; infamous as the final destination of Hogarth's fictional rake, 'Bedlam' was only just beginning to shed its unsavoury reputation as a popular freakshow for voyeuristic

38 See WO/116/5, fols 187–8.
39 Henry Fox to Commissary of Musters, James Pitcher, 12 June 1755 (WO/4/50, p. 357).
40 See WO/116/5, fol. 60.
41 At the Board of 3 April 1759, Thompson was simply described as 'Born in No. America' (ibid., fol. 31).
42 WO/116/5, fols 31; 54.

Londoners.[43] With these unfortunates there is no way of knowing the circumstances that triggered their illnesses. However, it was the unusual savagery of North American warfare that left one veteran of the 'American Army' suffering from what a later age would surely diagnose as 'post-traumatic stress disorder'. In 1762, John Knox of the 43rd Foot encountered the French priest Jean-Louis Le Loutre, who was being held as a prisoner-of-war in Jersey's Elizabeth Castle. The cleric's guards included a soldier who had suffered at his hands while himself a captive in Nova Scotia; Le Loutre had allegedly doomed this redcoat to the 'cruel fate' of being scalped alive. According to Knox, the priest had actually begun this operation, wielding a knife 'round the forehead and pole, in order to strip off the intire scalp' when the Englishman was spared. Recognising his old tormentor on Jersey, the soldier drew his bayonet with the intention of stabbing him to death. It was only with the greatest difficulty that this disturbed veteran was prevented from executing 'a just vengeance'. Indeed, Knox added, the soldier proved so persistent in his efforts to exact retribution that he eventually had to be exchanged into a regiment serving in England.[44]

Soldiers no longer fit for active service, but who were deemed capable of less arduous duties, were posted to the scattered companies of invalids that provided static garrisons for ports and other strong-points. For example, John Harrison, who was wounded at Quebec while serving in the 47th Foot, was ordered to perform the 'duty of garrison' at his home town of Hull.[45] Another veteran of the St Lawrence campaign, Charles Coyle of County Tyrone, had joined the 43rd Foot in 1755 at the age of sixteen. After seventeen years with that regiment he spent an equal period with the Earl of Eglington's Invalid Company at Edinburgh Castle. By 1789, three and a half decades of service had left Coyle lame in both legs and unfit even for garrison duty, and he was finally discharged and recommended to Chelsea. The same board that examined Coyle also dealt with 60-year-old Daniel Dormand, whose service had embraced nineteen years in the 43rd and sixteen in the Invalids at Edinburgh; it is tempting to imagine these two Irish veterans of the 'American Army' recalling their younger days

43 Eades, a 38-year-old 'white smith' with 20 years' service, was recorded as 'Mad in Bethlem'. He had been admitted to that establishment by the King's order on 5 February 1761 (WO/116/5., fol. 58). Bethlem (Bethlehem) Hospital, only closed its doors to paying 'visitors' in 1766. See R. Porter, *English Society in the Eighteenth Century* (London, 1982), p. 304.

44 *Knox's Journal*, I, 147 (note). Le Loutre likewise enjoyed some reputation for brutality among his own countrymen. The Jacobite exile James Johnstone, who served in Nova Scotia, described Le Loutre as a 'wicked monster' possessed of 'a murdering and slaughtering mind instead of an evangelical spirit'. See *The Campaign of Louisbourg: 1750–58: Literary & Historical Society of Quebec, Historical Documents* (Second Series, Quebec, 1868).

45 See WO/116/5, fol. 43 (Board of 18 March 1760).

at Quebec, Martinique and Havana as they contemplated the grimy tenements of 'Auld Reekie'.[46] When John Mackinnon was discharged in 1776 after 22 years in the Black Watch, the Chelsea Commissioners ordered him to Lord Elphinstone's Independent Company of Invalids at Fort George near Inverness. After twelve years with that unit, Mackinnon was once again recommended for a Chelsea pension. By now, as the fort's Lieutenant-Governor John Campbell certified, Mackinnon was 'intirely worn out' and too asthmatic to endure the trek from the Highlands to London.[47] The requirement for recommended men to 'pass the board' in person plainly caused great problems for the aged and infirm, particularly those based in the far-flung reaches of 'North Britain'. In the 1780s, the West Fencible Regiment mustered many Highland veterans of the Seven Years War. They included John McKenzie, who had been discharged from the regiment at Glasgow in April 1783, at the age of 72; on that occasion his discharge noted that he had served in Fraser's Highlanders throughout the Seven Years War. Besides an old wound to the head, he suffered from 'other infirmities peculiar to his age & [is] in every respect helpless with a large family to maintain or rather in a state of Beggary'. It was more than six years before McKenzie was able to appear at Chelsea. According to a note added to the discharge certificate on 30 May 1789, age and poverty had prevented McKenzie from applying for his pension; indeed, he could never have made the trip but for the 'charitable disposition of a Gentleman coming up from Scotland' who paid for his passage.[48] Philanthropy likewise assured the appearance of another Highland veteran at the same board. James Campbell, from Glen Orchy near Inveraray, was a sergeant in the colonel's company of the West Fencibles when discharged in 1783 at the age of 58. He had served in the Fencibles for nearly five years: his former career embraced four years as a private in the Royal Scots and another seven as a sergeant in Montgomery's Highlanders. Campbell had been discharged from the Fencibles because he was 'Consumptive & fairly worn out in the Service'. In his destitute situation, Campbell was unable to support a family which had recently undergone a substantial and unexpected increase, 'his wife having had three Children at one lying in'. Like McKenzie, the ailing Campbell had to wait six years before he could claim his pension; once again, it was only 'the Benevolent assistance of some Gentlemen, who know his distress' that had permitted the belated trip.[49]

46 Board of 13 March 1789 (WO/121/6).

47 Board of 13 June 1789, in ibid.

48 Ibid. McKenzie's original parchment discharge certificate from the 78th Foot, given at Quebec in September 1763, had recommended him for a Chelsea pension on the grounds of his head wound, and the loss of the use of his right side in consequence of sciatic pain. McKenzie was examined at Chelsea on 6 January 1764, but his application was dismissed. See WO/116/5, fol. 187.

49 Board of 13 June 1789 (WO/121/6).

Although the Fencibles were raised for home defence, service in their ranks was plainly no sinecure. Having returned unscathed after seven years of gruelling North American campaigning with Fraser's Highlanders, John Cameron was to prove less fortunate when he joined the West Fencibles in 1778. Five years later Cameron was discharged at Glasgow in a sorry state. Now aged 50, the unfortunate veteran had been among a party sent to seize a smuggling vessel at Port Glasgow. During the ensuing scrimmage 'he was wounded in the side and otherwise so much Beat & Bruised as to have occasioned a Severe Spitting of Blood and Violent Spasms in his Bowels which renders him totally unfit for service'. These injuries had prevented Cameron from attending the Chelsea Board before 1789; in consequence of his brutal treatment he was incapable of supporting himself or his family, who had been reduced to 'a helpless state of Beggary'.[50] The poignant fate of those soldiers who had once formed the 'American Army' provides a further reminder that such men deserve to be treated as individuals rather than as faceless and voiceless components in an oppressive military machine.

'A long past brilliant era in the British history'

Before the eighteenth century had run its course, the events of the 'Great War for Empire' were already garnering a romantic aura. In 1791, for example, an anonymous hack-writer ghosted an 'autobiography' of the veteran Highlander, Sergeant Donald Macleod.[51] The book's opening pages offered a colourful and clearly fictitious account of how the young Macleod, described as a native of Skye, cheerfully drubbed assorted braggarts and bullies – much in the fashion of the popular ballads of Robin Hood. However, Macleod's story becomes increasingly detailed and convincing when it deals with his exploits in the Seven Years War. In 1757, after the 42nd was sent to America, Macleod returned to Glasgow on recruiting duty and was drafted into Fraser's Highlanders as a drill sergeant. He fought with Fraser's at Louisbourg in 1758 and at Quebec the following year. According to his *Memoirs*, Macleod was then aged 70. It was after being wounded at Quebec that Macleod donated his plaid to carry Wolfe's body off the battlefield. The book adds that Macleod was sent home with Wolfe's corpse in the *Royal William* frigate in November 1759, being admitted as a Chelsea out-pensioner on 4 December. Recovering from his wounds, Macleod was

50 Board of 17 December 1789 (WO/121/7).

51 *Memoirs of the Life and Gallant Exploits of the Old Highlander, Serjeant Donald Macleod*... (London, 1791).

engaged in recruiting for Keith's and Campbell's Highlanders, and accompanied these units to Europe, where he was again wounded. At the outbreak of hostilities with the American colonists, Macleod once more tendered his services to the British Army, but was soon sent home. Concluding Macleod's story, his biographer made a surprisingly candid admission: 'With regard to his mental qualities, that which is most impaired is the faculty of memory, and of discriminating lively conceptions or ideas, from historical truths or realities.'[52]

Despite the ravages of time upon Macleod's confused old brain it would be wrong to dismiss his story as total fantasy. In the Chelsea pension register, under the date of 4 December 1759, are entered the names of twenty invalids of Fraser's Highlanders. Among them can indeed be found the name of Donald Macleod, described as a herdsman born on the Island of Skye. His age in 1759 was given as 60 rather than 70 – so putting him in his early 90s when the story of his life was published.[53] For all the fanciful interludes that pad his *Memoirs*, Macleod *had* served in North America as he claimed. Specific passages in the book can also be verified from independent evidence: for example, upon the formation of Fraser's and Montgomery's Regiments, Gaelic speakers from existing units were drafted into them as drill sergeants.[54] Even the dramatic peak of Macleod's service – the offering of the plaid to transport the stricken Wolfe – is not unlikely. Wolfe's redcoats had landed on 13 September without their blankets: their commander's corpse may indeed have been carried from the Plains of Abraham slung in a Highlander's plaid.[55] In addition, for all its flaws, Macleod's story illustrates phenomena about which there is less doubt: the extent to which Highland soldiers had ultimately transformed the image of their countrymen from dangerous rebels into popular heroes; and the growing popular fascination with the events of the Seven Years War.

Such interest even outlived the high drama of the titanic struggle against Revolutionary and Napoleonic France. One Black Watch officer who fought through these campaigns was David Stewart of Garth; despite his own experiences at Alexandria and elsewhere, he harked back nostalgically to the 1750s and 1760s as an era when the hallowed Highland code of behaviour remained sacrosanct, and the Highland

52 Ibid., p. 88.

53 WO/116/5, fol. 40.

54 On 25 January 1757, Barrington ordered ten battalions to contribute a total of 105 men 'who can speak the Highland Language' as NCOs for these two units (WO/4/53, p. 102).

55 See 'General Orders in Wolfe's Army', p. 52. It is interesting to note that Joseph Wilton's massive monument to Wolfe in Westminster Abbey, begun in the mid-1760s and finally erected in 1772, features a Highland sergeant watching over the dying General. See M. Whinney, *Sculpture in Britain, 1530 to 1830* (2nd edn, revised by J. Physick, London, 1988), pp. 265–6 (fig. 193).

regiments retained their true character, uncontaminated by Lowlanders, Irish, or worse still, Englishmen. When Stewart wrote his *Sketches* in the early 1820s, a handful of his regiment's veterans of the Seven Years War remained alive; they included John Peebles, who as a youthful volunteer had secured an ensign's commission for his bravery at Bushy Run, and John Grant, whose lively reminiscences have figured in this study. Indeed, Grant was still alive in 1826 when James Fenimore Cooper kindled interest in the picturesque events of the French and Indian War through his historical novel, *The Last of the Mohicans.*[56]

In the years after Waterloo, as the concept of a 'British Empire' gathered momentum, popular attention increasingly focused upon those men viewed as its founding fathers; such pioneers included the young conqueror of Quebec, James Wolfe. For Wolfe, the paths of glory had indeed led unerringly to the grave, yet the artistry of Benjamin West subsequently secured the General's resurrection to the pantheon of Britain's military heroes, while humble purveyors of street ballads preserved his name in folk-memory.[57] As Macleod's *Memoirs* indicate, some share of Wolfe's fame was reflected upon those old soldiers who had served alongside him on the Plains of Abraham. Such men included James Thompson, another venerable veteran of Fraser's Highlanders. Thompson was among those soldiers who chose to take their discharge in North America; according to an account of his career submitted on 31 July 1828 when he was in his 96th year, Thompson had subsequently served with the Engineers' Department at Quebec, helping to repulse the American attempt to capture the city at the outset of the Revolutionary War. In 1818, Thompson's link with Wolfe found him the blushing centre of attention when the Duke of Richmond visited Quebec.[58] In his twilight years, Thompson's growing celebrity gained him the friendship of no less a person than Quebec's governor, George Ramsay, Earl of Dalhousie. The Earl, who had pursued a varied military career from the West Indies to the Peninsula, revelled in the company of the old sergeant. Thompson proved a frequent guest at the 'Castle', where he gleefully

56 Stewart, *Sketches of the Highlanders*, I, 588, note. Peebles died in 1823, aged 84. See *John Peebles' American War. The Diary of a Scottish Grenadier, 1776–1782*, ed. I. R. Gruber (Stroud, 1998), p. 18. Grant refers to Cooper's novel when describing the scenery around Lake George ('Journal of John Grant', p. 67).

57 On the impact of West's *Death of General Wolfe* see S. Schama, *Dead Certainties (Unwarranted Speculations)*, (London, 1991); Colley, *Britons*, pp. 178–9. Wolfe ballads included 'The Death of General Wolfe', 'Brave Wolfe', and the 'Siege of Quebec'. The best-known song to feature the dramatic events of 1759, 'Bold General Wolfe', remained 'vastly popular ... throughout England' in the late nineteenth century, and was heard in Canada as recently as 1957. See Palmer, *The Sound of History*, pp. 274–5, and also his *A Ballad History of England* (London, 1979), p. 64.

58 GD 45/3/366, fol. 250; GD 45/3/422, fols 500–501. See also above, p. 285.

thrashed Lady Dalhousie at backgammon. As Dalhousie observed on 13 February 1822, after Thompson had dined with him accompanied by his three sons, 'his memory of Wolfes days here, as also that of the attack by Genl Montgomery in 1775, [is] perfectly clear and circumstantial mentioning Genl Townshend and many others by name as if the anecdotes had happened yesterday'.[59] Thompson's recollections soon reached a wider audience: on 10 May 1828, his account of the Louisbourg amphibious assault dominated the front page of a local newspaper *The Star and Commercial Advertiser* under the heading 'Anecdote of Wolfe's Army'.[60] That same year, as the lone survivor of the battle of Quebec, Thompson helped lay the foundation stone of a monument honouring Wolfe and Montcalm.[61] When it became apparent that Thompson had finally 'arrived at that stage of his existence which must soon terminate a long earthly career', one of his sons took the liberty of sending Dalhousie some memoirs that his father had dictated. The son adopted this course because of Dalhousie's 'lively interest' in 'an individual for whom his Lordship has on so many occasions shewn his friendship and conferred such substantial proofs of his favour'.[62]

Dalhousie's benevolence towards Wolfe's men had not always proved so unstinting. His Lordship's fondness for Thompson may have reflected Highland kinship; no such favouritism had been afforded to John Bell, an Irish veteran of the 58th Foot. Bell's case was brought to Dalhousie's attention by the Chief Engineer at Halifax, Lieutenant-Colonel James Arnold. At Arnold's instigation, Dalhousie had authorised that Bell should receive rations gratis. However, on learning that Bell was employed in the Engineer's Department at Halifax, and already received three shillings a day, Dalhousie changed his mind, observing that it was 'highly censurable in Lt Col Arnold to have obtained this from me without having stated that the person received so abundant remuneration from His Majestys Service'.[63] To his credit, Arnold stuck to his guns in defence of Bell, 'a poor old soldier, whose wants, and infirmities, the grave must shortly terminate!'.[64] Arnold had enclosed a sworn statement from Bell; the document remains a remarkable personal testimony of one redcoat's army career and subsequent fate. Bell declared:

59 Comment on letter from Thompson dated Quebec, 10 February 1822 (GD 45/3/366, fol. 248).

60 In GD 45/3/416, fol. 456. Dalhousie annotated the cutting: 'This is the style, phrase, & very words of old Thompson [who] has recounted to me many such stories, with astonishing recollection and accuracy of detail'.

61 See C. Rioux, 'Thompson, James', in *DCB*, VI, 768–70.

62 James Thompson Junior to Dalhousie, Quebec, 8 September 1828 (GD 45/3/422, fols 502–3). Thompson died on 25 August 1830, aged 97.

63 Single sheet containing two brief undated noted signed 'D' (Dalhousie), and another from Lt-Col. Arnold of 12 May 1820 (GD 45/3/345, fol. 86).

64 Arnold to Dalhousie, Halifax, 4 June 1820 (ibid, fols 87–8).

> That he was enlisted in the north of Ireland in the year 1757, in His Majestys 58th Regiment and served in it at the taking of Louisburg in the year 1758, from thence he came to Halifax, from Halifax he went to Quebec in the year 1759, and was in the above Regiment on the plains of abraham, as a private soldier under General Wolfe, when he was killed; – that he remained three years in the Canadas, and then marched overland to New York, & at that place he embarked for the Havannah, but was captured on the passage by a french man of War and was carried to France, and there remained a few weeks as a prisoner – that after his release, he joined the 58th Regiment again in Ireland, and remained there until the year 1768, when he volunteered into the 65th Regt and with that Corps he sailed for Boston – that after remaining there a few weeks, sailed for Halifax, and there remained as a private soldier for six years, and was then discharged, without any pension; – after that he served five years as a watchman in the Dock Yard, when he was discharged, that he went to Shelburne to cultivate land, and, by his industry, built a small House, after being about one year at that place, when, unfortunately, it took fire and was entirely consumed, with all that was in it, among which was his chest that contained all his cloths and discharge; that he came then to Halifax, and has ever since been employed in the Royal Engineer Department.[65]

Arnold respectfully requested Dalhousie's re-perusal of this affidavit, submitting that it contained 'a clear and undisguised statement of the services, and claims, of the veteran for whom I presumed to solicit the indulgence'. Indeed, it had not even occurred to Arnold to mention the pay received by Bell, as this was for his present services, and at the lowest rate given to a common labourer. Arnold had never imagined such meagre remuneration could affect any application for an allowance which he believed was indiscriminately granted to such survivors of 'a long past brilliant era in the British history'.[66] The outcome of the case is not recorded, but it is to be hoped that Dalhousie relented and allowed the old redcoat his rations.

65 Sworn statement of John Bell, Halifax, Nova Scotia, 10 May 1820 (GD 45/3/345, fol. 85). According to the 58th Foot's 'Succession Book', Bell was a weaver from Antrim and was amongst recruits of Lord Forbes's 61st Foot drafted into the 58th at Cork on 5 February 1758. Bell transferred from the 58th to the 65th on 30 September 1768. See WO/25/435, fols 67–8; 118–19.

66 Arnold to Dalhousie, Halifax, 4 June 1820, in GD 45/3/345, fols 87–8. Bell was not the only Seven Years War veteran of the 58th Foot alive at that time: Alexander Thompson had been admitted as a pensioner at Kilmainham on 21 July 1767 and died there on 2 October 1822. See WO/118/36, p. 101. Like Bell, Thompson was an Irish weaver and had entered the 58th as a draft from the 61st Foot (see WO/25/435, fols 85–6).

Unlike the eloquent Sergeant Thompson, Bell may have lacked the imagination or intelligence to grasp the significance of his own past; to an educated officer like Arnold, he none the less belonged to a distant and heroic age.

Army, empire and nation

Whether he realised it or not, old John Bell and his long-dead comrades of the 'American Army' were already part of a burgeoning legend of Britain's martial glory that they had themselves done much to found. Indeed, when Sir David Wilkie exhibited his acclaimed canvas *Chelsea Pensioners Reading the Gazette of the Battle of Waterloo* in 1822, the pivotal central figure portrayed just such another aged veteran of Quebec.[67] Commissioned by Wellington, Wilkie's painting commemorated the British Army's crowning victory over Napoleon: it has also been interpreted as a broader celebration of the 'Britishness' engendered by the long struggle with France that had culminated at Waterloo.[68] It could be added that the artist's decision to choose a survivor of the Plains of Abraham as the focal point of his painting was particularly significant: the Seven Years War – as epitomised by Wolfe's glorious victory at Quebec – had proved a crucial turning-point, not only for the British Army, but also for Britain's progress towards the status of global power.

By the opening decades of the nineteenth century the axis of Britain's empire had shifted decisively from west to east; indeed, 'The First British Empire' that reached its apogee in the wake of the Seven Years War was all too swiftly dismembered by the revolt of the Thirteen Colonies. Yet the spectacular territorial gains made during the war of 1756–63 had none the less injected a decisive impetus to the very concept of a 'British Empire'. Nowhere had these conquests proved more startling than in the American theatre that has formed the focus for this book. There is evidence that British soldiers who fought through the American campaigns of the Seven Years War were not unaware of the 'imperialist' overtones of that conflict. During the winter of 1758–59, in the brief lull between the fall of Louisbourg and the siege of Quebec, Lieutenant Thomas Webb of the 48th Foot gave the topic considerable thought; he justified his advocacy of a special Louisbourg medal on the grounds that the fortress's conquest had represented a significant 'Extension of Empire'. Webb, who would be

67 See H. A. D. Miles and D. Blayney Brown, *Sir David Wilkie of Scotland (1785–1841)* (Raleigh, N. Carolina, 1987), pp. 184–92. Wilkie's own catalogue note on the picture read: 'The Gazette is in the hands of an old pensioner, a survivor of the Seven Years' War, who was at the taking of Quebec with General Wolfe' (ibid., 189).

68 Colley, *Britons*, p. 365.

badly wounded during the coming St Lawrence campaign, was already looking ahead to the post-war problem of imperial defence. Anticipating the measure that was destined to instigate the rupture of the 'Empire' he was fighting to expand, Webb lobbied for a standing army in America itself. Indeed, he argued, Britain now had 'not only herself to defend, but also one of the finest and largest Countries in the World; whereof one single Province is almost equal to all England'.[69]

As this study has shown, the 'Great War for Empire' witnessed an unprecedented allocation of redcoats to North America and the West Indies: indeed, by the culminating Caribbean operations of 1762, at least 41 regular battalions were deployed in the Americas.[70] Whilst the coming of peace saw the customary reduction in the overall size of the Army, the establishment retained after 1763 was significantly larger than that which had survived the Peace of 1748. This swollen body of redcoats was also subject to a dramatically different pattern of distribution. Although the ratio of troops allotted to the British Isles remained relatively stable, a comparison of the Army's overseas commitments before and after the Seven Years War reveals a startling change in balance: nowhere was this more striking than in the Americas, where the pre-war garrison of five battalions had mushroomed to no less than 23 by 1764.[71] As a consequence of the victorious global conflict fought between 1755 and 1763 – not least the dramatic successes scored in the Americas – Britain's Army was set upon the imperial orientation that would continue to dominate its activities until the British Empire had ceased to exist.

It remains to consider the degree to which the 'American Army' responsible for lending such weight to Britain's growing imperial mission also acted as a conduit for concepts of 'Britishness'. This study has already argued that key underlying factors continued to ensure that the Army typically remained an unpopular institution far into the nineteenth century. It has likewise cautioned against overplaying the extent to which the services of Highland Scots during the 1750s and 1760s secured the speedy admittance of their countrymen into the British national fold. Yet while it would be unwise to suggest that the victories of the British Army at Quebec, Minden and elsewhere recast the redcoats as potent new symbols of British identity, it is none the less possible to argue that the Army itself provided an incubator for a shared Britishness that would mature more slowly outside its ranks.

69 Webb, *Military Treatise*, pp. 107; ibid., 3–6; *Knox's Journal*, III, 129.

70 The total excludes six companies sent to reinforce Jamaica, Gage's Light Infantry, independent companies and rangers.

71 See the diagrams in Houlding, *Fit For Service*, p. 412.

As has been shown, as early as 1757 the 'American Army' already fielded the substantial 'Celtic component' of Scots and Irish that has conventionally been taken to typify both the expanded British Army created after 1793 by the struggle against Revolutionary and Napoleonic France, and that which would continue to characterise the Victorian era.[72] Indeed, the 'American Army' absorbed the four component races of the British archipelago, added smaller but by no means negligible numbers of Americans and 'Germans', and ultimately welded these motley ingredients into a single and remarkably cohesive military machine. In response to local conditions, this force developed a distinctive group identity that transcended traditional national rivalries. The short-lived 'American Army' not only represented an highly innovative and flexible military force that gives the lie to enduring perceptions of a hidebound, ineffective and conservative organisation; it also served as an anvil upon which a precocious and all-embracing brand of 'Britishness' was roughly hammered into shape. Just as the 'American Army' offered a prototype for the reformed British forces destined to confront and defeat Napoleon's veterans from 1801, so it also proved the harbinger of the broad British identity that was finally tempered during the closing round of the long wars with France.

The 'American Army' and American independence

But what were the legacies of the 'American Army' for the continent that witnessed its brief but eventful career? Although this study has already cautioned against exaggerating the long-term consequences of tensions arising between regular soldiers and Americans during the Seven Years War, it is necessary to acknowledge other ways in which the redcoats' participation in that conflict influenced the destiny of British North America. First, by eradicating New France, the redcoats heralded an era in which colonial Americans could finally ponder a future free from the menace of their traditional foe. That same outcome prompted British politicians to contemplate overhauling the defence and administration of a burgeoning empire: their decision to maintain an expanded force of regulars in North America, and require the inhabitants of the Thirteen Colonies to contribute towards its cost, aroused vociferous opposition that crystallised thoughts of independence. Second, through the overwhelming nature of their conquests from Louisbourg to Havana, the redcoats virtually guaranteed that any revolt by Britain's American colonies

72 See J. E. Cookson, *The British Armed Nation 1793–1815* (Oxford, 1997), p. 126.

would attract the backing of a humiliated and vengeful France. So it transpired: between 1775 and 1783 the redcoats fought as doggedly as ever to maintain the integrity of the 'First British Empire'; from 1778, the unprecedented Franco-American alliance transformed colonial rebellion into a global war and thereby placed that objective beyond their powers.

Such sweeping theories of cause and effect clearly benefit from generous helpings of hindsight; yet it remains tempting to go further and identify other, more specific, legacies bequeathed to North America by the 'American Army'. As this chapter has demonstrated, alongside those Americans who served in the regular battalions during the Seven Years War, many British-born redcoats remained in the New World at the termination of their service. When war erupted between colonies and mother country, such men provided the trained kernel of loyalist provincial units sworn to uphold the *status quo*. For example, the Royal Highland Emigrants drew heavily upon those Highland veterans who had settled in Canada, Nova Scotia and New York after 1763.[73] Despite the undoubted importance of such former British soldiers to loyalist formations, it would be misleading to argue that those men who had once worn the red coat of King George automatically espoused his cause in 1775. Indeed, one of the Revolution's first heroes, the Anglo-Irishman Richard Montgomery, had previously served from Cape Breton to the Caribbean as an officer in the 17th Foot. With the rank of Brigadier-General in Congress's fledgling Continental army, Montgomery died amid a blast of grapeshot while leading the doomed assault upon Quebec on the last day of 1775. Quebec's defenders included veteran Highlanders like Malcolm Fraser and James Thompson, who had both fought alongside Montgomery at Louisbourg in 1758.[74] If the American War of Independence was also America's first *civil* war, it was not least because such former comrades were pitted against each other.

Handsome and dashing, the gallant Montgomery would be immortalised by the soldier-artist John Trumbull in the second and best of his famous Revolutionary War canvases. Trumbull completed *The Death of General Montgomery at the Battle of Quebec* in London with encouragement from his celebrated fellow countryman Benjamin West. Just as West's *Death of Wolfe* had provided Britons with a potent image of patriotic self-sacrifice, so Trumbull's 1786 masterpiece gave Americans

73 The extensive military experience of this unit's officers and men ensured that it ultimately gained regular status as the 84th Foot. See P. H. Smith, *Loyalists and Redcoats. A Study in British Revolutionary Policy* (Chapel Hill, North Carolina, 1964), pp. 67–9.

74 It was Fraser, now a captain in the Royal Highland Emigrants, who alerted Quebec's garrison to the impending assault. See Y. Desloges, 'Malcolm Fraser', in *DCB*, V, 330–31.

a military martyr of their very own.[75] As an exasperated James Thompson could testify, Montgomery swiftly attained cult status: following the failed Quebec attack, Thompson had supervised the burial of the General's body; he retained Montgomery's silver-mounted sword, and in his old age was pestered by 'a great number of American Ladies and Gentlemen' clamouring to see this hallowed relic.[76]

For all his significance as a revolutionary icon, Montgomery died before his military talents could be harnessed in the service of American liberty. Another former British officer of the 'American Army' was destined to strike a more telling blow for the cause of independence. Horatio Gates, whose victory at Saratoga in 1777 marked a turning-point in the Revolutionary War, first saw America in 1749 when he joined the garrison of Britain's new naval base at Halifax, Nova Scotia. After serving with the 45th Foot, Gates secured a captaincy in one of the New York Independent Companies; like his future superior and rival George Washington, Gates survived the massacre of Braddock's command on the Monongahela. Gates's administrative abilities did not go unrecognised: as one faithful reader of the *Gentleman's Magazine* noted in 1782, this prominent rebel general was the very same man who, as aide-de-camp to Robert Monckton, had been awarded the signal honour of delivering the despatches announcing the conquest of Martinique twenty years before.[77]

Stymied in their post-war military ambitions and out of step with those British politicians who sought to bridle the truculent inhabitants of New England, Montgomery and Gates had both returned to America in the early 1770s. They were soon joined by that outspoken admirer of the continent's natural beauties, the cantankerous Charles Lee. Following service with the 44th Foot at Ticonderoga and Niagara, Lee soldiered in Portugal and Moldavia: such extensive experience subsequently secured him a major-general's commission from Congress when war with Britain began. Lee proved an enthusiastic advocate for a guerrilla struggle waged by a citizen-militia.[78] The amateur soldiers that Lee championed fought stubbornly enough during the summer of 1775, administering a sharp

75 On the cult of Montgomery see C. Royster, *A Revolutionary People at War. The Continental Army and American Character, 1775–1783* (Chapel Hill, North Carolina, 1979), pp. 120–26; also J. D. Prown, 'John Trumbull as History Painter', in *John Trumbull. The Hand and Spirit of A Painter*, ed. H. A. Cooper (New Haven, 1982), pp. 22–92.

76 See 'Anecdote of Wolfe's Army – Captain Montgomery, afterwards General in the American Service', dictated by Thompson to his son James in August 1828 (GD 45/3/422, fol. 479).

77 *Gentleman's Magazine, 1782* (Dec.), p. 576.

78 On Lee's character and views see 'American Strategy: Charles Lee and the Radical Alternative', in J. Shy, *A People Numerous and Armed. Reflections on the Military Struggle for American Independence* (New York, 1976), pp. 133–62.

shock to British officers accustomed to the lack-lustre provincials of the previous conflict. Lieutenant-Colonel James Abercrombie was among those veterans of the 'American Army' who had initially doubted whether the militiamen beleaguering Boston would face British bayonets. On 17 June Abercrombie was granted an opportunity to put his theories to the test when he led the garrison's grenadier companies up the blood-slicked slopes of Breed's Hill. Three days later, as he lay dying of his wounds, Abercrombie conceded that 'the Rebells Behaved most Gallantly'; he warned his former general Jeffery Amherst – who had recently declined the King's invitation to return to America as commander-in-chief – that 'a few such Victories would Ruin the army'.[79]

Despite such unexpected successes against British regulars, the *rage militaire* that had drawn forth a 'virtuous militia' of solid and respectable citizens during the war's opening year dissipated beneath the determined royal riposte of 1776. As Congress now recognised, only a 'standing army' of professional soldiers could be relied upon to continue the fight. In remodelling the 'Continental army' for a prolonged war, its commander George Washington looked to neither the colonial militia nor the short-service provincials for his prototype: by contrast, the *regular* force that endured the privations of Valley Forge and ultimately savoured victory at Yorktown stemmed from a very different military tradition.

Over the past two decades, American scholars have confronted a powerful national mythology to suggest that far from comprising a selfless and patriotic host of stalwart yeoman freeholders, the Continental army was in fact recruited predominantly from among the 'have-nots' of colonial society; this reliance upon labourers, indentured servants, the unemployed and the unfree was only exacerbated after the introduction of drafting allowed the wealthy to avoid Continental service by paying fines and hiring substitutes; these rebel regulars, who included a hefty contingent of Irishmen, often enlisted in their teens and early twenties. Such men possessed an acute awareness of their 'rights' and would ultimately mutiny to preserve them.[80] The hard-bitten Continentals soon became notorious for excessive drinking and swearing – traits that the disapproval of civilians and a draconian discipline failed to curb. For their part, the Continental officers aspired to the status of 'gentlemen'

79 Abercrombie to Amherst, Boston, 7 May and 20 June 1775 (CKS U1350/080/1;3).

80 See C. P. Neimeyer, *America Goes to War. A Social History of the Continental Army* (New York, 1996); J. K. Martin and M. E. Lender, *A Respectable Army. The Military Origins of the Republic, 1763–1789* (Arlington Heights, Illinois, 1982); also R. K. Wright junior, '"Nor Is Their Standing Army to Be Despised": The Emergence of the Continental Army as a Military Institution', in *Arms and Independence*, pp. 50–74; and J. K. Martin, 'A "Most Undisciplined Profligate Crew": Protest and Defiance in the Continental Ranks, 1776–1783', in ibid., pp. 119–40.

and frequently duelled in defence of their honour.[81] In the teeth of their countrymen's indifference, suspicion and outright hostility, Continentals of all ranks drew strength and comfort from a growing professionalism and *esprit de corps*. The group portrait sketched here should strike a familiar chord with readers of this book: although it would perhaps be unwise to push the comparison too far – particularly as the social profile of the Continental army itself arouses continuing debate – it remains possible to suggest that in certain key respects the Continentals increasingly resembled the redcoats who had won the last American war, and who now faced them across the battlefield.

The revolutionaries' recourse to a professional 'mercenary' force based upon a European – and specifically British – pattern is even more noteworthy when it is appreciated that the very concept of a standing army remained ideological anathema to those promoting American independence after 1770. By providing the blueprint for the Continentals who did so much to preserve the Revolution after others had lost stomach for the fight, the redcoats gained a final, ironic victory of their own: here, as in other respects, the British army that failed to subdue America fell victim to the spectacular success of its victorious predecessor. Although unwilling witnesses at the birth of the American republic, the redcoats had none the less played their part in fathering the child: for the first 'American Army', therein lay the most remarkable legacy of all.

[81] Royster, *Revolutionary People at War*, pp. 75–80; 86–88.

Appendix: Statistical tables

Table 1. *Strength of British Army units in North America, summer 1757*

Unit	Officers	NCOs	Rank and File	Totals
2/1st	43	60	1064	1167
17th	35	48	700	783
22nd	46	60	1000	1106
27th	35	50	692	777
28th	34	50	696	780
35th	46	59	895	1000
40th	37	48	790	875
42nd	46	59	1000	1105
47th	45	60	991	1096
48th	44	60	786	890
55th	32	50	704	786
1/60th	22	28	379	429
2/60th	41	59	742	842
3/60th	46	59	801	906
4/60th	43	58	728	829
1st HB	45	60	1000	1105
NY Inds	16	20	260	296
Totals	**656**	**888**	**13 228**	**14 772**

Note: Returns are missing for the following units that were also present in North America in the summer of 1757: 43rd Foot, 44th Foot, 45th Foot, 46th Foot, the 2nd Highland Battalion (Fraser's Highlanders), three South Carolina Independent Companies, and the Royal Artillery. Some discrepancies exist between the totals provided in Table 1 and those appearing in Tables 2–6. This is because some units listed age, size and service for *all* ranks, whilst others supplied this information for NCOs and rank and file only. In other instances the records are incomplete in certain categories: for example, the returns of the 1st Highland Battalion fail to include any details of service. Despite these inconsistencies, the samples are large enough to provide reliable general patterns. Percentages have been rounded up or down to the nearest 0.5 per cent.

Sources: Tables 1–6 are based upon returns of the 'Service, Size [Height], Age and Country of Commission'd, Non Commission'd Officers and Private Soldiers' of the following units, made at Halifax (Nova Scotia), Charleston (South Carolina), or Fort Edward (New York), between 1 July and 18 September, 1757: 2/1st (LO 4011); 17th (LO 2533); 22nd (LO 2529); 27th (LO 4012); 28th (LO 1944); 35th (LO 6616); eight companies of the 40th (LO 1683); 42nd (LO 5661); 47th (LO 1391); 48th (LO 1384); 55th (LO 3936); five companies of the 1/60th (LO 6639); 2/60th (LO 1345); 3/60th (LO 6616); 4/60th (LO 4068); 1st Highland Battalion (Montgomery's Highlanders) (LO 6695); New York Independent Companies of Captains Gates, Wraxall, Cruikshanks and Ogilvie (LO 6616).

Table 2. *Age structure of British Army units in North America, summer 1757*

Age	Number in band	Percentage in band
18 and under	1417	10.0
20	3459	24.5
25	3718	26.5
30	2442	17.5
35	1582	11.5
40	781	5.5
45	396	3.0
50	139	1.0
55 and over	65	0.5
Total of sample	**13 999**	**100.0**

Table 3. *Height structure of British Army units in North America, summer 1757*

Height	Number	Percentage
5′ 6″ and under	5623	36.5
5′ 6.5″	1538	10.5
5′ 7.0″	1706	12.0
5′ 7.5″	1222	8.5
5′ 8″	1166	8.0
5′ 8.5″	739	5.0
5′ 9″	817	5.5
5′ 9.5″	560	4.0
5′ 10″	544	4.0
5′ 10.5″	286	2.0
5′ 11″	211	1.5
5′ 11.5″	112	1.0
6′ 0″	115	1.0
6′ 1″	42	0.5
6′ 1.5″	15	0.0
6′ 2″	22	0.0
Total of sample	**14 358**	**100.0**

Table 4. *Previous service of British soldiers in North America, summer 1757*

Years of service	Number	Percentage
1 or less	5402	41.0
2	2497	19.0
3	857	6.5
4	449	3.5
5	467	3.5
6	325	2.5
7	329	2.5
8	406	3.0
10	865	6.5
15	987	7.5
20	382	3.0
25	142	1.0
30	48	0.5
35 or more	22	0.0
Totals	**13 178**	**100.0**

Table 5. *Ethnic composition of rank and file and non-commissioned officers of British Army units in North America, summer 1757*

Unit	English	Scots	Irish	Foreigners enlisted in Europe	Natives of America	Foreigners enlisted in America	**Totals**
2/1st	121 (11%)	462 (41%)	444 (39.5%)	1 (0%)	68 (6%)	28 (2.5%)	**1124**
17th	375 (51%)	73 (10%)	290 (39%)	2 (0%)	–	–	**740**
22nd	431 (41%)	183 (17%)	439 (41.5%)	7 (0.5%)	–	–	**1060**
27th	371 (50%)	30 (4%)	340 (46%)	1 (0%)	–	–	**742**
28th	280 (38%)	46 (6%)	420 (56%)	–	–	–	**746**
35th	486 (51%)	84 (9%)	334 (35%)	4 (0.5%)	34 (3.5%)	12 (1%)	**954**
40th	432 (51.5%)	112 (13.5%)	136 (16%)	49 (6%)	74 (9%)	35 (4%)	**838**
42nd	–	1059 (100%)	–	–	–	–	**1059**
47th	432 (41%)	71 (7%)	293 (28%)	–	126 (12%)	129 (12%)	**1051**
48th	340 (40%)	83 (10%)	286 (34%)	–	102 (12%)	36 (4%)	**847**
55th	229 (30.5%)	421 (56%)	99 (13%)	5 (0.5%)	–	–	**754**
1/60th	88 (22%)	20 (5%)	100 (25%)	62 (15%)	44 (11%)	93 (23%)	**407**
2/60th	199 (25%)	52 (6.5%)	219 (27%)	126 (16%)	83 (10%)	122 (15%)	**801**
3/60th	212 (25%)	47 (5.5%)	207 (24%)	173 (20%)	72 (8%)	149 (17%)	**860**
4/60th	200 (25%)	49 (6%)	154 (19%)	177 (22%)	80 (10%)	143 (18%)	**803**
1st HB	–	1060 (100%)	–	–	–	–	**1060**
NY Inds	42 (15%)	15 (5%)	95 (34%)	–	72 (26%)	56 (20%)	**280**
Totals	**4238** (30%)	**3867** (27.5%)	**3856** (27.5%)	**607** (4.5%)	**755** (5.5%)	**803** (5.5%)	**14 126** (100.5%)

Table 6. *Ethnic composition of commissioned officers of British Army units in North America, summer 1757*

Unit	English	Scots	Irish	American	Foreign	**Total**
2/1st	3	18	19	2	1	**43**
17th	16	3	16	–	–	**35**
22nd	12	7	26	1	–	**46**
27th	7	1	27	–	–	**35**
28th	5	1	26	2	–	**34**
35th	8	6	29	3	–	**46**
40th	16	2	8	11	–	**37**
42nd	–	46	–	–	–	**46**
47th	26	6	9	4	–	**45**
48th	16	5	19	3	1	**44**
55th	16	6	10	–	–	**32**
1/60th	12	4	1	1	4	**22**
2/60th	10	15	3	6	7	**41**
3/60th	5	20	4	4	11	**44***
4/60th	4	17	3	3	16	**43**
1st HB	–	45	–	–	–	**45**
NY Inds	5	5	3	2	1	**16**
Totals	**161** (24.5%)	**207** (31.5%)	**203** (31%)	**42** (6.5%)	**41** (6.5%)	**654** (100%)

*Note: Although the total of officers in the 3/60th is listed as 46, ethnicity is only given for 44.

Table 7. *Age and service of British soldiers wounded in the Americas, 1755–59*

Sample	Sample size	Age range	Service range	Average age	Average service	Average enlistment age
(i) Monongahela 1755	44	21–50	1–23	34.0	10.3	23.7
(ii) Louisbourg 1758	14	24–37	3–18	27.8	5.8	22.0
(iii) Guadeloupe 1759	25	24–50	1.5–28	33.6	11.0	22.6
Combined averages	–	–	–	31.8	9.0	22.8

Sources: All samples are taken from Boards of Chelsea Royal Hospital in WO/116/5.
(i) 44th and 48th Foot: 22 March and 20 December 1756 (fols 4; 8). Also included is one man of the 44th examined on 21 January 1757 (fol. 8).
(ii) Boards held between 16 November 1758 and 20 July 1759 (fols 26–35). Applicants were from the following units: 2/1st, 17th, 22nd, 28th, 45th, 47th, 48th and 60th.
(iii) 4th and 63rd Foot: 7 September and 23 October 1759 (fols 35; 37).

Table 8. *Soldiers' occupations before joining the Army*

Sample Sample	Sample size	Labourers/ husbandmen	Weavers	Shoemakers/ cordwainers	Tailors	Others
(i) 58th Foot	558	196 (35%)	96 (17%)	38 (7%)	27 (5%)	201* (36%)
(ii) Chelsea	77	23 (30%)	14 (18%)	7 (9%)	5 (6.5%)	28** (36.5%)

Sources:

(i) 'Succession Book' of the 58th Foot (WO/25/435).

* Metalcrafts (needle-maker, cutler, button-maker, wire-drawer, founder, buckle-maker), 23; construction (tiler, mason, bricklayer/maker, stone-cutter, painter, slater, glazier, white-washer), 22; butcher, 12; extraction (tinner, collier, quarrier, miner), carpenter, barber, each 10; gardener and cooper, each 8; blacksmith and glover, each 7; flax-dresser and tanner, each 6; miller, 5; baker, basket-maker, potter, sawyer, wool-comber, dyer, pedlar/tinker, each 4; cabinet-maker, 3; sadler, hatter, breeches-maker, stay-maker, chandler, chair-maker, each 2; miscellaneous, 24.

(ii) Chelsea samples from WO/116/5 as given in Table 7 above.

** Carpenter, 3; button-maker, 2; clothier, 2; and one each of sailor, gunsmith, tanner, hatter, pin-maker, needlemaker, sawyer, dyer, baker, butcher, cutler, skinner, pedlar, bricklayer, brazier, gardener, nailer, stay-maker, waggoner, lead-miner and 'scribbler'.

Bibliography

Primary sources

1. Manuscripts

British Library, London

Add MSS 21,631–660: The Bouquet Papers, 1757–65.

Add MSS 21,661–892: The Haldimand Papers, 1756–90.

Add MSS 25,411: Grant Family Correspondence, Vol. VII, 1754–57.

Add MSS 45,662: Journal of Richard Humphrys, 28th Foot, 1757–62.

Map Library

King's Map K. 119.27.5. Tab. End (inset no. 2): 'Plan of the Battle and Situation of the British and French Armys on the Heights of Abraham the 28th of April 1760'.

Public Record Office, Kew

Admiralty

ADM 1: In-Letters.

Colonial Office

CO 5: America and West Indies.

CO 110: Guadeloupe.

CO 117: Havana.

CO 166: Martinique.

War Office

WO 1: In-Letters.

WO 4: Out-Letters, Secretary-at-War.

WO 12: Muster Books and Pay Lists.

WO 17: Returns.

WO 23: Registers of the Royal Hospital, Chelsea.

WO 25: General Registers.

WO 27: Inspection Returns.

WO 34: Amherst Papers.

WO 71: Courts Martial, Proceedings.

WO 116: Out-Pension Records, Royal Hospital, Chelsea (Admission Books).

WO 118: Royal Hospital, Kilmainham (Admission Books).

WO 119: Out-Pension Records, Royal Hospital, Kilmainham (Discharge Documents).

WO 120: Out-Pension Records, Royal Hospital, Chelsea (Regimental Registers).

WO 121: Out-Pension Records, Royal Hospital, Chelsea (Discharge Documents).

Gifts and Deposits

PRO 30/8: The Chatham Papers.

Maps

MP I/277: 'Fort Niagara, And Action in the Wood, 24th July, 1759'.

National Army Museum, Chelsea

NAM MSS 6707–11: Notebook of 'Lieutenant Hamilton', *c.* 1762.

NAM MSS 7808–93–1/2: Letters of Henry Browne, 22nd Foot, 1759.

NAM MSS 7905–48: Letters to Captain James Dalyell, 1761–62 (transcripts).

NAM MSS 8001–30: Diary of Captain Philip Townsend, 22nd Foot, 1756–58.

NAM MSS 9212–73: Order Book of Captain Henry Moore, 48th Foot, 1762–63.

Centre for Kentish Studies, Maidstone

U1350: Amherst Family Papers.

National Archives of Scotland, Edinburgh

Gifts and Deposits

GD 21: Cunningham of Thorntoun Muniments.

GD 24: Abercairny Muniments.

GD 45: Dalhousie Muniments.

GD 87: Mackay of Bighouse Muniments.

GD 125: Rose of Kilravock Muniments.

GD 248: Seafield Muniments.

Register House Series Microfilms

RH 4/22/2: Journal of Captain Thomas Stirling, 42nd Foot, 1765.

RH 4/77: Journal of Lieutenant John Grant, 42nd Foot, 1758–62.

RH 4/86/1–2: Papers of Brigadier-General John Forbes, 1755–59.

RH 4/98/2: Papers of Colonel Roger Townshend, 1757–59.

Huntington Library, San Marino, California

AB: Abercromby Papers.

LO: Loudoun Papers.

2. *Printed original sources*

An Account of the Expedition to the West Indies in 1759, by Major Richard Gardiner of the Marines (Birmingham, 1762).

An Account of the Remarkable Occurences in the Life and Travels of Col. James Smith During his Captivity with the Indians, in the Years 1755, '56, '57, '58 and '59 . . . Written by Himself (Lexington, Kentucky, 1799).

An Accurate and Authentic Journal of the Siege of Quebec, 1759, by a Gentleman in an Eminent Station on the Spot (London, 1759).

An Act for the Better Recruiting of His Majesty's Forces on the Continent of North America; and for the better Regulation of the Army, and preventing of Desertion therein (Boston, 1756).

Adventure in the Wilderness: The American Journals of Louis Antoine De Bougainville, 1756–60, ed. E. P. Hamilton (Norman, Oklahoma, 1964).

The Albemarle Papers: Being the Correspondence of William Anne, Second Earl of Albemarle, Commander-in-Chief in Scotland, 1746–1747, ed. C. Sanford Terry (2 vols, Aberdeen, 1902).

The American Rebellion. Sir Henry Clinton's Narrative of His Campaigns, 1775–1782, with an Appendix of Original Documents, ed. W. B. Willcox (New Haven, 1954).

The Army List

Colonel Samuel Bagshawe and the Army of George II, 1731–1762, ed. A. J. Guy (London, 1990).

'Thomas Barton and the Forbes Expedition', ed. W. A. Hunter, *Pennsylvania Magazine of History and Biography*, XCV (October, 1971), 431–83.

Boswell's London Journal, 1762–63, ed. F. A. Pottle (London, 1950).

Braddock's Defeat, ed. C. Hamilton (Norman, Oklahoma, 1959).

The Butiad, or political register; being a supplement to the British antidote to Caledonian poison … (London, 1763).

The Campaign of Louisbourg: 1750–58: Literary & Historical Society of Quebec, Historical Documents (Second Series, Quebec, 1868).

The Campaign of 1760 in Canada. A Narrative attributed to Chevalier Johnstone: Literary & Historical Society of Quebec, Historical Documents (Second Series, Quebec, 1887).

'The Capture of Quebec. A Manuscript Journal Relating to the Operations Before Quebec From 8th May, 1759, to 17th May, 1760. Kept by Colonel Malcolm Fraser. Then Lieutenant in the 78th Foot (Fraser's Highlanders)', ed. Brig. R. Alexander, *Journal of the Society for Army Historical Research*, XVIII (1939), 135–68.

The Case of the Infantry in Ireland … (Dublin, 1753).

Collection Des Manuscripts du Maréchal de Lévis: Volume I, Journal des Campagnes du Chevalier de Lévis en Canada De 1756 à 1760, ed. H. R. Casgrain (Montreal, 1889).

The Conquest of Louisbourg: A Poem by John Maylem, Philo-Bellum (Boston, 1758).

The Correspondence of the Earl of Chatham (4 vols, London, 1838).

Correspondence of Thomas Gray, eds P. Toynbee and L. Whibley (3 vols, Oxford, 1935).

The Correspondence of William Pitt, when Secretary of State, with Colonial Governors and Military and Naval Commissioners in America, ed. G. S. Kimball (2 vols, London, 1906; repr. New York, 1969).

The Deserted Village: The Diary of an Oxfordshire Rector James Newton of Nuneham Courtenay 1736–86, ed. G. Hannah (Stroud, 1992).

The Diary of a Journey to England in the Years 1761–1762, By Count Frederick Kielmansegge, trans. Countess Kielmansegge (London, 1902).

'The Diary of Rev. John Ogilvie 1750–1759', ed. M. W. Hamilton, in *Bulletin of the Fort Ticonderoga Museum*, X, 5 (Feb. 1961), 331–85.

The Diary of Thomas Turner, 1754–1765, ed. D. Vaisey (Oxford, 1984).

Documents of the American Revolution 1770–83, Colonial Office Series, ed. K. G. Davies (21 vols, Shannon, Ireland, 1972–81).

Documents Relative to the Colonial History of the State of New York, ed. E. B. O'Callaghan and B. Fernow (15 vols, Albany, 1853–87).

'George Durant's Journal of the Expedition to Martinique and Guadeloupe, October 1758 – May 1759', ed. A. J. Guy, in *Army Records Society: Military Miscellany I* (Stroud, 1997), pp. 1–68.

The East India Kalendar or Asiatic Register . . . For the Year 1794 (London, 1794).

The Expedition of Major General Braddock to Virginia . . . (London, 1755).

French and Indian Cruelty; Exemplified in the Life and Various Vicissitudes of Fortune, of Peter Williamson, A Disbanded Soldier . . . (1st edn York, 1757; 5th edn Edinburgh, 1762).

Robert Forbes, *The Lyon in Mourning*, ed. H. Paton (3 vols, Edinburgh, 1896).

General Orders in Wolfe's Army during the Expedition up the River St. Lawrence, 1759: Literary & Historical Society of Quebec, Historical Documents (Fourth Series, Quebec, 1875).

General Orders of 1757, issued by the Earl of Loudoun and Phineas Lyman in the Campaign Against the French, ed. Worthington. C. Ford (New York, 1899; repr. 1970).

'Thomas Gist's Indian Captivity', ed. H. H. Peckham, *Pennsylvania Magazine of History and Biography*, LXXX (1956), 285–311.

J. Hanway, *An Account of the Society for the Encouragement of British Troops in Germany and North America* (London, 1760).

An Historical Journal of the Campaigns in North America for the Years 1757, 1758, 1759, and 1760, by Captain John Knox, ed. A. G. Doughty (3 vols, Toronto, 1914).

The History of an Expedition Against Fort DuQuesne in 1755; Under Major-General Edward Braddock . . ., ed. W. Sargent (Philadelphia, 1855).

The History of the Life and Sufferings of Henry Grace, of Basingstoke in the County of Southampton. Being a Narrative of the Hardships He Underwent During Several Years Captivity Among the Savages in North America . . . Written by Himself (Reading, 1764).

'Journal of an Expedition to South Carolina, by Captain Christopher French', in *Journal of Cherokee Studies* (1977), 275–301.

The Journal of Jeffery Amherst. Recording the Military Career of General Amherst in America from 1758 to 1763, ed. J. C. Webster (Toronto, 1931).

'The Journal of Reverend John Cleaveland, June 14, 1758 – October 25, 1758', *Bulletin of the Fort Ticonderoga Museum*, X, 3 (1959), 192–233.

Journal of a Voyage to North America ... by Pierre Francois Xavier de Charlevoix (2 vols, London, 1761).

Journals of the Hon. William Hervey, in North America and Europe, from 1755 to 1814; with Order Books at Montreal, 1760–1763 (Bury St Edmunds, 1906).

Journals of the House of Commons.

The Journals of Major Robert Rogers, containing an account of the several excursions he made under the Generals who commanded upon the continent of North America during the late war (London, 1765).

'A Letter Describing the Death of General Wolfe', in *English Historical Review*, XII (1897), 762–3.

'The Letters of Captain Nicholas Delacherois, 9th Regiment', ed. S. G. P. Ward, *Journal of the Society for Army Historical Research*, LI (1973), 5–14.

'The Letters of Colonel Alexander Murray, 1742–59', in *1926 Regimental Annual. The Sherwood Foresters, Nottinghamshire and Derbyshire Regiment*, ed. Col. H. C. Wylly (London, 1927), pp. 181–220.

The Life, Adventures, And Surprising Deliverances of Duncan Cameron, Private soldier in the Regiment of Foot, late Sir Peter Halket's (3rd edn, Philadelphia, 1756).

' "Like Roaring Lions Breaking From Their Chains": The Highland Regiment at Ticonderoga', documents compiled and edited by N. Westbrook, *Bulletin of the Fort Ticonderoga Museum*, XVI, 2 (1999), 16–91.

'Lt. Gordon's Journal of the Siege of Louisburg', *Journal of the Royal United Service Institution* LX (1915), 117–52.

The Memoirs and Adventures of Robert Kirk, Late of the Royal Highland Regiment, Written by Himself ... (Limerick, 1770).

Memoirs of an American Lady ... By Mrs Anne Grant (London, 1808; repr. New York, 1901).

The Memoirs of Lieutenant Henry Timberlake ... (London, 1765).

Memoirs of the Life and Gallant Exploits of the Old Highlander, Sergeant Donald Macleod ... (London, 1791).

Military Affairs in North America, 1748–65: Selected Documents from the Cumberland Papers in Windsor Castle, ed. S. Pargellis (New York, 1936).

The Military History of Great Britain, for 1756, 1757, Containing a Letter from a British Officer at Canada, Taken Prisoner at Oswego. Exhibiting the Cruelty and Infidelity of the French, and their Savage Indians ... Also, a Journal (London, 1757).

The Military Journals of Two Private Soldiers, 1758–1775, ed. A. Tomlinson (Poughkeepsie, New York, 1855; repr. New York, 1971).

Military Sketches. By Edward Drewe, late Major of the 35th Regt of Foot (Exeter, 1784).

'Montcalm's Correspondence', in *Report of the Public Archives [of Canada] For the Year 1929* (Ottawa, 1930), pp. 31–108.

'The Monypenny Orderly Book', *Bulletin of the Fort Ticonderoga Museum*, II, 6 (July 1932), 219–51; XII, 5 (December 1969), 328–57; XII, 6 (October 1970), 434–61; XIII, 1 (December 1970), 89–116; XIII, 2 (June 1971), 151–84.

Governor Murray's Journal of the Siege of Quebec, from 18 September, 1759 to 25 May, 1760, ed. E. C. Kyte (Toronto, 1939).

Narratives of Colonial America, 1704–1765, ed. H. H. Peckham (Chicago, 1971).

The Northcliffe Collection (Ottawa, 1926).

The Papers of Henry Bouquet, eds S. K. Stevens, D. H. Kent, A. L. Leonard and L. M. Waddell (6 vols, Harrisburg, 1951–94).

The Papers of Sir William Johnson, eds J. Sullivan and A. C. Flick (14 vols, Albany, 1921–65).

John Peebles' American War. The Diary of a Scottish Grenadier, 1776–1782, ed. I. R. Gruber (Stroud, 1998).

A Plain Narrative of the Uncommon Sufferings, and Remarkable Deliverance of Thomas Brown ... (Boston, 1760).

Poems on several Occasions, by William Vernon, A Private Soldier in the Buffs (London, 1758).

Pierre Pouchot, *Memoirs on the Late War in North America Between France and England*, trans. M. Cardy, ed. B. L. Dunnigan (Youngstown, New York, 1994).

Proceedings and Debates of the British Parliaments Respecting North America, 1754–1783, eds R. C. Simmons and P. D. G. Thomas (6 vols, New York, 1982–87).

Proceedings of a General Court Martial ... For the Trial of a Charge Preferred By Colin Campbell, Esq Against the Honourable Major General Monckton (London, 1764).

Report Concerning Canadian Archives for the Year 1905 (Ottawa, 1905).

The Siege and Capture of Havana 1762, ed. D. Syrett (London, 1970).

The Siege of Detroit in 1763, comprising the Journal of Pontiac's Conspiracy and John Rutherfurd's Narrative of a Captivity, ed. M. Quaiffe (Chicago, 1958).

The Siege of Quebec and the Battle of the Plains of Abraham, eds A. G. Doughty and G. W. Parmelee (6 vols, Quebec, 1901).

A Soldier's Journal (London, 1770).

Philip Henry, 5th Earl Stanhope, *Notes of Conversations with the Duke of Wellington, 1831–1851* (4th edn, London, 1889).

Horace Walpole, *Memoirs of King George II*, ed. J. Brooke (3 vols, New Haven and London, 1985).

B. Willson, *The Life and Letters of James Wolfe* (New York, 1909).

B. Willson, 'Fresh Light on the Quebec Campaign – From the Missing Journal of General Wolfe', *The Nineteenth Century and After*, CCCXVII (March 1910), 445–60.

Writings of General John Forbes, Relating to His Service in North America, ed. A. P. James (Menasha, Wisconsin, 1938).

The Writings of George Washington, ed. J. C. Fitzpatrick (39 vols, Washington, 1931–44).

'Some Unpublished Wolfe Letters, 1755–58', ed. R. Whitworth, *Journal of the Society for Army Historical Research*, LIII (1975), 65–86.

Historical Manuscripts Commission, Reports

Marquess of Townshend Manuscripts (London, 1887).
Mrs Frankland-Russell-Astley Manuscripts (London, 1900).
Stopford-Sackville Manuscripts (2 vols, London, 1910).
Reports of Manuscripts in Various Collections, VIII (London, 1913).
Bathurst Manuscripts (London, 1923).

New-York Historical Society, Collections

1871: The Lee Papers, Volume One (New York, 1872).

1881: The Montresor Journals (New York, 1882).

1921: The Letters and Papers of Cadwallader Colden, Volume Five, 1755–1760 (New York, 1922).

1927: Papers of the Lloyd Family of the Manor of Queen's Village, Lloyd's Neck, Long Island, New York 1654–1826, Volume Two, 1752–1826 (New York, 1927).

1928: *The Letter Book of John Watts, Merchant and Councillor of New York, January 1, 1762 – December 22, 1765* (New York, 1928).

Military manuals

Humphrey Bland, *A Treatise of Military Discipline* ... (5th edn, Dublin, 1743).

Bennett Cuthbertson, *A System for the Compleat Interior Management and Oeconomy of a Battalion of Infantry* ... (originally published Dublin, 1768; new edn with corrections, Bristol, 1776).

Campbell Dalrymple, *A Military Essay. Containing Reflections on the Raising, Arming, Cloathing, and Discipline of the British Infantry and Cavalry; with Proposals for the Improvement of the Same* (London, 1761).

Col. David Dundas, *Principles of Military Movement, Chiefly Applied to Infantry. Illustrated by Manoeuvres of the Prussian Troops, and by An Outline of the British Campaigns in Germany, During the War of 1757* ... (London, 1788).

Robert Hamilton, *The Duties of a Regimental Surgeon Considered* ... (2 vols, London, 1787).

Thomas More Molyneux, *Conjunct Expeditions: Or Expeditions that have been carried on jointly By the Fleet and Army, with a Commentary on a Littoral War* (London, 1759).

Thomas Webb, *A Military Treatise on the Appointments of the Army* ... (Philadelphia, 1759).

Sermons

Nathaniel Appleton, *A Sermon Preached [upon] the Surrender of Montreal, and All Canada* (Boston, 1760).

Samuel Cooper, *Sermon Occasioned by the Reduction of Quebec* (Boston, 1759).

Andrew Eliot, *Sermon Preached ... For the success of the British Arms this Year* (Boston, 1759).

Thomas Foxcroft, *A Sermon Preached ... On the Occasion of the Surrender of Montreal, and the Complete Conquest of Canada* ... (Boston, 1760).

Jonathan Mayhew, *Two Discourses Delivered October 25th, 1759 ... For the Success of His Majesty's Arms* (Boston, 1759).

Newspapers and periodicals

The American Magazine and Monthly Chronicle for the British Colonies.
The Annual Register; or a view of the history, politicks, and literature of the year...
Boddely's Bath Journal.
The Derby Mercury.

Felix Farley's Bristol Journal.
The Gentleman's Magazine and Historical Chronicle ...
The London Gazette.
The London Magazine, or Gentleman's Monthly Intelligencer ...
The Pennsylvania Gazette.
The Scots Magazine.

Secondary sources

1. Books

J. Adair, *The History of the American Indians* (1775).

Adapting to Conditions: War and Society in the Eighteenth Century, ed. M. Ultee (Tuscaloosa, Alabama, 1986).

J. R. Alden, *General Gage in America* (Baton Rouge, 1947).

F. Anderson, *A People's Army: Massachusetts Soldiers and Society in the Seven Years War* (Chapel Hill, North Carolina, 1984).

F. Anderson *Crucible of War. The Seven Years War and the Fate of Empire in British North America, 1754–1766* (New York, 2000).

Arms and Independence. The Military Character of the American Revolution, eds R. Hoffman and P. J. Albert (Charlottesville, Virginia, 1984).

The Arsenal of the World. The Dutch Arms Trade in the Seventeenth Century, ed. J. P. Puype and M. van der Hoeven (Amsterdam, 1996).

R. Atwood, *The Hessians: Mercenaries from Hessen-Kassel in the American Revolution* (Cambridge, 1980).

J. Axtell, *The European and the Indian; Essays in the Ethnohistory of Colonial North America* (paper edn, New York, 1982).

C. Barnett, *Britain and Her Army, 1509–1970: A Military, Political and Social History* (London, 1970).

J. M. Beattie, *Crime and the Courts in England, 1660–1800* (Oxford, 1986).

J. Black, *European Warfare 1660–1815* (London, 1994).

J. Black, *Britain as a Military Power, 1688–1815* (London, 1999).

H. L. Blackmore, *British Military Firearms, 1650–1850* (London, 1961).

R. A. Bowler, *Logistics and the Failure of the British Army in America 1775–1783* (Princeton, 1975).

Britain and America: Studies in Comparative History, 1760–1970, ed. D. Englander (London, 1997).

The British Atlantic Empire Before the American Revolution, eds P. Marshall and G. Williams (London, 1980).

The British Navy and the Use of Naval Power in the Eighteenth Century, eds J. Black and P. Woodfine (Leicester, 1988).

British Politics and Society from Walpole to Pitt, 1742–1789, ed. J. Black (London, 1990).

A. Bruce, *The Purchase System in the British Army, 1660–1871* (London, 1980).

J. M. Bulloch, *Territorial Soldiering in the North-East of Scotland During 1759–1814* (Aberdeen, 1914).

L. Butler, *Annals of the King's Royal Rifle Corps: Volume One, The Royal Americans* (London, 1913).

C. G. Calloway, *The Western Abenakis of Vermont, 1600–1800. War, Migration, and the Survival of an Indian People* (Norman, Oklahoma, 1990).

N. Cantlie, *A History of the Army Medical Department* (2 vols, Edinburgh, 1974).

R. Chartrand, *The French Soldier in Colonial America* (Ottawa, 1984).

J. Childs, *Armies and Warfare in Europe, 1648–1789* (Manchester, 1982).

J. Childs, *The British Army of William III* (Manchester, 1987).

J. C. D. Clark, *English Society 1688–1832: Ideology, Social Structure and Political Practice During the Ancien Regime* (Cambridge, 1985).

Cadwallader Colden, *The History of the Five Indian Nations of Canada which are Dependent on the Province of New York ...* (3rd edn, 2 vols, London, 1755).

L. Colley, *Britons: Forging the Nation, 1707–1837* (London, 1992).

The Complete Barrack-Room Ballads of Rudyard Kipling, ed. C. Carrington (London, 1973).

S. Conway, *The British Isles and the War of American Independence* (Oxford, 2000).

J. E. Cookson, *The British Armed Nation 1793–1815* (Oxford, 1997).

James Fenimore Cooper, *The Last of the Mohicans* (first published 1826; Penguin Popular Classics edn, London, 1994).

D. H. Corkran, *The Cherokee Frontier: Conflict and Survival, 1740–62* (Norman, Oklahoma, 1962).

A. Corvisier, *L'Armée française de la fin du XVIIe siècle au ministère de Choiseul* (2 vols, Paris, 1964).

M. Craton, *Testing the Chains. Resistance to Slavery in the British West Indies* (London, 1982).

J. Cuneo, *Robert Rogers of the Rangers* (New York, 1959).

R. C. Dallas, *The History of the Maroons* (2 vols, London, 1803; repr. London, 1968).

K. Z. Derounian-Stodola and J. A. Levernier, *The Indian Captivity Narrative, 1550–1900* (New York, 1993).

Dictionary of Canadian Biography, ed. F. G. Halpenny (13 vols, Toronto, 1966–94).

Dictionary of National Biography, eds L. Stephen and S. Lee (63 vols, London, 1885–1900).

C. Duffy, *The Military Experience in the Age of Reason* (London, 1987).

B. L. Dunnigan, *Siege, 1759: The Campaign Against Niagara* (Youngstown, New York, 1986).

R. Durgnot and S. Simmon, *King Vidor, American* (Berkeley, California, 1988).

W. J. Eccles, *Essays on New France* (Toronto, 1987).

C. Eimer, *The Pingo Family and Medal Making in 18th-Century Britain* (London, 1998).

Empire and others: British encounters with indigenous peoples, 1600–1850, eds M. Daunton and R. Halpern (London, 1999).

John Entick, *The General History of the Late War, Containing its Rise, Progress and Events, in Europe, Asia, Africa and America* (5 vols, London, 1763–64).

Essays in Colonial American History, presented to Charles McClean Andrews by his students (Yale, New Haven, 1931).

J. E. Ferling, *A Wilderness of Miseries: War and Warriors in Early America* (Westport, Connecticut, 1980).

J. Fortescue, *A History of the British Army* (13 vols, London, 1899–1930).

G. Fregault, *Canada: The War of the Conquest*, trans. Margaret M. Cameron (Toronto, 1969).

S. R. Frey, *The British Soldier in America: A Social History of Military Life in the Revolutionary Period* (Austin, Texas, 1981).

J. F. C. Fuller, *British Light Infantry in the Eighteenth Century* (London, 1925).

D. Gates, *The British Light Infantry Arm, c. 1790–1815: Its Creation, Training and Operational Role* (London, 1987).

L. H. Gipson, *The British Empire Before the American Revolution* (15 vols, New York, 1936–70).

W. G. Godfrey, *Pursuit of Profit and Preferment in Colonial North America: John Bradstreet's Quest* (Waterloo, Ontario, 1982).

E. H. Gould, *The Persistence of Empire. British Political Culture in the Age of the American Revolution* (Chapel Hill, North Carolina, 2000).

W. H. Guthman, *Drums A'beating, Trumpets Sounding. Artistically Carved Powder Horns in the Provincial Manner 1746–1781* (Hartford, Connecticut, 1993).

A. J. Guy, *Oeconomy and Discipline: Officership and Administration in the British Army, 1714–63* (Manchester, 1984).

E. P. Hamilton, *The French Army in America* (Ottawa, 1967).

Handbook of the North American Indians: Volume 4, History of Indian–White Relations, ed. W. E. Washburn (Washington, 1988); *Volume 15, The North East*, ed. B. G. Trigger (Washington, 1978–79).

Hanoverian Britain and Empire. Essays in Memory of Philip Lawson (Woodbridge, Suffolk, 1998).

T. Hatley, *The Dividing Paths: Cherokees and South Carolinians Through the Era of Revolution* (New York, 1993).

D. F. Harding, *Smallarms of the East India Company 1600–1856* (4 vols, London, 1997–99).

R. Harding, *Amphibious Warfare in the Eighteenth Century: The British Expedition to the West Indies, 1740–1742* (Woodbridge, Suffolk, 1991).

J. R. Harper, *The Fraser Highlanders* (Montreal, 1979).

E. Harris, *The Townshend Album* (London, 1974).

D. Hay et al., *Albion's Fatal Tree: Crime and Society in Eighteenth-Century England* (London, 1975).

D. Hay and N. Rogers, *Eighteenth-Century English Society* (Oxford, 1997).

T. Hayter, *The Army and the Crowd in Mid-Georgian England* (London, 1978).

D. M. Henderson, *Highland Soldier: A Social Study of the Highland Regiments, 1820–1920* (Edinburgh, 1989).

J. M. Hill, *Celtic Warfare, 1595–1763* (Edinburgh, 1986).

An Historical Atlas of Canada, Volume I, From the Beginning to 1800, ed. R. Cole Harris (Toronto, 1987).

E. J. Hobsbawm, *Labouring Men* (2nd edn, London, 1968).

J. Houlding, *Fit for Service: The Training of the British Army, 1715–1795* (Oxford, 1981).

An Impartial Account of the Late Expedition Against St Augustine Under General Oglethorpe (London, 1742).

An Impartial History of the Late Glorious War (Manchester, 1764).

An Imperial State at War. Britain from 1689 to 1815, ed. L. Stone (London, 1994).

F. Jennings, *The Invasion of America: Indians, Colonialism, and the Cant of Conquest* (paper edn, New York, 1976).

F. Jennings, *Empire of Fortune: Crowns, Colonies, and Tribes in the Seven Years War in America* (New York, 1988).

J. M. Johnson, *Militiamen, Rangers and Redcoats: The Military in Georgia, 1754–1776* (Macon, Georgia, 1992).

E. C. Joslin, A. R. Litherland and B. T. Simpkin, *British Battles and Medals* (London, 1988).

L. Kennett, *The French Armies in the Seven Years War: A Study in Military Organisation and Administration* (Durham, North Carolina, 1967).

P. E. Kopperman, *Braddock at the Monongahela* (Pittsburgh, 1977).

P. Langford, *A Polite and Commercial People, England 1727–1783* (Oxford, 1989).

The Laws of War. Constraints on Warfare in the Western World, eds M. Howard, G. J. Andreopoulos and M. R. Shulman (New Haven, 1994).

D. E. Leach, *Arms for Empire: A Military History of the British Colonies in North America, 1607–1763* (New York, 1973).

D. E. Leach, *Roots of Conflict: British Armed Forces and Colonial Americans, 1677–1763* (Chapel Hill, North Carolina, 1986).

L. Leneman, *Living in Atholl. A Social History of the Estates 1685–1785* (Edinburgh, 1986).

B. Lenman, *Integration, Enlightenment and Industrialization: Scotland 1746–1832* (London, 1981).

B. Lenman, *The Jacobite Clans of the Great Glen, 1650–1784* (London, 1984).

C. Lloyd, *The Capture of Quebec* (London, 1959).

P. Mackesy, *The Coward of Minden. The Affair of Lord George Sackville* (London, 1979).

P. Mackesy, *British Victory in Egypt, 1801. The end of Napoleon's conquest* (London, 1995).

A. Mackillop, *'More Fruitful than the Soil': Army, Empire and the Scottish Highlands 1715–1815* (East Linton, 1999).

The Malefactor's Register; or, the Newgate and Tyburn Calendar . . . from the year 1700 to Lady-Day, 1779 (5 vols, London, 1779).

P. Malone, *The Skulking Way of War: Technology and Tactics Among the New England Indians* (Baltimore, 1993).

P. C. Mancall, *Deadly Medicine: Indians and Alcohol in Early America* (Ithaca, New York, 1995).

Thomas Mante, *The History of the Late War in North America and the Islands of the West Indies, including the Campaigns of MDCCLXIII and MDCCLXIV against His Majesty's Indian Enemies* (London, 1772).

J. K. Martin and M. E. Lender, *A Respectable Army. The Military Origins of the Republic, 1763–1789* (Arlington Heights, Illinois, 1982).

P. J. Marshall and G. Williams, *The Great Map of Mankind: British Perceptions of the World in the Age of Enlightenment* (London, 1982).

R. K. Marshall, *Bonnie Prince Charlie* (Edinburgh, 1988).

P. Mathias, *The Transformation of England: Essays in the Economic and Social History of England in the Eighteenth Century* (London, 1979).

R. May and G. Embleton, *Wolfe's Army* (Reading, 1974; revised edn 1997).

M. N. McConnell, *A Country Between: The Upper Ohio Valley and Its Peoples, 1724–1774* (Lincoln, Nebraska, 1992).

F. McLynn, *Crime and Punishment in Eighteenth-Century England* (Oxford, 1989).

G. McWhiney and P. D. Jamieson, *Attack and Die: Civil War Military Tactics and the Southern Heritage* (Alabama, 1982).

G. Metcalf, *Royal Government and Political Conflict in Jamaica 1729–1783* (London, 1965).

R. Middleton, *The Bells of Victory: The Pitt–Newcastle Ministry and the Conduct of the Seven Years War, 1757–1762* (Cambridge, 1985).

H. A. D. Miles and D. Blayney Brown, *Sir David Wilkie of Scotland (1785–1841)* (Raleigh, North Carolina, 1987).

A Military History of Ireland, eds T. Bartlett and K. Jeffery (Cambridge, 1996).

J. Namias, *White Captives: Gender and Ethnicity on the American Frontier* (Chapel Hill, North Carolina, 1993).

C. P. Neimeyer, *America Goes to War. A Social History of the Continental Army* (New York, 1996).

P. D. Nelson, *General James Grant: Scottish Soldier and Royal Governor of East Florida* (Gainesville, 1993).

B. Nosworthy, *The Anatomy of Victory. Battle Tactics 1689–1763* (New York, 1992).

C. Oman, *Wellington's Army, 1809–1814* (London, 1912).

The Oxford History of the British Empire. Volume Two: The Eighteenth Century Empire, ed. P. J. Marshall (Oxford, 1998).

The Oxford Illustrated History of the British Army, eds D. Chandler and I. Beckett (Oxford, 1994).

R. Palmer, *A Ballad History of England from 1588 to the Present Day* (London, 1979).

R. Palmer, *The Sound of History. Songs and Social Comment* (Oxford, 1988).

Parameters of British Naval Power 1650–1850, ed. M. Duffy (Exeter, 1992).

S. Pargellis, *Lord Loudoun in North America* (New Haven, 1993).

F. Parkman, *The Conspiracy of Pontiac* (2 vols, Boston, 1880).

F. Parkman, *Montcalm and Wolfe* (2 vols, Boston, 1884).

H. H. Peckham, *Pontiac and the Indian Uprising* (Princeton, 1947).

H. H. Peckham, *The Colonial Wars, 1689–1762* (Chicago, 1964).

M. G. H. Pittock, *Inventing and Resisting Britain. Cultural Identities in Britain and Ireland, 1685–1789* (London, 1997).

J. Prebble, *Culloden* (London, 1961).

R. Porter, *English Society in the Eighteenth Century* (London, 1982).

The Road to Waterloo: The British Army and the Struggle Against Revolutionary and Napoleonic France, 1793–1815, ed. A. J. Guy (London, 1990).

N. A. M. Rodger, *The Wooden World: An Anatomy of the Georgian Navy* (London, 1986).

A. Rogers, *Empire and Liberty. American Resistance to British Authority, 1755–1763* (Los Angeles, 1974).

H. C. B. Rogers, *The British Army of the Eighteenth Century* (London, 1977).

Robert Rogers, *A Concise Account of North America* (London, 1765).

C. Royster, *A Revolutionary People at War. The Continental Army and American Character, 1775–1783* (Chapel Hill, North Carolina, 1979).

J. Rule, *The Labouring Classes in Early Industrial England, 1750–1850* (London, 1986).

J. Rule, *Albion's People: English Society, 1714–1815* (Harlow, 1992).

J. Rule, *The Vital Century. England's Developing Economy, 1714–1815* (Harlow, 1992).

Sir Reginald Savory, *His Britannic Majesty's Army in Germany During the Seven Years War* (Oxford, 1966).

G. M. Sayre, *Les Sauvages Americains. Representations of Native Americans in French and English Colonial Literature* (Chapel Hill, North Carolina, 1997).

S. Schama, *Dead Certainties (Unwarranted Speculations)* (London, 1991).

A. Schutz, *William Shirley; King's Governor of Massachusetts* (Chapel Hill, North Carolina, 1961).

H. E. Selesky, *War and Society in Colonial Connecticut* (New Haven, 1990).

Sir Bruce Gordon Seton and Jean Gordon Arnot, *The Prisoners of the '45* (3 vols, Edinburgh, 1928).

1745. Charles Edward Stuart and the Jacobites, ed. R. C. Woosnam-Savage (Edinburgh, 1995).

A Short Account of the Late ... Dr Richard Huck Saunders, Physician, London ... From the Edinburgh Medical Commentaries ... (Edinburgh, 1786).

A Short History of the Highland Regiment; Interspersed with Some Occasional Observations As to the Present State of the Country, Inhabitants and Government of Scotland (London, 1743).

D. E. Showalter, *The Wars of Frederick the Great* (Harlow, 1996).

J. Shy, *Toward Lexington: The Role of the British Army in the Coming of the American Revolution* (Princeton, 1965).

J. Shy, *A People Numerous and Armed. Reflections on the Military Struggle for American Independence* (New York, 1976).

M. T. Smelser, *The Campaign for the Sugar Islands, 1759: A Study of Amphibious Warfare* (New York, 1955).

James Smith, *A Treatise on the Mode and Manner of Indian War ...* (Paris, Kentucky, 1812).

P. H. Smith, *Loyalists and Redcoats. A Study in British Revolutionary Policy* (Chapel Hill, North Carolina, 1964).

[William Smith] *An Historical Account of the Expedition Against the Ohio Indians in MDCCLXIV* (London, 1766).

C. P. Stacey, *Quebec, 1759: The Siege and the Battle* (Toronto, 1959).

G. F. G. Stanley, *New France. The Last Phase 1744–1760* (Toronto, 1968).

A. Starkey, *European–Native American Warfare, 1675–1815* (London, 1998).

I. K. Steele, *Betrayals: Fort William Henry and the 'Massacre'* (New York, 1990).

I. K. Steele, *Warpaths: Invasions of North America* (New York, 1994).

J. Stevenson, *Popular Disturbances in England 1700–1870* (London, 1979).

Col. D. Stewart, *Sketches of the Character, Manners and Present State of the Highlanders of Scotland, with Details of the Military Service of the Highland Regiments* (2 vols, Edinburgh, 1822).

J. Titus, *The Old Dominion at War. Society, Politics and Warfare in Late Colonial Virginia* (Columbia, South Carolina, 1991).

K. Tomasson and F. Buist, *Battles of the '45* (London, 1962).

John Trumbull, The Hand and Spirit of a Painter, ed. H. A. Cooper (New Haven, 1982).

C. Walton, *History of the British Standing Army, AD 1660 to 1700* (London, 1894).

War in the Early Modern World, 1450–1815, ed. J. Black (London, 1999).

W. E. Washburn, *The Governor and the Rebel: A History of Bacon's Rebellion in Virginia* (Chapel Hill, North Carolina, 1957).

M. Whinney, *Sculpture in Britain, 1530–1830* (London, 1966; revised edn, J. Physick, Harmondsworth, 1988).

R. White, *The Middle Ground: Indians, Empires and Republics in the Great Lakes Region, 1650–1815* (Cambridge, 1991).

R. Whitworth, *Field Marshal Lord Ligonier: A Story of the British Army, 1702–1770* (Oxford, 1958).

K. Wilson, *A Sense of the People. Politics, Culture and Imperialism in England, 1715–1785* (Cambridge, 1998).

2. *Articles*

C. T. Atkinson, 'A Colonial Draft for the Royals in 1757', *Journal of the Society for Army Historical Research*, XVI (1937), 215–17.

C. T. Atkinson,'The Highlanders in Westphalia, 1760–62 and the Development of Light Infantry', *Journal of the Society for Army Historical Research*, XX (1941), 208–33.

J. Axtell, 'The White Indians of Colonial America', *William and Mary Quarterly* (Third Series), XXXII (1975), 55–88.

J. M. Beattie, 'The Pattern of Crime in England 1660–1800', *Past and Present*, LXII (1974), 47–95.

H. Boscawen, 'The Origins of the Flat-bottomed Landing Craft 1757–58', *Army Museum '84 [National Army Museum Report, 1984]*, 23–30.

E. D. Branch, 'Henry Bouquet: Professional Soldier', *Pennsylvania Magazine of History and Biography*, LXII, 1 (January 1938), 41–51.

S. Brumwell, '"A Service Truly Critical": The British Army and Warfare with the North American Indians, 1755–1764', *War in History*, V, 2 (April 1998), 146–75.

S. Brumwell, 'Rank and File: A Profile of One of Wolfe's Regiments', *Journal of the Society for Army Historical Research*, LXXIX (Spring 2001), 3–24.

M. J. Cardwell, 'Mismanagement: The 1758 British Expedition Against Carillon', *Bulletin of the Fort Ticonderoga Museum*, XV, 4 (1992), 237–91.

J. Childs, 'Secondary Operations of the British Army During the Nine Years' War, 1688–1697', *Journal of the Society for Army Historical Research*, LXXIII (1995), 73–98.

J. Childs, 'War, Crime Waves and the English Army in the Late Seventeenth Century', *War and Society*, XV, 2 (October 1997), 1–17.

S. Conway, 'The Recruitment of Criminals into the British Army, 1775–81', *Bulletin of the Institute of Historical Research*, LVIII (1985), 46–58.

S. Conway, 'The Politics of British Military and Naval Mobilization, 1775–83', *English Historical Review*, CXII (1997), 1,179–1,201.

J. E. Cookson, 'The Napoleonic Wars, Military Scotland and Tory Highlandism in the Early Nineteenth Century', *Scottish Historical Review*, LXXVIII, 1 (April 1999), 60–75.

D. Daudelin, 'Numbers and Tactics at Bushy Run', *Western Pennsylvania Historical Magazine*, LXVIII (1985), 153–79.

W. J. Eccles, review of D. E. Leach, *Arms for Empire*, in *William and Mary Quarterly* (Third Series), XXXI (1974), 501–3.

L. V. Eid, '"National" War Among Indians of Northeastern North America', *Canadian Review of American Studies*, XVI, 2 (summer 1985), 125–54.

L. V. Eid, '"A Kind of Running Fight": Indian Battlefield Tactics in the Late Eighteenth Century', *Western Pennsylvania Historical Magazine*, LXXI (1988), 147–71.

J. Fortescue, 'Guadeloupe, 1759', *Blackwood's Magazine*, CCXXXIV (October 1933), 552–66.

S. R. Frey, 'Courts and Cats: British Military Justice in the Eighteenth Century', *Military Affairs*, XLIII, 7 (February 1979), 5–11.

E. W. H. Fyers, 'The Loss and Recapture of St John's Newfoundland, in 1762', *Journal of the Society for Army Historical Research*, XI (1932), 179–215.

A. N. Gilbert, 'The Regimental Courts Martial in the Eighteenth Century British Army', *Albion*, VIII (1976), 50–66.

A. N. Gilbert, 'Law and Honour among Eighteenth Century British Army Officers', *The Historical Journal*, XIX (1976), 75–87.

A. N. Gilbert, 'Army Impressment During the War of the Spanish Succession', *Historian*, XXXVIII (1976), 689–708.

A. N. Gilbert, 'Why Men Deserted from the Eighteenth Century British Army', *Armed Forces and Society*, VI, 4 (summer 1980), 553–67.

A. N. Gilbert, 'The Changing Face of British Military Justice, 1757–83', *Military Affairs*, XLIX, 2 (April 1985), 80–84.

W. S. Hadlock, 'War Among the Northeastern Woodland Indians', *American Anthropologist* (New Series), XLIX (1947), 204–21.

D. Hay, 'War, Dearth and Theft in the Eighteenth Century: The Record of the English Courts', *Past and Present*, XCV (1982), 117–60.

J. Hayes, 'Scottish Officers in the British Army, 1714–63', *Scottish Historical Review*, XXXVII (1958), 23–33.

J. Hayes, 'The Royal House of Hanover and the British Army, 1740–60', *Bulletin of the John Rylands Library*, XL (1957–58), 328–57.

D. Higginbotham, 'The Early American Way of War: Reconnaissance and Appraisal', *William and Mary Quarterly* (Third Series), XLIV (1987), 230–73.

J. M. Hitsman and C. C. J. Bond, 'The Assault Landing at Louisbourg, 1758', *Canadian Historical Review*, XXXV (1954), 314–30.

B. Knollenberg, 'General Amherst and Germ Warfare', *Mississippi Valley Historical Review*, XLI (December 1954), 489–94 (with letter from D. H. Kent, ibid., (March 1955), 762–3).

P. E. Kopperman, 'Medical Services in the British Army, 1742–1783', *Journal of the History of Medicine and Allied Science*, XXXIV (1979), 428–55.

P. E. Kopperman, 'The British Command and Soldiers' Wives in America, 1755–1783', *Journal of the Society for Army Historical Research*, LX (1982), 14–34.

P. E. Kopperman, 'The Stoppages Mutiny of 1763', *Western Pennsylvania Historical Magazine*, LXIX (1986), 241–54.

P. E. Kopperman, '"The Cheapest Pay": Alcohol Abuse in the Eighteenth-Century British Army', *Journal of Military History*, LX, 3 (July 1996), 445–70.

E. M. Lloyd, 'The Raising of the Highland Regiments in 1757', *English Historical Review*, XVII (1902), 466–9.

I. MacCulloch, 'Men of the 27th Foot: Two Portraits (i) Thomas Busby, Grenadier, 1735–1798', *Bulletin of the Fort Ticonderoga Museum*, XVI, 2 (1999), 119–27.

J. K. Mahon, 'Anglo-American Methods of Indian Warfare, 1676–1794', *Mississippi Valley Historical Review*, XLV (September 1958), 254–75.

R. Middleton, 'A Reinforcement for North America, Summer 1757', *Bulletin of the Institute of Historical Research*, XLI (1968), 58–72.

R. Middleton, 'The Recruitment of the British Army, 1755–1762', *Journal of the Society for Army Historical Research*, LXVII (1989), 226–38.

P. Muskett, 'Military Operations Against Smugglers in Kent and Sussex 1698–1750', *Journal of the Society for Army Historical Research*, LII (1974), 89–110.

M. L. Nicolai, ' "A Different Kind of Courage": The French Military and the Canadian Irregular Soldier during the Seven Years War', *Canadian Historical Review*, LXX (1989), 53–75.

F. T. Nichols, 'The Organization of Braddock's Army', *William and Mary Quarterly* (Third Series), IV (1947), 124–47.

S. A. Padeni, 'Forgotten Soldiers: The Role of Blacks in New York's Northern Campaigns of the Seven Years War', *Bulletin of the Fort Ticonderoga Museum*, XVI, 2 (1999), 152–69.

P. Paret, 'Colonial Experience and European Military Reform at the End of the Eighteenth Century', *Bulletin of the Institute of Historical Research*, XXXVII (1964), 47–59.

S. Pargellis, 'Braddock's Defeat', *American Historical Review*, XLI (1936), 253–69.

D. K. Richter, 'War and Culture: The Iroquois Experience', *William and Mary Quarterly* (Third Series), XL (1983), 528–59.

E. Robson, 'British Light Infantry in the Mid-Eighteenth Century: The Effect of American Conditions', *Army Quarterly* (1952), 209–22.

P. E. Russell, 'Redcoats in the Wilderness: British Officers and Irregular Warfare in Europe and America, 1740–1760', *William and Mary Quarterly* (Third Series), XXXV (1978), 629–52.

K. R. Stacy, 'Major General John Small, 1726–1796', *Journal of the Society for Army Historical Research*, LXXIV (1996), 102–4.

D. R. Starbuck, 'Anatomy of a Massacre', *Archaeology*, XLVI (1993), 42–6.

A. Starkey, 'War and Culture, a Case Study: The Enlightenment and the Conduct of the British Army in America, 1755–1781', *War and Society*, VIII, 1 (May 1990), 1–28.

G. A. Steppler, 'British Military Law, Discipline and the Conduct of Regimental Courts Martial in the Later Eighteenth Century', *English Historical Review*, CII (1987), 859–86.

J. Styles, 'Crime in 18th-Century England', *History Today*, XXXVIII (March 1988), 36–42.

D. Syrett, 'Living Conditions on the Navy Board's Transports during the American War, 1775–1783', *Mariner's Mirror*, LV (1969), 87–94.

D. Syrett, 'The British Landing at Havana: An Example of an Eighteenth Century Combined Operation', *Mariner's Mirror*, LV (1969), 325–31.

D. Syrett, 'The Methodology of British Amphibious Operations During the Seven Years and American Wars', *Mariner's Mirror*, LVIII (1972), 269–80.

T. Thayer, 'The Army Contractors for the Niagara Campaign, 1755–1756', *William and Mary Quarterly* (Third Series), XIV (1957), 31–46.

R. F. H. Wallace, 'Regimental Routine and Army Administration in North America in 1759', *Journal of the Society for Army Historical Research*, XXX (1952), 8–19.

M. C. Ward, '"The European Method of Warring is Not Practiced Here": The Failure of British Military Policy in the Ohio Valley, 1755–1759', *War in History*, IV, 3 (July 1997), 247–63.

P. Way, 'Rebellion of the Regulars: Working Soldiers and the Mutiny of 1763–1764', *William and Mary Quarterly* (Third Series), LVII (2000), 761–92.

L. S. Winstock, 'Hot Stuff', *Journal of the Society for Army Historical Research*, XXXIII (1955), 2–4.

R. L. Yaple, 'Braddock's Defeat: The Theories and a Reconsideration', *Journal of the Society for Army Historical Research*, XLVI (1968), 194–201.

G. S. Zaboly, 'The Use of Tumplines in the French and Indian War', *Military Collector and Historian*, XLVI, 3 (Fall 1994), 109–13.

3. Unpublished dissertations

S. Brumwell, 'The British Army and the North American Indian, 1755–1763', University of Leeds MA thesis (1994).

M. Odintz, 'The British Officer Corps, 1754–1783', University of Michigan PhD thesis (1988).

K. L. Parker, 'Anglo-American Wilderness Campaigning, 1754–64: Logistical and Tactical Developments', Columbia University PhD thesis (1970).

G. A. Steppler, 'The Common Soldier in the Reign of George III, 1760–1793', University of Oxford PhD thesis (1984).

Index

Note: 'n' following a page number denotes a note is referred to; 'f' following a number denotes a figure is referred to; 't' following a number refers to a table.